Risk Management and Insurance Planning for Physicians and Advisors

A Strategic Approach

David E. Marcinko, Editor

Chief Executive Officer and Provost
Institute of Medical Business Advisors, Inc.

JONES AND BARTLETT PUBLISHERS
Sudbury, Massachusetts
BOSTON   TORONTO   LONDON   SINGAPORE

World Headquarters
Jones and Bartlett Publishers
40 Tall Pine Drive
Sudbury, MA 01776
978-443-5000
info@jbpub.com
www.jbpub.com

Jones and Bartlett Publishers
Canada
2406 Nikanna Road
Mississauga, ON L5C 2W6
CANADA

Jones and Bartlett Publishers
International
Barb House, Barb Mews
London W6 7PA
UK

Library of Congress Cataloging-in-Publication Data

Marcinko.
    p. cm.

  ISBN (pbk.)
  1.

Production Credits
Executive Editor: Jack Bruggeman
Production Manager: Amy Rose
Editorial Assistant: Kaylah McNeil
Production Assistant: Tracey Chapman
Marketing Manager: Ed McKenna
Manufacturing Buyer: Therese Bräuer
Cover Design: Anne Spencer
Composition and Art: Bookwrights
Printing and Binding: Malloy, Inc.
Cover Printing: Malloy, Inc.

Printed in the United States of America
08 07 06 05 04   10 9 8 7 6 5 4 3 2 1

Table of Contents

About the Editor
Dedication
Foreword
Preface
Introduction for Condensed Reading and Review
Contributing Authors
Disclaimer xxxiii

Chapter 1. Insuring the Doctor's Life (Understanding Life Insurance . . . Personal Strategies for Physicians)
GARY A. COOK
Actuarial Sciences
Social Insurance
Retirement Benefits
Survivor Benefits
Disability Benefits
Health Insurance
Other Social Insurance Programs
Risk Management Principles
General Types of Insurance Policies for Physicians
Life Insurance Overview
Term Insurance
Annual Renewable Term Insurance
Level Term Insurance
Decreasing Term Insurance
Triple X
Term Insurance Summation
Permanent Insurance
Whole Life Insurance
Universal Life Insurance
Variable Life Insurance
Other Varieties of Life Policies
Survivorship Life Insurance
Joint First-to-Die Life Insurance
Interest-Sensitive Whole Life Insurance
Group Life Insurance

Single-Premium Life Insurance
The 5-100 Rule

Death Benefit Settlement Options
Life Insurance Taxation
Income Tax–Free Death Benefit
Transfer-for-Value Problem
Tax-Deferred Growth
Withdrawals and Loans
Violating the 2 out of 3 Rule
Policy Replacement: Section 1035 Exchanges
Modified Endowment Contracts

Annuity Overview
Deferred Annuities
Fixed Deferred Annuity
Variable Deferred Annuity

Immediate Annuities
Immediate Fixed Annuity
Immediate Variable Annuity
Qualified Annuities

Annuity Taxation
Qualified Annuity Taxation
Nonqualified Annuity Taxation
Wealth Transfer Issues

Health Insurance Overview
Disability Income Insurance
Disability Defined
Partial Disability
Elimination Period
Coordination of Benefits
Monthly Benefit Amount
Occupation
Inflation Protection
Renewability
Disability Income Taxation
Disability Income Summary

Long-Term Care Insurance
Medicare
Critical LTC Policy Features
ADLs

Long-Term Care Taxation

Chapter 2. Insuring the Doctor's Property and Possessions (Guarding Your Stuff . . . Against Man or Nature)

GARY A. COOK

General Types of Policies Covering Possessions

Homeowners (and Renters) Insurance Overview

Replacement Cost Versus Actual Cash Value

Inflation Protection

Other Homeowner Policy Endorsements

Title Insurance

Boat Insurance Overview

Automobile Insurance Overview

> *Liability Coverage*
>> Bodily Injury
>> Property Damage
>> Personal Injury
> *Physical Damage Coverage*
>> Comprehensive
>> Collision
> *Repairs After the Accident*
> *Uninsured–Underinsured Motorists Coverage*

Umbrella Liability Insurance Overview

Evaluating Insurance Companies and Policies

> *Introduction to Company Selection*
>> Financial Ratings
>> Bankruptcy
>> Lawsuits

Life and Health Insurance Policy Provisions

> *The Application*
> *The Underwriting Process*
> *Medical Information Bureau*
> *Final Underwriting Decision*
> *Contract Law (in brief)*
> *The Underwriting Decision*
> *Free Look Period*
> *Contract Language*
> *Policy Comparisons*

Policy Replacement
>   *Definition*
>   *The Process*
>   *Other Aspects to Consider*
>   *A Replacement Exception*
>   *Safeguards*

Lifetime (Viatical and Senior) Settlements

Needs Analysis Approach to Life Insurance

Chapter 3. Insuring the Doctor's Practice (Protecting the Business . . . Earning a Living)
GARY A. COOK

Business Uses of Life Insurance
>   *Key Person Insurance*
>   *Practice Continuation Funding*
>   *Executive Bonus Plan*
>   *Nonqualified Salary Continuation*
>   *Split-Dollar Plans*
>> Employer-Owned Method
>> Employee-Owned Method
>> Summary of Split-Dollar Method

Other Business-Related Insurance
>   *Workers' Compensation*
>   *Business Owner Policy*
>   *Professional Liability Insurance*

Miscellaneous Insurance Policies

Chapter 4. Risks of Medical Practice Noncompete Agreements (Restricted Covenants Vital . . . Often Contentious and Subject to Interpretation)
FREDERICK WILLIAM LACAVA

Restrictive Covenants Defined

Covenants for the Sale of a Medical Practice

Covenants as Part of a Medical Employment Contract

"Reasonable" Covenant Terms

Remedies for Covenant Breach

Agreements Restricting the Practice of Medicine

Chapter 5. Documentation and Medical Records Risks (No Longer a Reflection of Reality . . . Now, the Reality Itself)
FREDERICK WILLIAM LACAVA
Historic Purpose of Medical Records
The Medical Records Revolution
Documentation Guidelines for Evaluation &Management Coding
Legal Statutes Regarding Medical Billing

Chapter 6. Health-Care Compliance andrisk Management (An Impossible Task . . . But Doctors *Are* Responsible)
PATRICIA A. TRITES
The Compliance Process
Step 1. Know Which Rules You Have to Follow
Step 2. Outline the Rules in Written Policies and Procedures
Step 3. Assess the Organization's Current Compliance
Step 4. Training, Communication, and Enforcement
Step 5. Maintenance of the Compliance Program
The Rules
Billing and Reimbursement
Provider Numbers
Documentation of Medical Records
Proper Use and Billing of CPT and Diagnosis Codes
Use of Ancillary Personnel "Incident to" Services
Physicians at Teaching Hospitals
Medical Necessity and the Use of Advance Beneficiary Notices
Professional Courtesy and Waiver of Co-Pays and Deductibles
Proper Use of Certificates of Medical Necessity
Employment or Services of Excluded Providers or Entities
Occupational Safety and Health Act (OSHA)
Health Insurance Portability and Accountability Act (HIPAA)
Standardized Transaction and Code Set Rule
Privacy Rule
Security Rule
Limited English Proficiency (LEP)
Personnel and Employee Retirement Income Security Act (ERISA)
Clinical Laboratory Improvement Amendments (CLIA)

Chapter 7. Risk Management In Modern Medical Practice (It's Not Just About Medical Malpractice . . . Anymore!)

CHARLES F. FENTON, III, DAVID EDWARD MARCINKO

Medicare Recoupment Risks
Health-Care Fraud Risks
Medicare Fraud
Insurance Fraud
Misrepresentation
Provider Health-Care Fraud Considerations
The Kennedy-Kassenbaum (HIPAA) Act
The Balanced-Budget Act
The Federal False Claims Act
Money Laundering
Civil Asset Forfeiture Risks
Self-Referral Risks
Medicare Anti-Fraud and Abuse Statute
Medicare Safe Harbor Regulations
The Stark Amendment
Federal Agency Risks
Occupational Safety and Health Agency Risks
Drug Enforcement Agency Risks
Environmental Protection Agency Risks
Health and Human Services (Office of Civil Rights) Risks
Antitrust Risks
Business Practice Litigation Risks
Patterns of Practice Risks
Managed Care Contractual Risks
Historic Bars to Managed Care Lawsuits
Recent Trends
Implications for the Physician
The Contract Capitulation Dilemma
Employee Risks
Vicarious Risks
Employed Physicians
Members of a Group Practice
Certificates of Medical Necessity

Deselection Risks
Risks of Collateral Consequences
Medicare 5-Year Exclusion Risks
State Board Action Risks
Malpractice Risks
New Practice Risks
Expert Witness Risks
Peer Review Risks
On-Call Risks
Educational Debt Load Risks
Suggestions to Help Avoid Medicolegal Risks
Statistical Analysis and Fraud Investigations
The Bell-Shaped Normalization Curve
Appropriate Contracts
Practicing Bare
Staff Education and Training
Elimination of Risky Treatments

Chapter 8. Sexual Harrassment Risks In Medical Practice (He Said, She Said . . . There Is No Quid Pro Quo)

VICKI L. BUBA

Preferential Treatment
Hostile Medical Office Work Environment
Unreasonable Interference with Work Performance
Two-Pronged Test for Offensive Behavior
Examples of Sexual Harassment
> *Compliments*
> *Sexist Words*
> *Office Jokes*
> *Touching*
> *Invitations*
>> When "Yes" Becomes "No"
>> A Sense of Obligation
>> Listening for Clues
> *Demands or Threats*
Gender-Based Animosity
Same-Sex Harassment

Doctor-Employer Liability
> *Liability for Supervisor's Harassment*
> *Reporting Procedure*

Disciplinary Actions
Tangible Employment Action
Punitive Damages
Financial and Economic Costs
Commonsense Approach

Chapter 9. Medical Office Workplace Violence Risks (Pondering the Unthinkable . . . Preventing and Planning for the Horrific)
> W. BARRY NIXON

Introduction to Medical Workplace Violence
Case Example
Health-Care Workplace Violence Defined
Financial Risk Management Impact of Workplace Violence
Assessing the Risk of Workplace Violence
Contributing Factors to Workplace Violence
Focusing on Prevention: The Zero Incidents Approach
Establish a Workplace Violence Prevention Committee
> Focus on Eliminating At-Risk Behaviors
> Establish a Workplace Violence Prevention Policy
> Formulate a No Weapons in the Workplace Policy
> Define the Nature of the Risk to the Company
> Conduct Facility Risk Assessments
> Conduct Organizational Violence Assessments
> Make an Individual Threat Assessment
> Enhance Physical Security
> Synchronize Your Personnel, Security, and Safety Policies
> Develop Crisis Response Procedures
> Establish Emergency Protocol with Police
> Enhance Hiring Procedures
> Promote Your Employee Assistance Program
> Train Managers, Supervisors, Doctors, Nurses, and Employees
> Involve Health-Care Employees in the Prevention Effort

Disastrous Planning Mistakes
Analyzing the Business Impact of a Workplace Violence Incident
Cost of Implementing a Prevention Effort

The Hidden Cost of Conflict
> Wasted Time
> Reduced Decision-Making Quality
> Loss of Skilled Employees
> Restructuring Cost
> Sabotage, Theft, and Damage
> Lowered Job Motivation
> Lost Work Time
> Health Costs

Cost of Recovery After an Incident

Assessment

Chapter 10. Medical Malpractice and Tort Reform Risks (Crisis . . . or Red Herring?)

ROBERT JAMES CIMASI

Malpractice Insurance History
> The History of Medical Education and Practice

Background

The Corporate Tort Reform Movement
> Tort Lawsuits
> "Frivolous Lawsuits"

Physician Self-Regulation
> The State Licensing Process
> Self-Regulation
> Questionable Doctors: How Does the Public Know?
> Is It Always Gross Negligence?

The Medical Malpractice Crisis

Allegations of Greed: The Traditional Physician and Insurance Company–Based Arguments

The Proposed Tort Reform Solution: The Traditional Argument's Answers, Including Tort Reform

Patient Legal Protections: Checks and Balances on Abuse: Nontraditional Market-Based and Consumer Advocate-Based Arguments

Other Approaches to Controlling Premiums: Nontraditional Answers

Conclusion
> Summary
> Changes in the Technology and Practice of Medicine
> The Perfect Storm
> Table 9.1. Selected States' Medical Malpractice Liability Reform Measures

Chapter 11. The Capitation Liability Theory (Risk Retention Groups . . . Salvation or Ruination for the Malpractice Crisis?)

DAVID EDWARD MARCINKO, CHARLES F. FENTON, III

The Liability Insurance Industry
The Liability Premium-Setting Process
The Capitation Liability Theory
Premium Structures and Models
      Insurance Legislation Implications
      Indemnification Concerns
Liability Coverage Forms
The Contrary Viewpoint
      Pure At-Risk Capitated Model
      Reduced Fee-for-Service Model
      Hybrid Capitation/Reduced-Fee-for-Service Model
Miscellaneous Liability Factors
Current Trends
Specialty-Specific Insurers

Chapter 12. Medical Malpractice Trial Risks (A Necessary Evil . . . or Simply Evil?)

JAY S. GRIFE

Dear Doctor, You Have Been Served a Lawsuit
      First Steps
      Call Your Medical Malpractice Insurance Company
      Secure Personal Counsel
The Trial Players
Burden of Proof
Types of Trials
Discovery Process
Depositions
Motions *In Limine*
Jury Selection
      Voir Dire: Questioning the Jurors
      Challenges of Jurors
      Jury Selection Logistics
      Preliminary Instructions to the Jury
Opening Statements
Presentation of Evidence

Order of Evidence Presentation
Witnesses
Exhibits
Objections

Summation

Final Instructions

Jury Deliberations

The Verdict

Preventing and Reducing Incidents of Malpractice
Honesty
Medical Records

Chapter 13. Financial and Operative Risks of Divorce (Keeping it Civil and Equitable . . . Not Going Broke)
ANJU D. JESSANI

Domestic and Spousal Issues

Prenuptial Agreements

The Decision to Divorce
Divorce Mediation
Choosing a Divorce Attorney
Some Do's and Don'ts and Pitfalls as You Prepare to Separate

An Overview of Family and Divorce Law
Custody Options and Parenting Time Issues
Child Support and Other Financial Issues Related to the Children
Distribution of Marital Assets and Liabilities
Businesses and Professional Practices
Pension Plans (Defined Benefit Plans)
401(k) Plans and Other Qualified Plans (Defined Contribution Plans) and Individual Retirement Accounts (IRAs)
Real Estate or Marital Residence
Spousal Support or Alimony and Related Tax Issues Other Tax Considerations of Separation and Divorce
Filing Status
Exemptions for Dependents
Child Tax Credit
Child's Care Tax Credit
Education Credits
Earned Income Credit (EIC)

Child's Investment Income
The Jobs and Growth Tax Relief Reconciliation Act of 2003
Elimination of the Marriage Penalty
Physician Residents and Young Children
Staying Informed

Older Divorcing Medical Professionals

Chapter 14. Asset Protection Principles (What Is At Risk . . . How to Protect It!)

EDWARD J. RAPPAPORT, J. CHRISTOPHER MILLER

Getting Started
Appreciating the Risks
Asset Protection Tools
    Good Record Keeping
    Insurance
Malpractice Insurance
Life Insurance and Disability Insurance
General Liability Insurance
Natural Disaster Insurance
Layered Organizations
Practice Format
A Comparison of Business Entity Types
    An Ideal Approach
Qualified Retirement Plans
Joint Ownership of Assets
Gifting
Self-Settled Trusts
Complex Asset Protection Tools
    Avoiding Fraudulent Conveyance
    Relocation
    Homestead Exemption
Irrevocable Life Insurance Trusts
Family Limited Partnerships
Asset Protection Trusts
    Domestic Asset Protection Trusts
    Foreign Asset Protection Trusts
    Asset Protection Trusts and Divorce
Timing Is Everything

Chapter 15. Selecting Insurance Agents and Risk Management Advisors (Understanding Hidden Agendas . . . Wisely Choosing Consultants)

DAVID EDWARD MARCINKO, HOPE RACHEL HETICO. RACHEL PENTIN-MAKI

§ 15.01 Insurance Company Selection

[A] Financial Ratings

[B] Bankruptcy

[C] Lawsuits

Introduction to Insurance Agent Selection

Affinity Fraud

Promissory Note Scams

Illegal Investment Sales

Why Do Regulators Target Insurance Agents?

Insurance Agents Have a Built-In Customer Base

Many Physicians and Investors Are Looking for Yield and Safety Hiring the Right Insurance Agent

Brokers Versus Agents

Commissions

The State Insurance Department

Insurance Agent Titles andCredentials

The Life Insurance Agent

The Property and Casualty Agent

Medical Risk Management Societies and Specialists

Societies and Sources of Information and Products

Business and Medical Risk Management Degree Programs

The Role of Advisor/Agent Teamwork

David Edward Marcinko is a health-care economist and former private practitioner. He has edited three practice management textbooks and four personal financial planning books for physicians and healthcare professionals. His clinical publications are archived in the Library of Congress and the Library of Medicine at the National Institutes of Health. His economic thought leadership essays have been referenced by *Investment Advisor Magazine,* Medical Group Management Association (MGMA), American College of Medical Practice Executives (ACMPE), American College of Physician Executives (ACPE), JAMA.ama-assn.org, Healthcare Management Associates (HMA), CFP© Biz (*Journal of Financial Planning*), Financial Planner's Library Online, and the Business of Medical Practice, among others. A favorite on the lecture circuit, Dr. Marcinko speaks frequently to medical societies and financial institutions throughout the country.

Professor Marcinko received his undergraduate degree from Loyola College in Baltimore, his business degree from the Keller Graduate School of Management in Chicago, and his financial planning diploma from Oglethorpe University in Atlanta. He is a licensee of the Certified Financial Planner© Board of Standards in Denver, and holds the Certified Medical Planner© designation.

Professor Marcinko earned a Series #7 (general securities), Series #63 (uniform securities state law), and Series #65 (investment advisory) license from the National Association of Securities Dealers (NASD), and a life, health, disability, variable annuity, and property-casualty license from the State of Georgia. He is also a board-certified surgical fellow and a visiting scholar in the healthcare economics at the Keller Graduate School of Management, and instructor in finance for the University of Phoenix, Graduate School of Business and Management.

Dr. Marcinko was cofounder of an ambulatory surgery center that was sold to a publicly traded company and has been a Certified Professional in Healthcare Quality (CPHQ), an American Board of Quality Assurance and Utilization Review Physician (ABQAURP), a medical staff vice president of a general hospital, an assistant residency director; the founder of a computer-based testing firm for doctors, and president of a regional physician practice management corporation in the midwest.

Currently, Dr. Marcinko is Chief Executive Officer of the Institute of Medical Business Advisors, Inc., a national resource center and referral alliance providing financial stability and managerial peace-of-mind to struggling physicians clients.

Institute of Medical Business Advisors, Inc.
Peachtree Plantation - West
Suite 5901 Wilbanks Drive
Norcross, GA 30092-1141
770-448-0769 (voice)
775-361-8831 (fax)
www.MedicalBusinessAdvisors.com
info@MedicalBusinessAdvisors.com
MarcinkoAdvisors@msn.com

Dedication

It is indeed a privilege to edit *Risk Management and Insurance Planning for Physicians and Advisors (A Strategic Approach)*. One of the most rewarding aspects of my career has been the personal and professional growth acquired from interacting with financial professionals of all designations and medical professionals of all disciplines. The mutual sharing and exchange of ideas stimulates the mind and fosters advancement at many levels.

Creating this text for physicians and advisors was a significant effort that involved all members of our firm. Over the past year we interfaced with outside private and public companies to discuss its contents. Although it is impossible to list every person or company that played a role in its production, there are several people we wish to thank for their extraordinary assistance: Mike Jensen and Ruth S. Given, PhD, Director of Health Care Research at Deloitte Consulting and Deloitte & Touche; Robert J. Cimasi, ASA, and Timothy Alexander, MLS, of Health Capital Consultants, LLC, St. Louis, Missouri; Richard D. Helppie, Founder and CEO of the Superior Consultant Corporation (NASD-SUPC); Richard Melby of the Dell Computer Corporation Healthcare Division; Ahmad Hashem, MD, PhD, Global Healthcare Industry Manager of the Microsoft Corporation; Marvin W. Tuttle, CAE, of the Journal of Financial Planning; and Jack Bruggeman, Executive Editor of Jones and Bartlett Publishers.

Of course, this book would not have been possible without the support of my wife Hope and daughter Mackenzie, whose love and support gave me the encouragement to pursue it to completion. Above all, it is dedicated to our contributing authors, who crashed the development life cycle in order to produce time-sensitive material in an expedient manner. The knowledge I have gained and the satisfaction I have enjoyed from working with them are immeasurable.

David Edward Marcinko
Editor-in-Chief

Insurance is an important part of all our lives. This is especially true for physicians. I currently have no fewer than 10 separate insurance policies associated with my plastic surgery practice. I understand very little about the policies other than that somebody at some point told me I needed each and every one of them, and each made sense when I bought it. Am I overinsured and thus wasting money? Am I underinsured and thus at risk for a liability disaster? I never really had the means of answering these questions, until now.

Risk Management and Insurance Planning for Physicians and Advisors is an essential textbook because it explains to physicians and insurance professionals the background, theory, and practicalities of medical risk management and insurance planning. The insurance haze is lifted by editor and Certified Medical Planner© Dr. David Edward Marcinko and his team of contributing authors.

Doctors, like most people, tend to experience losses more intensely than gains, and they evaluate risks in isolation. So it's no surprise that goaded physicians might prefer vehicles like the guaranteed minimum death benefit of variable annuities, or the assurance that comes with disability or long-term care insurance, or traditional cash value life insurance policies, despite their decidedly higher costs and commissions. Similarly, physicians may enter a denial mode and eschew the potential business impact of HIPAA and the Balanced Budget Act risks; self-referral risks; OSHA, DEA, EPA, OCR, P&C, or managed care risks; managed care contract capitulation risks; employee, expert witness, peer review, and on-call risks; and even educational debt load risks, among so many others.

For insurance professionals, on the other hand, this is an exciting time to be practicing medical risk management, because there is much research and creative enlightenment occurring in academic and practitioner communities. However, one must be willing to abandon ancient thoughts and remain open to new ideas that identify and provide solutions to the contemporary problems of physicians. For example, the economist Christian Gollier revisits the raison d'être of insurance by asking: "Should one even buy insurance since the industry itself is so skilled at exploiting human foibles?" Although all this emerging work is descriptive, it is not yet time–tested. Some of it aspires to be normative, in that modern models of savings and consumption hint that insurance may deserve a smaller role in personal risk management than previously believed.

Risk Management and Insurance Planning for Physicians and Advisors is an invaluable tool for physicians wanting to make good decisions about the risks they face. It is also ideal for financial planners, insurance agents, and health-care business advisors wishing to reeducate and help doctors by adding lasting value to their client relationships. With time at a premium for all, and so much information packed into one well-organized resource, this book should be on the desk of every physician or financial advisor serving the health-care field.

Simply stated, if you read this compelling text with a mind focused on the future, the time you spend will be amply rewarded.

Lloyd M. Krieger, MD, MBA
Rodeo Drive Plastic Surgery
The Rodeo Collection
421 North Rodeo Drive
Beverly Hills, CA 90210
Phone: 310-550-6300
Fax: 310-550-6363
E-mail: lkrieger@ucla.edu
Website: www.RodeoDrivePlasticSurgery.com

In the current medical practice liability environment, *Risk Management and Insurance Planning for Physicians and Advisors (A Strategic Approach)* is of the greatest value to all doctors and their related financial and business advisors.

Traditionally, the physician protected his family with whole-life, disability, and long-term care insurance, and his practice with malpractice liability and business interruption insurance. For modern physicians, however, a comprehensive medical enterprise risk management plan must acknowledge more risks than ever before, and in an economically sound manner not counterproductive to individual components of the plan. These include risks not considered just a few years ago: sexual harassment and workplace violence risks; Medicare documentation, recoupment, and compliance risks; economic and personal divorce risks; and a plethora of risks associated with new legislative initiatives, such as the Health Insurance Portability and Accountability Act (HIPAA), Occupational Safety and Health Administration (OSHA) Act, Clinical Laboratory Improvement Act (CLIA), Environmental Protection Agency (EPA) Act, Limited English Proficiency (LEP) Act, Drug Enforcement Agency (DEA) Act, Civil Asset Forfeiture (CAF) Act, and Federal False Claims Act (FFCA), as well as Federal Trade Commission (FTC) anti-trust risks. The U.S. inspector general has declared health-care providers to be public enemy number two, behind drug and narcotics traffickers, for their fraud and abuse activities.

There is no question that real fraud exists. The Office of Inspector General (OIG) of the Department of Health and Human Services (HHS) saved American taxpayers a record $21 billion in fiscal year 2002, according to Inspector General Janet Rehnquist. Savings were achieved through an intensive and continuing crackdown on waste, fraud, and abuse in Medicare and in over 300 other HHS programs for which the OIG has oversight responsibility. The agency performed or oversaw 2,372 audits, conducted 70 evaluations of department programs, and opened 1,654 new civil and criminal cases, bringing to more than 2,700 the number of active OIG investigations. Additionally, the OIG excluded 3,448 individuals and entities from participation in Medicare, Medicaid, and other federally sponsored health-care programs, and its enforcement efforts resulted in 517 criminal convictions and 236 successful civil actions. Thus, the integration of risk management disciplines for physicians is no longer an academic luxury, but a pragmatic survival *imperative long recognized by the Medical Business Advisors, Inc. and contributing authors of this book.*

Source: http://oig.hhs.gov/publications/docs/semiannual/2002/fallsemiannual02pr.pdf.

And now, with the acceleration of private, state, and federal managed care initiatives, physicians may be facing the ultimate personal contingent liability by selecting the *wrong profession,* as suggested by Yale University economist Robert J. Shiller, PhD. In his new book, *The New Financial Order: Risk in the 21st Century,* Shiller states that a new risk-sharing paradigm to protect us from "gratuitous random and painful inequality" is required. The solution? *Livelihood insurance,* framed as a risk management contract!

Reassuringly, the risks and perils identified in this textbook are not quite as thought provoking as Shiller's ideas, although they are equally compelling and most applicable to solo and small-group medical practices. They are more pragmatic, however, and we are certain that this book will help all colleagues recognize and reduce their risks if these risks are appreciated, integrated, and managed with a trusted and knowledgeable advisor.

Dr. David Edward Marcinko, MBA, CFP©, CMP©
Editor

Introduction for Condensed Reading and Review

Risk Management and Insurance Planning for Physicians and Advisors (A Strategic Approach) is easy to read and written in prose format using nontechnical jargon. This style allows a large amount of information to be a condensed into a practical volume. It also allows the reader to comprehend an important concept in a single reading session, since a deliberate effort has been made to include germane examples with current information. The interested reader is then able to look up selected topics or perform additional research at leisure. Overlap of material is reduced, but important case models are included for increased understanding.

The textbook itself is divided into 15 logically progressive yet stand-alone chapters, written by 20 contributing authors.

Chapter 1 is a discourse on personal life insurance, the bedrock of financial planning for most indebted Americans, who are no different from the typical physician. Chapter 2 discusses how to effectively use insurance to protect the doctor's many possessions, and Chapter 3 focuses on insuring physician practice and business interests. These chapters inaugurate entry into the risk management process with an explanation of number theory and actuarial science, using real-life examples and scenarios identifiable to the practicing physician. Chapter 4 outlines the use and abuse of restrictive covenants in physician employment contracts, since more than 50 percent of contemporary doctors are employees rather than independent practitioners. Chapter 5, although brief in length, chillingly demonstrates the negative outcomes when medical record documentation is less than adequate, describing not only the results of claims nonpayments but also potential criminal sanctions. Similarly, Chapter 6 extols nuances of proper compliance principles in a skeptical payer environment, and it also reviews the civil and criminal penalties for both miscreants and the uninformed. Chapter 7 provides information for effective nonclinical risk management strategies, and Chapter 8 represents a legal discourse on sexual harassment issues as manifested in the health-care setting. Again, the topics are frightening. Of course, no book on risk management would be complete after 9/11 without a discourse on medical office workplace violence. Chapter 10 provides a current update to the traditional conundrum of professional medical liability, but with a decidedly economic perspective. A new corporate entity in the malpractice industry is presented, in the form of the Capitation Liability Theory, in Chapter 11, and Chapter 12 walks the physician or his or her advisor through an actual medical malpractice trial, from voir dire to verdict. Chapter 13, on physician divorce, is another topic not typically addressed until too late, and its corollary topic of asset protection is presented in Chapter 14. Finally, the book rightly ends with Chapter 15, which explains agency law and how to select the insurance professional that's right for you.

As you read, study and reflect on this challenging textbook, remembering the guiding philosophy of Eric Hoffer: "In a time of drastic change; it is the learners who will inherit the future. The learned find themselves equipped to live in a world that no long exists."

Hope Rachel Hetico
Rachel Pentin-Maki
Author's Editors

Vicki L. Buba, JD
Stone, Pregliasco, Haynes, and Buba, LLP
First Trust Center
200 South Fifth Street
Suite 404 South
Louisville, KY 40202
Voice mail: 502-568-4700
Fax: 502-568-9190
E-mail: vlbla@aol.com
Ms. Vicki L. Buba is a partner in the law firm Stone, Pregliasco, Haynes, and Buba, LLP. Her emphasis is on employment law and commercial litigation. She received her undergraduate degree from Indiana University School of Business and graduated cum laude from the University of Louisville Brandeis School of Law. She is a noted legal authority who conducts educational seminars for attorneys and has been a national speaker for companies such as Dun & Bradstreet, AT&T, the Kentucky Legislative Research Commission, and Norex Computer Group.

Robert James Cimasi, ASA, AVA, CBA, FCBI, CMP©
Health Capital Consultants
9666 Olive Blvd, Suite 375
St. Louis, MO 63132-3013
Voice mail: 314-994-7641
Fax: 314-991-3435
Phone: 1-800-FYI-VALU
E-mail: info@healthcapital.com
Robert Cimasi has 20 years of experience serving clients in 35 states. His professional focus is on the financial and economic aspects of health-care service sector entities, including valuation consulting, litigation support, business intermediary and financing services, and health-care transactions, including sales, mergers, and acquisitions. He is a nationally known speaker on health-care industry topics who has served as conference faculty or presenter for such organizations as

the American Society of Appraisers (ASA), the Institute of Business Appraisers (IBA), the International Business Brokers Association (IBBA), the American Institute of Certified Public Accountants (AICPA), the American College of Healthcare Executives (ACHE), the National Association of Healthcare Consultants (NAHC), the National CPA Health Care Advisors Association, and the National Litigation Support Services Association (NLSSA), among others. He has been certified and has served as an expert witness on cases in several states and has provided testimony before federal and state legislative committees. Mr. Cimasi has published articles, chapters, and books and presented papers and case studies before national conferences, and he is often referenced in professional publications.

Gary A. Cook, MSFS, CFP©, CLU, ChFC, RHU, LUTCF, CMP©
COSS Development Corp.
13420 Reese Blvd, West
Huntersville, NC 28078
Voice mail: 704-948-4103
Fax: 704-948-4612
E-mail: gacook@palm.net
Gary A. Cook received a degree in mathematics from the Indiana University of Pennsylvania and his Master of Science degree, in financial services, from the American College in Bryn Mawr. As an accredited estate planner, he has taught courses in that discipline, as well as insurance, business and finance planning, and is past president of the Chester Country Estate Planning Council. He is a professional author and a sought-after public speaker and television guest for the Insurance Broadcast System, Inc. He is also a member of the Society of Financial Service Professionals, the Financial Planning Association, and the Association for Advanced Life Underwriting. Mr. Cook was formerly Assistant Vice President, Advanced Market and Sales Support, for AIG Life Insurance Companies (USA), and is now Content Manager for COSS Development Corporation.

Dr. Charles F. Fenton, III, JD
Law Offices: Suite 101
1145 Cockrell Court
Kennesaw, GA 30152-4760
Voice mail: 404-233-4350
Fax: 404-231-0853
Website: www.MedicalBusinessAdvisors.com
Dr. Charles F. Fenton is a board-certified surgeon from Temple University who received his law degree as class valedictorian from Georgia State University; he currently practices in Atlanta, Georgia. His clients include physicians involved in audits and recoupment actions, as well as in disputes with insurance or managed care companies. He is a contributing author to many books on health-care law and

medical practice, as well as many other medicolegal publications for physicians and the bar. Currently, he is Chief Legal Officer for the *Institute* of Medical Business Advisors, Inc.

Dr. Jay S. Grife, MA, JD
Malpractice Consultants, LLC
Post Office Box # 56320
Jacksonville, FL 32241
Voice mail: 904-886-4477
Fax: 904-880-8446
Dr. Jay S. Grife is a physician-attorney admitted to practice law in the state of Florida. His focus is medical malpractice and health law topics, and he works with counsel of other states. He received a Master of Arts degree in legal history from the University of Florida, and a Juris Doctor degree from the University of Florida, College of Law. He is an Assistant Professor of Law Studies at the University of North Florida and Adjunct Professor of History and Political Science for the University of North Florida. His professional affiliations include the ABA, the Florida Bar Association, the Association of Trial Lawyers of America, and the American College of Legal Medicine.

Hope Rachel Hetico, RN, MHA
Institute of Medical Business Advisors, Inc.
Suite 5901, Wilbanks Drive
Norcross, GA 30092-1141
Voice mail: 770-448-0769
Fax: 775-361-8831
Website: www.MedicalBusinessAdvisors.com
Hope Rachel Hetico received her nursing degree from Valpariso University and her Master's Degree in Healthcare Administration from the College of St. Francis in Joliette, Illinois. She is author's editor for a dozen major textbooks and a nationally known expert in reimbursement, case management, utilization review, and HR, OSHA, NACQA, HEDIS, and JCAHO rules and regulations. Prior to joining the *Institute* of Medical Business Advisors as President, she was a financial advisor, licensed insurance agent, and Certified Professional in Healthcare Quality (CPHQ). She was also Eastern Regional Director for Quality Improvement at Apria Healthcare in Costa Mesa, California.

Anju D. Jessani, MBA, APM
Accredited Professional Mediator and Arbitrator
Divorce with Dignity
223 Bloomfield Street, Suite #104
Hoboken, NJ 07030

Voice mail: 201-217-1090
Fax: 201-217-1220
E-mail: divorcewithdignity@hotmail.com
Website: www.divorcesource.com/NJ/dwd.html
Anju D. Jessani is a divorce mediator and founder of the firm Divorce with Dignity. She received her Association for Conflict Resolution education from the Center for Family and Divorce Mediation in New York, and her practical education through the Hudson County Court's Mediation Program in New Jersey. Currently, she serves on the Parenting Time Committee of the New Jersey Administrative Office of the Courts. She is an editor for *The Children's Advocate*, an Advanced Practitioner Member of the Association for Conflict Resolution, and an Accredited Mediator by the New Jersey Association of Professional Mediators. Ms. Jessani contributes to numerous professional journals and media talk shows. She holds an MBA from the Wharton School and a BA from Rutgers University. Prior to founding Divorce with Dignity, she was a manager with Price Waterhouse and a Vice President with J.P. Morgan.

Dr. Frederick William LaCava, JD
LaCava & Buba Law Firm
5146 East 75th Street
Indianapolis, IN 46250
Voice mail: 317-577-2249
Fax: 317-577-1320
E-mail: LaCavaLaw@aol.com
Dr. Frederick William LaCava, also known as "Duffy,", earned his BA from Emory University, Atlanta, a doctorate in English from the University of North Carolina, Chapel Hill, and a JD from Indiana University School of Law, Bloomington, Indiana. He practices health law at the LaCava Law Firm in Indianapolis, Indiana.

J. Christopher Miller, JD
Robinson, Rappaport, Jampol, Aussenberg & Schleicher, LLP
500 North Winds Center West
11625 Rainwater Drive, Suite 350
Alpharetta, GA 30004
Voice mail: 770-667-1290, Ext 227
Fax: 770-667-1690
E-mail: cmiller@roblaw.com
Mr. J. Christopher Miller holds an economics degree, magna cum laude, from Emory University, as well as a juris doctorate from the Emory University School of Law. He is a well-known author who served as managing editor of the *Bankruptcy Developments Journal,* and he is a member of the Atlanta Bar Association's Estate

Planning and Probate Section and the American Bar Association's Real Property, Probate and Trust Law Section.

W. Barry Nixon, MS
National Institute for Prevention of Workplace Violence, Inc.
22701 Woodlake Lane
Lake Forrest, CA 92630
Voice mail: 949-770-5264
Fax: 949-597-0977
Website: www.workplaceviolence911.com
E-mail: wbnixon@aol.com
W. Barry Nixon is the Executive Director for the National Institute for Prevention of Workplace Violence. Previously, he studied at the Executive Management Program, University of Hawaii, and earned a Master's degree in Human Resource Development from the New School for Social Research (New School University) and a Bachelor's degree in Business Administration from Northeastern University. He has completed the Advanced Human Resource Management Program of Babson College; the certification programs in organization development from National Training Laboratories, in systems thinking from MIT, and in equal employment opportunity and affirmative action from Cornell University's School of Industrial Relations; and the "Creating Competitive Advantage Through Human Resources" program from the University of Michigan's School of Industrial Relations. He is board-certified in workplace security by the National Safety Council and a trained mediator. Mr. Nixon is also the workplace violence consultant for the state of California and many private companies, such as Canon USA, Beckman-Coulter, Gillette, CALTRANS, Southern California Edison, Public Utilities Commission, City of Pasadena, City of Irvine, and the National Transit Institute. Additionally, he is a writer and speaker who teaches at several universities and hosts a radio talk show entitled *Workplace Violence Today.*

Rachel Pentin-Maki, RN, MHA
Institute of Medical Business Advisors, Inc.
Peachtree Plantation – West
Suite 5901, Wilbanks Drive
Norcross, GA 30092-1141
Voice mail: 770-448-0769
Fax: 775-361-8831
Website: www.MedicalBusinessAdvisors.com
Rachel Pentin-Maki received her nursing degree from the Community College of Springfield, Ohio, and her Master's Degree in Healthcare Administration from Lewis University in Evanston, Illinois. Formerly, she helped edit several medical and business textbooks and is a nationally known expert in business staffing and human resource management. Prior to joining the *Institute* of Medical Business

Advisors as Chief Operating Officer, she was the Administrator and Director of Human Resources at the Finnish Retirement Hospital, Lantana, Florida. Currently, she is on the Board of Directors at Finlandia University (Suomi College) in Hancock, Michigan, while leading *i*MBA's European initiative to Helsinki.

Edward J. Rappaport, JD, LLM
Burr & Forman LLP
One Georgia Center, Suite 1200
600 West Peachtree Street
Atlanta, GA 30308
Phone: 404-815-3000
Fax: 404-817-3244
Mr. Edward J. Rappaport graduated from the University of Georgia School of Law and received his LL.M in taxation from the University of Florida. He has a tax, estate, and general business planning practice in Atlanta that represents closely held business interests. He lectures regularly at and is a frequent contributor of scholarly works for the bar. Mr. Rappaport is past president of the North Atlanta Tax Council and is active in the Atlanta Tax Forum and the Fiduciary Law Section of the State Bar of Georgia.

Patricia A. Trites, MPA, CHBC, CPC, CHCC, CHCO
Healthcare Compliance Resources
507 West Jefferson
Augusta, MI 49012
Voice mail: 616-731-2561
Phone: 800-973-1081
Fax: 616-731-2490
E-mail: info@complianceresources.com
Patricia Trites is CEO of Healthcare Compliance Resources who holds a Master's Degree in Public Administration, specializing in health care, from Western Michigan University. She is a college instructor in health-care administration with intensive coding and reimbursement training protocols. She is also a noted speaker for national health-care industry conventions and conducts compliance guidance in the areas of billing and reimbursement, OSHA, CLIA, and employment law. Her professional memberships and affiliations include the American Compliance Institute, the Medical Group Management Association (MGMA), the Independent Accountants Association of Michigan, the National Association of Health Care Consultants, the Institute of Certified Professional Healthcare Consultants, the American Academy of Professional Coders and Trustee, and the Institute of Certified Healthcare Business Consultants.

Disclaimer

The information presented in this textbook is not intended to constitute insurance, risk management, legal, or financial planning advice. Prior to engaging in the type of activity described, you should receive independent counsel from a qualified professional. Examples are generally descriptive and do not purport to be accurate in every regard. The financial and managerial health-care industry is evolving rapidly, and all information should be considered time-sensitive.

Unlike Cassandra of Greek mythology, prescience is not a quality we claim to possess at the *Institute* of Medical Business Advisors, Inc. To stockbrokers, insurance agents, and other financial product vendors, however, the economic future represented an orgy of sales commissions from ill-informed physicians. But, if you were of this philosophical ilk prior to reading this handbook, we hope that you now realize that the bulk of financial planning activities for physicians will now take place on a deeply informed consultative basis, in conjunction with a fiduciary, Certified Financial Planner,© and/or Certified Medical Planner©.

For physicians and financial planners to succeed in this market-driven transformation to health-care specificity, they will need to consider the example of our contributing authors and take certification courses to augment their health-care niche knowledge. Hopefully, this text will prove useful in this regard and serve as a valuable resource for every doctor, advisor, planner, broker, and agent in the country.

Do not be complacent, for as onerous as it seems, physicians and financial consultants may not survive to serve the medical profession without utilizing this sort of information, because the bar to a new level of health-care specific advice has been raised in this decade. Although we will still need insurance and financial products, we believe that all financial advisors will look back on the year 2005 and recognize it as the turning point in the health-care advisory imbroglio. Already there are growing signs of this sea change away from product-driven salesmanship and toward advice-driven practices, as indicated by the popularity of online CFP© and CMP© certification programs and iMBA books, subscriptions, journals, seminars, and class-ware courses.

As the professional marketplace for investment and practice management advice grows, the financial future of physicians will improve through our research and development initiatives in:

- Personal income taxation for physicians
- Medical practice taxation and accounting
- Managed care reimbursement and business decision making
- Medical practice cost analysis and modeling
- Activity-based costing and medical managerial accounting

- Investing, investments, and portfolio management
- Hedge and market neutral fund analysis
- Medical practice financial statements, ratio analysis, and benchmarking

Therefore, as doctors and advisors, please realize that we all face the same issues as you. And, although the multicertified and multidegreed experts of this textbook may have a particular expertise, we should never lose sight of the fact that, above all else, financial planning advice should be delivered in a personal manner, with physician-client interest rather than self-interest, as our guiding standard. *Omnia pro aegroto*, or "all for the client."

Good medicine, good risk management, and good day!

Fraternally,

David Edward Marcinko

Hope Rachel Hetico

Rachel Pentin-Maki

Chapter 1

Insuring the Doctor's Life

(Understanding Life Insurance . . . Personal Strategies for Physicians)

Gary A. Cook

Should one even buy insurance since the industry itself is so skilled at exploiting human foibles?

Christian Gollier, Ph.D.

The Geneva Papers on Risk and Insurance Theory

Yes and no. This book has abundant case examples in Chapters 1–3; the companion financial planning book contains the theory but does not have any of the real-life examples. Unless you are a financial services professional advising physicians, there will be a strong tendency to immediately skip this chapter. The word *insurance* seems to have that effect on many doctors. The physician is assured, however, that each topic, although important, will not be covered in laborious detail.

Acturial Sciences

Although the insurance industry's numerous marketing departments may believe it to be an art, the basis for much of today's insurance evolved from the 17th-century study of probabilities and what is called the Law of Large Numbers. It is not an art, but rather a science. Actually, it's the language of science—mathematics—and more precisely, statistics. Statistically, whenever a potentially random event is to be predicted, the more events recorded or tested, the more likely the final outcome will match the predictions—

this is the first concept of the Law of Large Numbers. Actuaries believe this instinctively. It seems that the rest of us are always trying to beat the odds.

Certainly we all try to be the exception to the rule, the statistical anomaly. For example, looking at all the readers of this chapter as a sample set, and assuming that they are all licensed drivers, we could predict that the reader has been involved in a minor automobile accident at some time in his or her lifetime. If only one person ever reads this section, the likelihood of this prediction being wrong is fairly high. The more people that read it, however, the more likely this prediction will be right on target.

Depending on the reader's age and sex, the number of miles driven in a year, his or her particular area of the country, and some other factors, the actuary can actually predict how often this will occur and, to an uncanny degree, even the extent of the damage. Accuracy of the predictions, then, leads to profits.

Expanding on this second concept within the Law of Large Numbers, the marketing department is tasked with enticing enough drivers (readers) into the company's risk pool to ensure the frequency distribution (experience accuracy) of the actuarial predictions. Insurance coverage can generally be obtained for car-related accidents, tornado damage, cancer expenses, theft losses, cost of repairing tooth decay, being killed by a falling space lab, or any other statistically predictable event. The potential of finding an insurance underwriter willing to predict the event and develop rates usually depends equally on finding enough willing buyers to make the predictions accurate. It's not personal; it's just business.

Social Insurance

Although the efficiency of the private sector has routinely been light years ahead of the bureaucracy of most governments and government agencies, our country's collective desire to assist the underprivileged and downtrodden has legislated the socialization of more and more "insurance" coverage. When potential insurance losses either make coverage unavailable or the premiums unaffordable, the government must aid or supplant private insurance market endeavors if insurance is to be provided.

Social Security, also referred to as OASDI-HI, is very much the socialized foundation of our capitalistic society. A mid-1999 poll taken for Lincoln Financial Group and *Money* magazine by Roper Starch Worldwide Inc. reported that 81 percent of the 50–64 age group, which includes the baby boomers, said they expected Social Security to be a key source of their retirement income. Here, then, is social insurance for the masses—mandated life insurance, retirement savings, disability income insurance, and medical coverage for the elderly. Let's briefly review each of these benefits in some detail.

[A] Retirement Benefits

This is the OA portion of the Social Security acronym (OASDI-HI)—old age. To qualify for this benefit, the worker must have 40 quarters of coverage. The amount of monthly retirement benefit is calculated by the Social Security Administration (SSA) based on the career average earnings, after some minor adjustment for the effects of inflation. A full benefit is then available at the normal retirement age (NRA). The NRA is age 65 for persons born before 1938, but rises gradually to age 67 for persons born after 1954. For those with an NRA of 65, an early retirement is available at age 62, but it is actuarially reduced to 80 percent of the full benefit. For those with an NRA of 67, early retirement is still available at age 62, but the benefit is now approximately 71 percent of the full benefit. Nonworking spouses, at their NRA, can generally expect a benefit of 50 percent based on the working spouse's record.

[B] Survivor Benefits

This is the S portion of the acronym OASDI-HI. Qualification for benefits to be paid to surviving family members is from 6 to 40 quarters of coverage, depending on the deceased worker's age. For young families, unmarried dependent children under the age of 18 years are generally eligible for a "child's benefit." The surviving spouse is also eligible for what is commonly referred to as the "mother's benefit" and is eligible for this payment until the last dependent child under his or her care turns 16 years old. Both benefits are subject to a family maximum. The surviving spouse's benefits do not start again until the surviving spouse reaches the age of 60 years. This could be a considerable period of time and is commonly referred to as the black-out period. It is considered a prime reason to consider personal life insurance on the life of the worker.

These survivor benefits are really what were referred to earlier as "mandated life insurance." Although not payable in lump sum, the monthly benefits paid to the family operate in the same manner as if they had come from a life insurance policy.

There is also an arcane payment of $255 paid to the family of a deceased worker. This figure has not been changed since 1952 and was reported to be originally intended to help pay for a casket. Experience has shown that most funeral homes routinely help the family apply for and receive this benefit as part of their overall service and then show it as a credit on their final bill.

[C] Disability Benefits

This is the DI portion of the acronym OASDI-HI. To qualify for this benefit, the worker must generally have at least six quarters of current coverage and meet very strict guidelines. For example, the qualifications include the inability to perform any substantial gainful work *and* the expectation of being unable to work for at least twelve months or the expectation of an earlier death. Should a worker be unfortunate enough to meet these requirements and to pass the application and screening process, he or she will be eligible for the first monthly check at the end of the sixth month. Each dependent child under the age of 18 years can generally expect a benefit of 50 percent of the worker's benefit. There is, however, no spousal benefit.

[D] Health Insurance

This is the HI portion of the acronym OASDI-HI. It is more commonly referred to as Medicare, and coverage begins when workers reach 65 years, whether they are retired or still working. Spouses can qualify at age 65 years based on their own work record or their working spouse's work record, even when the working spouse has not yet attained the age of 65 years. Persons with severe kidney disease and those who have been entitled to Social Security disability benefits for 2 years are also eligible for Medicare.

Medicare consists of two parts: Hospital Insurance (Part A) and Supplemental Medical Insurance (Part B). Part A is mandatory and considered paid from the FICA (Federal Insurance Contributions Act) withholding tax. Part B is voluntary, with retirees paying an ever-increasing monthly premium from their retirement benefits. Both Part A and Part B contain deductibles and co-pay insurance. These features change annually, so the medical professional or his or her advisor is encouraged to research further as to the current year's specifics.

Medicare coverage for nursing home care will be discussed in the Long-Term Care section.

One last note of possible interest: the above-described benefits are scheduled to be adjusted for the effects of inflation every January 1. This adjustment is based on the annualization of the cost of living reported as occurring during the third quarter each calendar year. This gives the Bureau of Economic Affairs (BEA) time to calculate the rate and the SSA adequate time to react to the figures and program its computers. Contrary to popular belief, the third quarter is not the calendar quarter that has historically shown the least effect of inflation. Based on the published reports since 1980, it's a pretty fair estimate for the entire year.

[E] Other Social Insurance Programs

It is beyond the limited space available in this section to review all the other programs that could be included under socialized insurance. Medicaid, FAIR (Fair Access to Insurance Requirements) Plans, the National Flood Insurance Program, and the various state assigned-risk auto insurance programs would also be eligible for this category.

Risk Management Principles

Risk can be defined in many ways. For one speculating in the stock market, risk has a very different meaning than for one operating a sailboat. For our general discussion of insurance risk, we will define it as the chance of financial loss due to a nonspeculative hazard. Risk comes as a major aspect of our environment. In general, there are four methods of dealing with risks.

1. **Risk Avoidance.** Some risks can be avoided. The risk of airplane accidents can pretty much be avoided by not flying. The risk of a sport-related injury can be

avoided by not playing sports. For the majority of us, however, risk avoidance is not a practical solution for the many risks involved in our daily routines.

2. **Risk Assumption.** The assumption (or retention) of risk can occur as a result of denial or careful consideration. Concern for our exposure to risk can be neglected because of its unrecognized existence, or it can be so inconsequential that we assume it naturally. When we leave the house in the morning, we assume a multiplicity of risks. Driving without a spare tire is an example of assuming a risk. The consequences of smoking, unfortunately, are another many have seen fit to assume.

3. **Risk Reduction.** If avoidance is impossible and assumption is unthinkable, it may be possible to take positive action to reduce (or minimize) the risk. Within this category we could include certain aspects of daily living, such as thoroughly cooking meat, scheduling for periodic maintenance on our vehicles, and installing smoke detectors within our living environment. The overall risk remains, but in a somewhat modified and possibly diminished capacity.

4. **Risk Transfer.** Some of the most important risks faced by individuals and businesses cannot be avoided or assumed, and reduction doesn't provide adequate peace of mind. A method must then be identified to shift the risk to others. One noninsurance method could be to form a corporation. Here the stockholders would limit their risk to their investment, while the creditors would assume much of the remaining risk. Another noninsurance method would be subcontracting. In this case, the general contractor shifts a portion of the risk to the subcontractors. Yet another might be to use mass transit rather than driving our own vehicle. This solution, however, exposes us to other risks, so most people (outside major metropolitan areas) have collectively decided to ignore this option.

Insurance is, by design, an excellent device for transferring risk. When the frequency of the occurrence is low but the potential severity of the financial loss is high, insurance can usually be conveniently priced and thus becomes a viable solution in managing risk.

There are two major categories of insurance policies: those that cover people and those that cover possessions. People can generally be covered by three types of insurance policies: life insurance, annuities, and health insurance. Possessions, or property, are collectively insured through P&C (property and casualty) insurance, also referred to as property-liability insurance.

General Types of Insurance Policies for Physicians

[A] Life Insurance Overview

Life insurance transfers the financial loss resulting from death. A myriad of different families of life insurance policies exists, but they basically have two main branches: term insurance and permanent insurance.

[B] Term Insurance

Term insurance is the simplest form of life insurance and is a sensible place to begin any discussion of life insurance. Term insurance is exactly what the name implies: it provides life insurance coverage for a specified period of time, that is, the term. At the end of the term, the policy is either canceled or continued, typically by paying higher premiums.

[1] ANNUAL RENEWABLE TERM INSURANCE

The oldest form of term insurance is that of annual renewable term (ART). These polices have premiums that typically begin very low but increase steadily each year. At the end of each year, the policyholder has the option to renew coverage at the higher premium or cancel the coverage. By the time an insured reaches age 60 years and the probability of dying becomes more pronounced, the premiums start to rise drastically. The increased premium is simply a reflection of the increased chance of dying combined with the obvious fact that there are fewer lives at that age over which to spread the risk.

ART insurance has lost much of its popularity recently since level-premium term products have captured more market share. Nonetheless, ART policies are appropriate when a very short-term life insurance need exists, for example, to cover a 5-year loan balance.

[2] LEVEL TERM INSURANCE

Level term policies offer a premium that remains level for a specified period of time, usually 5, 10, 15, 20, 25, or 30 years. The most popular products have premiums that are guaranteed to remain level for the prescribed period. Be aware, however, that policies do exist whereby the insurance company has the right to change the premiums during this period. The medical professional should be absolutely sure as to which type of policy is being bought.

Following the selected level-premium period, the term policy is typically canceled, although the owner may keep the policy in force by paying higher premiums. The premiums, however, may increase drastically, sometimes even to an absurd degree.

The affordability (during the selected term period) and simplicity of these products have made them very popular. It is easy to see why a 40-year-old medical professional or health-care practitioner would be attracted to a term policy that guarantees its premium for 20 years. It is entirely reasonable for many to obtain affordable coverage that will end exactly when it is anticipated that it will no longer be needed—at retirement. It is a seemingly very nice fit, unless justification can be made for longer coverage.

> **Example:** Dr. Simms, 32 years old and married, just purchased a house and just had her second child. Before returning to her practice, she decides to purchase $1,000,000 of life insurance. Being a nonsmoker and in good

health, she could purchase a 20-year term policy for about $650 per year. This premium is guaranteed to remain level for 20 years. Thus, for a very low rate, this policy will cover her until her youngest child is about to graduate from college.

If Dr. Simms wanted to keep this coverage after the 20th year, the premium at age 53 years could be as high as $7,000 and grow to $12,000 by age 60 years. The premium will continue to rise each year.

No matter which type of term policy is purchased, it is always highly recommended that the policy offer a conversion feature. A conversion feature allows the owner to convert the term policy into a permanent policy at the same original underwriting class as the term policy, regardless of the actual health at the time of conversion. This is a very valuable feature that provides the term policyholder with both flexibility and security in the event of a change in health.

Example: Dr. Simms's 20-year term policy also has a 15-year conversion feature. In the 12th policy year (age 44 years), Dr. Simms becomes seriously ill. She realizes her term policy will only cover her for 8 more years (she decides the anticipated premiums after year 20 are just too expensive to justify). She also realizes that she still has an excellent chance of living beyond those 8 years. Since her family will depend on her income for longer than the 8 years, she asks her financial planner/insurance agent for assistance.

Because of her recently diagnosed health issues, a newly underwritten permanent policy is not attainable: she is currently considered uninsurable. Fortunately, her term policy has a conversion feature. She converts her term policy to a permanent policy with the same company and for the same preferred health rate that she had on the original term policy. The new premium of $5,900 per year is much higher than the current term premium because this product now offers lifetime coverage, but it is still affordable. More importantly, she can be sure her family will receive the insurance proceeds regardless of when she dies.

If the same situation happened and Dr. Simms's policy did not have the conversion feature, she would be forced to continue the term policy beyond the 20th year by paying ever-increasing premiums (see previous example) or terminate the coverage.

[3] DECREASING TERM INSURANCE

Decreasing (or reducing) term is another common style of term insurance that not only lasts for a specified period of time but also reduces death benefits each year. These are often recommended by lenders to cover mortgages as the mortgage balance decreases each year. These policies have become very rare because level term insurance is so affordable that it makes little sense to buy decreasing coverage.

Currently marketed term products generally have excellent premiums that allow a policyholder to purchase substantial coverage for a very affordable price. But it is important to keep in mind why the premium is so affordable—because the vast majority of term policies never pay a death benefit. The simple reason for this unexpected fact is that most people outlive the term period or their policies are not in force when they die.

[4] TRIPLE X

One more item needs to be mentioned, that of Regulation XXX—also referred to simply as Triple X. This is a model regulation from the National Association of Insurance Commissioners (NAIC) that was implemented on January 1, 2000. This regulation has substantially changed the manner in which an insurance company must set aside reserves for any term policy with a premium guarantee longer than 15 years, or a universal life policy with a secondary guarantee of more than 5 years (this will be covered soon).

It basically requires higher reserves for policies with longer guarantee periods. Higher reserves generally result in the insurance companies increasing their premiums. As a direct result, if the medical professional or health-care practitioner has a current policy with a premium or death benefit guarantee longer than 5 years, the policy should probably not be replaced or lapsed without some serious thought (see Policy Replacement for more information).

[5] TERM INSURANCE SUMMATION

In summary, term insurance is generally intended as pure protection (death benefit) for a finite period of time. The death benefit, as discussed, can be level or decreasing. The premium paying period can be for 1 year (ART) or levelized for a period of time. Term insurance is routinely referred to as temporary insurance, both because of its renewability feature and because of the nature of the short-term risk needing to be protected.

[C] Permanent Insurance

Permanent insurance differs from term insurance in two major ways. First, it is usually designed to last to age 95 or 100 years (commonly referred to as the maturity date) without any future requirement to requalify for the coverage by providing proof of good health. Some newer contracts, in fact, have no maturity date at all and are being illustrated as lasting until age 115 years. Second, permanent policies have some form of cash value accumulation. This feature will be discussed later.

One permanent insurance policy can cover a single life, two lives, or an entire family. Policies covering two lives can provide a death benefit either on the first death or the last death. These policies and their uses will be described later in this section.

Generally, permanent insurance has a predefined level-premium payable until a stated maturity, but the premium-paying period can potentially be shortened in a number of ways. Regardless, the predefined premium is substantially higher in a permanent policy than in a comparable face-amount term insurance policy. This higher premium results in the aforementioned aspect of an internal accumulation of cash value.

This accumulation was originally designed by actuaries to help level the premium over longer periods of time. It has since, however, been seen by many as a convenient method of accumulating funds in a tax-deferred manner. Taxation will be discussed later in this section.

Permanent insurance comes in four standard variations: whole life, variable life, universal life, and variable universal life. Do not be fooled by the title *permanent*, however. Today's life insurance products are very complex, and few policies are truly permanent. Events can occur that result in policies lapsing or paying reduced benefits, even when specified premiums have been submitted in a timely manner. The word *permanent* simply reflects the fact that these policies are expected to last until the insured's death no matter when that may be.

[1] WHOLE LIFE INSURANCE

Whole life, also called straight life or ordinary life, is the oldest and the most classic type of permanent insurance. It typically has the highest required premium of the four standard variations, but it is also the least risky for the policyholder. Whole life remains in force until maturity and is guaranteed to pay the full death benefit if the required premiums are paid in a timely manner. The whole life family of policies also includes those referred to as Life Paid-Up at 65, 83, 85, 95, etc.

Whole life premiums are fixed; that is, they cannot be arbitrarily changed from year to year, and they must be paid in a timely manner if the entire death benefit is to be kept intact. Whole life is more rigid than universal life, but it counters by offering the highest level of guarantees. Whole life, like all permanent policies, offers growing cash values that can be borrowed by the policyholder if needed.

Because whole life is considered expensive, companies have created ways, such as through term riders, to reduce the premium to more affordable levels. However, the drawback of these term riders is that more risk falls upon the policyholder. When term riders are added to a whole life policy, the premium becomes cheaper, but the entire policy is no longer guaranteed to last to maturity and/or may pay reduced death benefits under some situations.

> **Example:** Dr. Jones, age 40 years, can purchase a $200,000 20-year term policy with a conversion feature for $250. His insurance agent also quotes him a $200,000 whole life policy for $3,150, or a $100,000 whole life policy with a $100,000 term rider for $1,650.
>
> Dr. Jones's term policy is expected to only be in force for 20 years, but both whole life policies are expected to remain in force until death—thus the extra cost. However, under some scenarios, the whole life with rider will only pay $120,000 death benefit, but the *pure* whole life will always pay the $200,000 as long as premiums are paid on time.

An Overview of Common Types of Life Insurance

Pure Protection Only

Cost = Mortality Charges and Administrative Expenses (M & E)

	Generic description	Investment possibilities	Investment flexibility	Access to funds	Premium flexibility	Face value flexibility	Common uses
_?_ YEAR DECREASING TERM	Reducing face value protection for _?_ years; lowest cost	NONE	NONE	NONE	NONE (miss a premium and the policy LAPSES)	NONE (decreases by schedule)	Ideal for loan or mortgage protection
ANNUAL RENEWABLE TERM	Level face value to age 70 or 100 years; lower cost, but increases annually	NONE	NONE	NONE	NONE (miss a premium and the policy LAPSES)	NONE (must buy another)	Ideal for short-term need or limited cash flow
_?_ YEAR LEVEL TERM	Level face value for _?_ years; low cost, but increases often	NONE	NONE	NONE	NONE (miss a premium and the policy LAPSES)	NONE (must buy another)	Ideal for short- to intermediate-term need
Protection COMBINED with Tax Advantaged Cash Values Cost = Mortality Charges and Administrative Expenses (M & E) PLUS Expenses Associated with Investment Opportunities							
WHOLE LIFE	Level cost for entire life (may be shortened using dividends)	Insurance company decides	NONE	Borrow* or surrender	NONE (miss a premium and it becomes a LOAN)	NONE (must buy another)	Appeals to older ages; maximum guarantees
VARIABLE LIFE	Level cost for entire life WITH investment options	Fixed account, balanced account, stock accounts, bond accounts, etc.	MAXIMUM (you choose and can change periodically)	Borrow* or surrender	NONE (miss a premium and it becomes a LOAN)	NONE (must buy another)	Sophisticated buyers, for whom protection is primary concern

	Generic description	Investment possibilities	Investment flexibility	Access to funds	Premium flexibility	Face value flexibility	Common uses
UNIVERSAL LIFE	Variable cost with current interest rates	Insurance company decides	NONE	MAXIMUM withdraw, borrow,* or surrender	MAXIMUM Cash value must support M&E, but premium can vary greatly	MAXIMUM Reduce anytime, increase only if still healthy	Great premium flexibility if short-term rates are satisfactory
VARIABLE UNI-VERSAL LIFE	Variable cost with investment options	Fixed account, balanced account, stock accounts, bond accounts, etc.	MAXIMUM (you choose and can change periodically)	MAXIMUM Withdraw, borrow,* or surrender	MAXIMUM Cash value must support M&E, but premium can vary greatly	MAXIMUM Reduce anytime, increase only if still healthy	Great premium flexibility AND investment control

Borrowers should be aware of the possibility of "phantom income" should the policy lapse.

Note: This chart is intended for educational purposes only and does not constitute an endorsement or offer for any particular product or company. Prior to the purchase of any variable product, the consumer should receive the appropriate Prospectus containing complete information on the product and the separate accounts.

READ ANY PROSPECTUS CAREFULLY BEFORE YOU INVEST OR SEND MONEY.

When a whole life contract is purchased, the death benefit is fully guaranteed, as long as the premium is paid on time every year. At the maturity date, the internal cash values (to be discussed later) will equal the amount of guaranteed death benefit: this is called endowment.

If the insurance company offers a participating policy and has good experiences with its business over the years—that is, fewer people die than expected—the company may illustrate that the policy receives dividends.

Dividends are paid to participating policies and are considered a return of the policyholder's premium and are, therefore, not taxable income. A policyholder can generally take them in cash, use them to buy paid-up additions, use them to buy 1-year term additions, or have them accumulate at interest, like an additional savings account. Using the dividend to buy paid-up additions or allowing them to accumulate at interest will provide the policyholder with an additional source of future premiums.

At some point in the policy's life, these funds may be sufficient to allow the policyholder to cease paying premiums and direct the insurance company to take its annual premium from these excess values. This is sometimes called a "vanishing premium," a "short pay" premium, or a "premium offset." The premiums are still due and still paid each year, but instead come from the excess external policy values rather than the owner's pocket.

A life insurance agent may illustrate this discontinued premium flow as a benefit of the policy. Beware! This is a *projection*, meaning the company is not guaranteeing the ability to stop paying premiums. This may possibly occur if the company keeps doing well, but it is not guaranteed!

Many whole life policies were sold this way in the past, and although some policies actually did allow the owner to stop paying premiums, many policies did not. This surprised many policyholders who were expecting to cease their premiums. Medical professionals or health-care practitioners must make sure they understand what policy aspects are guaranteed and what are merely projections.

A well-informed purchaser, when purchasing a whole life policy, will ask his or her insurance agent to check the *A.M. Best's Annual Historical Dividend Report.* This report tells how a company's actual dividends compared to its projections for each year. It is wise to be leery of illustrations from companies that consistently fail to meet their projections.

Before a whole life product is purchased, ask to see what happens to the death benefit and premiums if the company experiences a lower dividend scale (worse business conditions). This will allow the purchaser to see how sensitive the policy is to different business conditions. Beware of whole life policies that are very sensitive to reduced dividend scales.

[2] UNIVERSAL LIFE INSURANCE

Universal life was developed in the late 1970s and became a very popular product in a very short time. Generally, in terms of price and risk to the policyholder, it falls between term and whole life.

Universal life is similar to a bank savings account that has automatic monthly withdrawals to pay for the death benefit. An explanation may be in order. Each universal life premium goes into the policy and becomes part of the cash value just as a bank savings deposit becomes part of a savings account. Some policies have a premium expense charge that generally is designed to pay the individual state premium tax. The cash value also has monthly debits to pay for the death benefit and/or any riders, and most also charge a monthly administrative fee. The resulting cash value of the policy earns a competitive rate similar to a money market interest rate. Finally, policy owners receive an annual report that itemizes all relevant costs, to the penny. Universal life has often been called "whole life unbundled" because of this feature.

On the following page is a representative example of how certain nonguaranteed annual policy values and charges might look for a 55-year-old male with a $1,000,000 policy. Such a break-out of charges is typically available from the insurance company for both universal life and variable universal life.

Clearly, the cash value of the universal life policy will depend on which is greater: the amount going into the policy (premiums and interest) or the amounts leaving the policy (the cost of the death benefit and the monthly administrative fees). Additionally, the charges for the death benefit will rise over time as the insured gets older (just like ART rates).

Typically, in the early policy years, the amounts flowing into the policy are greater than the internal charges and the subsequent cash value increases. If, at some point, the outflows exceed the inflows, the cash value will cease growing and may even decline. If the cash value falls to zero, the policy generally lapses unless more premiums are paid.

The policyholder can periodically adjust the amount and timing of the universal life premiums and even skip premiums (without incurring a loan, which is the result with whole life). Any change in premium amount or mode of payment will also change the cash value projections on a policy illustration. Skipping premiums will cause a drop in cash values and possibly cause a policy to lapse. If ample cash value has accumulated in the contract, the ability to skip a premium without adverse consequences becomes more probable. This flexibility is one of the reasons for the popularity of universal life policies.

Because universal life polices are very interest rate sensitive, a policyholder needs to keep track of the policy values each year to make sure the policy is performing as expected. When a policyholder receives his or her "Annual Report," it is a good idea to use this as a reminder to request (from the agent or the company) a reprojection of future amounts based on the then current assumptions. This is commonly called an inforce projection or midstream proposal.

Just as with "vanishing premium" whole life projections, there have also been problems with universal life. In the 1980s, interest rates were very high, and this appeared to make universal life policies appear very inexpensive compared to whole life. Unfortunately, interests rates have declined dramatically, and those polices have been credited far less interest than was originally illustrated. As a result, the cash values were lower than expected and policy owners had to either increase their premiums or risk the policies lapsing.

If purchasing a universal life policy, the health-care professional should definitely ask to see illustrations reflecting declining interest rates. Typically these do not need to be to the guaranteed rate. Ask the agent or broker for a history of the company's rates and gauge your request accordingly. If policy performance is drastically affected, commit to a higher premium so that coverage is not jeopardized in the event of falling interest rates.

> **Example:** Dr. Bob Boucher is about to purchase a $250,000 universal life policy. Based on the current credited interest rate of 6.5 percent and the expected cost of insurance in the policy, he commits to a premium of $3,000 per year. He wisely asks to see what would happen to the cash values if, with this premium, the interest rate fell to 5 percent after he bought the policy. The agent shows him that the policy would likely lapse (zero cash value) at Bob's age of 80 years.
>
> Bob decides this isn't safe enough and instead commits to a premium of $3,300. With this new premium and a 5 percent crediting rate, Bob's policy is now projected to last until his age of 95 years. Bob has thus partially self-insured against further interest rate declines.

Besides being interest rate sensitive, the insurance company can also change the internal cost of the death benefit on a universal life policy. Obviously, increasing these charges could cause the cash values to drop and the policy to lapse. Companies try to avoid doing this, but it can and does happen. A potential buyer should also inquire as to the company's history of "mortality cost" increases before purchasing any universal life policy. Avoid companies that have a history of raising their insurance costs or that fail to provide this vital information.

[3] VARIABLE LIFE INSURANCE

Variable life is a type of permanent insurance that comes in the same two forms discussed above: universal life and whole life.

The same general design of whole life and universal life, as just described, also applies to variable whole life and variable universal life. The only real difference is the availability of investment choices for the cash value of the policy. With whole life and universal life, the insurance companies generally invest the money in fixed income investments like bonds and mortgages. The insurance company then declares the interest rate, which gets credited to the company's policies (except term, which has no cash value).

With variable policies, the company offers the policyholder a choice of investment options. These investment options are called separate accounts and resemble traditional mutual funds. Good variable life policies should offer a wide array of investment choices to include money market funds, bond funds, balanced funds, stock funds, and international funds. It is not unusual to find policies offering in excess of 30 such separate accounts.

The policyholder then chooses the account, or accounts, that match his or her investment risk. Most policy owners put a majority of their premium dollars into equity accounts because they have historically provided better returns than most other investments. Of course, the higher the actual returns of the separate accounts, the more the cash value grows.

> **Example:** Dr. Jason Green, age 42 years, and his twin brother, Dr. Ben, both purchase a $300,000 policy and both pay the same $2,500 premium each year. Jason's policy is a variable universal life because he believes in the continued growth of the stock market. Ben's policy, on the other hand, is a traditional universal life because he has a low risk tolerance and is afraid of losing money in market crashes.
>
> If, over the next 15 years, Jason's choice of separate accounts experiences a 10 percent per year average, his policy will have a potential cash value of $36,000. Ben's policy, however, if only credited 6.5 percent, will have a potential cash value of $29,500.
>
> On the other hand, if the separate accounts Jason chose earned only a 7 percent per year average, then the potential cash value would be $28,000, less than Ben's policy even though 7 percent was a higher return than Ben's 6.5 percent average return.

This seemingly odd result occurs because the internal policy expense costs of a variable policy are typically higher than the internal costs of a fixed interest rate policy. It therefore takes a higher return inside of a variable life to offset the effect of these higher internal costs. Generally, one should not purchase a variable policy unless one expects the separate accounts to earn an average of at least 8.5 percent per year.

Variable life policies give policyholders more control over how their premium dollars are invested. These polices allow greater potential returns, but at greater risk, which the policyholder assumes. Variable policies have become very popular over the last 10 to 15 years because of the recent bull market. These products are most appropriate for policy owners with a moderate to high risk tolerance, who believe in the long-term superiority of equities as investments, and who have a long-term time horizon.

The same principles that apply to investing in general also apply to variable policies. A wise variable policyholder will invest his or her premiums in several separate accounts to achieve diversification. Most variable policies will also allow dollar cost averaging and asset rebalancing.

[4] OTHER VARIETIES OF LIFE POLICIES

[a] Survivorship Life Insurance

Survivorship life is commonly referred to as second-to-die life insurance. Unlike the typical life insurance policy, which has one primary insured and pays a death benefit when that person dies, a survivorship life policy generally has two insureds and only pays a death benefit when both of the insureds are deceased.

Survivorship products have existed for about 30 years, but they became very popular after passage of the unlimited marital deduction in the Economic Recovery Tax Act

(ERTA) of 1981. These policies are used almost exclusively in the estate planning realm, where the husband and wife have a combined net worth of more than two times the current unified credit, that is, $2.0 million in year 2003, and $3.0 million in year 2004. Wealthy couples, typically between the ages of 50 and 70 years, purchase survivorship insurance to assist in providing adequate liquidity for estate transfer and settlement costs routinely due at the second death.

In 1996, a new feature was seen in universal life and, in particular, survivorship universal life policies—that of a secondary guarantee. The primary guarantees in these policies were those of a guaranteed minimum credited interest rate and a maximum amount of monthly charges, and, specifically, a maximum charge for mortality. The earlier versions of these policies illustrated poorly with regard to guaranteed cash values, unless a whole life type of premium was paid.

Secondary guarantees have also been called no-lapse guarantees. Basically, these policies are guaranteed to stay in force for a specified number of years as long as the policyholder pays a required cumulative premium as of a particular date, even if the underlying primary guarantees would allow the policy to otherwise lapse. Most importantly, the new no-lapse premiums were still considerably lower than that of a whole life policy. Unfortunately, Triple X regulations have forced most insurance companies to remove these products from sale or substantially increase their premium requirements for this benefit.

Survivorship insurance comes in all the forms already mentioned: whole life, universal life, variable whole life, and variable universal life.

[b] Joint First-to-Die Life Insurance

Just as with survivorship life insurance, a joint first-to-die policy generally insures two people. Unlike survivorship, however, a joint first-to-die pays upon the death of the first insured.

Joint first-to-die policies typically make sense in family insurance planning for households where both parents work, and occasionally they are used for mortgage (loan) protection. The vast majority of joint first-to-die plans, however, are used in the business world. These policies are particularly well suited for multiple key person plans or for stock redemption (entity) buy–sell plans.

It is important to remember that when the first insured dies under a joint first-to-die policy, the death benefit is paid and the policy is terminated: coverage no longer exists on the remaining insured(s). This problem can be solved by buying a guaranteed insurability option on the policy that allows the remaining insured to purchase a new joint policy with no underwriting immediately after the first death.

Another rider that should be considered when joint policies are purchased for business planning reasons is a substitute insured rider. This allows the policyholder to exchange an insured with a new insured. This rider comes in very handy if one of the insureds leaves the business and is replaced by someone else. Many insurance companies, unfortunately, have withdrawn this rider because of the difficulty in administering it.

Joint first-to-die policies are certainly more complex and cause a different set of potential planning issues than individual policies. For that reason, extra care must be used when considering these policies.

[c] Interest-Sensitive Whole Life Insurance

Interest-sensitive whole life, also referred to as current assumption whole life, is a hybrid of whole life and universal life. Like whole life, the premiums are fixed. Some companies fix the premium for the life of the policy, but most fix the premium only for a specified period of time. As with universal life, the current internal mortality charges are lower than for a whole life policy, but the insurance company retains the right to raise them. Also as with universal life, a competitive interest rate is credited to the policy cash values each month. These polices are currently not very common.

[d] Group Life Insurance

Group life insurance coverage is very common, and the vast majority of people have this form of coverage at work and/or have the opportunity to purchase more group life insurance coverage through their employer or other associations to which they belong. Most group life insurance policies are group term because term is affordable and easy to understand, but group universal life and group variable universal life policies exist as well.

Many employers, especially larger ones, typically offer a minimum of group life insurance as an automatic employee benefit. Since current tax code provisions allow up to $50,000 of group coverage as a totally tax-free benefit, this is often the initial amount of coverage. Many employers also offer the employee the ability to purchase additional group life insurance with the premium being deducted from each paycheck. The main advantage of group life insurance is its convenience.

The major disadvantages concern the lack of flexibility. It may not be easy to change your coverage under a group life policy, and if you leave your company, it may not be possible to take the coverage with you. For this reason, most people prefer to purchase their own individual life insurance policy for the bulk of their life insurance protection.

[e] Single-Premium Life Insurance

Single-premium life is exactly as the name implies: the owner pays one premium for lifetime coverage. Clearly, the premium will be much larger than in any other type of insurance for an equivalent death benefit.

These policies have become quite rare since the Modified Endowment Contract (MEC) rules were established to discourage large premiums early in the life of a policy (see Life Insurance Taxation later in this chapter). Nonetheless, these polices still have a limited number of uses. They may be appropriate if tax-deferred growth is desired and the money is not expected to be needed during the insured's lifetime.

> **Example:** Dr. Warbucks wants to make a sizable lifetime charitable gift to his local hospital, for which he will receive an income tax deduction. He has plenty of money and prefers to just "get the gift out of the way" rather than

commit to an annual donation. He therefore purchases a single premium life policy and gifts it to the hospital. When Dr. Warbucks dies, his local hospital will receive the death benefit. He also hopes the policy will be a good investment while he is living and will increase substantially in death benefit by the time of his death.

[f] The 5-100 Rule

With any universal life insurance policy (and certainly all variable life policies), fluctuating rates of return, the actual timing of the premium payments, and potential internal policy changes by the insurance company all contribute to results that will probably differ substantially from the original illustration. The 5-100 rule states that as a result of accounting for these elements, all initial projections of cash value beyond 5 years will necessarily be 100 percent incorrect when compared to actuality. A prudent policyholder should therefore keep on top of any changes and react accordingly. If a policyholder ignores his or her policy for even 5 years, any adverse changes could be so drastic as to make rectifying them very costly.

[D] Death Benefit Settlement Options

Settlement options refer to the different ways a beneficiary can receive the death benefit payable upon the death of the insured. A beneficiary commonly receives the entire death benefit in a lump sum, but that is certainly not the only choice. Another possibility is the interest-only option, whereby the beneficiary leaves the death benefit with the insurer and receives the monthly interest. Another common option is the lifetime annuity option, whereby the death benefit is paid out as a guaranteed lifetime income (see the discussion of annuities later in this chapter).

Settlement options can be left to the discretion of the beneficiary. In this way, the beneficiary can hopefully make an informed choice based on his or her particular situation at the time. Alternatively, the policyholder can specify a particular settlement option. During the life of the insured, the policyholder can instruct the insurance company to pay the beneficiary according to a design the policyholder feels is appropriate. However, a better alternative would be to establish a trust for any beneficiary unable to manage his or her funds, rather than use a restrictive settlement option.

Life Insurance Taxation

As mentioned earlier, the word *insurance* evokes unusual responses in most people. If there were ever two concepts that together inspired both dread and boredom in an audience, insurance and taxation would be high on the list. Putting them together is, assuredly, not glamorous, but life insurance does have a number of tax advantages that can be potentially rewarding. However, there are also some pitfalls that should be avoided.

[A] Income Tax–Free Death Benefit

Let's start with the simplest tax advantage, that of the death benefit being received by the beneficiary income tax free. When the insured dies, the named beneficiary generally receives all death proceeds free of any income taxes. The word *generally* is used because there are situations that can cause the entire death benefit, or a large part of it, to become subject to income tax.

[B] Transfer-for-Value Problem

This is a situation that can cause the death benefit of a life insurance policy to be income taxable. This can be a complicated topic, and the situation may arise unexpectedly, especially when life insurance is used for business purposes.

Generally, if an existing life insurance policy is transferred to a new owner for some type of consideration (money, exchange of property, or a quid pro quo arrangement), then the death benefit becomes taxable to the beneficiary to the extent that the proceeds exceed the basis in the policy. Basis becomes the amount of consideration paid at the time of transfer and all future premiums following the transfer, which are paid by the new owner.

There are five exceptions to this rule:

1. Transfers by any person or company of ownership to the person insured by the policy
2. Transfers by a business partner (in the strictest sense, that is, not a coshareholder) to another partner in the same business
3. Transfers to a partnership by any of the partners
4. Transfers to a corporation in which the insured is a stockholder or officer
5. Transfers between corporations (under certain conditions) in a tax-free reorganization

If a transfer for value falls under one of these exceptions, then the policy retains its tax-free death benefit status.

Medical practitioners may use life insurance as part of their business plan, for example, as part of a buy–sell arrangement. Anytime the practitioner is the transferor or transferee of ownership in an existing life insurance policy, experienced counsel should be consulted to make sure the transfer for value rule is not violated. Even naming a beneficiary in exchange for something in return could inadvertently cause the proceeds to be taxable to the beneficiary. A bona fide gift, however, is not a transfer for value.

[C] Tax-Deferred Growth

Another tax advantage of life insurance is its income tax–deferred cash value growth. As mentioned earlier in this section, life insurance products, other than term, have cash accumulation potential. The cash values will depend on the policy style, the amount of the premiums, and also the general economic environment. If there is growth in the cash value, the growth will be tax deferred, under current tax laws.

[D] Withdrawals and Loans

Income taxes are not generally an issue unless cash values are removed from the policy while the insured is still alive. There are three methods of accessing a policy's cash value while the insured is living. The first choice is to surrender the policy. If the policy is surrendered and the cash value is greater than the total premiums paid, the difference is subject to ordinary income tax. A policyholder must give careful consideration before surrendering because if a policy is surrendered, the policy no longer exists.

What if you want to access a portion of the cash value but not lose the coverage? There are two methods by which to accomplish this: through withdrawals and through loans. A withdrawal, also called a partial surrender, does not cause the policy to terminate, but it does lower the death benefit of the policy by the amount of the withdrawal. If a withdrawal is requested, then under the current FIFO (first in, first out) accounting rules, the total amount of premiums paid into the policy are removed first, and, more importantly, without any income tax liability. Any withdrawals removed in excess of the gross premium paid would be income taxable.

Because withdrawals beyond a policy's basis are taxable, loans are often used at this point, because policy loans are not taxable. If the insured dies while a loan is outstanding, the insurance company repays itself from the death proceeds, and the remaining death benefit goes to the named beneficiary. In other words, the death proceeds will decrease by an amount equal to each loan. Also, unless the interest charged on the loan balance is paid annually, the size of the loan will increase as the interest accrues to the loan. So when withdrawals and loans are combined, a significant portion of a policy's cash value can be accessed while the policy is still in force.

A word of caution is in order. Any policyholder using this technique must be very vigilant that the policy remains in force until the insured's death. Should the policy lapse for insufficient cash value, the entire outstanding loan, including the accrued interest on the debt, would immediately become taxable. Expressed in the slang of today, "This is not a good thing." Basically, other than through the receipt of death proceeds, if the policyholder receives more money from the policy than was paid into the policy, income taxes may be assessed on the difference.

> **Example:** Fifteen years ago, Dr. Russell purchased a $500,000 universal life policy on his own life. He named his wife as beneficiary. The total premiums paid into the policy are $60,000 and the current cash value is $150,000. Dr. Russell's children are in college, and he could use a little extra money for their tuition payments this year.
>
> If Dr. Russell takes a $50,000 withdrawal from his policy, no taxable event occurs because it is less than his total premium paid. Dr. Russell's death benefit will also drop by $50,000 to $450,000, and his basis from

$60,000 to $10,000. If, during the next year, Dr. Russell decides to remove $20,000 more from his policy, then $10,000 would be taxable because his total withdrawals would exceed his basis. The death benefit would now be $430,000.

To avoid taxes on the $10,000, Dr. Russell could get the same basic results by taking a $10,000 withdrawal followed by a $10,000 loan. This way the total withdrawals would not exceed his remaining basis. Future premiums could be recharacterized as loan repayments until the loan is extinguished. Loan interest would not be deductible.

If, instead of taking any withdrawals, Dr. Russell decides to surrender the policy and receive the entire $150,000 cash value, then $90,000 is taxable to Dr. Russell. Of course, by surrendering the policy he ensures that his coverage no longer exists.

[E] Violating the 2 out of 3 Rule

Another common mistake involves an issue of gift taxation. Violating the 2 out of 3 rule can result in a policyholder unwittingly making a sizable gift of the entire death benefit and wasting a major portion of his or her unified credit as a consequence. The *3* refers to the parties to the policy: the insured, the policyholder, and the beneficiary. *Two* of these *three* parties should almost always be the same.

Example: Dr. Beck wishes to purchase life insurance on his partner Dr. Kelly so that if Dr. Kelly dies, he can purchase Dr. Kelly's share of their practice from Dr. Kelly's wife. Dr. Beck is the owner of the policy, Dr. Kelly is the insured, and Dr. Beck is the beneficiary. This is an appropriate design. If Dr. Kelly dies, Dr. Beck receive the proceeds from the policy and can use them to immediately purchase Dr. Kelly's half of the practice from his wife.

If, however, Dr. Beck is the owner, Dr. Kelly is the insured, and Dr. Beck decides to name Mrs. Kelly as the beneficiary, this would cause the death proceeds received by Mrs. Kelly to be a gift from Dr. Beck. This gift would most certainly be in excess of the $11,000 annual gift exclusion and consequently cause Dr. Beck to file a gift tax return and to use his unified credit in the process. This is a very inappropriate design for a buy–sell arrangement.

[F] Modified Endowment Contracts (MEC)

Modified endowment contracts is the last tax issue to be addressed with regard to life insurance policies. Because the cash values inside a life insurance policy grow tax deferred, many policy owners once recognized this advantage and deposited large, single premiums into their policies. Unfortunately, this was perceived by Congress as abusive. It was clear that these people were buying life insurance primarily as a means of escaping income taxation and not actually for the life insurance death benefit.

As a result, the laws were changed in 1984 to discourage putting very large amounts of money into life insurance contracts in the early years. Based on the age, sex, and size of the death benefit, an MEC premium (also referred to as the TAMRA 7-pay guideline) is established for each policy. For the first 7 years of the policy, the policyholder cannot have paid cumulative premiums greater than the cumulative MEC premium.

> **Example:** Based on Dr. Salvatore's age and death benefit, the MEC premium for his life insurance policy is $20,000 per year. Dr. Salvatore pays $10,000 of premiums in year 1, $21,000 in year 2, and $50,000 in year 3. Even though the year 2 premium is more than the annual MEC premium, Dr. Salvatore's cumulative premium after year 2 is only $31,000, whereas the cumulative MEC premium is $40,000. Therefore, it is not an MEC after year 2. However, at the end of year 3, Dr. Salvatore's cumulative premium is $81,000 and the cumulative MEC premium is $60,000. Thus, this policy is now an MEC.

If a policy is classified as an MEC, then it is treated as an annuity contract, and not a life insurance policy, for any and all lifetime withdrawals or loans. Taxable interest earnings are removed before basis is recovered; that is, all funds removed from the policy in excess of basis will be immediately taxable. If the insured is under 59½ years of age, there will also be a 10 percent tax penalty. Thus, one of the basic tax benefits of life insurance is destroyed. Remember from our example that withdrawals of non-MEC policies are not taxable until the withdrawals exceed the cumulative premiums. Finally, once an MEC, always an MEC.

> **Example:** Ten years later, the same Dr. Salvatore (from the previous example) desires to withdraw $25,000 to purchase a car for his daughter. Although the policy may have $150,000 of cash value and he has paid $81,000 of premiums, the policy is looked at for tax purposes as an annuity. The entire $25,000 is taxable, and if Dr. Salvatore is under 59½ years old, he will have an additional 10 percent penalty to pay.

In summary, life insurance cash values can be accessed by the policyholder. However, the tax treatment can be confusing, and there are a couple of methods available for accessing that value: through withdrawals or loans. Consequently, whenever a policyholder is looking to take money from a policy, a life insurance agent or financial planner should be consulted.

Health Insurance Overview

Health insurance transfers the potential financial hardship caused by severe or chronic health conditions resulting from accidents or illnesses (morbidity), whereas life insurance is concerned with death (mortality). Health insurance, like life insurance, also has families of policies. There are medical expense/hospital policies, disability income policies, and long-term care policies. Since the physician and health-care worker should already be familiar with the medical expense/hospital family of policies, they will not be discussed here.

[A] Disability Income Insurance

Disability income insurance is designed to transfer the financial risk of wages lost because of an accident or illness to an insurance company. The actual benefits may be received for as short a period as 6 months in some short-term group policies, to age 65 years in both group long-term and many individual policies, and possibly even to a lifetime for some individual "professional" policies. The length of the benefit period is one of the main factors in determining the premium to be charged by the insurance company.

[1] DISABILITY DEFINED

Arguably, the most important issue when purchasing disability insurance is the definition of disability found within the policy. Disability insurance pays a monthly benefit to the insured if he or she satisfies this definition of disability. Unlike a life insurance policy death claim, a disability income claim can be a far more difficult issue. Different policies from the same insurance company can define disability differently, and medical professionals or health-care practitioners must be sure they are comfortable with the definition found in their policy.

The more liberal the definition of disability in any given policy, the easier it will be to meet that definition, and the more likely the insurance company will pay benefits. Consequently, these are also the most expensive policies. Many agents and financial planners recommend paying the extra premium so that you have a higher chance of receiving benefits. The last thing an insured wants to do after becoming seriously injured is have to fight an insurance carrier over benefits.

There are two common definitions of disability:

- The ability to perform the substantial and material duties of your occupation
- The ability to perform any gainful occupation for which you are reasonably trained

Some aggressive insurance companies have even gone so far as to define the disability in terms of occupational specialties. Regardless, the definition will almost always end with the words "and under a physician's care."

> **Example:** Dr. Stein, a board-certified surgeon, loses some dexterity in his right hand because of a car accident. He can no longer operate, but he can teach in a medical school or become a family practitioner.
>
> Under the first definition, Dr. Stein could receive disability benefits. But under the second definition, he would not receive benefits. The policy with the first definition would likely have a higher premium because it is more likely to pay benefits.

Some polices will pay benefits under the first definition for a couple of years and then use a second definition thereafter. This design permits the insured full monthly benefits immediately after a disability and then time to rehabilitate and establish a new career.

[2] PARTIAL DISABILITY

Some policies also allow fractional benefits for a partial, or residual, disability. Partial benefits can be available under two circumstances:

1. During a disability whereby the insured cannot perform some of the duties of his or her occupation, or
2. When the insured can still perform all the duties of his or her occupation, but for a limited period of time during recuperation.

> **Example:** Jon Riba, a nurse, has a disability policy that pays $3,000 per month if he becomes fully disabled. It also has a partial disability benefit provision. Because of a back injury, Jon can only work half of the hours he used to work. His policy will pay $1,500 per month in benefits while this condition persists.

Medical professionals or health-care practitioners should pay particular attention to the partial disability benefit language in their policy. Some companies require total disability prior to any partial claims payment. Other companies may have no such provision and, in fact, may even pay a full benefit for the first 3 months of partial disability.

[3] ELIMINATION PERIOD

Another aspect used in the development of a disability income insurance premium is the waiting period, the period of time that elapses prior to the payment of any benefits during which the insured must generally be continuously disabled. This is also referred to as the elimination period and in individual contracts is usually specified as 30, 60, 90, 180, or 365 days.

The shorter the elimination period, the higher the potential premium. In short-term group policies, the standard elimination period is the first day for accidents and the seventh day for sickness. Long-term group policies traditionally begin after 6 months. Medical professionals and health-care practitioners with ample savings should consider a longer elimination period in order to save premium dollars, but those with fewer savings should obviously choose a shorter elimination period.

[4] COORDINATION OF BENEFITS

Coordination between short-term group and both long-term group and individual contracts is often possible to complete an overall portfolio of coverage. Since most long-term group policies have a provision for coordination of benefits (insurance for "reduction of benefit payments") with individual coverage purchased subsequent to the group policy effective date, many financial service professionals will look for the opportunity to place substantial amounts of individual coverage prior to writing the group coverage.

[5] MONTHLY BENEFIT AMOUNT

Yet another aspect to be taken into consideration for developing the premium to be charged is the monthly benefit amount. The amount of coverage that can be initially purchased is dependent on the current level of predisability earnings. Insurance companies have usually been willing to insure 50 percent of current income (for the highest wage earners), to up to 70 percent of current income (for moderate to lower-income workers).

[6] OCCUPATION

The hazard category of the insured's occupation is also important to develop an adequate premium. Obviously bus drivers, firefighters, cardiovascular surgeons, and financial service professionals face different risks during their typical day. These occupation classifications also take into account the claims experience related to that occupation. For example, dentists at one time were in the same top classification as physicians. However, because of poor claims experience, many companies have since lowered their classification, that is, raised their premiums.

Note ■ Unfortunately, "your own occupation" policies are rapidly disappearing from the marketplace and are being replaced by loss of income contracts, which simply indemnify for loss of income, regardless of whether a physician can work at his or her occupation or not.

[7] INFLATION PROTECTION

When a disability income policy is purchased, it is strongly recommended that it include an inflation rider. In the event of disability, this rider will increase the benefit each year in an attempt to keep pace with inflation. Without this rider, if a young insured becomes totally disabled, his or her monthly benefit will certainly lose its purchasing power over the years. If the insured is young enough, a level benefit may become almost meaningless 20 to 30 years in the future. An inflation rider will cost extra, but it is money well spent.

[8] RENEWABILITY

The last major issue to be considered when purchasing a disability policy is the renewal feature of the policy. The typical renewal features are the following:

- Conditionally renewable
- Guaranteed renewable
- Noncancelable

Conditionally renewable policies allow the insurance company a limited ability to refuse to renew the policy at the end of a premium payment period. The insurance company may also increase the premium. Most policies sold to medical professionals will not contain this limitation.

Guaranteed renewable means the insurance company cannot cancel the policy, except for nonpayment of premium, but it can change the premium rates for an entire class of policies. As long as the owner pays the premium in a timely manner, the policy will remain in force. Simply, you are guaranteed the right to renew the policy, but it may be at a higher premium rate.

Noncancelable means the insurer cannot cancel the policy, nor can it change the rates. This added level of security means that noncancelable policies are more expensive than guaranteed renewable policies.

Although redundant, many disability income policies specify that they are both "noncancelable and guaranteed renewable."

[B] Disability Income Taxation

The general rule for taxation of disability benefits is that if the policyholder pays the premiums from his or her own funds, then any benefits received as a result of the disability are income tax free. If the policy owner's employer pays the premiums as an employee benefit, then any benefits are taxable. Therefore, when choosing a monthly benefit amount, the medical professional or health-care practitioner should always factor his or her individual tax status of the benefits into the calculations.

[C] Disability Income Summary

How important is disability insurance? In a word, VERY. Almost everyone understands the importance of adequate life insurance, especially when they have children and a mortgage. But many seemingly intelligent professionals overlook disability insurance.

These professionals fail to recognize that the chance of becoming disabled at least once during their lifetime and not being able to work for months, or even years, is greater than the chance of dying. For those health-care professionals working for someone else, ask this question: "Will my employer pay me if I am in a car accident and can't work for 6 months?" What if the disability is so severe that you can never work again and you're only 35 years old? Will your employer still pay you for the next 30 years?

Statistics

At age 30 years, long-term disability is 4.1 times more likely than death.

At age 40 years, long-term disability is 2.9 times more likely than death.

At age 50 years, long-term disability is 2.2 times more likely than death.

Risk of Disability Within Groups of People

At age 30 years, there is a 46.7 percent chance of any one person having a 90-day disability before age 65 years.

At age 40 years, there is a 43 percent chance of any one person having a 90-day disability before age 65 years.

At age 50 years, there is a 36 percent chance of any one person having a 90-day disability before age 65 years.

At age 30 years, there is a 71.6 percent chance of any one person out of any two people having a 90-day disability before age 65 years.

At age 40 years, there is a 67.5 percent chance of any one person out of any two people having a 90-day disability before age 65 years.

At age 50 years, there is a 59 percent chance of any one person out of any two people having a 90-day disability before age 65 years.

Source: 2003 National Underwriter Field Guide.

Do not overlook disability insurance. In fact, adequate disability and life insurance protection should be the foundation of any financial plan. Medical professionals and health-care practitioners should consider covering these risks before they invest in stocks or anything else.

Life and Health Insurance Policy Provisions

[A] The Application

After the decision has been made to buy insurance, the next step is usually to fill out an application. The application itself generally consists of a number of different parts:

- The initial section usually asks for basic personal information (name, address, Social Security number, etc.).
- The next area contains the parties to the life insurance contract. This requires the applicant to name the owner of the policy, the insured, the beneficiary, and any contingent owners or beneficiaries.
- The medical questions section will consist of an in-depth inquiry into the insured's medical history. It will generally include the current doctor's name and address, along with a request for detail on any recent surgery or current medications. It may also include short medical questions about the insured's parents and siblings.
- The financial history section may include the approximate value of the estate and the salary history of the insured(s) and owner.

- The style of policy being requested and the choice of numerous riders, plan options, and premium payments are usually found in the plan or product section.
- Finally, a miscellaneous provisions section may include a request for employment history, address history, HIV waiver, driving records, a Medical Information Bureau (MIB) request, replacement forms, automatic bank withdrawal authorization, and any supplemental paperwork required for a variable life insurance product.

After the application has been completed and signed, it can be submitted with or without an initial payment of a premium by the consumer. If any payment is submitted, a conditional receipt should be issued containing a temporary insurance agreement. This temporary agreement may bind the insurance company up to a set limit, pending the results of the underwriting process. The medical professional or health-care practitioner should pay particular attention to the conditions contained within this agreement.

[B] The Underwriting Process

Following submission of an application, one of the next things the agent or broker will do is to schedule a paramedic or medical exam for the insured. That is correct; the insurance professional will be scheduling a medical exam for the medical professional or health-care practitioner, with a company-approved physician or nurse, typically not the insured's physician.

The amount of medical underwriting, or medical testing, will depend on a number of factors. The first factor is the age of the insured. In general, the older the insured, the less insurance he or she can buy without a medical exam.

Second is the amount of insurance applied for. If the insured is applying for a very large amount of life insurance, the underwriting becomes more stringent. For example, a $5,000,000 policy may require a physician exam to include urine, blood, a stress EKG, and a chest X-ray.

[C] Medical Information Bureau (MIB)

Third is the insured's prior medical history. Not only do insurance companies require the insured to answer a number of medical questions, but they may also request an insured's medical dossier from the attending physicians listed on the application. The insurance company will also routinely request information through the Medical Information Bureau (MIB), a clearinghouse of medical information that insurers share. This particular resource also helps identify those insureds who may lie about their medical history on their application.

The MIB is made up of over 700 member insurance companies. Members are required to report relevant results from their underwriting process to the MIB. The member companies must report both favorable and unfavorable medical information, as well as any nonmedical but pertinent information, such as dangerous hobbies like race car driving. All information is reported in codes to ensure confidentiality, and only member companies have access to the MIB reports. The insured must sign an authorization to allow the insurer to check the MIB.

[D] Final Underwriting Decision

Once all the required information is gathered, the home office underwriter assigned to review the insured's policy will issue a medical classification for the insured. Classifications normally range from "preferred" or "select" for the very healthy, to "standard" for those of average health. Additionally, there may be a substandard rating assigned to those insureds who have particular chronic or life-shortening medical conditions. For those insureds with extremely serious medical conditions, the underwriter may assign a rating of "uninsurable." Besides these classifications, being a smoker will also affect an insured's rating and result in a higher premium amount.

Lastly, medical underwriting is not an exact science, and the ratings assigned to the same potential insured may differ drastically between insurance companies. It is often recommended in large cases that the insured submit an application to more than one insurance company, for two reasons. First, it provides a greater chance of receiving the best possible health classification from at least one of the insurers. Second, it also allows the owner to divide the coverage among multiple insurers, thus decreasing the impact if one of them fails.

A final word of caution is in order. Don't be fooled by the actual name assigned to the underwriting classification. Although the rates may be determined by actuaries, the marketing department may be involved with how it is eventually labeled. One company's preferred classification may be priced cheaper than another company's select. Don't get hung up on the name. The actual costs and values are what should be compared.

Some insurance companies even have grades within their "select," or best classification. Too often, the illustration that is used in the initial sales interview will reflect the best possible classification in order to provide the lowest premium and the greatest potential cash values. Keep this illustration, and request another one after the underwriter has made his or her decision. Make sure you understand any differences.

Working in the health-care field, the medical professional surely understands the many privacy and confidentiality issues involved in handling medical information. The life insurance underwriting process is strictly confidential. Insurers do not share medical underwriting information with the agent or broker, or with each other, unless the insured signs an authorization for them to do so.

[E] Contract Law (in brief)

Three important concepts in contract law are offer, acceptance, and consideration.

The application can be an offer, or a request for an offer. If the application is submitted without money (the consideration), it is considered a request for an offer. The final underwriting decision and the printing of the policy then become the offer. The applicant can accept or reject, and with the payment of a premium upon acceptance, the contract is in force.

If money is submitted with the application, an offer has been made to the insurance company. Some coverage may be present during the underwriting process as specified in the restricted temporary insurance agreement. If the insurance company issues a policy "as applied for," acceptance is complete and the policy is in force.

If the insurance company modifies the application or issues the policy "other than as applied for," the printed policy becomes a counteroffer and the applicant is then in a position to accept or reject the contract.

[F] The Underwriting Decision

Once the underwriting process has been completed, one of three things will happen.

1. The policy will be approved "as applied for." At that point, if accepted by the applicant, the contract will be delivered and the parties will be bound by the final agreement.

2. Underwriting will decline the policy based on the medical information received. Depending on the medical reason for the declination, the insured will have the option to pursue insurance through any number of specialized carriers in order to receive life insurance protection. If the policy is declined, any temporary insurance agreement will cease to exist.

3. The policy may come back "rated" differently than that applied for. The applicant must then make a decision. The applicant can either accept the policy and probably pay an additional premium, or decline the policy and attempt to obtain a more favorable classification from another insurance company.

[G] Free Look Period

If a policy is accepted by the insured, every state has a "free look period." This encourages owners to read their contracts and, if they change their mind, provides them the opportunity to cancel the contract. Upon cancelation during the free look period, the insurance company must return all premiums paid. If cancelation is attempted after the free look period has expired, the owner will usually only receive the surrender value of the contract. In the first few years, this surrender value will likely be considerably less than the amount of premium paid.

[H] Contract Language

The policy itself will have a number of different provisions and clauses. The provisions outline the details of the agreements and define the terms in order to protect each party from possible future misunderstandings or misinterpretations. The provisions are usually divided into three major categories:

- **Obligations:** Each party has certain obligations to the contract. They can include the obligation to pay premiums when due, or the company's obligation to pay a benefit upon death.
- **Rights:** The rights of the parties to the contract will be clearly outlined. For instance, a policy owner's right to cash value will be explained in detail in a permanent life insurance contract.
- **Conditions:** The contract will list specific conditions that designate any restrictions, limitations, or exclusions of the policy issued. This may include when a term rider will expire, or the surrender charge associated with an early withdrawal of cash value.

The clauses will vary by contract and policy type. A few of the more common clauses include the following:

- **The Insuring Clause:** This outlines the obligation of the insurance company.
- **Consideration Clause:** This outlines the obligation of the policy owner.
- **Execution Clause:** This states that the contract is executed when both parties meet the specified conditions.
- **Ownership Control Clause:** This is used when the insured is a minor and designates the initial owner and whether the control will pass automatically at a particular age.
- **Incontestable Clause:** This prevents the insurance company from voiding the contract for any reason other than nonpayment of premium after a certain amount of time has passed, usually 2 years. This protects the consumer from having a minor misstatement jeopardize the status of the policy.
- **Suicide Clause:** This ensures that a beneficiary will receive the full death proceeds even if the insured were to commit suicide, as long as the suicide occurs after a specified time period has been satisfied from the policy issue (usually 2 years).
- **Grace Period:** This prevents the insurance company from immediately canceling a policy for nonpayment of premiums. Typically the insured is given a 30- or 31-day period in which to pay an overdue premium.
- **Reinstatement Clause:** This states the conditions by which a policy can be reinstated if the policy owner has exceeded the grace period.
- **Misstatement of Age Clause:** This allows for the adjustment of premium or death benefit due to a mistake in the stated age of the insured.
- **Privilege of Change Clause:** This describes the conditions by which the policy can be changed for a different policy.
- **Automatic Premium Loan Provision:** This permits the insurance company to automatically use the cash values of an existing whole life policy to pay premiums following the expiration of the grace period. Because of the design of the universal life policy, this provision is not relevant and is not contained within those contracts.

- **Nonforfeiture Options:** These outline the values in a policy that must be made available to a policyholder should he or she stop paying for the policy. It is typically a table of guaranteed cash values, a table of reduced paid-up insurance values, and a table of periods during which reduced term insurance would be in force. Again, it is a whole life insurance concept and not typically contained in universal life policies.

- **Policy Loan Provisions:** This stipulates the insurance company's policy regarding policy loans and includes the specified interest rate charged or the index used to determine it.

- **Settlement Options:** This provides a summary of the options that a beneficiary may select when receiving the proceeds of the death benefit.

- **Policy Riders:** This will list any riders selected and their descriptions.

The preceding is a summary of many of the provisions and clauses a policy owner will find in a life insurance policy contract. This information, when located in the insurance policy, can be difficult to understand because it was likely written by attorneys. Do not be afraid to request clarification of any contract issues that are of concern. Answering questions should be one of the main responsibilities of the selling agent or broker.

[I] Policy Comparisons

An insurance purchaser will likely need to compare two or more different products when purchasing new coverage or when considering the replacement of an existing policy. In the case of purchasing a new policy, the applicant will probably wish to compare two or more new policies, whereas with a replacement situation, the applicant must compare the current policy to the proposed new policy. In either circumstance, a policy comparison is not easy. This is truly where a qualified and trustworthy insurance advisor is of great value.

There are numerous ways to compare different policies. Some people will naively make superficial comparisons, such as between premiums and nothing else. "Product A has a $400 premium and Product B has a $500 premium so Product A is better." This is obviously dangerous.

What if Product A provides no cash value, but Product B guarantees $10,000 cash value in 10 years? Product B, all of a sudden, looks a lot better. What if Product B comes from an insurer with an A+ financial rating and Product A comes from a company with a B financial rating? What if Product B comes from a company that two of your coworkers have policies with and who are very satisfied with the company, whereas no one you know has a policy with Company A? In this example, I can make a strong case that Product B is the better choice given our current information.

The better product was simple to select in this example once all of the pertinent information was revealed. But often many of the characteristics of different policies are roughly equal. Product A may be better in some areas whereas Product B may be better in others. Now the decision is not easy. What can you do if two products provide all of the characteristics and benefits you deem important?

If the selection of a policy comes down to comparing the policy illustrations, the internal rate of return (IRR) can be very useful. It is an excellent tool for comparing products with different premiums, different cash values, and different death benefits. The IRR measures the return your premium dollars generate in regard to the death benefit (IRR can also be run for cash value). In other words, the calculation, for any given year, looks at the cumulative premium paid in and compares it to the expected death benefit (or cash value) and determines what rate of return would need to be generated to achieve that particular result.

Put another way, if a policy owner took his or her premiums and invested them instead of paying premiums, what would that investment have to earn each year in order to have accumulated a pot of money equal to the death benefit (or cash value) for that year?

> **Example:** We wish to compare two policies based on their year 40 IRR in regard to death benefit and cash value. Product A has a premium of $4,800, and product B has a premium of $7,000. An overly simple analysis may conclude that product A is the "better deal" because the premium is less.
>
> But using an IRR analysis, the better deal could be product A.

	Product A	Product B
Annual premium	$4,800	$7,000
Cumulative premium	$192,000	$280,000
Expected cash value	$315,283 (IRR = 2.26%)	$960,880 (IRR = 5.30%)
Expected death benefit	$500,000 (IRR = 4.22%)	$1,008,924 (IRR = 5.51%)

By year 40, product A has an expected IRR on cash value of 2.26 percent, and product B has an expected cash value IRR of 5.30 percent. Product B also has a higher expected death benefit IRR in year 40. If the purchaser can only afford a premium of $5,000 or less, Product A is likely the better product for that individual. If the purchaser can afford either product, product B provides better expected long-term performance. The additional $2,200 of annual premium may be money well spent if the policy is held for the long term.

As with any life insurance illustration, you must remember that the future values are just projections and are based on assumptions that may or may not be true over the next 40 years.

IRR analysis is an excellent way to compare different premiums with different death benefits and different cash values. A qualified insurance advisor will be able to provide the medical professional or health-care practitioner with this type of analysis.

Annuity Overview

Annuity contracts transfer the financial risk of living too long, that is, outliving one's savings. Annuities are deferred or immediate, fixed or variable, and tax qualified or non tax qualified.

[A] Deferred Annuities

The deferred annuity contract, like a permanent life insurance policy, has been found by some to be a convenient method of accumulating wealth. Funds can be placed in deferred annuities in a lump sum, called single-premium deferred annuities, or periodically over time, called flexible-premium deferred annuities. Either way, the funds placed in a deferred annuity grow without current taxation (tax deferred).

[1] FIXED DEFERRED ANNUITY

Fixed deferred annuities provide a guaranteed minimum rate of return (usually around 3 percent per year) and typically credit a higher, competitive rate based on the current economic conditions. Fixed annuities are usually considered conservative investments.

> **Example:** Mrs. Park, a retired therapist, desires a safe financial vehicle for $100,000 of her savings. She doesn't need the earnings of this investment for current income and also wants to reduce her income tax liability. She decides to purchase a fixed deferred annuity with her $100,000. The annuity guarantees a 3 percent annual return, and the current rate is 6 percent.
>
> After the first year, $6,000 of interest is credited to the annuity, and Mrs. Park has no current income taxes as a result. If the 6 percent interest rate does not change, after 3 years, the annuity will have $119,102 of value.

[2] VARIABLE DEFERRED ANNUITY

Recently, variable deferred annuities have become very popular. Like fixed annuities, variable deferred annuities offer tax-deferred growth, but this is where the similarities end. Variable deferred annuities offer separate accounts (similar to mutual funds) that provide different investment opportunities. Most of the separate accounts have stock market exposure, and therefore variable annuities do not offer a guaranteed rate of return. But the upside potential is typically much greater than that of a fixed annuity.

The value of a variable deferred annuity will fluctuate with the values of the investments within the chosen separate accounts. Although similar to mutual funds, there are some key differences:

- A variable annuity provides tax deferral whereas a regular mutual fund does not.
- If a variable annuity loses money because of poor separate account performance, and the owner dies, most annuities guarantee at least a return of principal to the heirs. It is important to note that this guarantee of principal only applies if the

annuity owner dies. If the annuity value decreases below the amount paid in, and the annuity is surrendered while the owner is alive, the actual cash value is all that is available.

- When money is eventually withdrawn from a deferred annuity, it is taxable at ordinary income tax rates. With taxable mutual funds, they can be liquidated and taxed at lower, capital gains rates.

- There is also a 10 percent penalty if the annuity owner is under 59½ years old when money is withdrawn. There is no such charge for withdrawals from a mutual fund.

- The fees charged inside a variable annuity (called mortality and expense charges) are typically more than the fees charged by a regular mutual fund.

Variable deferred annuities are sensible for people who want stock market exposure while minimizing taxes. Most planners recommend regular mutual funds when the investment time horizon is under 10 years. But if the time horizon is more than 10 years, variable annuities may become more attractive because of the additional earnings from tax deferral.

Both types of deferred annuities are subject to surrender charges. Surrender charges are applied if the annuity owner surrenders the policy during the surrender period, which typically runs for 5 to 10 years from the purchase date. The charge usually decreases each year until it reaches zero. The purpose of the charge is to discourage early surrender of the annuity.

[B] Immediate Annuities

Immediate annuities provide a guaranteed income stream. An immediate annuity can be purchased with a single deposit of funds, possibly from savings or a pension distribution, or it can be the end result of the deferred annuity, commonly referred to as annuitization. Just like deferred annuities, immediate annuities can also be fixed or variable.

Immediate annuities can be set up to provide periodic payments to the policyholder annually, semiannually, quarterly, or monthly. The annuity payments can be paid over life or for a finite number of years. They can also be paid over the life of a single individual or over two lives.

[1] IMMEDIATE FIXED ANNUITY

Immediate fixed annuities typically pay a specified amount of money for as long as the annuitant lives. They may also be arranged to only pay for a specified period of time, for example, 20 years. Either way, they often contain a guaranteed payout period, such that, if the annuitant lives less than the guaranteed number of years, the heirs will receive the remainder of the guaranteed payments.

> **Example:** Dr. Jones is 70 years old and retired. He is of average wealth, but is concerned that if he lives too long, he could deplete his savings. He

decides to use $100,000 and purchase a lifetime immediate annuity with 20 years certain. The insurance company promises to pay him $7,000 per year as long as he lives.

If Dr. Jones dies 4 years after purchase, he will only have received $28,000 out of a $100,000 investment. However, his heirs will receive $7,000 for the next 16 years. If Dr. Jones survives to the age of 98, he will receive $196,000 (or 28 years of $7,000).

[2] IMMEDIATE VARIABLE ANNUITY

Immediate variable annuities provide income payments to the annuitant that fluctuate with the returns of the separate accounts chosen. The theory is that since the stock market has historically risen over time, the annuity payments will rise over time and keep pace with inflation. If this is indeed what happens, it is a good purchase, but it cannot be guaranteed. Some companies will, at a minimum, provide a guarantee of a low minimum monthly payment no matter how poorly the separate accounts perform.

[C] Qualified Annuities

The term *qualified* refers to those annuities that permit tax-deductible contributions under one of the Internal Revenue Code (IRC) sections, that is, § 408 Individual Retirement Accounts (IRA), § 403(b) Tax Sheltered Annuities, and § 401(k) Voluntary Profit Savings Plans. Qualified annuities can also result from a rollover from such a plan.

Nonqualified annuities, then, do not permit deductible contributions.

At the writing of this section, there is much debate as to whether an annuity, which is tax deferred by nature, should also be used as a funding vehicle within a tax-qualified plan, that is, as a tax shelter within a tax shelter. Since the investment options within the annuity are also generally available to the plan participant without the additional management expenses of the annuity policy, it is felt that this could be a breach of fiduciary responsibility.

Annuity Taxation

The tax treatment of annuities is extremely dependent on whether it is a qualified or nonqualified annuity. Although both permit the tax-deferred growth of the investment and both have penalties for early distributions, they are governed under different sections of the IRC. Since qualified annuities were just discussed, we will start with them.

[A] Qualified Annuity Taxation

Qualified annuities are treated no differently than any other tax-qualified retirement investment. Growth of the investment, whether based on fixed interest or variable interest, escapes current taxation under one of the 400-series IRC sections. Additionally, if the funds are withdrawn prior to age 59½ years, there is a 10 percent penalty. As the money is withdrawn, every dollar is taxed as ordinary income. Finally, fund distributions must begin no later than April 1 of the calendar year following the year in which the owner turns age 70½ years.

[B] Nonqualified Annuity Taxation

The taxation of nonqualified annuities is generally contained within IRC § 72. Again, the annuity is provided tax-deferred growth and the 10 percent penalty for early withdrawal. The manner in which distributions are taken, however, will determine the nature of their taxation.

If funds are withdrawn other than by annuitization, they are taxed under the LIFO (Last In First Out) accounting rules. Under these rules, the first funds withdrawn are considered the investment earnings, that is, the last funds credited to the annuity. Ordinary income taxes will be paid until all earnings have been removed, at which time only the original principal remains. This principal, having already been taxed, can then be withdrawn without any further income taxation.

On the other hand, if annuitization is chosen, an exclusion ratio is developed by the insurance company using governmental tables. This permits a portion of each payment received to be considered a return of principal, and thus only a portion of each payment is taxable. This exclusion ratio remains in effect until the insurance company has returned all of the original principal to the owner. After that, each payment received will be considered 100 percent earnings and totally subject to ordinary income taxation.

> **Example:** Dr. Cook has retired and purchased an immediate annuity with part of his retirement funds. He will receive $2,000 a month for the rest of his life.

[C] Wealth Transfer Issues

Regardless of whether the medical professional or health-care practitioner has a qualified or nonqualified annuity, extreme care must be given when specifying beneficiaries. Although these investments have great potential for appreciating sizable amounts of wealth during a lifetime, they are, unfortunately, very poor vehicles for the transfer of this wealth to successor generations after death.

Upon the death of an annuity owner, an annuity can be subject to both federal estate and federal income taxes. This double taxation often results in a 40 to 70 percent loss of annuity value before the heirs can receive it. Retired medical professionals should seek wealth transfer advice if they hold a large portion of their wealth in annuities or other qualified plans such as IRAs.

Long-Term Care Insurance

Long-term care (LTC) insurance is considered one of the newest forms of personal coverage insurance. LTC insurance is designed to transfer the financial risk associated with the inability to care for oneself because of a prolonged illness, disability, or the effects of old age. In particular, it is designed to insure against the financial cost of home health care or an extended stay in a nursing home, assisted living facility, adult day care center, or hospice. It has been estimated that two out of every five Americans now over the age of 65 years will spend time in a nursing home. As life expectancy increases, so does the potential need for LTC.

[A] Medicare

Any discussion of LTC must begin with an understanding of what Medicare is designed to cover. Currently, the only nursing home care that Medicare covers is skilled nursing care, and it must be provided in a Medicare-certified skilled nursing facility. Custodial care is not covered. Most LTC policies have been designed with these types of coverages, or the lack thereof, in mind.

To qualify for Medicare Skilled Nursing Care, an individual must meet the following conditions:

1. One must be hospitalized for at least 3 days within the 30 days preceding the nursing home admission.

2. One must be admitted for the same medical condition that required the hospitalization.

3. The skilled nursing home care must be deemed rehabilitative.

Once these requirements are met, Medicare will pay 100 percent of the costs for the first 20 days. Days 21 to 100 are covered by Medicare along with a daily copayment, which is indexed annually. After the initial 100 days, there is no additional Medicare coverage.

Medicare Home Health Services cover part-time or intermittent skilled nursing care, physical therapy, medical supplies, and some rehabilitative equipment. These are generally paid for in full and do not require a hospital stay prior to home health service coverage.

[B] Critical LTC Policy Features

According to the U.S. Department of Health and Human Services and the Health Insurance Association of America, there are seven features that should always be included in a good LTC policy.

1. It should be guaranteed renewable (as long as premiums are paid, the policy cannot be canceled).

2. It should cover all levels of nursing care (skilled, intermediate, and custodial care).

3. Premiums should remain level (individual premiums cannot be raised due to health or age, but can be raised only if all other LTC policies as a group are increased).

4. Benefits are never reduced.

5. The policy should offer inflation protection.

6. There should be full coverage for Alzheimer's disease (earlier contracts tried to eliminate this coverage).

7. There should be a waiver of premium (during a claim period, further premium payments will not be required).

In addition, another seven features are considered to be worthwhile and should be included in the better LTC policies:

1. Home health care benefits

2. Adult day care and hospice care

3. Assisted living facility care

4. No prior hospital stay required

5. Optional elimination periods

6. Premium discounts when both spouses are covered

7. Medicare approval not a prerequisite for coverage

[C] ADLs

Most LTC policies provide benefits for covered insureds with a cognitive impairment or the inability to perform a specified number of activities of daily living (ADLs). These ADLs generally include those listed below, and the inability to perform two out of six is generally sufficient to file a claim:

1. **Bathing:** Washing oneself in either a tub or shower, or by sponge bath, including the task of getting into and out of the tub or shower without hands-on assistance of another person.

2. **Dressing:** Putting on or taking off all necessary and appropriate items of clothing and/or any necessary braces or artificial limbs without hands-on assistance of another person.

3. **Toileting:** Getting to and from the toilet, getting on and off the toilet, and performing associated personal hygiene without hands-on assistance of another person.

4. **Transferring:** Moving in and out of a bed, chair, or wheelchair without hands-on assistance of another person.

5. **Eating:** The ability to get nourishment into the body without hands-on assistance of another person once it has been prepared and made available.

6. **Continence:** The ability to voluntarily maintain control of bowel and/or bladder function, or in the event of incontinence, the ability to maintain a reasonable level of personal hygiene without hands-on assistance of another person.

Another issue concerning ADLs is whether the covered insured requires "hands-on" assistance or merely needs someone to "stand by" in the event of difficulty. Obviously, policies that read the latter are more liberal.

[D] Long-Term Care Taxation

Some LTC policies have been designed to meet the required provisions of the Kassenbaum-Kennedy health reform bill, passed in 1996, and subsequently are "Tax Qualified Policies." Insureds who own policies meeting the requirements are permitted to tax-deduct some of the policy's premium, based on age, income, and the amount of total itemized medical expenses. The major benefit of the tax-qualified LTC policy is that the benefit, when received, is not considered taxable income. There are several initiatives in Congress, however, that would expand and simplify these deductibility rules.

Regardless, medical professionals or health-care practitioners should investigate the opportunity afforded them through their current form of business for any purchase of an LTC policy. Currently, small businesses can deduct LTC premiums on a discriminatory basis.

Additional Readings

1. Baldwin, Ben: *New Life Insurance Investment Advisor* (2nd edition). McGraw-Hill, New York, 2002.
2. Black, K: *Life Insurance*. Prentice Hall, New York, 1993.
3. Gastel, Ruth: *Re-Insurance Fundamentals*. Insurance Information Institute, 1995.
4. *Life Insurance Fact Book*. Washington, DC. American Council of Life Insurance, 2004 and annual.
5. Skipper, Harold: *Life and Health Insurance*. Prentice Hall, New York, 1999.
6. Vaughn, Emmett: *Fundamentals of Risk and Insurance* (13th edition). John Wiley, 2002.

Websites

The following URL addresses have also been found to contain worthwhile insurance information:

- www.insure.com - consumer-oriented guide to insurance and insurance-related questions; this site discusses all forms of insurance, insurance company guides, etc.

- www.sunamerica.com - visit the link to insurance information and "Your Retirement" for new perspectives on whether you are doing everything correctly
- www.bisis.com (phone = 0031-40-2789901) info@bisis.com
- www.taxresourcesgroup.com (phone = 800-578-3498)
- www.GlennDaily.com
- www.fincalc.com - another site for simple calculations for life insurance, loans, college funding, retirement and savings, income taxes, etc.

Chapter 2

Insuring the Doctor's Property and Possessions

(Guarding Your Stuff . . . Against Man or Nature)

Gary A. Cook

For doctors, most medical practice enterprise liability problems are predictable, and avoidable. Yet, physicians often leave themselves open to a myriad of implicit and explicit risks, sans the obvious malpractice issues. As an anonymous attorney speaking at an insurance seminar once commented, "you can show doctors the best risk reduction plan possible, but if it isn't tainted with some abuse or illegality, they're just not interested." The audience of insurance agents applauded enthusiastically, as all knew exactly what was meant. For too many doctors, the axiom "investigate, then invest" is an unheeded motto, as product vendors using the balm of "trust" grease the road to physician sales. For whenever a scheme involves more risks than rewards, it's a safe bet that marketers will make an easy sale to time-compressed doctors.

Glenn S. Daily, CLU, ChFC, CFP©

Fee Only Insurance Consultant

The insurance policies discussed in this chapter generally provide coverage for the financial risks involved with two aspects of physician ownership: property and casualty (P&C). An insurance company may combine one or both of these into a single contract covering a particular possession. Unlike those insurance policies covering people, discussed in Chapter 1, which are mostly a matter of personal choice, most of these coverages are virtually required by law.

General Types of Policies Covering Possessions

This section will discuss P&C coverage for the most common possessions that the medical professional or doctor generally needs to protect.

[A] Homeowners (and Renters) Insurance Overview

The basic model of the homeowners contract began in 1958 and contains three areas of coverage: property, theft, and liability. There are seven standard forms of homeowner contracts (to be discussed shortly), and the aforementioned coverages are contained in two sections.

Section I is for property and theft coverage and typically includes coverage for the following:

- The structure itself (commonly called the dwelling)
- Appurtenant structures (unattached buildings, fences, swimming pools, etc.)
- Unscheduled personal property (commonly just called contents within the structures and only those not itemized by endorsement)
- Additional living expenses (the increased cost of living during the period after damage occurs while the structure is uninhabitable)

Contents coverage is typically 50 percent of the dwelling coverage for on-premises losses. Off-premises coverage is usually worldwide but is limited to 10 percent of the limit for contents coverage. Typically, there are other restrictions, with some types of personal property being totally excluded and others having a dollar limitation applied against them. This is one area of the homeowner's form that physicians should pay particular attention to.

It is important to have a basic inventory of your property in an off-site location, possibly a safe deposit box. This is often conveniently accomplished by periodically taking pictures of each of the rooms in the house. Should there be a fire damaging that section, the picture may assist in bringing to mind property that was destroyed and for which a claim needs to be filed.

Section II, the liability protection section, covers personal liability for bodily injury to others or for damage to their property and includes reasonable medical payments for their injuries. Section II is identical in all seven forms. Liability protection often begins at $100,000 with medical payments at $1,000 per person.

Briefly, the seven forms are as follows:

1. **HO-1: The Basic Form** insures against fire, lightning, removal, vandalism or malicious mischief, glass breakage, and theft. It also provides what is called "extended coverage" for damage from wind, civil commotion, smoke, hail, aircraft, vehicles, explosion, and riot. The dwelling protection is specified as a dollar

amount, the contents are covered at 50 percent of this amount, and the additional living expenses are covered at 10 percent. Many states do not permit this form to be used.

2. **HO-2: The Broad Form** gets its name from broadening the extended coverage perils of the HO-1. Coverage is now extended to include damage from falling objects; damage from weight of ice, snow, or sleet; accidental damage to steam or hot water heating systems; accidental discharge of water or steam from those systems or domestic appliances; freezing of those systems or appliances; and electrical surge damage. Again, the dwelling protection is specified and the contents are covered at 50 percent. Additional living expenses are increased to 20 percent of the dwelling coverage amount.

3. **HO-3: The Special Form,** also called the "all-risk" form, expands on the HO-2 by providing coverage for the dwelling, appurtenant structures, and additional living expenses on an all-risk basis. Rather than naming each peril to be covered, this form covers all perils not specifically named as an exception, such as flood, earthquake, war, and nuclear accidents. Coverage for the dwelling, contents, and additional living expenses is identical to the HO-2.

4. **HO-4: The Tenants Form** is basically the same as the HO-2 and provides a named-perils basis for the contents of renters. Additional living expenses are provided at 20 percent of the amount of coverage purchased for the contents.

5. **HO-5: The Comprehensive Form** is seldom seen anymore. It is identical to the HO-3 except that contents are covered at 50 percent of the dwelling amount for both on and off premises.

6. **HO-6: The Unit Owners Form** is also referred to as the "condominium form." It is very similar to the tenants form except that additional living expenses are provided at 40 percent of the amount of coverage purchased for the contents. There are other unique differences with regard to insuring additions and alterations by the unit owner and the availability of optional coverage to protect against the exposure to losses from assessment by the condominium association for uninsured property damage or liability claims.

7. **HO-7: The Modified Coverage Form** is designed specifically to provide coverage for older dwellings. Many older homes contain elaborate carvings and specialty features that would cause the replacement value to substantially exceed current market value. This form of coverage has no replacement cost provision, but it substitutes a "functional replacement" concept for any losses.

[B] Replacement Cost Versus Actual Cash Value

Actual cash value settlements provide payments for claims that generally start with the cost today to replace a lost, stolen, damaged, or destroyed item. However, they then take into account the length of time the item was owned or in service to develop a deduction for depreciation. Often, this depreciation amount is substantial and severe.

Under replacement cost coverage, insureds are able to collect for their losses without the deduction for appreciation, up to the limits of the policy. This is an automatic but optional provision of all homeowner forms. To take advantage of this provision, the amount of insurance on the dwelling must be at least 80 percent of its replacement cost at the time of claim.

[C] Inflation Protection

The easiest way for a homeowner to ensure replacement cost coverage is with the addition of a rider that automatically adjusts the value of the dwelling coverage by the inflation rate for his or her community as calculated by the insurance company. This coverage adjusts policy limits periodically to maintain appropriate levels of coverage.

[D] Other Homeowner Policy Endorsements

The homeowner is well advised to also consider a multitude of endorsements and/or potential increases in policy limits:

- Scheduling personal property, such as jewelry, furs, golf equipment, and computers, that have been exempted from coverage or for which coverage has a severe dollar limitation
- Increasing liability coverage to take advantage of the minimums needed for "umbrella liability," to be covered shortly
- Theft extension endorsement to remove the exclusion for loss of unattended property from a motor vehicle, trailer, or watercraft
- Earthquake and/or sinkhole collapse coverage
- Increasing the deductible from the standard $250 to a convenient self-insurance amount

[E] Title Insurance

As a routine part of any home purchase, a history of the title to the property, as well as any liens or conveyances, is completed. This is referred to as title insurance, and typically protects the mortgage lender from any title defects. If a title defect causes loss, the title insurance company will indemnify the lender, not the homebuyer, to the extent of the loan. These are single-premium policies of indefinite duration, but they can terminate when the loan is retired. Title insurance is usually required by the lender at the time of settlement. If the state does not require this coverage to be paid by the seller, its payment can certainly be negotiated by the parties involved.

Medical professionals or health-care practitioners should also inquire as to the cost of their own title insurance policy. This second policy would protect them rather than the mortgage lender. Although it would undoubtedly add to the expense of closing, there is no harm in requesting that the seller be responsible for providing this protection to the purchaser as well.

[F] Boat Insurance Overview

Watercraft and small pleasure boats are usually covered within a homeowner policy, but generally only for $1,000. More expensive boats are often insured either under a separate inland marine policy or as a personal articles floater (attachment) to the homeowner's policy. The decision between these two alternatives usually involves the liability risk element. There is no provision in the personal articles floater for liability, and although it could be increased on the homeowners insurance policy, it is usually preferable to use a separate policy. Other items to consider are the size of the craft, maximum speed, engine horsepower, waters navigated, and special uses, such as water skiing or racing.

Yacht insurance is usually written in the traditional terms of ocean marine insurance, with both "hull" coverage and "protection and indemnity" liability coverage. It is quite different from an inland marine policy and is beyond the scope of this section.

Automobile Insurance Overview

With the possible exception of the handgun, the automobile represents the greatest single item of ownership that is capable of inflicting death, injury, and damage. America's fascination with the automobile has resulted in a marked increase in the power and potential speed of our vehicles. The latest trend in sports utility vehicles (SUVs) has also witnessed a substantial increase in damage because of their higher ground clearance and heavier frames. The owners and operators of any vehicle must be financially able to respond to any resulting claims, or they need to transfer the risk through insurance. All states require some minimal coverage for personal vehicles.

The most frequently used policy to insure individual private passenger vehicle risks is the family automobile policy (FAP). It provides two major types of coverage: liability and physical damage. Liability coverage includes both bodily injury and property damage. Physical damage, on the other hand, includes comprehensive and collision coverage.

[A] Liability Coverage

The liability section of the FAP is contained within most policies as Part A: Liability and Part B: Personal Injury Protection.

[1] BODILY INJURY

Bodily injury liability coverage generally includes sickness, disease, and death and is expressed in dual limits: per person and per occurrence. Nearly half of the states require minimums of $25,000 per person and $50,000 per occurrence. Higher limits of $100,000 per person and $300,000 per occurrence are often required for consideration of umbrella coverage.

[2] PROPERTY DAMAGE

Property damage liability is coverage for damage or destruction to the property of others and includes loss of use. Liability coverage limits usually include property damage limits as the third number, for example, $100/300/25. The coverage here would be for $25,000 of property damage. As automobiles become more expensive, however, coverage to $50,000 is not considered excessive.

[3] PERSONAL INJURY

Personal injury coverage is provided for medical expenses, funeral expenses, and loss of earnings for anyone sustaining an injury while occupying your vehicle, or from being struck by your vehicle while a pedestrian.

Liability insurance follows the vehicle, not the driver. Coverage is extended to the vehicle owner and any resident in the same household. It also covers anyone using the insured vehicle with the permission of the owner *and* within the scope of that permission.

Newly acquired vehicles are usually covered automatically for liability for 30 days after acquisition, but physical damage must have been on all currently covered vehicles to be included. Coverage is also typically extended to a temporary substitute automobile, but only if this vehicle is used in place of the covered automobile because of its breakdown, repair, servicing, loss, or destruction.

[B] Physical Damage Coverage

[1] COMPREHENSIVE

Comprehensive physical damage includes coverage for theft, vandalism, broken windshields, falling objects, riot or civil commotion, and even damage from foreign substances, such as paint. Comprehensive is often described as coverage for all those hazards other than collision.

[2] COLLISION

Collision involves the upset of the covered vehicle and collision with an object, usually another vehicle, and is not enumerated in the discussion of comprehensive. Colliding with a bird or animal is considered under the comprehensive coverage.

The distinction between comprehensive coverage and collision coverage is more than technical. The deductible provisions of the FAP often show a considerable difference in these areas, with the collision deductible typically being much greater.

Damage to tires can be covered by provisions in either comprehensive or collision. Exclusions typically include normal wear and tear, rough roads, hard driving, or hitting or scraping curbs.

[C] Repairs After the Accident

Following a collision, the insurance company will assign a claims adjuster to determine the extent of damage and the cost of repairs. If these repairs exceed the estimated value of the vehicle, it may be "totaled." Experience tells us that the value of the vehicle to the owner nearly always exceeds that estimated by the insurance company.

The medical professional or health-care practitioner is therefore strongly urged to consider purchasing replacement cost coverage rather than accepting actual cash value, which is the depreciated value of the vehicle. The cost may be higher for this coverage, but accepting a larger deductible will often make up the difference. Paying a little more toward the deductible could easily be worth it if the damage is extensive.

[D] Uninsured–Underinsured Motorists Coverage

Uninsured motorist coverage provides protection from the other driver who is operating his or her vehicle without any insurance coverage. It covers expenses resulting from injury or death as well as property damage. There are currently a dozen states where it is estimated that over 20 percent of the vehicles on the highway are being operated without any insurance. This is not coverage that should be rejected when buying automobile insurance.

Underinsured motorist coverage provides protection from the other driver who purchased only the state-mandated minimum liability insurance coverage. Again, this is not coverage that the medical professional or health-care practitioner should thoughtlessly reject when buying automobile insurance.

Umbrella Liability Insurance Overview

Negligence is generally the basis for liability insurance. Negligence is the failure on the part of an individual to exercise the proper degree of care required by the circumstances. It may consist of the failure to do something, or doing something that should *not* have been done. It is the omission to do what a reasonable and prudent person would have done in the ordinary conduct of human affairs.

Umbrella policies should be considered anytime the medical professional or health-care practitioner has a substantial current income or has accumulated a sizable estate and is concerned about asset protection from potential litigation. Umbrella policies vary greatly in structure, so care should be taken to examine all of the various aspects of the policy carefully.

Not only do umbrella policies vary in structure, but they also can be arranged with many different endorsements to meet the specific needs of the medical professional. A few examples would be the following:

- The addition of personal injury coverage (to include libel, slander, and defamation of character)

- Incidental business pursuits (to include coverage to personal automobiles where the business activity is incidental and not the primary purpose of the use of the car)
- The broadening of personal automobile coverage (to the insured regardless of whose vehicle he or she was driving and the coverage afforded that vehicle)

Evaluting Insurance Companies and Policies

[A] Introduction to Company Selection

The medical professional or health care practitioner may have heard of Standard & Poor's, Moody's, and A.M. Best, possibly as a result of doing research for an investment. These are a few of the better-known companies that monitor the strengths and weaknesses of the thousands of insurance companies that conduct business in the United States (and around the world). Independently, these rating services assign a rating to the insurance carrier based on their in-depth research.

Standard & Poor's, for example, will research a company's financial records, interview senior management, and base its rating on the company's ability to pay under its existing insurance policies and contracts. A company that specializes in selling life insurance will be rated according to its ability to pay outstanding death benefit obligations. A property and casualty company will be rated on its ability to pay claims associated with property damages or losses.

[1] FINANCIAL RATINGS

What do the financial strength ratings mean? It depends on the rating service. From our earlier example, Standard & Poor's rates companies from AAA (extremely strong) to CC (extremely weak). Within those ratings it may also assign a subrating of a plus (+) or a minus (–), which reflects the company's strength or weakness within the corresponding strength rating.

Table 2-1 shows a summary of the three ratings companies. The categories are grouped to reflect the similar ratings classes for each company, but they may not show the actual wording used by the rating service.

How important is the financial strength of an insurance company? Well, how important is it for a patient to be treated in one of the best-rated hospitals in America? The answers to these questions will likely vary with each consumer or patient. If someone is shopping for the least expensive insurance product, he or she may be willing to overlook a poor financial strength rating to get the least expensive price. On the other hand, if a consumer wants a company that has an exceptional financial strength rating, he or she should be willing to pay a little more for the security of knowing that the company chosen has a good chance of being there to pay any future claims.

Table 2-1 *Summary of the Three Ratings Companies*

	A.M. Best	*Standard & Poor's*	*Moody's*
Superior/excellent	A++/A+/A/A–	AAA/AA+/AA/AA–	Aaa/Aa 1–3
Strong		A+/A/A–	
Very good/good	B++/B+/B/B–	BBB+/BBB/BBB–	A 1–3/Baa 1–3
Fair/moderate	C++/C+	BB+/BB/BB–	Ba 1–3
Marginal			
Weak/vulnerable	C/C–	B+/B/B–	B 1–3
		CCC+/CCC/CCC–	
Poor/very poor	D	CC	Caa/Ca/C
Extremely weak			
State supervision	E	R	
Regulatory action			
Liquidation	F		

Then again, because of the competitive marketplace, medical professionals and health-care practitioners will likely notice that many of the more highly rated insurance companies will have a competitive price and, in some cases, be less expensive than those companies rated lower. Their decision, as consumers, should depend on how much risk they are willing to take with something as important as insurance protection. For many consumers it is worth a few extra dollars to get a little more peace of mind.

[2] BANKRUPTCY

What would happen if an insurance company were to go bankrupt? Although a relatively rare occurrence, the bankruptcy of an insurance company is still a very real and frightening possibility. Most cases of insolvency can be blamed on one of three circumstances: poor business decisions, corruption, or catastrophe.

Poor business decisions refer to how well a company invests its assets. Much like any business, a few bad economic cycles, coupled with mismanagement, can force an insurance company to declare bankruptcy. Because of the booming economy, this has not been a major cause of bankruptcy in the recent past. According to the National Organization of Life and Health Insurers Guaranty Associations (NOLHIGA), only two companies were declared insolvent in 2000 because of poor investment-related business decisions, with one in 2001 and a few more in 2002–2003, despite the 9/11 incident at the World Trade Center in New York City.

Unfortunately, corruption and embezzlement are not eliminated by a strong economy. A recent case involved the loss of $950 million, included nine insurance companies, and spread through six southern states. This loss occurred when a company that was supposed to invest money for the nine insurers instead transferred it into a variety of untraceable accounts. As a result, over 100,000 policyholders were affected.

Catastrophes cannot be controlled or predicted. In the property and casualty industry one natural disaster can wipe out a small company. According to the National Conference of Insurance Guaranty Funds, Hurricane Andrew caused 12 insolvencies alone.

So now that we know that the improbable can happen, what happens to the policyholder? The good news is that it is highly likely that a policyholder would receive insurance coverage, thanks to the state guarantee laws.

Every state has a "guaranty fund" or "guaranty association" created by law. This law ensures that any insurance company bankruptcy will be "insured," much like the FDIC insures the potential insolvency of banks. Also similar to the FDIC, state guaranty funds will only protect a consumer's insurance interests up to a specified monetary limit, usually $300,000 for auto, home, and life policies. NOLHGA estimates that upwards of 90 percent of all insurance policyholders affected by a bankruptcy will be fully protected.

In many instances, a financially stable insurance company may take advantage of an industry bankruptcy and purchase all or part of the financially troubled company for a bargain price. The acquiring insurance company would then assume financial responsibility for the insolvent company's policyholders.

What should the medical professional or health-care practitioner do if his or her insurance carrier becomes insolvent? Usually no direct action will need to be taken. Each policyholder will typically be contacted by the insurance company, his or her state's guaranty association, or his or her state's insurance department.

Do negative ratings signify an increased chance for bankruptcy? Although there is no guarantee, common sense seems to indicate that, if a company is in a strong financial position, there is less likelihood of it being forced into bankruptcy because of a few bad economic cycles or a couple of unforeseen natural disasters. For example, a large company that conducts multiple lines of business all over the world is likely to be in a far better position to financially survive an earthquake in California than a company that only conducts homeowners business in California.

[3] LAWSUITS

It seems we live in an age in which lawsuits are very common and a natural cost of doing business—and unfortunately the insurance industry is no exception. Lawsuits against insurance companies have lately involved misleading sales practices and improper compliance procedures.

The good news is that the industry is working at improving its reputation and increasing its collective commitment to compliance and sales practices. Not only are most companies more active in regulating themselves through various internal and external safeguards, but also the states' insurance departments and court systems have taken a more active role in protecting the consumer in recent years.

Policy Replacement

[A] Definition

Replacement is a term that has always generated the attention of the states' insurance commissioners, especially for life insurance. Whenever a new policy is issued and an older, similar policy is lapsed, surrendered, reduced, or subsequently modified, a replacement has occurred. The new policy may be issued by the same company (an internal replacement) or by a competitor (an external replacement).

The rationale for the replacement is sometimes the generation of another commission payment. Replacement, as a general rule, rarely makes sense. Unfortunately, the industry's reliance on commission income makes sales abuses a real possibility.

There *are* occasions when policyholders are better off replacing an existing product. For example, term insurance rates have dropped sharply in recent years, often making it possible to buy a longer term policy for less premium than what the owner currently has.

[B] The Process

Educated consumers can often judge the validity of a recommended replacement by being aware of their state's mandated replacement procedures. If the medical professional or health-care practitioner has been recommended to change his or her existing policies as described in Chapter 1, a number of things should occur.

First, review the application thoroughly. Make sure that the agent has clearly marked that this new policy will be replacing another policy. This is usually a yes or no check mark.

Second, most states require that a formal notification be made to the replaced policy's company and be signed by the applicant. This properly affords that company an opportunity to conserve its business. It is possible that it will offer the applicant a more favorable alternative in order to keep the insured as a client.

Third, a fair number of states also require a detailed 4- to 6-page explanation by the replacing agent and company as to why this is in the best interest of the applicant. This should include a projection into the future of the old policy as well as the illustration for the new policy. This obviously takes time to complete, but it is another safeguard for consumers. A copy of all these documents should be kept by the physician applicant.

If a replacement is occurring and none of this happens, the medical professional or health-care practitioner is well advised not to relinquish possession of any older policies, not to write a check for the first premium, and to immediately seek a second opinion. In general, it is always wise to be skeptical when a replacement is recommended.

[C] Policy Replacement: Section 1035 Exchanges

If a policyholder intends to replace an existing policy with a new policy, he or she has two choices regarding the existing policy. Once the new policy is issued, the policyholder can simply surrender the first policy and receive the cash value, if any. Income taxes will be due if there is a gain in the policy.

However, most policy owners would transfer the cash value from the old policy into the new policy, rather than actually receive it. If this is the case, the policyholder can take advantage of an Internal Revenue Code Section 1035 exchange. This section of the tax code allows a policyholder to transfer cash value from one life insurance policy *directly* to a new policy. The main advantage of a Section 1035 exchange, unlike a regular surrender, is that the transfer is tax free, even if the first policy had a large gain.

Section 1035 exchanges have a definite procedure that requires the insurance companies to conduct the exchange of money, much as in the trustee-to-trustee transfer of qualified funds. Additionally, this procedure only permits the transfer of a life insurance policy to another life insurance policy or an annuity policy. Annuities can only be transferred to annuities.

> **Example**: Dr. Jones has a 5-year-old policy into which he has paid $15,000 of premiums, and it currently has a cash surrender value of $19,000. Because his current company recently had a severe ratings downgrade from the major ratings companies, Dr. Jones is concerned about the long-term health of the company. As a result, he wishes to buy a new life insurance policy from a different company for the same face amount as his current policy.
>
> Dr. Jones and his advisor decide on a universal life policy from Company A. Dr. Jones fills out the 1035 exchange forms and other required replacement forms along with the application for the new product. About a month later, the new product from Company A is issued and the $19,000 of cash value is transferred directly to his new policy. No taxes are due.
>
> If Dr. Jones simply surrendered the first policy, he would owe tax on $4,000.

Unfortunately, policy replacement is probably recommended more often than it is really necessary. If replacement and a Section 1035 exchange are recommended, the medical professional or health-care practitioner should carefully review the proposal. Ensure that the assumptions made for projecting the old policy into the future are consistent with those assumptions for the new policy. Also, if replacement is warranted, a policyholder should never cancel an existing policy until the new policy is in force. Replacement will be covered again later in this chapter.

[D] Other Aspects to Consider

If replacement is warranted, the procedures of a Section 1035 exchange (described in Chapter 1) will usually prove to be an additional benefit. The potential tax ramifications of not using a Section 1035 exchange can be costly.

Beyond any tax consequences and potential premium savings, there may be a substantial surrender charge, or contractual penalty, by your existing company for surrendering or transferring your old policy. Replacing a policy still in the surrender period may cost the owner thousands of dollars in cash value, and this may take years to recover in the new policy.

The American Society of Financial Service Professionals has issued a very helpful replacement questionnaire to help guide agents and their clients in determining if a policyholder should consider the replacement of a contract. If an agent does not cover the pitfalls and issues surrounding the replacement of a policy, the best thing to do is take it as a warning sign that he or she might not be the appropriate insurance professional for you.

[E] A Replacement Exception

When a term policy is converted, it is considered replaced. But if the conversion occurs within the same company, it is an exception to the preceding rules. See the section on term insurance in Chapter 1 for more information on term conversions.

If a term policy is being converted and the new policy is with a different company, it probably is not an exception and, also, probably not a conversion. A true term conversion requires no underwriting, so if the selling agent or broker wants to covert a term policy and an exam is necessary, it is a replacement and should be viewed accordingly.

[F] Safeguards

The insurance industry has instituted a number of safeguards to protect consumers from unwarranted and unethical replacements:

- The policing and investigation of complaints by the state's insurance department
- Numerous state specific forms and application supplements that need to be completed and read by the consumer before a replacement is processed
- Internal company reviews of known replacement activity and patterns of abuse

Lifetime (Viatical and Senior) Settlements

A lifetime settlement is made when a life insurance policyholder sells his or her life insurance policy to a company that specializes (and speculates) in purchasing life policies as an investment. Lifetime settlements began as viatical settlements and were originally created in the late 1980s as a way to provide HIV-infected individuals with much needed additional income to pay for their increasing medical expenses or for experimental drug treatment. Viatical settlements expanded quickly to include any terminally ill policyholder. Later, they evolved into acceptance of any elderly policyholder.

In the past, when a policy owner determined that a particular policy no longer served a purpose, it could be surrendered for any existing cash value, or merely lapsed without value. Now the policy owner can sell it to a lifetime settlement company as another alternative.

The lifetime settlement company may purchase the policy for a percentage of its death benefit value. If the policy owner would not receive more money through this sale than he or she would through simply surrendering the policy, then the lifetime settlement concept should be dropped.

The price set by the lifetime settlement company will depend on the insured's age and medical condition. The lower the projected life expectancy, the higher the price paid by the company. To receive from 40 to 80 percent of a life insurance policy's death benefit while still alive could be very helpful to a family struggling with medical bills and other debts.

Once a policy is purchased by a lifetime settlement company, that company becomes the owner of the policy and continues to pay the premiums until the insured dies. The settlement company then receives the full death benefit. The company's profit is the death proceeds minus the amount it paid to the original owner.

As a result of the Health Insurance Portability and Accountability Act of 1996, the money received by the insured in a viatical settlement may not be subject to income taxes. If the insured is terminally or chronically ill, the money is generally considered an early payment of the death benefit and is not income taxable. If the insured, however, is healthy and just doesn't need the policy any longer, any payment received over the insured's original cost basis will be taxed as ordinary income.

Beware! ■ Lifetime settlements are not always as attractive as they might seem. When such a company purchases a life contract, it is wagering on the death of the insured. The faster the insured dies, the more profit for that company. The various state insurance departments have been slow to respond to this growing trend, and regulation of this activity is sporadic.

What should the medical professional or health-care practitioner do if approached about a lifetime settlement? The best thing to do is to keep a number of guidelines in mind.

- Call your state insurance department to find out if the settlement company is licensed or regulated in your state.
- Consult your attorney or financial advisor. Review the current tax ramifications of the recommendation. If you are terminally ill, the viatical settlement will probably be exempt from federal income tax as a result of the Health Insurance Portability and Accountability Act of 1996.
- Make sure you contact a number of different settlement companies. Settlements can vary greatly between different companies, and the Viatical Association of

America encourages potential "viators" to get at least three different offers before selling.

- Request that the settlement company set up an escrow account for you when you accept the settlement so that the funds will be ensured. Any reputable firm should not have a problem with this request.

- Talk with your current beneficiaries. Your decision may affect their lives as well, and if they will be saddled with large, unpaid medical bills upon your death, a viatical or senior settlement may not be the best decision.

- A viatical settlement will likely affect any financial need-based public assistance you may otherwise be eligible for.

- Such settlements are normally fair game for creditors.

- Check into alternatives. Find out how much cash is available in your policy without selling it, and check if your policy has an accelerated death benefit. An accelerated death benefit will typically allow terminally ill insureds to access a portion of the total death benefit (usually 50 percent) while still alive.

Unlike in a viatical settlement, the lifetime settlement policy is still owned by the original policy owner. Thus, when the insured passes away, the named beneficiary will receive the remaining death benefit. This results in all of the death benefit going to the original parties of the contract rather than a viatical company getting a piece of the pie.

The lifetime settlement industry has flourished in recent years, partly because company and agent sales practices have largely gone unchecked. Not only do different insurance industry groups have an interest in the regulation of these companies, but so does the securities industry. Many individuals have invested in the promised returns of lifetime settlement companies.

States are generally split as to how and who should regulate this industry. There are three different alternatives: the securities regulator, the insurance department, or no regulation at all. As lifetime settlements become more popular, both as an investment and a settlement option, they can expect more attention and scrutiny from a number of regulators.

> **Example:** Dr. Dread has recently learned that he has an inoperable brain tumor. His doctor has given him 6 months to a year to live.
>
> He knows that his health insurance will cover most of the bills, but he realizes that his wife would have to pay for the difference from his estate. Although they have not saved excessively, he does own multiple life insurance policies totaling over $2 million in death benefits. His wife has an excellent job, and they do not depend on his income to survive financially.
>
> After talking it over with his wife, Dr. Dread decides to opt for a viatical settlement on $1 million worth of insurance. He shops for his policies through a number of different viatical firms and receives an offer of 70 percent of the death benefit from Viaticals-R-Us. Dr. Dread can then use the $700,000 to take himself and his wife on the vacation they always dreamed

of, knowing his wife will still have $1 million in death benefit to cover any outstanding medical bills, if needed, or to supplement her income.

Needs Analysis Approach to Life Insurance

Needs analysis is a generic term used within the insurance industry to identify a process that helps quantify a variety of financial needs, including life insurance. The techniques for calculating the need can vary considerably, and there exist a variety of computer and work sheet models that can calculate the financial objective. The insurance professional assisting the medical professional or health-care practitioner should request the following:

- An in-depth discussion of your goals, both financial and personal
- A review of your current insurance (life, health, disability, property and casualty, etc.), financial holdings, and investment assets and their projected growth potential
- A review of your current estate plan, including any current wills and trusts
- Any personally owned practice business information

The length and detail of the needs analysis, or financial plan, can vary based on the model used or the detail of the results requested. Whereas a broker or agent may use a simple needs analysis designed to pinpoint a certain life insurance amount, a model by a certified financial planner (CFP®) should include a more thorough review of insurance needs and a long- and short-term financial analysis.

Keep in mind that there should be a difference between using an agent or broker for this service and using a CFP®. An agent or broker should not normally charge a fee for this service. A CFP® will generally charge a set amount that could range from $200 to $5,000, depending on the size of the estate being analyzed.

Once the needs analysis model has been completed, the agent, broker, or financial planner will then take the information and produce a recommendation. The results are only as good or correct as the information provided the advisor. This process can be time consuming, but the results are usually worth the trouble.

Lastly, things change. A comprehensive financial plan, or a simple needs analysis, must be reviewed regularly. A simple review should be done yearly, and a more thorough review is recommended at each phase of the life cycle or at each major family event, such as the birth of a child.

The life cycle is typically thought of as consisting of four different stages (different insurance professionals may have different names for these stages):

1. Early career and/or growing family
2. Peak accumulation

3. Preretirement

4. Retirement

At each of these stages, an in-depth analysis or comprehensive plan should be performed. This will ensure an accurate, up-to-date plan for the future.

Additional Readings

1. Bryis, Eric: *Insurance: From Underwriting to Derivatives.* John Wiley, New York, 2001.

2. Cummins, David: *Changes in the Life Insurance Industry.* Kluwer Academic Publishers, 1999.

3. Hardy, Mary: *Life Insurance Investment Guarantees.* John Wiley, Boston, 2003.

4. Lowe, Terry: *Business of Insurance.* Health Insurance Association, Washington, DC, 1998.

5. Rubin, Harvey: *Dictionary of Insurance Terms.* Barron's Business Guides, New York, 2002.

Websites

The following URL addresses have also been found to contain worthwhile property and casualty insurance information:

- www.taxresources.com - an excellent location for research on any insurance tax matter

- www.knowledgeservice.com - a resource for insurance, estate planning, and business information; this includes sample agreements and some free software you should use for a risk-free and comfortable retirement

Chapter 3

Insuring the Doctor's Practice

(Protecting the Business . . . Earning a Living)

Gary A. Cook

Make sure the fiduciary firms you rely on are established, have adequate references, carry insurance and are bonded, if applicable. It will not be difficult to find some of the largest accounting, investment and banking firms in the world. Don't skimp on these services . . . the security of your funds depends on it.

Celia Clark, JD, LL.M., and David B. Mandell, JD, MBA

There are three parts to any life insurance policy: the policy owner, the beneficiary, and the covered life. This unique policy format allows life insurance to indemnify a medical practice and ensure its successful business continuity. Examples will be used in this chapter to illustrate these applications.

Business Uses of Life Insurance

[A] Key Person Insurance

If a key physician were to die prematurely, what would potentially happen to the medical practice? In many cases, especially in smaller practices, it would have a devastating affect on the bottom line, or even precipitate a bankruptcy. In these circumstances, a form of business insurance, called key person coverage, is recommended in order to alleviate the potential financial problems resulting from the death of that employee.

The practice would purchase and own a life insurance policy on the key person. Upon the death of the key doctor employee, the life insurance proceeds could be used to do the following:

- Pay off bank loans for the practice
- Replace lost profits of the practice
- Establish a reserve for the search, hiring, and training of a physician replacement

> **Example**: Main Lion Hospital has gained national recognition for innovating a new procedure for laser eye surgery. Not only has it invested an enormous sum of money in the equipment used, but it is also very dependent on the talents and continued employment of Dr. Williamson, who helped design the equipment and procedure.
>
> Fearing the economic consequences if Dr. Williamson were to die, the hospital has purchased an insurance policy on his life to help pay for the immediate replacement and the training of another specialist.

[B] Practice Continuation Funding

A medical practice continuation, or buy–sell agreement, stipulates how the different shares of the practice must be sold or continued upon the death or disability of a physician business partner, shareholder, or sole proprietor In a typical buy–sell agreement, the sole proprietor, shareholder, or partner is the insured of a life insurance policy, which can create the funds to complete the agreement.

There are a number of keys to creating a successful buy–sell agreement:

- It must be decided who will buy the practice from the disabled proprietor, shareholder, or partner, or his or her heirs upon death. It may be the remaining shareholders, partner(s), or the business entity itself or, in the case of a sole proprietor, a key employee or relative.
- The buy–sell agreement must be stipulated as mandatory. According to the IRS, if the agreement is not mandatory, the value of the practice is not considered fixed. As a result, the IRS would not consider the agreement binding in determining the value of the business for estate tax purposes.
- Be specific as to what is to be purchased. This can include land, buildings, inventory, licenses, and even good will.
- The most important key is determining the correct value for the practice or share in question. The IRS will rarely challenge a value for being set too high, but it will challenge those deemed to be valued too low. Valuation should not be taken lightly and can be a fixed dollar amount or based on a formula. There are many different formulas that can be used, such as adjusted book value and capitalization of earnings. It is usually recommended to use a formula rather than a fixed dollar amount.

There are a number of different forms of buy–sell agreements. The following is a quick overview of four different variations.

1. **Sole Proprietor Buy-Sell Agreement:** Since a sole proprietor does not have a partner, other than a spouse, he or she usually must look elsewhere for a buyer. Therefore, the sole proprietor is likely to turn to a valued employee, a competitor, or a family member in order to continue the business. In this case, life insurance is purchased by the future business owner on the life of the solo doctor. The agreement is signed between the current and the future owners, providing the guidelines for the future practice. In addition to being the owner of the policy, the future practice owner typically names himself or herself beneficiary.

2. **Cross Purchase Buy-Sell Agreement:** This type of buy–sell agreement is normally used for any business with multiple owners, although it is best used for agreements with only two owners. In this arrangement, each physician practice owner purchases insurance on each of the other owners' lives. Again, the owner of each policy names himself or herself beneficiary as well. Upon the death or disability of one partner or shareholder, the remaining partner(s) or shareholder(s) is(are) provided the funds to purchase a pro rata share of the deceased or disabled individual's practice interest.

3. **Entity Purchase Buy-Sell Agreement:** This form is used for multiple physician owners, and/or when the owner(s) of the business want(s) to use the assets of the practice to fund the insurance policies. In this arrangement, the practice owns the policies on each physician partner or shareholder, and it is also listed as the beneficiary of each policy. Upon the death or disability of the partner or shareholder, the business would be able to purchase the shares from the disabled partner or shareholder, or the deceased's heirs.

4. **Optional Purchase/Wait and See/Buy-Sell Agreement:** This type of agreement allows either the business or the individual partner(s) or shareholder(s) the option of purchasing the deceased or disabled shareholder's or partner's interest in the business. Normally, if the practice does not initially exercise its option to buy within a set period, the remaining partner(s) or shareholder(s) would then have a period in which to exercise their option. If they do not buy the outstanding interest, the practice would then be forced to purchase the shares.

Often a "trusteed" agreement is advisable. It can be used with all four agreements just mentioned. It is not unusual to find situations in which the practice partners work together smoothly and efficiently. Their spouses, however, are another story. To remove personalities from the transfer of ownership interests for money, especially at a very stressful point in their lives, it is often a good idea to let a disinterested third party (a trustee) conduct the transfer.

> **Example:** Dr. Martin has been the sole owner of the Family Physician Group, which includes six other physicians and 12 other employees, for

over 10 years. He has often thought about who will continue this successful practice.

In the past month he has decided that Dr. Rogers is the best candidate for the job. She has also expressed an interest in becoming the successor to Dr. Martin.

As a result, they have decided to set up a trusteed sole proprietor buy–sell agreement that would provide for the smooth, mandatory transfer of the practice in the case of the death or disability of Dr. Martin. Once the practice is correctly valued, she plans to purchase a life insurance policy on the life of Dr. Martin, which will be owned by a third-party trust, who will also be the beneficiary. Upon the death or disability of Dr. Martin, the terms of the agreement will be executed by the trustee, and Dr. Rogers would then be the sole owner of the Family Physician Group.

[C] Executive Bonus Plan

An executive bonus plan (or § 162 plan) is an effective way for a company to provide valued, select physicians or other employees an additional employment benefit. One of the main advantages to an executive bonus plan, when compared to other benefits, is its simplicity. In a typical executive bonus plan, an agreement is made between the employer and employee whereby the employer agrees to pay for the cost of a life insurance policy, in the form of a bonus, on the life of the employee.

The major benefits of such a plan to the employee are that he or she is the immediate owner of the cash values and the death benefit provided. The only cost to the employee is the payment of income tax on any bonus received. The employer receives a tax deduction for providing the benefit, improves the morale of its selected employees, and can use the plan as a tool to attract additional talent.

> **Example:** Dr. Stern is a sole practitioner in rural West Virginia. Among his employees is Nurse Jackson, who has been with him for over 10 years. She is the single parent for two boys. Although he pays well and provides additional benefits, he has been looking for a way to selectively reward Nurse Jackson for her years of service and hard work. Recently Nurse Jackson has expressed a concern for her children if she were to die prematurely.
>
> Dr. Stern chooses to provide an executive bonus plan by allowing Nurse Jackson to purchase a life insurance policy on her life. Dr. Stern will provide the premium payments in the form of a bonus to her. Nurse Jackson must simply pay the tax on this additional income. Dr. Stern's practice will get a tax deduction for the premium and improve the morale of an important employee. Nurse Jackson will get needed protection for her family.

[D] Nonqualified Salary Continuation

Commonly referred to as deferred compensation, this is a legally binding promise by an employer to pay a salary continuation benefit at a specific point in the future in exchange for the current and continued performance of its employee. These plans are normally used to supplement existing retirement plans.

Although there are different variations of deferred compensation, in a typical deferred compensation agreement, the employer will purchase and own a life insurance policy on the life of the employee. The cash value of the policy grows tax deferred during the employee's working years. After retirement, these cash values can be withdrawn from the policy to reimburse the company for its after-tax retirement payments to the employee.

Upon the death of the employee, any remaining death benefit would likely be received income tax free by the employer. (Alternative minimum taxes could apply to any benefit received by certain larger C corporations.) The death benefit could then be used to pay any required survivor benefits to the employee's spouse, or to provide partial or total cost recovery to the employer.

In a typical plan, the terms of the agreement are negotiated as to the amount of benefit received by the employee, when retirement benefits can begin, how long retirement benefits will be paid, and if benefits will be provided for death or disability. The business has established what is commonly referred to as "golden handcuffs" for the employee. As a result, the benefit will only be received if the employee continues to work for the company until retirement. If the employee is terminated for cause or quits prior to retirement, the plan will end and no benefits will be payable.

> **Example:** Dr. Young has been working for Northeast Chiropractic for almost 7 years. His employer knows that he has been approached by a number of other chiropractic firms in regards to joining them in the future.
>
> Northeast Chiropractic wants to keep Dr. Young on its staff for many years and needs to create an incentive program for Dr. Young to want to stay. It has agreed to enter into a deferred compensation plan with Dr. Young.
>
> According to the agreement, Dr. Young will agree to continue to work for Northeast Chiropractic until normal retirement age. In exchange for his continued services, the company will provide him, or his surviving spouse, an additional $50,000 per year starting at age 65 years and lasting for 20 years.
>
> In order to fund this plan, Northeast Chiropractic has astutely decided to purchase a life insurance policy on Dr. Young. As the cash value grows tax deferred, it will eventually be available to provide the company reimbursements for the after-tax additional retirement benefit. Should Dr. Young die prematurely, the policy's death benefit would be available to provide the agreed benefit for his surviving spouse. It has also been designed to provide some key person coverage.

[E] Split-Dollar Plans

Split-dollar arrangements can be a complicated and confusing concept for even the most experienced insurance professional or financial advisor. This concept is, in its simplest terms, a way for a business to share the cost and benefit of a life insurance policy with a valued employee. In a normal split-dollar arrangement, the employee will receive valuable life insurance coverage at little cost to himself or herself. The business pays the majority of the premium, but it is usually able to recover the entire cost of providing this benefit.

Following the publication of IRS Notices 2002-8 and 2002-59, there are currently two general approaches to the ownership of business split-dollar life insurance: employer owned or employee owned. (In addition, Proposed Regulation 164754-01, if finalized in present form, would substantially change split-dollar arrangements even further. The practitioner should research this area thoroughly before making any recommendations.) Regardless of the method used, a written agreement must be prepared to spell out the rights and obligations of the parties.

[1] EMPLOYER-OWNED METHOD

In the employer-owned method, the employer is the sole owner of the policy. A written split-dollar agreement usually permits the employee to name the beneficiary for most of the death proceeds. The employer owns all the cash value and has the unfettered right to borrow or withdraw it as necessary. At the end of the formal agreement, the business can generally (1) continue the policy as key person insurance, (2) transfer ownership to the insured and report the cash values as additional income to the insured, (3) sell the policy to the insured, or (4) use a combination of these methods. This is commonly referred to as "rollout."

Medical practitioners and their advisors should be careful not to include rollout language in the split-dollar agreement. Many plans are set up with the intent—although not in writing—to transfer the policy to the insured after a certain number of years. The reason the rollout should not be included is that if the parties formally agree that, after a specified number of years (or following a specific event, related only to the circumstances surrounding the policy), the policy will be turned over to the insured, the IRS could declare that the entire transaction was a sham and that its sole purpose was to avoid taxation of the premiums to the employee. If that happens, the IRS may deem that the premiums paid should be considered income to the employee when they were paid. If this comes up in an audit year after the inception of the agreement, it may generate substantial interest and penalties in addition to the additional taxes due.

The death proceeds available to the insured employee's beneficiary are considered a current economic benefit. Also called reportable economic benefit (REB), they are an annually taxable event to the employee. If an individual policy is involved, the REB is calculated by multiplying the face amount times the government's Table 2003 rates or the insurance company's alternative term rates, using the insured's age. If a second-to-die policy is involved, the government's PS38 rates or the company's alternative PS38 rates will be used. IRS Table PS 38 rates are for a second-to-die life policy. The IRS tables have been an accepted method of valuing the insurance portion of a life insurance policy for more than three decades. Any part of the premium actually paid by the employee is used to offset any REB dollar for dollar.

The employer-owned method is primarily used when the employer wishes to maintain as much control as possible over the life insurance policy or when there are officers and executives of publicly held corporations. This employee perquisite can be used to reward key employees with current inexpensive death protection and simultaneously provide a potential handcuff for them by informally funding a deferred compensation agreement.

[2] EMPLOYEE-OWNED METHOD

With the employee-owned method, the insured-employee is generally the applicant and owner of the policy. Any premiums paid by the business are deemed to be loans to the employee, and the employee reports as income an imputed interest rate on the cumulative amount of loan based on Code § 7872. A collateral assignment is made for the benefit of the business to cover the cumulative loan amount. In some cases, the assignment may allow the assignee to have access to the cash values of the policy by way of a policy loan. This method is unavailable for officers and executives of publicly held corporations because of the current restrictions on corporate loans (the Sarbanes-Oxley Act).

The employee-owned method is somewhat similar to the older collateral assignment form of the split-dollar plan. The benefits for the employee are both the ability to control large amounts of death proceeds and the ability to develop equity in the policy. Whether this new method catches on will depend greatly on the imputed interest rate published by the IRS every July. If set low enough, this may be an excellent opportunity for the employee to use inexpensive business dollars to pay for life insurance. In September 2003, for example, the rate was 2.35 percent.:

[3] SUMMARY OF SPLIT-DOLLAR METHOD

The preceding summaries are not intended to be a complete treatise on the split-dollar concept. There are many different variations that continue to change and develop daily. Because of the complexity of the split-dollar plan and its potential tax implications, one should consult an experienced team of advisors whenever one is considering a split-dollar arrangement.

> **Example**: Dr. Tryon is a valuable member of a team of surgeons at St. Mary's Hospital. He has recently developed a new technique for treating brain aneurysms. The hospital would like to keep him on staff for years to come.
>
> Dr. Tryon is married and has one small child and his wife is pregnant. He has requested that the hospital provide him with more life insurance. The

hospital's board of directors meet with a number of financial advisors to review their options, and they settle on an employer-owned split-dollar arrangement.

As a result, they will purchase and pay for a life insurance policy on Dr. Tryon, providing him the bulk of the death benefit for his family as long as he is a member of their hospital staff. They have also agreed to bonus Dr. Tryon the amount equal to the reportable economic benefit in order to keep his insurance cost at a minimum.

Other Business-Related Insurance

[A] Workers' Compensation

Workers' compensation is reported to be the largest line of commercial insurance, possibly because it is also a statutory obligation for employers who have common law employees. Workers' compensation provides coverage for lost income due to on-the-job accidents or work-related disability or death, and benefits vary by state. Its purpose is not only to provide these benefits but also to reduce potential litigation. Employees accepting the benefit payments from a workers' compensation claim generally forego the right to sue their employer. Workers' compensation rates are established by job descriptions and commercial rates; for the medical professional's office, they are some of the lowest available.

There are three methods of providing workers' compensation coverage:

1. Private commercial insurance
2. Governmental insurance funds
3. Self-insurance

There are, however, seven "monopolistic" states—Nevada, North Dakota, Ohio, Washington, West Virginia, and Wyoming—that do not permit private commercial insurance.

The medical professional may be inclined to the third method, self-insurance, especially in larger offices. Since the weekly benefits are typically below $500, this would seem to make a lot of sense. Since in larger groups the officers and owners can elect not to be covered, it is usually more convenient for the medical professional to cover this risk with personal disability income insurance.

Larger offices or companies that wish to take more direct control of costs and benefit management should consider self-insuring only after receiving expert advice. This is one form of coverage that truly requires a trusted, knowledgeable insurance advisor.

[B] Business Owner Policy

Business owner policies are offered on a simplified package basis. Much like homeowner policies, they contain both property and liability coverage. Property coverage is available on either an actual value or replacement value basis, and it can be purchased for named perils or on an all-risk basis.

Also as with homeowner policies, the medical professional or health-care practitioner should compile a basic inventory of property to be covered. Medical records and important papers are typically covered for a flat amount. Don't forget to allow for supplies and leased equipment.

Liability coverage protects the business owner from claims arising from bodily injury or property damage while the claimant is on the premises. Liability insurance pays not only the damage awarded to the claimant but also the attorney fees and other costs associated with any defense of the suit.

Coverage under a business owner policy is typically very broad and can be tailored to fit almost any practice. Since coverage under this policy can often be coordinated with other business-related insurance, it should be handled by the same trusted insurance advisor.

[C] Professional Liability Insurance

Professional liability insurance is also known as malpractice insurance or "errors and omissions insurance." The intent of this coverage is to provide for professional acts only and avoids any liability coverage for criminal acts. Some policies also exclude acts of the insured and assistants while under the influence of drugs or alcohol.

It is generally very important to the medical professional or health-care practitioner that the insurance company is not able to unilaterally settle a claim without the express consent of the insured. Such a provision recognizes the extreme importance of the medical professional's reputation.

Almost all professional liability contracts today are written on a claims-made basis. These policies pay claims that are made only during the coverage period subsequent to the retroactive date. This is the inception date of the first policy written on a claims-made basis for the insured.

Professional liability coverage is also almost universally offered through professional organizations or associations.

Miscellaneous Insurance Policies

The following insurance policies should be carefully considered before they are purchased, since they may be unnecessary or too expensive, may provide only minimal benefits, or may be duplicated in your other policies. These include credit life or home mortgage insurance (decreasing term), life insurance for children, accident policies for students, hospital indemnity policies, dread disease insurance, credit card insurance, pet health insurance, life insurance for the elderly, funeral insurance, flight insurance, prepaid legal insurance, and most extended warranties on automobiles, televisions, stereos, home computers, and the like.

On the other hand, the following types of coverage may be important in selected cases: trip cancelation insurance, termite insurance, and flood and earthquake insurance.

Additionally, according to fee-only life insurance expert Peter C. Katt of Kalamazoo, Michigan, doctors should be on guard against believing in the existence of perfect retirement vehicles funded through springing cash value life insurance plans. These plans reportedly feature payments of very large premiums while the policy is subject to favorable tax treatment, and then transfer the policy to the insured doctor when it appears to have no taxable value, after which the cash value *springs* to life. Unfortunately, in the real world, one cannot create tax-deductible contributions and tax-free benefits without resorting to fraud or deception. Particularly notorious are the so-called continuous group insurance and VEBA (Voluntary Employee Benefit Association) prepaid retiree plans, despite the fact that the latter have been mistakenly endorsed by state medical societies in certain cases.

Always remember that no matter how professional and sincere marketers appear, there are no life insurance policies that can legitimately provide tax-deductible insurance with tax-free retirement benefits. Therefore, you should always consult a qualified professional for further information regarding your specific needs.

Additional Readings

1. Babbel, David: *Investment Management for Insurers.* John Wiley, Boston, 1999.
2. *Business Insurance Concepts* by Pictorial, Inc. 1-800-428-4215. (This is very basic and easy to read. It is a great starting point if you know very little.)
3. Current Year's *Field Guide to Estate Planning, Business Planning, and Employee Benefits,* by Donald F. Cady, JD, LLM, CLU, published by the National Underwriter Company (1-800-543-0874).
4. Current Year's *Guide to Health Insurance for People with Medicare,* developed jointly by the National Association of Insurance Commissioners and the Health Care Financing Administration of the U.S. Department of Health and Human Services.
5. *Introduction to Life Insurance* by Pictorial, Inc. 1-800-428-4215. (Again, this is very basic information and a great starting point.)

Websites

The following URL addresses have also been found to contain worthwhile risk management and insurance information:

- www.brentmark.com - a free insurance software site; more complex calculators and soliciting for sales; look under "Demo Disks" for free programs
- www.medicare.gov - get your Medicare insurance information firsthand at their website
- www.leimberg.com - Steve Leimberg is an insurance industry legend; this website contains current information on many business and charitable aspects of life insurance

Chapter 4

Risks of Medical Practice Noncompete Agreements

(Restrictive Covenants Vital . . . Often Contentious and Subject to Interpretation)

Frederick William LaCava

The enforceability of covenants not to compete has been a widely litigated issue. Restrictive covenants, within the context of the delivery of health care services, is particularly complex. Such covenants must be reasonable in terms of duration, scope and geography and they must be tailored to protect a legitimate business interest.

Hall, Render, Killian, Heath & Lyman, P.S.C., www.HallRender.com

The angriest individuals I have ever met in my life are parties to litigation over contractual covenants not to compete. Not medical malpractice cases, not even divorces, produce the fury, the expense, the feelings of betrayal and fraud that infect doctors fighting over whether, if, and how a paragraph in what was once a friendly business deal should be interpreted. The anger and grief probably spring from a failure of the parties to achieve mutual understanding at the time that the agreement is negotiated. These covenants are still necessary, but overreaching by one side or the other leads to terrible legal conflicts.

Restrictive Covenants Defined

The covenants in question are agreements that in certain circumstances one of the parties is committing himself or herself not to practice his or her profession for a period of time within a geographical area or with members of a defined population. They arise in two sets of circumstances: the sale of a practice or as a term of an employment agreement. The law treats the two types quite differently, favoring agreements as part of the sale of a practice and entertaining challenges to covenants in employment contracts.

A covenant not to compete is legally based on preservation of a protectable interest in good will. Though good will is an intangible property right, it is very much a real one. Accountants and the IRS have recognized methods of quantifying it. The federal government's fraud and abuse enforcement arm is very interested in it to make sure that it is not in fact a disguised kickback, and divorce lawyers love it when divorce prompts an evaluation of marital property. Good will is the value attributed to an ongoing practice's name recognition, location, telephone numbers, business names, and all those things that would make a potential patient come to one doctor's office rather than another's. The law recognizes that a practitioner has the right to protect that value from a competitor who unfairly tries to appropriate it.

Covenants for the Sale of a Medical Practice

Good will should be protected in a sale of a practice because much of the value of such a practice is encompassed by the element of good will. A practice may include a building or suite of offices, either owned or leased; the equipment, furniture, and supplies on hand; records of patients; and other financial interests. But the biggest value of a practice is the propensity of existing patients to come to that location for medical services. The good will has been created by the practitioners who have provided those services in the past. To the extent that patients have liked Dr. Washington and have been satisfied with his medical treatment, they will tend to come to his office after Dr. Adams has acquired the practice. A large part of what Dr. Adams has paid for is the likelihood of transfer of that patient loyalty from Dr. Washington to him. A necessary part of the sale of the practice, then, is a commitment from Dr. Washington not to compete with Dr. Adams in that location or nearby for some reasonable amount of time. If Dr. Adams were not to require such a commitment from Dr. Washington, Dr. Washington would be free to open a new office across the street from the old one and attract the patients who were loyal to him in the old office to come to the new office. Unless Dr. Adams only bargained for some secondhand equipment and shopworn office space, he would not have gotten the good will he paid for.

Covenants not to compete that are incident to the sale of a practice are favored by the law, almost universally enforced, and play a logical and necessary part of the sale or transfer of good will. Disputes and litigation over these covenants arise when the seller tries to find a way to get around the commitment. For example, the seller might say, "Yes, I signed the covenant not to compete with Dr. Adams, but my wife, Dr. Martha Washington, did not. She can start up a competing practice across the street from the old office. She doesn't use the business name *Washington Internal Medicine Associates* that I sold to Dr. Adams; she uses *Dr. M. Washington Internal Medicine, P.C.* I don't practice medicine in any way at her office; I just sit out in the waiting room and drink coffee and chat with the patients."

Sellers who try such tactics usually lose. In negotiating the sale of a practice, either as seller or as buyer, use an attorney who is expert in the area of covenants not to compete. Don't use a real estate lawyer, your tax attorney, or your divorce attorney. Don't use your brother's former college roommate just because he would do it cheap. You would never have a psychiatrist set your broken leg; so pay for the appropriate specialist. Make sure that the terms of the covenant are reasonable. A covenant whose terms are draconian may be voided by a court, leaving the purchaser with no protection at all.

Covenants as Part of a Medical Employment Contract

A covenant not to compete that is part of a contract of employment (or part of a stockholder's agreement) is far more likely to result in litigation because these covenants are far more likely to be used or avoided unfairly. Many an employer would like the covenant to punish an employee who would dare to leave a job with an ongoing practice and compete with it in any conceivable fashion. Many an employee has signed an employment contract without ever giving thought to the possibility that the covenant would be enforced against him or her, or worse, thinking that the covenant could not be enforced. If the covenant is drafted to be reasonable, it will be enforced, and should be enforced. The reasons are easy to see.

Young associate, Dr. Johnson, joins elder practitioner, Dr. Lincoln, in an ongoing practice with good will created by Lincoln. Dr. Johnson gets to know Dr. Lincoln's patients and impresses them with his own abilities. Dr. Johnson and Dr. Lincoln do not agree on an extension of the employment contract, and Dr. Johnson is notified that he may not practice medicine within the terms of the covenant not to compete contained in his employment contract. Dr. Lincoln has a protectable interest in the good will of his practice that Dr. Johnson should not be allowed to appropriate and use against his former employer as a competitor. If the covenant is reasonably drafted, it will do no more than protect that defined interest belonging to Dr. Lincoln. The problem is defining what interest may be reasonably protected.

"Reasonable" Covenant Terms

A covenant not to compete will not be upheld by a court if its effect is to go beyond the interest that Dr. Lincoln has in his good will. Current patients who have a current relationship of trust with Dr. Lincoln should be recognized as a legitimate interest. But, what about persons who have never been patients of Dr. Lincoln, patients who may never have heard of Dr. Lincoln? What about patients who have not seen Dr. Lincoln in years and who may no longer have any tendency to consult with him on a new problem? The courts have struggled with this concept, and decisions can be found that both enforce and strike down covenants that cover future or possible patients.

The covenant must be for a reasonable amount of time. How long is there a reasonable expectation that a patient would come back to a doctor who treated him or her earlier? Covenants up to 2 years have been almost uniformly upheld, but covenants longer than that period have had varying fates.

The covenant must extend over no more than a reasonably necessary geographical area to effectuate protection of the legitimate interest. That geographical area may be far wider in a rural area than within a metropolis. The size of the geographical area may also vary with the kind of business interest being protected. In some cases an area of a whole county is too big, whereas in others an area of 12 states is deemed reasonable. The definition of the geographical area is often given little review by a court, and, instead, another covenant with protection of one county or a 50-mile radius is cited with a conclusion that a similarly sized area is also reasonable. A more particular examination of the facts of the particular case may distinguish it from that other case.

An alternative to a geographical limitation is a specification of certain persons whose business may not be solicited by the former employee, usually a designation of "current" patients or customers who have been served by the employer within the time of the associate's employment. In these cases, there is no geographical area of coverage, and the patient or customer may reside anywhere. Courts approve of these current customer limits.

A covenant may be declared unenforceable if one of its terms is unreasonable and cannot be separated from the remainder of the covenant. The law will not apply a "blue pencil" to rewrite the terms of a covenant to bring it within the scope of reasonability, but it will strike down a term that is unreasonable that can be isolated from the other terms of the covenant. However, a covenant may contain a *cy pres* clause (medieval French for "as close"), which directs the court to enforce the covenant within the limits of the law as closely to the meaning of the parties as possible.

Remedies for Covenant Breach

Remedies are the things that courts can do to protect or compensate a person who has been harmed by violation of a covenant not to compete. The possible remedies are (1) an award of actual damages proven after the fact, that is, how much monetary loss can be attributed directly to the unfair competition of the former employee; (2) liquidated damages calculated in advance at the time the covenant was drafted; and (3) injunction, that is, a court order that the former employees stop violating the covenant immediately. The first remedy is almost never used and is included in this analysis to show why the other two remedies are used instead. Actual damages after the fact require that the whole period of the covenant run before any remedy can be considered. Employers argue that they could be put out of business before they ever got to be heard in court. Employers also argue that it would be so difficult as to be impossible to calculate. I have my doubts about how impossible it would be, but it is not very practical. I will come back to liquidated damages and why they are far more appropriate for physicians later.

An injunction is an order by the court, that is, the government, that a doctor not practice his or her area of medicine within the area and time limits of the covenant. In order for a court to issue an injunction, the court must find that the damages that may be done to the former employer are irreparable, that is, that no amount of money that can be reasonably calculated can compensate the former employer for the harm done by the former employee's competition. Further, the court must determine that it is in the public interest to issue the injunction. Most frequently, an employment agreement with a covenant not to compete will include recitations that the parties agree that damages to the employer would be irreparable and that it would be in the public interest that an injunction would be issued to enforce the covenant; in other words, the covenant tries to supply these necessary areas of proof by incorporating them into the language of the covenant. No court is bound by such recitations. It is only the court that determines the public interest, not the parties, and it is only the court that can determine that an alleged damage is or is not irreparable.

There are a million arguments and counterarguments between medical practitioners over whether the financial damages that may be done between them can or cannot be calculated. However, once a court turns to damages that may be done to patients, arguments tend to be more one-sided. Courts are beginning to pay serious attention to the public interest, which may be affected by the issuance of an injunction if it can be shown that an injunction would endanger members of the public who may need a particular specialty of medicine or even someone with the ability to perform a specific procedure within that specialty. They also pay attention if an injunction would prevent a community hospital from having physicians available to make full use of its facilities.

Arguments have also been made that a covenant between doctors is or should be against public policy because the enforcement of such an agreement forbids a patient from seeing the physician that he or she prefers without allowing the patient any say in the matter. The *Opinions of the Council on Ethical and Judicial Affairs of the American Medical Association* (1986, 1994, 1996), Section 9.02, provides for agreements restricting medical practice.

Agreements Restricting the Practice of Medicine

The Council on Ethical and Judicial Affairs discourages any agreement between physicians that restricts the right of a physician to practice medicine for a specified period of time or in a specified area upon termination of employment or a partnership or a corporate agreement. Such restrictive agreements are not in the public interest.

However, the AMA appears not to frown on covenants not to compete. Courts in some states have taken the position that the covenants are void as against public policy. You must consult with an attorney to find out the legal handling of covenants not to compete between physicians involving injunctions.

Liquidated damages are specifications within a contract, in advance of any breach, that reasonably determine what monetary damages are likely to result from a breach of the covenant not to compete. The liquidated damages may set a specific figure or provide a certain formula for calculating the damages based on specified elements, such as collections at a particular office. If the covenant is for longer than a year, the contract may provide that liquidated damages for breach during the first year will be one amount, and a breach after one year would be another amount. The law highly favors liquidated damages because the two parties have calculated the amount in advance and have relieved the court of having to determine damages from the many different ways by which they can be calculated.

It is my own position that a specification of liquidated damages in a contract eliminates the claim for injunctive relief as well. The basic argument for injunctive relief is that a monetary award cannot compensate for the injuries done. Liquidated damages specify that amount and eliminate that claim. However, some courts have granted both damages and injunctive relief, perhaps because the parties did not raise the logical conflict before the court. I personally advise my clients to seek or offer provisions for liquidated damages because I find it repugnant to use the power of the state to tell a patient that he or she may not seek medical treatment from Dr. Kennedy or Dr. Nixon. The patient's choice is not to be sacrificed for a business concern, and the monetary damages will protect the loss of any good will that may be suffered.

Liquidated damages, however, have their own set of abuses. The amount of the damages may not bear a logical relationship to any reasonable way to calculate damages. An amount that is obviously in excess of a reasonable estimation is legally a penalty on the person violating the covenant rather than compensation of injuries sustained by the complaining party. The law will not enforce a penalty or private punishment. An employer who overreaches may find himself or herself with no protection at all.

Conclusion

When faced with the prospect of drafting or signing a covenant not to compete, consult a lawyer experienced in this area of law. Such a covenant is a reasonable and appropriate protection for the legitimate property right of good will, but such covenants will lead to bitter conflict if they attempt to restrict competition beyond what is legitimately protectable.

References

1. *Dick v. Geist,* 107 Idaho 931, 693, P.2d, 113 (1985).
2. *Duffner v. Alberty,* 19 Ark App. 137, 718 SW 2d 111 (1986).
3. *Ellis v. McDaniel,* 95 Nev 455, 596, P.2d, 222 (1979).

Additional Readings

1. *Lowe v. Reynolds,* 75 A 2d 967, 428, NY 2d 358 (1980).
2. *Wagler v. Excavating Corp v. McKibben Cobnst., Inc.,* 679 NE 2nd edition, 155 (Ind. App. 1997).

Chapter 5

Documentation and Medical Records Risks

(No Longer a Reflection of Reality . . . Now, the Reality Itself)

Frederick William LaCava

It's like a game: Get the doctor to add the word "sepsis" to the chart as opposed to "urinary tract infection," and the hospital can bill for a higher-paying DRG. Or prompt the doctor to write down "acute respiratory failure" instead of "chronic obstructive pulmonary disease exacerbation," and the hospital can once again charge for a more lucrative DRG. But unless there is a clinical context for additional diagnoses or complications and co-morbidities, Medicare auditors may see this as an attempt by the hospital to exaggerate a patient's medical condition and inappropriately squeeze more DRG reimbursement from Medicare. That's why hospital documentation improvement programs must focus on giving physicians the knowledge and tools necessary to translate their clinical thought processes into specific and detailed words that truly reflect the patient's medical conditions and treatment—and steer clear of shortcuts that rely on adding a few magic terms to generate additional Medicare reimbursement.

Report on Medicare Compliance, www.AIShealth.com

Physicians of all persuasions are having trouble adjusting to the radically new use of medical records in the present era of managed care and review of billing practices. An inadequately documented medical chart can mean civil and criminal liability to the sloppy and/or unwary practitioner. A brief look at the history of keeping medical records puts this new risk in some perspective. Medical records were previously used to aid in the quality of medical care. Now they are also *the* basis for payment for services, not as a record or reflection of the care that was actually provided, but as a separate justification for billing. The lack of appropriate documentation no longer threatens only nonpayment for services; it also threatens civil money penalties and criminal charges.

Historic Purpose of Medical Records

As little as a hundred years ago, detailed medical records were likely to have been compiled by medical researchers such as Charcot and Hughlings-Jackson. The medical record was an *aide memoire* for detecting changes in patients' conditions over time, solely for the benefit of the physician in treating the patient. As health care became more institutionalized, medical records became a communications device among health-care providers. Doctors made progress notes and gave orders. Nurses carried them out and kept a record of patient responses. A centralized record, theoretically, allowed all to know what each was doing. The idea was that if the doctor were unable to care for the patient, another physician could stand in his or her shoes and assume the patient's care.

Then came pressures from third-party payers. As insurance and then government programs became larger players in the compensation game, they wanted to know if the care they were paying for was being delivered efficiently. Why were these tests ordered? Why weren't these studies done? Why had the patient remained hospitalized after his temperature had returned to normal for so many hours and no pain medications had been required? Why couldn't this preoperative work be done on an outpatient basis? Though the real push behind these questions was the desire to save money, utilization review also directly contributed to better patient care. A patient who was being given inefficient care was getting substandard care as well.

Utilization review, however, was mainly retrospective; denial of compensation was rarely imposed, and suasion by peers was the main effector of change. Though "economic credentialing" was shouted about, it rarely showed itself in public. Even managed care, which openly admitted economic incentives as one of its motivators, preferred to find some other reason for deciding not to admit Dr. Jones to its panel of providers or not renewing Dr. Smith's contract with the HMO. The medical record remained essentially a record of patient care that was good or not, efficient or not. If the record was not complete, the doctor could always supplement it with an affidavit, use information from somewhere else, or provide explanations.

The Medical Records Revolution

To understand the revolution that has since occurred, put yourself for a moment in the position of the third-party payer. You want to know if Dr. Brown actually gave the care for which he is submitting a bill. You want to know if that care was needed. You want to know that the care was given to benefit the patient, rather than to provide financial benefit to the provider beyond the value of the services rendered. You cannot send one of your employees to follow Dr. Brown around on his or her office hours and hospital visits. You cannot see what actually happened in Dr. Brown's office that day or why Dr. Black ordered a CT scan on the patient at the imaging center. What you can do is review the medical record that underlies the bill for services rendered from Dr. Blue. Most of all, you can require the doctor to certify that the care was actually rendered and was indicated. You can punish Dr. White severely if one motive for referring a patient to another health-care provider was to obtain a benefit in cash or in kind from the health-care provider to whom the referral had been made. You can destroy Dr. Rose financially and put him in jail if his medical records do not document the bases for the bills he submitted for payment.

This nearly complete change in function of the medical record has precious little to do with the quality of patient care. To illustrate that point, consider only an office visit in which the care was exactly correct, properly indicated, and flawlessly delivered, but not recorded in the office chart. As far as the patient was concerned, everything was correct and beneficial to the patient. As far as the third-party payer is concerned, the bill for those services is completely unsupported by required documentation and could be the basis for a False Claims Act charge, a Medicare audit, or a criminal indictment. We have left the realm of quality of patient care far behind. Shall we change it back to the way it was? That is not going to happen.

Instead, practitioners must adjust their attitudes to the present function of patient records. They must document as required under pain of punishment for failure to do so. That reality is infuriating to many, since they still cling to the idea of providing good quality care to their patients and disdain such requirements as hindrances to reaching that goal. They are also aware that full documentation can be provided without a reality underlying it. "Fine, you want documentation? I'll give you documentation!"

Some have given in to the temptation of making "cookbook" entries in their charts, or canned computer software programs, listing all the examinations they should have done, all the findings that should be there to justify further treatment. I have personally seen records of physical examinations that record a patient's ankle pulses as "equal and bounding bilaterally" when the patient had only one leg; hospital chart notes that describe extensive discussion with the patient of risks, alternatives, and benefits in obtaining informed consent when the remainder of the record demonstrates the patient's complaint that the surgeon has never told her what he planned to do; and operative reports of procedures done and findings made in detail that, unfortunately, have no correlation with the surgery that was actually performed.

Whether electronic medical records (EMR) will be helpful in the future is still not known. It is at best naive and more frequently closer to a death wish to think that a practitioner can beat the system with either handwritten or computer-generated fabricated documentation.

Documentation Guidelines for Evaluation & Management Coding

The most important document with which every medical practitioner should be intimately familiar is *Documentation Guidelines for Evaluation and Management Services,* published jointly by the American Medical Association and the Health Care Financing Administration in 1997. Those guidelines were revised in December 2000 and are available on CMS's web page. The changes being proposed are almost all in the direction of requiring more detail in documentation. One of the really nasty, unfair requirements that the guidelines impose is that the records be legible: if the entries cannot be read, then there is no documentation at all. You do not want to join the list of practitioners who, at deposition, under oath, have to admit that they cannot read their own handwriting. By the way, whether you can read the entries is irrelevant—it is the reviewer who must be able to read them.

The guidelines rank all patient–practitioner encounters by level of intensity of services rendered and require levels of documentation consistent with those intensity levels. The documentation at every level must include "history, examination and medical decision making."[1] If you look at the suggested guidelines, you will find our old friend SOAP lurking beneath. "Subjective" and "objective" are combined in the first entry; then come "assessment" and "plan." Added to the standard list is a requirement for the date of service and the identity of the doctor providing it. The guidelines suggest beginning with chief complaint. Please note that few patients complain that they have "paroxysmal nocturnal dyspnea." They are more likely to say, "I wake up in the night choking for air." I personally advocate keeping subjective reports separate from objective examination to handle those cases when the two do not match up, such as when the patient says, "My back is killing me," but has no trouble hopping up onto the examining table.

The detail required for recording the patient's history of the present illness, past medical history, and family history and/or social history varies according to the level of intensity of the encounter. However, the only exception in the proposed changes in the guidelines for the required, detailed history is for emergency conditions, which take up so much time and skill of the practitioner that he or she cannot take the time to obtain those facts. The review of systems may be included in the history, and all positive findings must be recorded. The proposed changes, however, no longer allow silence to indicate that there were no significant negative findings. Significant negative findings are proposed to be required as well.

What is new in the guidelines is the requirement that the process the practitioner goes through in determining how to handle a patient's problem be apparent from the documentation. There must be an indication in the records of *why* a test was ordered, for example. This requirement aids a reviewer in judging whether the expense of the test was justified. Another requirement is that if an addendum is made to the record, it must be dated on the day that it was added to the record, not the date of service. This requirement can be troublesome for practitioners who dictate all or a portion of their records and have the typed dictation inserted into the record when the dictation is transcribed. A detailed discussion of the guidelines is beyond the scope of this book, but detailed examination of them is recommended for all practitioners.

Legal Statutes Regarding Medical Billing

After the guidelines in importance (but not far behind) are the statutes that punish providers for submitting false claims for services. There is a special False Claims Act for Medicare[2] and a general False Claims Act.[3] The original of the False Claims Act was passed during the Civil War period when unscrupulous traders were bilking the government for war material. The special act provides for coordination of state, federal, and insurance company efforts to monitor and investigate false claims for medical services. The general act provides severe penalties for any person who bills the U.S. government for items or services not actually provided and/or falsely billed. What every practitioner needs to know is that A BILL FOR A SERVICE THAT IS INADEQUATELY DOCUMENTED IS A FALSE CLAIM. Read this sentence over a few times and believe it.

It does not matter if the care was actually given, given properly, or if the patient benefited.[4] A bill for those services is not to be submitted unless the documentation is there before the bill is submitted. If the bill is sent (claim made) without the level of documentation required, then the claim is false. Submitting a false claim is a civil wrong done to the government and may constitute a crime as well. The consequences are so horrendous that they are hard to imagine.

The False Claims Act allows the government to get not only its money back for improperly billed claims, but double or triple that amount. Next come fines called civil money penalties beginning at $5,000 and going up to $10,000 for *each bill submitted*. Finally, criminal punishment can be imposed for knowing violation of the act. In the case of the False Claims Act, there is a special definition of "knowing" and "knowingly": they mean that a person, with respect to information,

1. has actual knowledge of the information;
2. acts in deliberate ignorance of the truth or falsity of the information; or
3. acts in reckless disregard of the truth or falsity of the information, and no proof of specific intent to defraud is required.[5]

The case of *U.S. v. Krizek*[6] provides a shocking example of a physician falling afoul of the False Claims Act. A psychiatrist had his wife bill the government for alleged healthcare services and did not check her bills in any way. The bills amounted to more than 24 hours of service in a 24-hour period, so that the government did not have to review the individual documentation to show that the claims were false. Both the doctor and his wife were held liable, and the impossibility of the care having actually been provided was held to be sufficient to amount to knowledge of the falsity of the claims. A chilling detail of this case is that the government wanted to charge a civil money penalty not just for each bill submitted but for each diagnostic code listed on each bill.

Billing for medical services at a higher reimbursement level than was justified by the services actually provided constitutes a false claim. In *U.S. v. Lorenzo*,[7] a dentist billed for a separate oral examination for cancer that was actually only a part of his regular dental checkup examination. So-called "upcoding" is a basis for a False Claims Act charge, and it can take a number of forms. For example, if a patient comes into the office for a diagnostic test or a session of some therapy that is not personally delivered by a practitioner, and the practitioner tacks on an office visit to the bill, the claim is obviously false. A more troublesome area of potential liability, however, arises when the code and the actual intensity of care match up but the documentation does not. The practitioner may have done all the care needed to justify the billing code, but if the documentation is lacking, the claim may be false. Upcoding levels of intensity of care causes false claims to be submitted.[8]

Potential liability for damages is not linked directly to the amount of money that was lost by the government in the false billing. Although the amount of damages starts with triple the government's losses, the civil money penalties can soon overwhelm that amount. In the case of *United States v. Greenberg*[9] the court awarded the government $78,000 against Dr. Greenberg despite the fact that he only gained $549.09 from the false claims he submitted for his medical services.

The False Claims Acts contain "whistle-blower" provisions for immunity. A person acting in good faith who reports possible false claims to governmental authorities is immune from prosecution for doing so.[10]

Many defendants in such actions have attempted to bring complaints of theft or conversion of trade secrets against those who bring records to the offices of prosecuting attorneys. They have not had much success except when records have actually been stolen rather than copied.[11]

A *qui tam* action may also be brought by civilians on behalf of the government under 31 U.S.C. § 3730. The civilian, known as a relator, brings the claim on behalf of the government to recover the amount of the false claim. (All of those cases that begin "U.S. ex rel." are *qui tam* actions.) If the relator has insider knowledge that allows the claim to succeed, then the relater is entitled to a percentage of the damages ultimately recovered for the government.

Finally, in almost an ironic return to the original reason for medical records, False Claims Act suits have been maintained on the basis of claims that the care actually provided to patients was not good enough in quality to justify the claims being submitted. In other words, if the care provided fell below the standard of care provided, not only did the practitioner commit medical malpractice, but he or she also submitted a false claim![12] Therefore, always remember that today medical records are not a reflection of reality; they are the reality.

References

1. Guidelines, p. 2.
2. 42 U.S.C. 1320a-7c.
3. 31 U.S.C. 3729.
4. U.S. ex rel. Pogue v. American Healthcorp, Inc., 914 F. Supp. 1507 (M.D.Tenn.1996).
5. 31 U.S.C. §3729(b).
6. 111 F.3d 934 (D.C. App. 1997).
7. U.S. v. Lorenzo, 768 F. Supp. 1127 (E.D. Pa. 1991).
8. U.S. ex rel Trim v. McKean, 31 F. Supp. 2d 1308 (W.D. Okla. 1998).
9. 237 F. Supp. 439 (S.D.N.Y. 1965).
10. 42 U.S.C. § 1320a-7c (B)(iii); Mann v. Olsten Certified Healthcare Corp., 49 F. Supp. 2d 1307 (M.D. Ala.1999).
11. U.S. ex rel. Mikes v. Straus, 931 F. Supp. 248, *motion to certify appeal denied*, 939 F. Supp. 301 (S.D.N.Y. 1996).
12. *See* Report on Medicare Compliance, Vol. 9, No. 44, 12-14-00 (billing abuses by physicians visiting patients in long-term care facilities) and Report of Medicare Compliance, Vol. 10, No. 3, 1-25-01 (Maryland Medicaid Fraud and Abuse Unit's prosecution of long-term care facilities under False Claims Act and other statutes for substandard health care).

Chapter 6

Health-Care Compliance Risk Management

(An Impossible Task . . . But Doctors Are Responsible)

Patricia A. Trites

The health-care industry operates in a heavily regulated environment with a variety of identifiable risk areas. An effective compliance program helps mitigate these risks.

Corporate Responsibility and Corporate Compliance,
A Resource for Health Care Boards of Directors, www.OIG.gov

L et's imagine a world without compliance: no rules, regulations, or laws and no fines or other legal consequences. This would mean there would be no speed limits, anywhere; no requirements for construction, like building codes; and no rules about how cars, appliances, or toys were made; credit card companies and mortgage companies could charge whatever interest rate they chose; and that is just the beginning. We actually thrive on making rules and following them. Unfortunately, we also have certain perceptions about "the rules," such as "If we don't get caught breaking the rules, then it is okay" and "If everyone else is breaking the rules, then it must be okay." But if our children even hint at either of these two statements, we have customized responses, and we have all heard them or said them at one time or another.

Compliance in health care is no different. We cajole, appeal, and sometimes even frighten patients with the consequences of not complying with their medical treatment, in order to gain compliance. This chapter is about compliance with the regulations that surround the business of health care, and, more importantly, how this compliance will make your organization more profitable and improve the quality of health care to patients. From a risk management perspective, it is first identifying the organization's risks (lack of compliance, partial compliance, or excellent compliance) and managing those risks by implementing compliance programs.

Knowledge of rules and expectations = Increased morale and understanding = Increased patient satisfaction and increased profit = Better quality of health care

Compliance is a behavior. Most people expect employees to follow the rules that are set within the organization. They don't hire employees who they believe will not comply with the organization's rules, who they believe will steal from the organization, who they believe will take shortcuts, or who they believe will alienate the other staff members or patients. Most people have high expectations for everyone within the organization. It is these expectations that, if nurtured, will prove to be the basis of a superior health-care organization.

The Compliance Process

[A] Step 1. Know Which Rules You Have to Follow

People who understand what they are supposed to do, and how to do it, are more productive and happier. They understand the rules they are expected to follow. Most employers begin the process of teaching the rules with a Personnel Policy Manual that explains what the employer expects on a day-to-day basis. At the same time, this manual should encompass the employer's obligations by addressing the pertinent employment laws. There is also the opportunity to develop and implement a Corporate Compliance Program that outlines the organization's expectations, shows the organization's commitment to legal and ethical behavior, and delineates the exact policies and procedures that are to be adhered to by all members of the workforce.

The Health Insurance Portability and Accountability Act of 1996 (HIPAA) increased the amount of documentation that is required to comply with the rules of privacy and security. These are also elements that must be presented to the staff to ensure their understanding of compliant behavior. Written documentation of the organization's understanding and compliance with the HIPAA Administrative Simplification Rules is mandatory.

Billing and reimbursement rules come from many sources, including the federal and state health programs and private payers. Unless a provider delivers services on a 100 percent cash payment basis, these rules must be understood and followed by all members of the health-care organization. In most instances, a written compliance program for billing and reimbursement is voluntary, but it is an excellent means to convey the rules and the expectation of compliant behavior to the members of an organization.

OSHA compliance is also a mandatory element for employers, regardless of industry. Health-care organizations have specific standards that have been formulated and enacted to protect the safety and health of employees. Health and safety have always been a predominate focus of the health-care profession, and it would stand to reason that compliance with these rules and regulations would be "second nature"; unfortunately, this is not the case in many organizations.

There are other sets of rules and regulations that apply to specific health-care organizations, but not all. If a health-care entity performs any type of laboratory test, then it must comply with the rules of the Clinical Laboratory Improvements Act (CLIA). If a health-care organization receives federal assistance monies, then it must comply with the Limited English Proficiency (LEP) regulations. Different medical specialties, such as radiology and practices performing clinical research, have additional rules and regulations.

Specific rules are discussed in more detail later in the chapter.

[B] Step 2. Outline the Rules in Written Policies and Procedures

This is a formal process that will take time and effort on the part of staff. It is important that those responsible for formulating and documenting these policies and procedures receive the necessary time and resources to accomplish the task, since a review of all of the appropriate and applicable rules and regulations must be made in order to formulate compliant policies and procedures. It is not enough to know which rules must be followed; each employee must understand how the rules can and will be followed within the scope of his or her individual job description.

[C] Step 3. Assess the Organization's Current Compliance

This step allows the organization to take its own "vital signs." When there is an understanding of what rules must or should be followed and also how the individual organization plans to implement its policies and procedures, there can be an accurate assessment of "where we are now" and "where we want to be." Many organizations find that they are not compliant in many areas, even though they always intended to follow the rules.

[D] Step 4. Training, Communication, and Enforcement

The health-care organization must introduce and train its employees about the rules that are to be followed. This is accomplished with an effective communication process and with the support of management. It takes only one person to circumvent and sabotage an organization's compliance initiatives, so it is important that everyone understands and adheres to the rules, policies, and procedures that have been adopted by the organization. It is also essential to deter noncompliance with consistent enforcement of the penalties associated with violations.

[E] Step 5. Maintenance of the Compliance Program

The process continues indefinitely because the makeup of the health-care organization changes and the rules change. More rules are added, and sometimes some are removed. To ensure that the organization continues to operate in a compliant manner and that each individual understands his or her role in the process, the organization must evaluate its policies and procedures at least annually.

The Rules[1]

[A] Billing and Reimbursement

Billing and reimbursement rules and regulations vary according to payer type, geographic region, and place of service. Each health-care provider should have a thorough understanding of the specific rules that apply to its organization. This begins with an understanding of each of the contracts or provider agreements that the organization or provider has signed. Because Medicare is one of the principal payers and promulgator of rules, we will concentrate on its rules.

[B] Provider Numbers

It is important to use the correct provider identification number for each claim for service that is submitted for payment. Claims for services that have been performed by a provider who does not have a current provider identification number need to be "held" until the identification numbers can be obtained.[2] This will slow the cash flow for the organization, but the risk of submitting false claims and the subsequent penalties outweigh the inconvenience.

A locum tenens physician is one who is filling in for another physician and is an independent contractor (nonemployee) of the organization. He or she may provide these temporary services for up to 60 consecutive days. The claim for service(s) is billed using the provider number of the absent physician with the HCPCS modifier, "-Q6."[3]

[C] Documentation of Medical Records

Evaluation and management services make up approximately 75 percent of all services performed by physicians. The nature and the amount of work vary by the type of service, the place of service, and the patient's condition or status. It is important that the provider's documentation reflect this information for both good patient care and compliance with the documentation guidelines. (See Table 6-1 for the CMS documentation requirements.) Documentation is the foundation of a successful practice, because without complete documentation it is almost impossible to accurately report services and achieve optimal reimbursement.

[D] Proper Use and Billing of CPT[4] and Diagnosis Codes

After completing the documentation of a service provided to a patient, the next step is to "code" the procedure and the diagnosis. These codes are updated annually, and each health-care organization should make sure that it is using current codes. It is also impor-

Table 6-1 *General Principles of the Medical Record*

1. The medical record should be complete and legible.
2. The documentation of each patient encounter should include:
• reason for the encounter and the relevant history, physical examination findings, and prior diagnostic test results;
• assessment, clinical impression, or diagnosis;
• plan for care; and
• date and legible identity of the observer
3. If not documented, the rationale for ordering diagnostic and other ancillary services should be easily inferred.
4. Past and present diagnoses should be accessible to the treating and/or consulting physician.
5. Appropriate health risk factors should be identified.
6. The patient's progress, response to, and changes in treatment, and revision of diagnosis should be documented.

tant to make sure that the use of these codes is not contingent upon whether payment will be made for the service, but should reflect the service(s) and the reason for the service(s) provided.

Much has been written on selecting the correct procedure codes and the associated documentation that is required for each level of service. There are also rules associated with selecting the correct diagnosis code. To determine if a provider can be paid for its services, the provider must show that there was a medically justifiable reason for performing the procedure or service. This is established primarily by looking at the CPT or procedure code that was billed in relation to the ICD-9 or diagnosis code that was given as the reason for the encounter or procedure. If medical necessity can be shown, the likelihood is that the bill will be paid. The basic requirement is that the diagnosis must justify the procedure. If the following five rules are followed, there is a much better chance that the claim(s) will be paid.

1. Code all diagnoses to the ultimate specificity.
2. Use additional code(s) and code any underlying diseases when necessary.
3. Code all the conditions encountered during the service to fully describe the encounter.
4. Choose the appropriate principal diagnosis and sequence all secondary codes correctly.
5. Avoid using .8 and .9 "catch-all" codes.

[E] Use of Ancillary Personnel "Incident to" Services

Using physician extenders such as physician assistants and nurse practitioners is one way of increasing the productivity of the health-care office or clinic. These nonphysician practitioners may see patients and bill for their services at 85 percent of the Medicare

Physician Fee Schedule. Each organization must review its contracts with other third-party payers to ensure that these insurers recognize the services of nonphysician practitioners as credentialed or payable services.

Another use of physician extenders is "incident to" the physician's service. After the nonphysician practitioner sees a patient, the billing is submitted under the physician's name. This is perfectly acceptable under the Medicare guidelines, if the rules are followed. Again, each organization must check with its third-party contractors to make sure that this type of service or billing is allowed.

There has been a recent change in the "incident to" rules.[5] The change allows independent contractors to both perform the services and fulfill the direct supervision requirements. The rules are listed below.

- The service must be an integral part of the physician's (or other practitioner's) diagnosis or treatment of an injury or illness. In other words, there must be a prior established plan of care developed by the physician (or other practitioner) for the patient being seen. The physician or other practitioner who developed the plan of care may be an employee or an independent contractor.

- The service must be provided under the "direct supervision" of a physician (or other practitioner). This means that the person who is providing the supervision must be (a) on site **and** (b) immediately available. A definition of "on site" would be within the same office suite.

- The service must be performed by auxiliary personnel. The term *auxiliary personnel* is defined as any individual who is acting under the supervision of a physician (or other practitioner), regardless of whether the individual is an employee, leased employee, or independent contractor of the physician (or other practitioner) or of the same entity that employs or contracts with the physician (or other practitioner).

The service must be something ordinarily done in a physician's office or clinic. This equates to providing services in a noninstitutional setting to noninstitutional patients.

[F] Physicians at Teaching Hospitals

The supervision and billing rules for teaching physicians have been defined more clearly since the arrival of the Physician at Teaching Hospital (PATH) audits. These rules are fairly extensive and include exceptions and specific instructions for specific services, but the documentation rules are fairly straightforward. The complete set of regulations can be found at http://www.cms.hhs.gov/manuals/14_car/3b15000.asp#_15016_0.

According to the Medicare guidelines, teaching physicians do not have to write detailed documentation on initial E&M visits if the resident has already documented the encounter. However, the physician must write a brief summary of comments to confirm and/or revise the information obtained by the resident. Teaching physicians must document all the key portions of the encounter, including the relevant facts regarding the history of present illness and any prior diagnostic tests, major findings in the physical exam, his or her assessment and clinical impression, and the plan of care.[6]

The billing of the evaluation and management service is to be based upon the teaching physician's documentation. "If a teaching physician documents his/her presence and participation in the E/M service, the level of service may be selected based on the extent of history and/or examination and/or the complexity of the medical decision making required by the patient and documented in his/her personal entry in the medical record which may include references to notes entered by the resident."[7]

What has been a significant problem in the teaching setting is the requirement of the teaching physician's presence and the documentation that must be recorded by the teaching physician. Except as indicated in the "Exception for E/M Services Furnished in Certain Primary Care Centers" section of the Medicare Regulations, the teaching physician must be physically present during the portion of the service that determined the level of service billed. In all cases, the teaching physician must personally document his or her presence and participation in the services in the medical records. This documentation by the teaching physician may be in writing or via a dictated note.[8]

[G] Medical Necessity and the Use of Advance Beneficiary Notices

Medical necessity was discussed in the preceding diagnosis coding section. What was not addressed was when an item or service is not "medically necessary" for billing purposes (in other words, a payable diagnosis) but may be perfectly necessary for the health or welfare of the patient. This is where Advance Beneficiary Notices (ABNs) can save the health-care organization a lot of time and money in the billing process.

Advance Beneficiary Notices are statements that are given to the patient to read and sign whenever a provider believes that the item or service may not be covered (paid) by Medicare. This may occur when there are a limited number of services that can be performed in a specific time frame, such as mammography, PSA, colonoscopy, etc. It can also be used when a patient insists on a specific treatment or test, even when the physician believes the service is unwarranted or unnecessary but understands that failing to provide the service may put him or her at risk under professional liability standards.

When an Advance Beneficiary Notice has been signed by the patient, it removes the risk of nonpayment from the provider. Advance Beneficiary Notices cannot be given to every patient or for all procedures or services. There must be a reasonable expectation that payment will be denied because there is a lack of medical necessity (for billing and payment). To access complete instructions for the use of ABNs and copies of the specific form that must be used for Medicare patients, go to www.cms.hhs.gov/medlearn/refabn.asp.

[H] Professional Courtesy and Waiver of Co-pays and Deductibles

Professional courtesy and the waiver of co-pays and deductibles is a very controversial subject to health-care practitioners. It appears to most people that it should be up to each physician to decide if he or she wants to waive payment for services or to discount the service. Unfortunately, this practice is illegal in most instances. There are only a few instances when this "tradition" is legally allowable, such as in the case of indigence of the patient or when the practitioner provides services to an immediate relative or household member.[9]

According to the Department of Health and Human Services, "routine waiver of deductibles and co-payments by charge-based providers, practitioners or suppliers is unlawful because it results in (1) false claims, (2) violations of the anti-kickback statute and (3) excessive utilization of items and services paid for by Medicare."[10] When the patient has insurance other than Medicare, waiving the co-payment, deductible, or the entire charge is violating both the insured's contract with his or her insurance company and the physician's or other provider's contract or participation agreement.

As stated previously, financial or medical indigence is an exception. The provider may reduce or waive his or her fee if the rules are followed. A simple statement by the patients that they are unable to pay their share of the service is not enough. Medicare requires that the provider ask and document the answers to these specific questions:

1. Does the patient have any other source that may be legally responsible for his or her medical bills? Examples: Medicaid or legal guardian.
2. Can the patient provide information for the practice to perform an analysis of total resources? Examples: assets (only those convertible to cash and unnecessary for the patient's daily living), liabilities, and income and expenses.

This information should be reviewed at least annually and documented in the patient's financial file.

[I] Proper Use of Certificates of Medical Necessity

Certificates of Medical Necessity (CMNs) are used for the authorization of both durable medical equipment (DME) and home health services. These certificates have specific requirements, depending on the services requested. According to the Medicare regulations, improper certification of medical necessity may subject a physician to significant criminal, civil, and administrative penalties. Even if physicians do not receive any financial or other benefit from providers or suppliers for signing incomplete or erroneous CMNs, they may be liable for making false or misleading certifications.

The special fraud alert issued by the Office of the Inspector General (OIG) states, "While the OIG believes that the actual incidence of physicians' intentionally submitting false or misleading certifications of medical necessity for durable medical equipment or home health care is relatively infrequent, physician laxity in reviewing and completing these certifications contributes to fraudulent and abusive practices by unscrupulous suppliers and home health providers."[11] The physician must make sure that the entire CMN has been completed before signing the form. The physician's signature is an attestation that the information is complete and accurate to the best of his or her knowledge and that the form is complete. The CMN must have an actual signature and date; stamps are not acceptable.

[J] Employment or Services of Excluded Providers or Entities

Employment of excluded providers or entities is becoming a significant area of risk in health-care organizations. As of this writing, there are over 29,000 excluded individuals and entities listed on the Office of the Inspector General's listing.[12] The risk of a ten thousand dollar ($10,000) fine seems small in comparison to the possible risk of any services provided by the excluded individual or entity being regarded as nonpayable (and hence must be refunded).

Each organization is responsible for querying the OIG's listing and also the General Services Administration's (GSA) List of Parties Excluded from Government Procurement and Non-Procurement Services.[13] The most common reason a physician is placed on the OIG's sanctioned list is not for abusive or fraudulent behavior, but because he or she has defaulted on student loans. This listing also includes billing companies, laboratories, nurses, dentists, and many other types of health-care professionals. It is an important element of an organization's compliance program to first query the systems for the names of each of its employees and subcontractors and then to monitor the listing on a regular basis. The OIG's excluded listing is issued monthly and can be reviewed at the OIG's website.

[K] Occupational Safety and Health Act (OSHA)

The Occupational Safety and Health Act (OSHA) was enacted in 1970. It requires all employers to comply with specific rules and regulations in an effort to protect the safety of employees. There are rules promulgated by the federal OSHA administration and approximately 30 state OSHA administrations. When there is a state OSHA administration, this organization enforces both the state and federal regulations. As with all federal versus state issues, whichever entity has passed a stricter rule or regulation is the one that must be followed.

In the health-care industry there are specific, additional regulations that must be adhered to that do not apply to all industries, such as the Occupational Exposure to Hazardous Chemicals in Laboratories, the Bloodborne Pathogen Standard, and the Tuberculosis Guideline or Standard.[14] There are annual training and monitoring requirements as well as record-keeping standards that must be complied with by all health-care industry employers.

An important note is that, regardless of whether there are federal or state standards regarding specific issues, there is a "General Duty Clause" that requires employers to protect their employees from almost any recognized hazard. Section 5 (a)(1) of OSHA states: "Each employer shall furnish to each of his employees employment and place of employment which are free from recognized hazards that are causing or are likely to cause death or serious physical harm to his employees." Violations of this section of OSHA can only be cited when there is no standard that applies to a particular hazard.

It is the hazard, not the absence of a particular means of abatement, that is the basis for a General Duty Clause citation. There are four required elements for an OSHA representative or inspector to document before issuing a General Duty Clause violation:

- The employer failed to keep the workplace free of a hazard to which employees of that employer were exposed.
- The hazard was recognized.
- The hazard was causing or was likely to cause death or serious physical harm.
- There was a feasible and useful method to correct the hazard.

Compliance with the OSHA regulations reduces the risk of employee injuries and illness. Reduced injuries and illness also reduce the employer's workers' compensation premiums and the risk of OSHA fines.

[L] Health Insurance Portability and Accountability Act (HIPAA)

The Health Insurance Portability and Accountability Act, known as HIPAA, has received a great deal of publicity in the last few years. This is a comprehensive law that impacts many facets of the health-care industry, including the portability of health insurance for employees, increases in fines, and funding for fraud and abuse in both the public (Medicare, Medicaid and other federal- and state-funded health-care programs) and the private (nongovernmental) health-care programs. This law also enacted a new category of "federal health-care offenses," which include health-care fraud, theft, and embezzlement; making false statements; obstruction of criminal investigations; and money laundering. These criminal offenses apply to both federally funded and private health-care programs. The administrative simplification provisions of HIPAA include a standardization of health-care claims submission, privacy of patient information, and security of electronic health information.

HIPAA exemplifies the statement "Be careful what you ask for." The health-care industry asked for a standardized system of health-care claims submission, and it received just that. It is the administrative simplification rules that have received the largest amount of press in the health-care journals and as topics of speeches at health-care seminars. This is because we are in a technology-driven, electronic environment, and it was necessary to implement systems for security and privacy of the health information. Health-care providers have traditionally understood the importance of privacy when it comes to patients and their medical records, but it is now just as important to ensure that these "traditions" are understood, embraced, and followed by the entire organization. In order to do this, providers must document their development, implementation, and continued compliance with the HIPAA rules.

[M] Standardized Transaction and Code Set Rule

There has been a lot of discussion about the cost of implementing the HIPAA rules, but little has been said about the cost savings that will undoubtedly occur because of the implementation of a standardized health-care claims process. Today, providers must fill out different types of claim forms or fill out the same forms in different ways for each individual third-party payer. There are even submission differences between the regional Medicare carriers and intermediaries. There are differing "codes" used by the insurers, such as non-current-year CPT and ICD-9 codes, explanation of benefit codes, and payer-specific codes and modifiers, that are contrary to or in addition to the American Medical Association HCPCS codes. Currently, each provider must submit claims in the correct format according to each payer's rules. This causes increased risk for errors and a slowing of the organization's cash flow.

The ability to transmit billing and claims information in one standard format will certainly save both providers and payers a significant amount of money. There will eventually be one set of forms that will be submitted and received electronically that will streamline the billing and payment systems. The forms outlined by the HIPAA legislation to date are Health Claims, Health Plan Eligibility, Enrollment, and Disenrollment, Payments for Care, Health Insurance Premiums, Claims Status, First Report of Injury, Coordination of Benefits, and Other Related Transactions.

One of the advantages of using the standardized format is that organizations will be able to send a claims status inquiry to the payer at least twice a month, either as a batch or real time. The payer will then send a response to the status request and will use a standard set of codes to explain the status of the claim. One of the major reasons a claim is rejected (30 to 40 percent of the time) is that there is a missing or incorrect member identification number. One California Medical Association survey showed that half of these rejected claims are never resubmitted.

Another advantage will be that the provider's staff will not need to submit "paper claims" for secondary claims because there will be no need to copy the explanation of benefits forms (EOBs) to attach to the paper claims. The standardized electronic transmission will include detailed coordination of benefit (COB) information, such as the previous payer's payment, adjustments, and so on. More information can be transmitted at one time on one claim form, such as up to 8 diagnosis codes (currently only 4 can be transmitted), 19 different dates at the claim level and 15 at the service line level, as many as 8 different providers, and additional information for ambulance, chiropractic, home health, DME, etc. This again will save time and effort on the part of the health-care staff.

Many providers have not taken advantage of automatic posting of payments and electronic deposit of funds, but if and when they do, their organizations will be able to post payments automatically, take write-offs and roll responsibility to the next payer or to the patient, and, again, save time and money because there will doubtless be a significant decrease in posting errors. This equates to the staff being able to perform more important duties, such as patient care, or a decrease in the number of full-time-equivalent (FTE) staff members required to conduct the day-to-day operations of the organization.

Significant savings will be realized when the Referrals and Authorization Transactions Form and System are implemented. One example of this cost savings is verification of a patient's eligibility for services. A California Medical Association study estimated that there is a 30-minute average call time just to verify eligibility information for a patient and that the current system of manual referrals costs $20 a referral for specialists and $40 a referral for primary care physicians. These savings should offset and exceed any hardware or software upgrades that are necessary to perform and submit standardized transactions.

[N] Privacy Rule

It is the Privacy Rule portion of HIPAA that many people believe will cost each organization a considerable amount of time, effort, and money to implement and maintain. Unfortunately, there are enumerable myths and misinterpretations of this portion of the legislation. When the Privacy Rule is basically "common sense," most organizations are operating in compliance with the majority of the law. The areas that are necessary, but in most organizations need to be developed, are the written policies and procedures, the training, and the documentation that the requirements have been met. An excellent source of information for the interpretation of the Privacy Rule was published by the Office of Civil Rights, the governmental agency that has been charged with oversight of the Privacy Rule. This guidance document can be found on the Internet at http://www.hhs.gov/ocr/hipaa/.

This Privacy Rule allows for the transfer of protected health information (PHI) for the purposes of treatment, payment, or health-care operations (TPO) without specific authorization from the patient. Except as otherwise allowed by law,[15] or for the health and safety of the public, patients must specifically authorize any other release or disclosure of their protected health information.

Contrary to the early interpretations of the Privacy Rule, patients do not have to sign a HIPAA consent form to allow the physician to treat and bill for the services. The consent provision that was in the original Privacy Rule was modified when it became apparent that this would be a barrier to health-care access. Consent was not completely removed from the rule, but it became nonmandatory. What is necessary to obtain, if possible, is an "Acknowledgment of Receipt" from patients when they are given a copy of the organization's Notice of Privacy Practices. If the patient is unable or refuses to sign this acknowledgment, then the staff member who gave the patient the copy of the Notice of Privacy Practices should document this on the acknowledgment form. The patient may still be treated and the organization may still use the patient's protected health information for treatment, payment, and health-care operations.

Training is a requirement of this legislation. Members of the health-care organization's workforce must receive training relevant to the functions they perform as they pertain to protected health information. Privacy training must be provided to current members of the workforce no later than the compliance date of April 14, 2003. Privacy training must be provided to each new member of the organization (including volunteers, subcontractors, etc.) within a reasonable period of time after the person begins work-related duties. The organization must also ensure that members of the workforce whose job functions are affected by a material change to the policies or practices required by the Privacy Rule are retrained within a reasonable period of time after such material change.

Essential elements of privacy training include the following:

- The rights of individuals
- Duties and responsibilities of a covered entity
- Duties and responsibilities of business associates
- The specific impact this rule has on each employee's day-to-day work environment, including specific policies and procedures and sanctions or discipline for violation

[O] Security Rule

The Final Security Rule was published February 20, 2003. For the majority of health-care organizations that meet the definition of "covered entity," the implementation date of the Security Rule is April 21, 2005. The final Security Rule's emphasis is on each covered entity performing a risk analysis or assessment of its organization. In this way the organization can determine which parts of the Security Rule are applicable to the organization and how to address them. This is actually a somewhat flexible and more commonsense approach to development and implementation. As the organization goes through the provisions of the Security Rule, it will develop policies and procedures to comply with the 20 required components and will either develop policies and procedures for the remaining and applicable "addressable" components or document why it has not or does not need to comply with the component.

The HIPAA Security Rule has four general requirements: (1) Each covered entity must ensure the confidentiality, integrity, and availability of all electronic protected health information (EPHI) that it creates, receives, maintains, or transmits. (2) The organization must protect against any reasonably anticipated threats or hazards to the security or integrity of the information. (3) It must protect against any reasonably anticipated uses or disclosures of such information that are not already permitted or required by the Privacy Rule. (4) The organization or covered entity must ensure compliance of its workforce.

The language in the final Security Rule states that covered entities must "conduct an accurate and thorough assessment of the potential risks and vulnerabilities to the confidentiality, integrity, and availability of electronic protected health information held by the covered entity." It also states, "The required risk analysis is also a tool to allow flexibility for entities in meeting the requirements of this final rule." [16,17]

Initial and annual training is also a vital part of the Security Rule. For each of the elements for which the organization develops policies and procedures, it must provide training to the workforce about their role in the security plan. Documentation of the policies and procedures, as well as any documentation of risk assessments, training, violations, and remedies, should be maintained and retained by the organization to demonstrate its compliance with this law.

[P] Limited English Proficiency (LEP)

Title VI of the Civil Rights Act of 1964 prohibits discrimination because of a person's national origin. The legislation we know as HIPAA mandated that the Department of Health and Human Services Office of Civil Rights prepare and distribute guidance to the health-care industry regarding its obligations for providing free language assistance to people who have limited English proficiency (LEP). This guidance was released in January 1998 to address appropriate assistance when language barriers cause LEP persons to be excluded from or denied equal access to HHS-funded programs.

To comply with this legislation, any provider of health-care services who receives funding from Health and Human Services must implement a compliance program policy that includes the following four components:

1. Assessment
2. Written policy on language access
3. Training of staff
4. Vigilant monitoring

The minimum requirement pertains to providers with fewer than 100 persons in a language group eligible to be served or likely to be directly affected by the provider's services. These providers do not have to translate written materials, but they need to provide written notice in the primary language of the LEP language group of the right to receive free, competent oral translation of written materials. There are also requirements for competent translation of written materials for those providers who have larger numbers of LEP patients. These guidelines can be found at http://www.hhs.gov/ocr/lep.

[Q] Personnel and Employee Retirement Income Security Act (ERISA)

Personnel compliance is probably the most important part of an organization's compliance-related risk management system. People who do not understand what they are supposed to do or who have the feeling that no one has an interest in their work are more likely to place the organization at risk for potential fines, significant refund events, alienation of patients or other staff members, and/or poor-quality work, resulting in lost income. Employees who feel that both they and their work are respected and appreciated usually are more productive and convey the same respect and appreciation to their coworkers and to the patients.

It does not take a lot of effort or expense to provide a pleasant, respectful workplace. If an organization currently does not have the cooperation and respect of the employees, it will take time to alter the existing perceptions.

The first step in this process is to fully outline and explain each employee's responsibilities. This is accomplished through a detailed job description. Next, detailed procedure manuals will clearly define how each job function should be accomplished. This not only aids the person who regularly performs the task(s) but also provides a backup system when that person is temporarily or permanently absent.

The organization also needs to outline and explain, in writing, the expectations and prohibitions that are associated with employment. This can be accomplished through a personnel policy manual. The personnel manual should include the organization's rules for such things as full- and part-time employment; vacation, sick, and PTO benefits; lunch and break periods; procedures for filing complaints or concerns; and policies regarding company property, Internet and phone use, and other matters. It is just as important to communicate to the employees when laws or regulations do not apply to the organization, such as the Family Medical Leave Act, the employment provisions of the Americans With Disabilities Act, or continuation of health benefits under COBRA. These benefits only apply to organizations with a specific number of employees, so smaller organizations are not necessarily required to offer these benefits.

Private employers are not required to offer benefits to their employees, but this will make it difficult to hire or keep good employees. If an organization offers any welfare or retirement benefits, it must comply with the Employee Retirement Income Security Act (ERISA). This legislation imposes an obligation on the employer to (1) operate its welfare and/or retirement plans in accordance with the rules, (2) inform the employees, in writing, of their benefits and how to access them, and (3) comply with any annual reporting requirements (this does not apply to all benefits). Although the risk of fines or penalties may be an impetus to follow these rules, it is the productivity and morale of the workforce that is a better motivation for employment and ERISA compliance.

[R] Clinical Laboratory Improvement Amendments (CLIA)

The Clinical Laboratory Improvement Amendments (CLIA) were passed in 1988 and pertain to any health-care provider or entity that performs *any* laboratory test. This legislation established quality standards for all laboratory testing in order to ensure the accuracy, reliability, and timeliness of patient test results, regardless of where the test was performed. Providers must register with the Centers for Medicare and Medicaid Services (CMS) by filling out an application and paying the required fees. These fees vary upon the type or complexity of certificate requested. After completing all of the requirements, the provider will receive a CLIA Certificate. The four types of certificates are Waived Complexity, Provider Performed Microscopy (this is a subgroup of Moderate Complexity), Moderate Complexity, and High Complexity.

In 1997 CMS enacted a new regulation that requires providers to include their CLIA number on all claim forms (e.g., HCFA/CMS 1500) that contain requests for payment for clinical laboratory services. This is to ensure that (1) the provider has a current CLIA certificate and (2) the provider is performing only the laboratory tests that are allowed for the particular level of certificate.

There are specific regulations and documentation requirements for the different levels of service. A recent study (1999–2001) found that a large percentage of clinical laboratories are not in compliance with the regulations. It has been recommended that increased inspection, both announced and unannounced, be instituted to better ensure the quality of laboratory services. The CLIA requirements can be found at http://www.cms.gov/clia.

Conclusion

Our lives may be our own, but when we have an impact on any other person or entity, there are rules that must be followed. It does not matter if we are speaking about driving a vehicle, manufacturing a product, or providing a service such as mortgage loans or health care. There are risks that have to be assessed, and each person or entity must determine if (1) it is in compliance or (2) what are the consequences of noncompliance. In health care the rules have been specifically developed to protect patients and employees, but in reality when the rules are followed there is a greater chance of increased profits and increased quality of patient care to be realized by the health-care organization. Just as physicians manage the risk of their patients' health, they should also manage the risk of their business's health.

References

1. This is only an overview of some of the major rules that must be followed. It is not intended to be a complete list of all of the health-care compliance rules and regulations.
2. http://www.trailblazerhealth.com/pub/partb/all/2000/01-011.pdf. Provides quality services to Medicare beneficiaries and health-care professionals in selected states throughout the country.
3. Medicare Carrier Manual, 14-3-3060.7.
4. *Physician's Current Procedural Terminology*, Copyright American Medical Association.
5. Federal Register, Vol. 66, No. 212, Thursday, November 1, 2001.
6. Medicare Carrier Manual, Part 3, Chapter 15, Section 15016.
7. Trailblazer Health Enterprises, LLC, *Supervising Physicians in a Teaching Setting*.

8. Ibid.

9. Medicare Carriers Manual, 14-3-2332, Charges Imposed By Immediate Relatives of Patient or Members of Household.

10. DHHS/Office of the Inspector General, Special Fraud Alert: Routine Waiver of Co-payments or Deductibles Under Medicare Part B, Issued May 1991.

11. DHHS/Office of the Inspector General, Physician Liability for Certifications in the Provision of Medical Equipment and Supplies and Home Health Services, Issued January 1999.

12. http://oig.hhs.gov/fraud/exclusions/database.html.

13. Excluded Parties List, http://www.epls.gov.

14. Some states have developed a TB Standard that is stricter than the TB Guideline issued by the federal OSHA.

15. *Required by law* means a mandate contained in law that compels a covered entity to make a use or disclosure of protected health information that is enforceable in a court of law. *Required by law* includes, but is not limited to, court orders and court-ordered warrants; subpoenas or summons issued by a court, grand jury, a governmental or tribal inspector general, or an administrative body authorized to require the production of information; a civil or an authorized investigative demand; Medicare conditions of participation with respect to health-care providers participating in the program; and statutes or regulations that require the production of information, including statutes or regulations that require such information if payment is sought under a government program providing public benefits.

16. HIPAA Says Software, Version 1.0.7, Healthcare Compliance Information Systems, 2003.

17. 45 CFR 164.

Chapter 7

Risk Management in Modern Medical Practice

(It's Not Just About Malpractice . . . Anymore!)

Charles F. Fenton, III
David Edward Marcinko

The greatest challenge facing health care providers is to preserve and improve the quality of health care services in the face of diminishing resources. A major part of this challenge is the prevention of financial losses from litigation. These losses may be in the form of direct costs, such as legal fees and insurance premiums, or indirect costs, such as unnecessary medical tests performed in a misguided attempt at "defensive" medicine. Whether direct or indirect, such losses reduce the resources available for necessary patient services. . . . Such is the task of virtually all risk management efforts in medical practice.

Edward P. Richards, III, JD, MPH, www.LawGeneCentre.org

In the past, the term *risk management* in the medical arena referred to methods of avoiding medical malpractice claims. *Defensive medicine* and *risk management* were often synonymous terms. Medical malpractice insurance companies provided "risk management seminars" to instruct physicians and staffs on methods of defensive medicine to limit the malpractice risk. However, the emphasis on medical risk management as a method of limiting the chances of a medical malpractice lawsuit under the current legal and political environment of medicine is completely misplaced. A medical malpractice action is mainly about money—and in most of the cases, the insurance company's money. The risks attendant in medical practice today are much greater than the risks involved in a medical malpractice action. The risks today are also mostly about money—*your* money.

In today's medicolegal environment, the physician faces risks from many directions. Risks come from the federal government (including the Health Care Financing Administration, the Occupational Safety and Health Administration, the Drug Enforcement

Agency, the HHS Office of Civil Rights, and the Environmental Protection Agency), the state government (including state medical boards), insurance companies (including health maintenance organizations, preferred provider organizations, and even indemnity plans), patients, and even one's own employees and prospective employees. The practicing physician almost needs to have a law degree to keep track of all the rules and regulations attendant with practicing.

Medicare Recoupment Risks

Historically, the main risk that the practicing physician faced that would place the physician's own assets at risk was the threat of a Medicare recoupment. Although many practitioners act surprised when receiving the notice of recoupment, this should not be the case. After all, the majority of recoupment requests are preceded by a request for copies of medical records. The practitioner has therefore been forewarned of the risk of recoupment. Many practitioners, upon receiving a request to forward copies of several patients' medical records, simply assign the task to a clerk and forget about the incident. That is a mistake. Whenever a request for medical records is received, whether from Medicaid, Medicare, or another third-party payer, there is a golden opportunity.

The medical records in question should be thoroughly reviewed prior to their release. The guidelines of the requester, as well as the current procedural terminology (CPT) definitions of the billed CPT codes, should be reviewed, and both of these should be compared to the record to ensure that proper-level codes and proper documentation were used. Often it is prudent to write an accompanying letter that points out to the reviewer why the documentation is proper. Remember Rule Number One: DO NOT ALTER THE MEDICAL RECORDS! That does not mean that you cannot "complete" your medical records. Medical records should be completed according to your office's previously established written medical record policy. That policy should include methods for ensuring the completion of all medical records before filing, methods for random auditing of medical records, and methods for completion of medical records that are found to be incomplete, either by audit or by chance. The medical record policy of your local hospital can be used as a guide, or you may choose legal assistance.

It is much easier to make your case at this juncture than to have treatment denied, have a recoupment request, and have to request additional hearings. If you are not sure how to develop such a document justifying your treatment, then you should consult with a knowledgeable health-law attorney or a CPT consultant. In fact, the prudent practitioner will not assign this task to a clerk, but rather will have a health-care attorney respond to the request.

If, having demonstrated the medical necessity of the treatments, a recoupment letter still is received, then the practitioner should retain an attorney to preserve all legal rights. Generally, there is a right to request a *fair hearing* before a *hearing officer*. At the fair hearing, the practitioner is given the opportunity to present justification of the treatments to the impartial hearing officer. If the fair hearing results are adverse to the practitioner, there is a right to request a hearing before an *administrative law judge.* Even if the practitioner is unsuccessful at that level, there may be additional appeal rights.

These processes are long and drawn out. The amount of time necessary will result in larger and larger attorney's fees. It is simpler, easier, faster, and cheaper to retain an attorney for assistance when the first request for medical records is received. Although retaining an attorney at this juncture is no guarantee of success, it is the best opportunity to "nip it in the bud." Finally, be aware that some malpractice insurance policies may contain an Administrative Defense rider that might assist you in such an instance.

Health-Care Fraud Risks

The greatest risk to the practicing physician's fiscal fitness in the current medicolegal environment is the fraud risk. With the federal and state governments, as well as the private insurance companies, seeking to reduce health-care costs, active investigations into health-care fraud have increased. It is relatively easy for an administrative billing error to be labeled as fraud. In this manner, an innocent act becomes a criminal act, which the practitioner must now defend.

[A] Medicare Fraud

The federal government has many weapons in its arsenal to investigate and prosecute Medicare and Medicaid fraud. Some of these include the Medicare and Medicaid Anti-Fraud and Abuse Statute, the RICO statute, the Federal False Claims Act, money-laundering laws, and civil asset forfeiture laws.

[B] Insurance Fraud

The federal government now has the power to investigate and prosecute fraud involving private insurance companies. The new federal crime of *health-care fraud* authorized in 1996 gives the federal government wide scope of authority. A practitioner being investigated for Medicare fraud may also end up defending against a charge of private health-care fraud.

[C] Misrepresentation

The reader may feel that once the medical practice is sold and the reader is retired, the chances of being sued for fraud would disappear. However, the very act of selling the medical practice can potentially expose the seller to fraud accusations by the buyer. Consider the following case:

A physician decided to sell the practice and move to another state to practice. The physician sold the practice to another physician in the same specialty. The value of the sale was based, in part, on the yearly gross of the practice. The physician sold his practice, accepted installment payment terms from the buyer, and moved to the new state. The buyer began to practice medicine at his new office. Although he was busy, his gross never approached the gross of the prior physician. Eventually the buyer defaulted on the loan. The buying physician sued for the deficit. The defaulting physician, who still had all of the seller's patient and computer records, began to do an in-depth evaluation of the seller's practice. The buyer noticed some discrepancies in the billing patterns and practices of the seller. Considering these discrepancies to constitute Medicare and insurance billing fraud, the buyer countersued the seller on the grounds of misrepresentation, the buyer's theory being that because the seller allegedly committed Medicare and insurance fraud, the gross receipts of the practice, and hence the ultimate purchase price of the practice, were grossly inflated. Therefore, the buyer determined that the seller had fraudulently misrepresented the potential of the practice.

But the buyer did not stop at simply filing a countersuit. The buyer also notified state and federal authorities and filed complaints of insurance fraud against the seller. The seller thought that he would move to the good life in the new state, but his old practice kept him in constant legal trouble.

Provider Health-Care Fraud Considerations

Fraud in the health-care arena has become a high priority for the United States Department of Justice. Health-care fraud ranks close behind terrorism and drug crimes as one of the department's top priorities. Because physicians are engaged in delivering health-care services, and because a high percentage of those services are delivered to patients covered by federal plans (e.g., Medicare, Medicaid, CHAMPUS), many physicians may soon find themselves subject to a federal investigation. As the investigators seek to uncover health-care fraud, many innocent or unsuspecting physicians may find themselves the subject of investigation.

During the 1980s physicians dealt with fears from the malpractice crisis. During the 1990s, physicians saw their practices and income shrink because of the managed care crisis. The new millennium may become the time of the health-care fraud crisis, along with a *malpractice liability redux*. Whereas a claim of malpractice involves only money and, in most cases, the insurance company's money, a charge of health-care fraud will not only involve your personal assets, but may very well involve your liberty. During the late 1990s, many physicians found their professional and personal lives devastated with charges of health-care fraud.

In fiscal year 2003, the Office of the Inspector General (OIG) conducted over 2,000 audits and evaluations, recouping $21 billion. The OIG opened over 1,654 new civil and criminal cases, winning over 517 criminal convictions and over 236 civil actions. It also excluded over 3,448 individuals from participation in federal health-care programs, (see http://oig.hhs.gov/publications/docs/semiannual/2003/SemiannualFall03.pdf for the full report). It is almost as if the federal government prides itself on the number of cases and excluded individuals. It can only increase those numbers by going after *you* (after all, there is no point in going after those 3,448+ excluded individuals this year— they are excluded). How much of the money that you earned from treatment of patients will you pay back to the federal government this year?

In the past practitioners feared an audit because it meant the possibility of paying back prior reimbursements. Often this repayment placed a financial burden on the practitioner. Now, with the increased emphasis on fraud, the repayment of such amounts will seem insignificant compared with the burden of paying back those amounts, paying civil penalty fines, paying lawyer fees, being subject to forfeiture, and being placed in jeopardy of going to jail.

The government has always had an arsenal of laws to deal with health-care fraud. These included the Medicare and Medicaid Anti-Fraud and Abuse Statute, the Stark Amendments, the Federal False Claims Act, and mail and wire fraud laws. Recently, the federal government's arsenal has been significantly augmented.

The Kennedy-Kassenbaum (HIPAA) Act

The Health Insurance Portability and Accountability Act of 1996, also known as the Kennedy-Kassenbaum health-care bill, provides a whole section on fighting health-care fraud. In particular, the bill authorizes a new crime: health-care fraud. It changes the intent requirement to include "reckless disregard of the truth" or "deliberate ignorance" of the truth. This intent definition is important because it will probably eliminate the provider's defense that the billings in question were "clerical errors," or the defense that "the E/M codes are too difficult to understand, so I never bothered to learn them." The report *Documentation Guideline for Evaluation and Management Services*, AMA-CMS, May 1997, is most helpful in this regard.

The Kennedy-Kassenbaum bill increases the civil money penalties from $2,000 per line item to $10,000 per line item. Even 1 erroneous item can be devastating for the provider. Add 20 or 30 such items and many physicians will see their net worth drop to near zero. The bill also makes it easier for money-laundering charges and civil asset forfeiture to be brought against health-care professionals. Furthermore, unlike in the past, when the federal government concerned itself with fraud in federal programs, the law extends the federal government's power to include *all* health plans, public and private. The practitioner could potentially face civil asset forfeiture for alleged claims of fraud involving an HMO, PPO, or MCO.

The bill also authorizes the usage of bounty hunters in the pursuit of health-care fraud. If an individual provides information to the government that results in a recovery of only $100, then the whistle-blower will share in the recovery. The frightening fact is that now your own patient (or their relatives) or employee may become a bounty hunter against you. Additionally, the bill authorizes Centers for Medicare and Medicaid Services (CMS) to contract with private entities to pursue health-care fraud on a wide scale. Private entities will now have financial incentives to investigate health-care providers in an attempt to uncover health-care fraud. Practitioners will find their activities under scrutiny from different sides.

The preceding provisions are commonly termed HIPAA, part one, to distinguish them from HIPAA, part two—those provisions dealing with the recently required Privacy Rule and Transaction Standards.

The Balanced Budget Act

The Balanced Budget Act of 1997 provided some additional tools that the federal government can use in its fight against health-care fraud. In particular, physicians convicted of three health-care crimes can be permanently prohibited from Medicare.

The Federal False Claims Act

A Civil War era law, titled the False Claims Act (*qui tam* [in the name of the king]), is increasingly popular with prosecutors who pursue inappropriate billing mishaps by physicians. This is because in 1990 the health-care industry accounted for about 10 percent of all false claims penalties recovered by the federal government. By 1998, the health-care share was almost 40 percent.

This act allows a private citizen, such as your patient, your employee, or a competing podiatrist, to bring a health-care fraud claim against you on behalf of and in the name of the United States of America. The "relator" who initiates the claim is rewarded by sharing in a percentage of the recovery from the health-care provider. Essentially, this act allows informers to receive up to 30 percent of any judgment recovered against government contractors (Medicare, Medicaid, CHAMPUS, prison systems, American Indian reservations, or the Veterans Administration systems). With a low burden of proof, triple damages, and penalties of up to $10,000 for each wrongful claims submission, these suits are the enforcement tools of choice for zealous prosecutors pursuing health-care fraud. All that must be proven is that improper claims were submitted with a reckless disregard of the truth. Intentional fraud is irrelevant to these cases, even if submitted by a third party, such as a billing company. Therefore, it is imperative that attending physicians review all bills before they are submitted to any state or federal agency.

Money Laundering

Charges of money laundering may seem foreign to the practice of medicine. The term *money laundering* evokes visions of a suitcase of drug cash being brought into a legitimate business and being transformed into that business's receipts and later tunneled through legal channels. In medicine the route begins with receipt of a claim payment check (i.e., a check as opposed to the drug dealer's cash). The check is then deposited into the professional corporation's checking account. The funds are then paid to the physician in the form of wages. Those wages are deposited into the physician's personal checking account. Those funds and other similarly situated funds are then accumulated until a check is written to pay for a sports utility vehicle. The money received from the alleged fraudulent insurance claim has successfully been "laundered" into a hard asset (a new SUV).

Civil Asset Forfeiture Risks

We have all heard stories of civil asset forfeiture run amok and out of control. The family that lost their home because a child had marijuana in his bedroom, the man who lost his boat because a friend who (unknown to the owner) borrowed it and used it to smuggle drugs. These cases will pale in comparison to what can happen if civil asset forfeiture is applied to health-care professions. Just like the drug dealer who has his Cessna plane seized because it was used to smuggle drugs, a health-care provider may find that his practice is seized because the office was the conduit for committing a crime. Furthermore, the practitioner's house, furnishings, car, bank account, and retirement assets could likewise be seized, because they constitute "fruits" of the illegal activities.

Civil asset forfeiture is a "seize now, ask questions later" activity. This appears on the surface to constitute punishment without due process. However, in civil asset forfeiture there is due process; it just comes AFTER the seizure. Civil asset forfeiture is to property like an arrest is to the person. A warrant is issued stating in essence that the property did something wrong. The property is "arrested" (i.e., seized), and a hearing or trial will follow at some later date to determine the facts.

Self-Referral Risks

The federal and state governments have enacted several overlapping laws to deal with the issue of financial inducement in the referral of patients. These laws create a virtual maze of regulations, which can easily snare the unwary. The extent of the federal regulation in the area of self-referral includes the Medicare Anti-Fraud and Abuse Statute, the Medicare Safe Harbor Regulations, and the Stark Amendment.

[A] Medicare Anti-Fraud and Abuse Statute

The federal government has addressed the issue of physician fraud and abuse in the Medicare Anti-Fraud and Abuse Statute (anti-fraud statute). This statute applies equally to any abuses in the Medicaid system. However, the statute does not apply to abuses involving private patients. The statute states the following:

> *Whoever knowingly and willfully offers or pays any remuneration (including any kickback, bribe, or rebate) directly or indirectly, overtly or covertly, in cash or in kind to any person to induce such person*
>
> *(A) to refer an individual to a person for the furnishing or arranging for the furnishing of any item or service for which payment may be made in whole or in part under a Federal health care program, or*
>
> *(B) to purchase, lease, order, or arrange for or recommend purchasing, leasing, or ordering any good, facility, service, or item for which payment may be made in whole or in part under a Federal health care program,*
>
> *shall be guilty of a felony and upon conviction thereof, shall be fined not more than $25,000 or imprisoned for not more than five years, or both. [42 U.S.C. 1320a-7b(2)]*

The anti-fraud statute applies only to persons receiving kickbacks for referring Medicare or Medicaid. There are many examples of physicians who ran afoul of the law. These included several chiropractors that were paid "handling fees" for collection and transmission of lab specimens to a certain laboratory. In another case, cardiologists who received "interpretation fees" for referring patients to a certain cardiac lab were found guilty of violating the statute. Additionally, a hospital administrator was found guilty when he received perks from an ambulance company to whom he had referred patients. Succinctly, any benefit given or received in exchange for referral of a Medicare or Medicaid patient will violate the statute.

[B] Medicare Safe Harbor Regulations

The Medicare Safe Harbor rules were passed in an effort to identify areas of practice that would not lead to a conviction under the anti-fraud statute. The Safe Harbor regulations provide for 11 areas in which providers may practice without violating the anti-fraud statute:

1. *Large-Entity Investments.* Investment in entities with assets over $50 million. The entity must be registered and traded on national exchanges.
2. *Small-Entity Investments.* Small-entity investments must abide by the 40-40 rule: no more than 40 percent of the investment interests may be held by

investors in a position to make referrals. Additionally, no more than 40 percent of revenues can come through referrals by these investors.

3. *Space and Equipment Rentals.* Such lease agreements must be in writing and must be for at least a 1-year term. Furthermore, the terms must be at fair market value.

4. *Personal Services and Management Contracts.* These contracts are allowable as long as certain rules are followed. Like lease agreements, these personal service and management contracts must be in writing for at least a year's term, and the services must be valued at fair market value.

5. *Sale of a Medical Practice.* There are restrictions if the selling practitioner is in a position to refer patients to the purchasing practitioner.

6. *Referral Services.* Referral services (such as hospital referral services) are allowed. However, such referral services may not discriminate between practitioners who do refer patients and those who do not.

7. *Warranties.* There are certain requirements if any item of value is received under a warranty.

8. *Discounts.* Certain requirements must be met if a buyer receives a discount on the purchase of goods or services that are to be paid for by Medicare or Medicaid.

9. *Payments to Bona Fide Employees.* Payments made to bona fide employees do not constitute fraud under the Safe Harbor regulations.

10. *Group Purchasing Organizations.* Organization purchases of goods and services for a group of entities or individuals are allowed, provided certain requirements are met.

11. *Waiver of Beneficiary Co-Insurance and Deductible.* Routine waiver would not come under the Safe Harbor regulations.

Physicians' actions that come under the Safe Harbor regulations will not violate the Medicare Anti-Fraud and Abuse Statute. However, the provider must still abide by the Stark amendments and must also abide by applicable state law.

[C] The Stark Amendment

The Stark Amendment to the Omnibus Budget Reconciliation Act of 1989 was a step by the federal government to prohibit physicians from referring patients to entities in which they have a financial interest. Originally, the Stark Amendment applied only to referral of Medicare patients to clinical laboratories in which the physician had a financial interest.

The Stark Amendment provides that if a physician (including a family member) has a financial interest in a clinical laboratory, then he or she may not make a referral for clinical laboratory services if payment may be made under Medicare. A financial interest is an ownership interest, an investment interest, or a compensation arrangement.

Exceptions to the Stark Amendment are made if a physician personally provides the service or if a physician or employee of a group provides the services. Like the Safe Harbor regulations, the Stark Amendment also permits physician investment in large entities and provides an exception for rural providers. Under the Stark Amendment, large entities are defined as publicly traded entities with assets greater than $100 million.

There are certain other exceptions that are similar to the Safe Harbor regulations. They include items such as provision for rental of office space, employment and service arrangements with hospitals, and certain service arrangements. These arrangements must be at arm's length and at fair market value.

Stark II was passed in 1993 to modify and expand the Stark Amendment. In particular, it acts to bring numerous other entities, besides clinical laboratories, within the prohibitions of the Stark Amendment.

Self-referral and overutilization may become less of a problem as managed care makes further inroads in medical practice control and quasi-subrogation. Future legislation is likely to address the concerns of the financial incentives toward underutilization of ancillary medical services.

Federal Agency Risks

As politicians continue to tout the "right" to health care and as they enact piecemeal regulations and statutes to control health-care delivery in the United States, more and more federal agencies will regulate physicians. For example, the practitioner has to deal with agencies such as the Occupational Safety and Health Agency (OSHA), Health and Human Services (HHS), the Drug Enforcement Agency (DEA), and even the Environmental Protection Agency (EPA).

Occupational Safety and Health Agency Risks

OSHA has several standards with which the physician must comply. Physicians are covered generally under OSHA simply by the fact that they have employees, but they also have two specific standards that they must follow. These include the Bloodborne Standard and the Hazardous Communication Standard and general provisions for games.

Drug Enforcement Agency Risks

The Drug Enforcement Agency (DEA) controls the issuance of DEA numbers that permit physicians to prescribe controlled substances to their patients. The use of controlled substances is important to almost all medical specialties. Family practitioners use codeine to treat coughs and surgeons use narcotics to manage pain.

There will always be a rogue physician willing to sell narcotic prescriptions. These physicians cause the DEA to cast a jaundiced eye toward all physicians. However, there are simply too many stories of physicians who "overuse" controlled substances in a practice designed to ease the suffering of their patients.

The physician never knows when a patient comes into the office complaining of pain and asking for pain medication whether that patient is truly in pain or is an undercover agent for the DEA. This risk and paranoia (combined with the risk of a malpractice claim of "hooking" the patient) generally cause physicians to underprescribe pain medication.

Environmental Protection Agency Risks

The practitioner may not think about the Environmental Protection Agency (EPA) when thinking about the possible risks of practicing, but that agency can be a nightmare for the unsuspecting physician. A physician who improperly disposes of developing fluid, silver wastes, bodily fluids or biohazardous materials, and/or other wastes may become a target of the EPA.

Health and Human Services (Office of Civil Rights) Risks

There is now a new and recent risk. Part II of HIPAA, the Privacy Rules, went into effect on April 14, 2003. Patients must be informed of their privacy rights and physicians must adhere to certain regulations in order to safeguard the privacy of their patients. Failure to do so can result in civil money penalties of $100 per incident up to a maximum of $25,000 per year. There are also substantial criminal penalties (jail and fines) for certain transgressions of the HIPAA Privacy Rule.

Antitrust Risks

The following are some antitrust rules:

1. *Monopolistic* risks are reduced when more than a few networks or contracts are available in the local area for excluded providers to join.
2. Fee schedule managed care organization (MCO) contracts, per se, are not generally considered price fixing, provided the providers have not conspired with one another to set those prices. Moreover, any such network pricing schedule should not spill over into the nonnetwork patients.

3. Individual providers may be excluded from a network if there is a rational reason to do so. It is much more difficult to exclude a *class* of providers than it is to exclude an *individual* provider.

4. A *safety zone* can be created if networks or other contractual plans require a substantial amount of financial risk sharing among plan participants, since Stark II laws have been relaxed. Such zones have been created by the Department of Justice (DOJ) and the Federal Trade Commission (FTC) in recent policy statements.

5. The FTC and DOJ are not likely to challenge an exclusive provider independent physicians' association (IPA) that includes no more than 20 to 25 percent of the doctors within the panel who share financial risk. Such panels are likely to fall within a Safe Harbor regulation.

6. *Tying arrangements* (e.g., the requirement to buy one item or service in order to buy another item or service) are suspect if not reasonably justified. For example, a patient should not be required to obtain a brace prescription from a specific provider in order to purchase the device from a laboratory that the doctor owns.

7. *Nonexclusive* provider panels will not usually be challenged if no more than 30 percent of the providers are included (another Safe Harbor provision).

8. Physician networks are often analyzed according to *four criteria:* (1) anticompetitive effects, (2) relevant local markets, (3) procompetitive effects, and (4) collateral agreements.

9. Anti-Trust Considerations consist of analyzing *market power*. This consists of two factors: (a) geographic power and (2) product power. *Geographic power* is difficult to define in today's environment. In the past, the geography that was analyzed when medical practices merged was the immediate neighborhood. Currently, the geographical area could consist of an entire metropolitan area. In the past, individual patients would often seek a physician whose office was close to work or home. Now they seek a physician based on inclusion in a health plan. Now, health plans choose physicians based on needs within an entire metropolitan area.

Product power relates to the specific service being performed. There are two products in today's environment: (a) primary care and (b) specialty care. Since there are so many primary care physicians in practice, it would be difficult for all but the largest group to acquire product power.

It is easier for specialists to develop product power. However, certain specialists may never be able to obtain product power. For example, foot care is provided by many types of physicians. Primary care physicians, emergency physicians, chiropractors, physical therapists, orthopedic surgeons, nurse practitioners, and podiatrists all provide foot care. Therefore, it would be difficult, even for a large group of podiatrists, to obtain significant product power.

Business Practice Litigation Risks

A recent report stated that 25 percent of all suits filed in Federal District Court relate to a growing field of law loosely called "business practices litigation." That percentage is only likely to grow in the coming years. Business practices litigation encompasses a wide variety of issues, but they mostly revolve around the relationship between a business and its employees and customers.

The issues include, for example, racial and sexual discrimination, sexual harassment, wrongful termination, and violations of the Americans With Disabilities Act. These claims are not confined to big corporations; they can also affect the sole proprietor physician.

For example, a Georgia physician recently paid $5,000 in settlement of an employment claim. Apparently, the physician would have won the claim, but only after paying over $20,000 in legal fees. That $5,000 settlement was not paid by the malpractice insurance carrier, but by the individual physician himself.

Patterns of Practice Risks

One of the next big areas of risk that will surface in the near future is the *pattern of practice risk. Pattern of practice* refers to the way that a particular physician practices medicine. With computers, standardized diagnosis and treatment codes, and the budgetary restraints inherent in medical practice, it is becoming easy to analyze a physician's method of practice.

The treatment and diagnosis codes that a physician uses and submits to third-party payers can be quantified and compared to those of colleagues in the same or similar specialties. Statistical *outliers* can be identified. These outliers will then be further audited and required to justify their treatments. If no rational basis exists for the statistical differences, the outlier may find himself or herself the subject of a fraud investigation.

Managed Care Contractual Risks

Attorneys are becoming more aggressive in suing HMOs and other managed care companies. Historical bars to such suits are declining simultaneously with recent federal ERISA (Employee Retirement Income Security Act of 1974) protection erosion. The upshot is that more litigation against managed care companies, their affiliates, and their health-care providers is likely. Health-care providers need to be aware of these trends, need to evaluate their own situation, and may need to take certain steps to limit these new evolving risks and potential liabilities.

For example, the usual method of protection for the practicing physician, the use of the corporate form of business, is usually no benefit when signing managed care contracts. Most managed care companies credential the individual physician and hence require that the individual physician and not the professional corporation sign the contract. *This puts all of the physician's personal assets at risk.*

Historic Bars to Managed Care Lawsuits

Historically, managed care companies have been afforded immunity from negligence and malpractice lawsuits. Several state and federal bars, including ERISA, have insulated managed care companies from liability relating to the treatment of patients. Likewise, managed care companies have historically been immune from malpractice committed by a health-care member of their panel of providers.

On a state law basis, the *corporate practice of law* often insulated managed care companies from such liability. The theory underlying this protection was essentially uncomplicated; since corporations are prohibited under the Corporate Practice of Law Doctrine from practicing medicine, they should not be held liable for medical negligence and malpractice.

However, in recent years, it has become apparent that managed care companies do in fact "practice medicine." These companies tell their panel of providers how to practice, whether it is in a generalized or specific field of medicine. They establish a formulary of approved drugs, limiting those medications available to their subscribers. They review and then approve or deny needed medical care. They create economic incentives for patients to be undertreated or treated in a predetermined manner. They effectively minimize referrals to specialists, often at the peril of the patient subscriber and the health-care provider seeking that consultation.

In the federal arena, ERISA has been the primary deterrent to suits against managed care companies. Under the theory of federal preemption, even the lowest federal regulation takes precedence over any and all state laws. However, ERISA has been described as possessing "*superpreemption*." That term was coined to express the special deference that courts have displayed to potential defendants who allege defensive protection based upon ERISA. In the past, most providers ran into the ERISA preemption when a health plan governed by ERISA was contrary to a state law, such as a state antidiscrimination law (i.e., a state law prohibiting insurance payment discrimination based on degree). In the context of this chapter, the reader should understand that liability claims, such as medical malpractice claims, are state law causes of action. Since the federal ERISA law trumps state laws, bringing a medical malpractice action against an ERISA entity is almost impossible.

[A] Recent Trends

Recent cases would imply that the days of ERISA preemption applicable to the vast majority of managed care companies might be numbered. At first blush, this might sound like good news to the health-care provider. After all, everyone (the patient, the public, and the provider) tends to dislike the depersonalization that has occurred in medicine since the advent of managed care.

But a closer look into the facts will show that this change of events is a very bad omen for the health-care provider. It is axiomatic that the actual providers of medical services, even if employed by a managed care organization, can and usually do shoulder the enormous liability for medical malpractice, even if conforming to the directives of the managed care company. State legislatures are becoming more aggressive in making the managed care companies liable for their actions. Likewise, federal courts are increasingly willing to permit claims against managed care companies. Yet, most employment contracts between the health-care provider and the managed care entity allow for subrogation of the managed care entity's potential liability, including defense counsel costs, to that of the individual provider.

In one case, the court found that ERISA does not preempt the patient's negligence claim against an HMO-employed physician. A U.S. district court held that preemption is inapplicable to a patient's negligence claim against a physician who was employed by an HMO [*Edelen v. Osterman*, 943 F. Supp. 75 (D.D.C., 1996)].

In one federal case [*Dukes v. U.S. Healthcare, Inc.*, 57 F.3rd 350 (3d Cir.) (1995)], the court implied that medical malpractice cases against health-care plans based on vicarious liability may not be preempted by ERISA. Under this case and its progeny, it appears that the managed care company can be held vicariously liable for the actions of its independent providers. Several courts have tended to follow the Dukes precedent, but this trend is certainly far from uniform throughout the United States. Again, this may appear to be a favorable turn of events, but it can spell disaster for the provider.

The state of Texas has a statute, upheld in 1998, that allows a patient to sue a health plan if the patient was injured because of denial or delay in approval of treatment. Many more states are likely to follow suit.

With the ERISA shield melting away, lawyers are chomping at the bit to sue these managed care companies. A recent legal publication instructed the reader about several potential theories of liability to pursue in civil litigation against managed care companies for negligence of their panel of health-care providers. The same journal had an additional shorter article instructing the reader in ways to avoid ERISA when suing managed care companies. It seems apparent that if this current trend continues in the future, the likelihood of managed care companies becoming defendants or codefendants in medical malpractice actions will rapidly escalate. Such an occurrence brings up certain issues for the individual health-care practitioner. With such acceptance of ERISA meeting, there has been much debate in state legislatures and in Congress concerning reducing the liability protections that many managed care companies have thus far enjoyed. When the shield from medical negligence liability is finally broken, the floodgates will open for plaintiffs and lawyers to sue the managed care company as a specifically named defendant for its own negligence.

Lawyers have several options when suing managed care companies. The lawyer can opt to institute a direct suit against the company, or he or she can bring a derivative suit based on vicarious liability. In a direct suit, the lawyer alleges that the managed care company did something wrong, that is, that its negligence damaged his or her client. Such claims can take the form of direct negligence, corporate liability, or contract. In a derivative suit based on vicarious liability, the lawyer contends that the managed care company is liable because the contracted provider was negligent. Causes of action can take the form of nondelegable duty by contract (the patient's contract with the managed care company), nondelegable duty under state statute, joint venture (of the managed care company and the provider), or under various agency principles. It is this type of suit that is more likely to cause later problems for the provider.

If an attorney knows that the managed care company is protected through a Hold Harmless Clause in its provider agreement, the reader may wonder why the attorney would sue the company and not just sue the provider. The answer is simple: *money.* The company is the deep pocket. Even if the provider has malpractice insurance, the limit is usually $1 million per incident. However, a recovery from the managed care company could potentially be larger. If the attorney is successful against the company, then the attorney will not care if the company files an indemnity or subrogation action against the provider. The attorney will already have his or her settlement.

[B] Implications for the Physician

Participating in managed care is like a double-edged sword. The practitioner has to participate in managed care, but the contract that is signed creates many potential risks for the individual. The main risk is the Hold Harmless Clause prevalent in most managed care contracts. Although these clauses cannot be negotiated out of the contract, they are still binding upon the signer.

In a malpractice action, the plaintiff has several options. The plaintiff can sue the provider or name the HMO as a codefendant. In some cases, the plaintiff may decide to forego suing the provider (if the provider does not have insurance) and instead sue the managed care company directly.

If a patient sues the physician and the managed care company and if a Hold Harmless Clause exists, the individual physician may be liable for any settlement or award made by the managed care company to the patient. Even if the managed care company were to win a defense verdict at trial, under these clauses, the individual physician would be liable for the managed care company's attorneys' fees. This could be tens of thousands of dollars, even though the defense won!

Some examples of Hold Harmless Clauses will help the reader understand the import of what they are signing. Following are several examples with commentary. *These examples have been taken from actual managed care contracts,* contracts that physicians *are signing.*

> **EXAMPLE 1.** *"The Provider further agrees to indemnify and to hold the Company, its officers, directors, shareholders, employees, agents, and representatives harmless from and against any claims or liabilities, from any cause whatsoever, arising under this Agreement or the provision or rendering of*

Healthcare Services. Any claims or liabilities which arise out of this Agreement or the provision or rendering of Healthcare Services are the sole responsibility of the Provider."

This clause is very broad and one-sided. It is obvious that any claims against the company that are related to alleged malpractice by the provider would eventually become the responsibility of the provider. Moreover, since the clause also covers "any claims or liabilities, from any cause whatsoever, arising under this Agreement or the provision or rendering of the Healthcare Services," it is arguable that the provider might also end up liable for acts of the company, such as denial of services, adverse results related to the drug formulary, or practice guidelines established by the company.

Since this clause is skewed and is also so broad, the provider should not sign this agreement. The provider should either negotiate out the clause or should sign the agreement in the name of the provider's corporation.

> **EXAMPLE 2.** *"Specialist shall indemnify Company for any losses, judgments, costs, claims or expenses (including, without limitation, attorney's fees) that Company may incur because of the negligent or intentional actions or omissions of Specialist or any of Specialist's employees or agents or due to any limitation, lack of coverage, revocation or suspension of Specialist's malpractice insurance."*

This clause is more specific than the clause in Example 1. However, this clause clearly shifts the burden to the specialist if the company is sued for any alleged malpractice by the specialist. It clearly states that the specialist is responsible for "attorney's fees." The reader should realize that even if the company receives a defense verdict, the specialist will be responsible for the company's attorneys' fees, even though the specialist had no input into the attorneys' selection, hourly rate, or amount of hours dedicated to the case.

> **EXAMPLE 3.** *"Provider further agrees to indemnify and to hold harmless the Company against any claims or liabilities arising under this Agreement."*

This clause is very succinct. The physician should not be lulled into complacency by its brevity. It has the same impact as the clause in Example 2!

> **EXAMPLE 4.** *"Neither the Provider nor the Company shall be liable for defending or for the expense of defending the other party, its agents, employees or representatives against any claims, suits, actions, dispute resolutions or administrative or regulatory proceedings arising out of or related to such other party's actions or omissions. Neither party shall be liable for any liability of the other party or its agents, employees or representatives, whether resulting from judgment, settlement, award, fine or otherwise, which arises out of such other party's actions or omissions."*

This clause appears to be a mutual clause. Each party indemnifies the other party. Such mutuality often leads the reader into a false sense of security. Remember that the contract was written by the managed care company's attorney for the sole purpose of protecting the company. The purpose of this clause, like the purpose all of the other clauses, is to render the provider responsible for any suits against the company based on any alleged malpractice of the provider.

This clause has a red flag that should jump out at the reader. It makes the provider liable for "any liability . . . resulting from . . . settlement." Therefore, if the company decides to settle a pending case, then it can seek reimbursement from the provider. The company can seek reimbursement from the provider for the settlement, even though the provider had no input whatsoever regarding the terms or the amount of the settlement.

> **EXAMPLE 5.** *"Neither the Company nor the Provider nor any of their respective agents or employees shall be liable to any third parties for any act or omission of the other party."*

This is another brief clause essentially similar to Example 4.

The Contract Capitulation Dilemma

The dilemma that providers will have to consider when facing the adverse effects of a Hold Harmless Clause is the prospective detriment to their practice if they do not capitulate to the managed care company's demand to provide indemnification for a settled case. The provider has the option to fight the issue in court. In some cases, the provider may prevail, but it is likely to be a futile and expensive effort.

In any event, if providers do not indemnify the managed care company, most likely they will find themselves deselected from the panel. Such a deselection is likely to create a domino effect of deselection from other panels. These events could destroy the provider's practice.

Employee Risks

Practice employees have *inside information* concerning the practice and the physician's patterns of practice. In most cases the staff members are trained by the doctor. The staff's frame of reference is thereby limited to what they have been taught. However, more credit should be given to the office staff. Staff members deal every day with insurance companies (including Medicare), and they field a wide array of patient questions and complaints. An astute staff member will soon realize if the physician is miscoding insurance submission.

An informed, irate employee can be your biggest risk. Many medical malpractice lawsuits have been brought by patients because terminated employees have informed the patient that "something was wrong" with their treatment. Likewise, OSHA investigations have been instituted by disgruntled employees. In these cases the employees had nothing to gain but revenge against real or perceived injustices from their former employer. Now, employees also have a financial incentive to bring health-care fraud charges against their former physician-employer.

Vicarious Risks

In certain situations, the doctor may be at risk for vicarious fraud charges, even if he or she never submitted a questionable claim. The two classes of practitioners that may have such risk are employed (or contracted) physicians and physicians who are members of a group practice.

[A] Employed Physicians

You may think that simply because you are an employed physician that you are not at risk. However, in some cases, your risk could be greater. For example, if you work for a physician who employs you to see patients at a contracted nursing home and you get paid either per patient or per day, you should realize that Medicare is being billed under your name as the provider of services. Although you may never get receipt of the money, since the billing was done under your name, if there is a question of fraud, you would be the one liable. The point is that whether you are self-employed, a member of a group, or an employed physician, you should personally ensure that the billing being conducted under your name and signature is proper.

[B] Members of a Group Practice

If you are a member of a group and your income is at all dependent upon the income of another member of a group (as with expense sharing or production-based income), then you may be liable for the fraud of another member of your group. The rationale is that every member of the group benefits financially from the money received secondary to the fraudulent activity. This can put a practitioner in a very difficult position. One must choose whether to continue in practice with a practitioner employing questionable billing techniques or to dissolve the group.

[C] Certificates of Medical Necessity

Physicians are asked daily to sign Certificates of Medical Necessity (CMNs). Under the new law, you may be liable if you sign a CMN and the product or service is later found to be not medically necessary. In most cases, a physician should have no problem with this rule. Practitioners should be careful in signing CMNs that come into their office unsolicited. *For example*, you may be asked to sign a CMN for transportation of a Medicaid patient to your office. But was that transportation, or the particular level of transportation, medically necessary? Extreme caution should be employed when signing a CMN for transportation. In most cases, transportation to your office will be nonemergency transportation of an ambulatory patient. Unscrupulous transportation companies have been known to bill for stretcher transportation of ambulatory patients. Do not allow yourself to be swept into another's fraudulent scheme. Be careful what you certify as medically necessary!

Deselection Risks

In the current medical environment a physician's practice does not consist of a collection of individual patients or of the "charts." A physician's practice consists of a number of managed care contracts that allow the physician to be a member of a panel and listed in the individual subscriber's insurance book. The patients merely flow from those managed care contracts. Without the contracts, there would be no patient flow.

Therefore, the physician faces the risk of being deselected from an individual, or several, managed care panels. Each deselection will have an adverse effect on the physician's practice. In actuality, the revenue lost from deselection will come disproportionately from the net revenue of the practice. Often one deselection will snowball into several deselections, until the physician barely has a practice remaining.

Risks of Collateral Consequences

Many risks inherent in medical practice also have collateral consequences. For example, making a payment in response to a medical malpractice claim requires reporting to the National Practitioner Data Bank. Often such a report instigates an investigation by state boards and hospital staffs. The result is that the medical license of staff privileges can be placed in jeopardy.

Medicare 5-Year Exclusion Risks

Medicare rules provide for a mandatory exclusion of a provider who has been convicted of certain crimes. For example, a physician who is convicted of insurance fraud (unrelated to the Medicare program) could also be excluded from Medicare participation during a 5-year period.

State Board Action Risks

Many of the state medical board actions are "piggyback" actions, meaning that the disciplined physician may find himself or herself subject to action by an out-of-state state board where he or she holds an additional license. The grounds will be that the practitioner had been disciplined by the practitioner's home state and therefore the foreign state has grounds for action against the medical license in that state. Some states investigate all closed malpractice cases, even cases that have settled. The investigation in these cases is to determine whether the practitioner is engaging in practice patterns that would be adverse to the public benefit.

It is easy to see how one incident can snowball. The risk is great. Take the example of a physician who settles a malpractice claim. The physician's state board investigates the matter and determines that there is enough evidence for a reprimand. Next, an out-of-state board takes action simply because of the action taken by the home state.

All of these actions are subsequently reported to the National Practitioner Data Bank. When the physician's local hospital appointment is up for re-appointment, the hospital (as required by law) checks the National Practitioner Data Bank. Seeing the adverse actions taken against the physician, the hospital restricts the physician's privileges. Finally, the managed care companies, of which the physician is a panel member, learn of all these actions and deselect the physician. The physician's ability to earn a living is therefore significantly impaired.

In the past, a physician could afford an adverse ruling in a legal action (e.g., state board, Medicare, hospital) so long as the penalty was not very severe and so long as the physician kept his or her license and malpractice insurance. However, with the advent of the "managed care revolution," every legal action, no matter how small, can pose a threat to the livelihood of the physician.

Managed care companies provide their subscribers with "panels" of physicians from which they can choose their primary care physician and specialists. The managed care companies limit the number of physicians on their panels. If a physician is terminated from the panel, there are plenty of other physicians who would be happy to join the panel. Managed care companies have application and reapplication procedures. During these procedures, the companies investigate certain aspects of the physician's background. These include items such as malpractice history, state board or federal agency action, and Medicare suspensions and sanctions.

An adverse legal action can potentially prevent a physician from gaining access to a panel or could cause the physician to be terminated from a panel. Such an action therefore would have a detrimental effect on the physician's income. If the physician has been removed from one panel, the effect could snowball and the physician could find himself locked out of many panels. Such a situation would ultimately lead to the collapse of the physician's practice.

Malpractice Risks

Although medical risk management is no longer about medical malpractice, the reader should not get the impression that reducing the risk of medical malpractice is no longer important. Malpractice claims can have adverse consequences beyond the payment by the malpractice carrier.

For example, an adverse malpractice ruling can result in an increase in malpractice premiums, nonrenewal by the malpractice carrier, and difficulty in getting replacement insurance. Although such results are not likely following one claim, they may be more likely with one large payout or several small payouts. Also, an adverse malpractice claim can result in collateral consequences, as already discussed. Therefore, risk management still encompasses reducing malpractice risk.

New Practice Risks

It seems that the potential liability associated with medical practice is limitless, since the following three additional risks have recently been identified.

[A] Expert Witness Risks

In the past, a physician expert witness for the plaintiff was merely an opposing opinion by a learned and/or like colleague. Today, it is becoming a risk management minefield because the AMA and other groups are urging state medical licensing boards to police expert witnesses, which might require that expert testimony be considered the practice of medicine. This seems especially true with the American Association of Neurological Surgeons (AANS) based in Rolling Meadows, Illinois. Currently, a member of the AANS can file a complaint against any fellow member for testimony as either an expert witness for the plaintiff or defense witness for the doctor. A committee of four then reviews the court records and requires the accuser to face the accused in a formal review. Sanctions range from 3 months to a year, to complete expulsion from the association. In the past 20 years, the program has reviewed 27 cases, all involving plaintiff testimony. One led to expulsion and 10 to suspension.

Since 2001, the courts have begun to take the AANS process seriously. After years of operations without strong legal backing, the program was upheld by the Seventh Circuit Court of Appeals in Chicago by a neurosurgeon whom the group suspended in 1997. So always remember, if you testify falsely or too far from the norm, you may be at risk.

[B] Peer Review Risks

The Center for Peer Review Justice is a group of physicians, podiatrists, dentists, and osteopaths who have witnessed the perversion of medical peer review by malice and bad faith. Similar to the AANS, they have seen the statutory immunity, which is provided to "peers" for the purposes of quality assurance and credentialing, used as a cover to allow those "peers" to ruin careers and reputations to further their own, usually monetary, agenda of destroying the competition. Therefore, the group is dedicated to the exposure, conviction, and sanction of doctors and affiliated hospitals, HMOs, medical boards, and other such institutions that would use peer review as a weapon to unfairly destroy other professionals. PeerReview.org is a rallying point and resource center for any medical professional who finds himself or herself in the midst of an unfair and bad faith attack by unethical, malicious "peers."

[C] On-Call Risks

Being on call is getting more expensive these days as physicians are electing not to take this responsibility because of decreased reimbursement rates. Others opt out because of a desire to spend more time with family or because of scheduling conflicts. Whatever the reason, there is a growing revolt of specialists against hospital on-call duties that threatens to violate federal law and to make hospitals lose their status as trauma centers. Specialties most likely to refuse include plastic surgery; ear, nose, and throat; psychiatry; neurosurgery; ophthalmology; and orthopedics.

Refusing to respond to assigned call is a violation of federal law and carries fines of as much as $50,000 per case. In contrast, refusing to sign up for call does not violate the law, and more physicians are taking this option. The problem is especially acute in California, where hospitals are combating the issue by increasing compensation, reporting refusing physicians to the authorities, or threatening to remove them from staff completely. In turn, doctors are fighting back with lawsuits.

Education Debt Load Risks

Managed care is a prospective payment method by which medical care is delivered regardless of the quantity or frequency of service, for a fixed payment, in the aggregate. Among the many reasons that doctors are financially unhappy, some might even say desperate, is that a staggering medical student loan debt burden of $100,000 to $250,000 is not unusual for new practitioners. For example, the federal Health Education Assistance Loan (HEAL) program reported that for the year 2002–2003, student numbers and default totals included the following:

- Allopathic medicine 194, $20,495,446
- Chiropractic 926, $74,781,238
- Clinical psychology 40, $3,051,546
- Dentistry 342, $40,158,139
- Health administration 4, $285,543
- Optometry 29, $2,481,808

- Osteopathy 39, $4,988,389
- Pharmacy 33, $1,320,457
- Podiatry 127, $17,797,564
- Public health 7, $569,733
- Veterinary medicine 1, $32,602
- **Total for all disciplines: 1,742, $165,962,465**

   Source: www.defaulteddocs@hrsa.gov

Suggestions to Help Avoid Medical or Legal Risks

"Will the defendant please rise." These words should strike terror in all that hear them. By taking certain measures now, one can hopefully avoid hearing them. There are actions that can be taken by the practitioner now in an attempt to limit charges of fraud. They include an awareness of the statistics that third-party payers have about billing patterns, changing certain outlying patterns, and changing questionable documentation. Here are some positive defensive steps to take.

[A] Statistical Analysis and Fraud Investigations

To determine where an audit is likely to take place, one only needs to find out "where the money is," to quote noted bank robber Willie Sutton. Luckily, the federal government has provided adequate statistics so that the provider can determine risk, at least to a certain extent. Whether you are charged with health-care fraud first depends upon whether you are audited and upon the results of that audit.

The Health Care Financing Agency (HCFA) compiles data concerning fee charges and payments by all physicians. These data are broken down into various categories, such as by current procedural terminology (CPT) code, physician specialty, and state. Each and every physician should obtain a copy of this report and review it thoroughly. This information is available through HFCA or can be downloaded from its Internet website (http://www.hcfa.gov). The report contains valuable yearly statistical information concerning the rendering of services to Medicare beneficiaries. By comparing the statistics of this report with the statistics of your office, you can determine your risk of an audit.

Since the likelihood of an audit is dependent upon "where the money is," the nationwide average and the placement of your state in the table can indicate the likelihood of your being audited. Therefore the risks are that many physicians in high reimbursement states will be audited and few physicians in low reimbursement states will be audited. This is not as arbitrary as it may seem. There must be a reason why the average physician's Medicare charge in one state is higher than that of the national average. Unfortunately, only an audit will determine the reason why, whether the reason is due to valid treatments or health-care fraud.

These statistics are available to Medicare. Since "knowledge is power," you should familiarize yourself with the data that Medicare will use in targeting audit candidates. By knowing where a likely audit will take place, the practitioner can alter procedures and policies to ensure that he or she has the ability to withstand an audit.

[B] The Bell-Shaped Normalization Curve

Although a bell-shaped normalization curve will not ensure that you will not be audited, it can go a long way to disprove any intent to defraud a third-party payer. Understanding your options is the first step in visualizing the bell curve.

There are five new patient E/M codes (99201, 99202, 99203, 99204, 99205) and five established patient E/M codes (99211, 99212, 99213, 99214, 99215). A normal bell curve for most physicians would probably see most of the visits spread fairly evenly over the different levels of codes of each group, with a smaller amount in the level 1 and 5 codes.

You can use your computer to evaluate whether your CPT codes, especially the E/M codes and the other codes all fall within a bell curve. If these codes do not fall within a bell curve, then you should consider whether to adjust your coding patterns to bring them into a bell curve. Staying within the bell curve is a prudent defensive step.

[C] Appropriate Contracts

The first and most obvious step that every provider should take is the one that is most often skipped. The provider should read every managed care contract. Most providers simply sign and return every contract that comes across their desk. In recent years, with so much of the population participating in some form of managed care, many providers feel that they have no choice but to sign the contract. Remember that even if the terms are not negotiable, you still have a choice of not signing the contract. If you do sign the contract, you should fully understand the risks that you are undertaking. It is okay to assume a risk, but only if you understand the risk you are assuming and are willing to assume that risk.

It is often not reasonable to expect that the provider will fully understand the import of many of the clauses in current managed care contracts. For that reason, it is prudent to have an attorney review every contract that you intend to sign. Although it costs more initially to pay legal fees to review the contract, it could potentially save a lot of problems and money at a later date.

Once you become aware of a risk or a clause in the managed care contract that is contrary to your interests, your first defensive step is to attempt to negotiate the clause out of the contract. Unfortunately, the individual provider has very little leverage in negotiating such contracts, and the clause is likely to remain.

The *next defensive step* to take is to *"just say no!"* Many readers will balk at that statement and will declare: "I don't have a choice. If I don't sign the contract, I will not have any patients!" *The point is that you do have a choice.* If you choose to sign the contract, then what becomes important is what you do after you sign the contract.

If you choose to sign the contract, then you should sign the contract in the name of your professional corporation and as an agent of your professional corporation *(i.e., do not sign the contract in your personal capacity).* By signing the contract on behalf of your corporation, your liability (in most cases) becomes limited to your equity in the corporation.

Unfortunately, the usual method of protection for the practicing physician, the use of the corporate form of business, is usually no benefit when signing managed care contracts, because most managed care companies credential the individual physician and hence require that the individual physician and not the professional corporation sign the contract. This puts all of the physician's personal assets at risk.

Nonetheless, the provider should attempt to sign all such contracts in the name of the corporation. Some contracts are likely to be accepted by the managed care company. When the company requires the provider to sign in his or her individual capacity, then the provider can make the decision at that time.

It is important to realize that the risks delineated in this chapter apply not only to affluent physicians, but also to any physician who signs a managed care contract. A typical example resonates when the provider requests legal analysis of the contract and is quoted a fee for this professional service. More often than not, the health-care provider will reject this as costing too much, yet in reality, the fee, when juxtaposed to the fees charged for medical services, is generally fair and equitable. A young physician with unpaid student debt load that finds himself or herself on the wrong end of a Hold Harmless agreement with a managed care company may find himself or herself forced into bankruptcy.

[D] Practicing Bare

Many providers in practice would not think of "practicing bare." In the past, the term *practicing bare* meant that the provider did not have malpractice insurance. Current managed care contracts often require that the provider not only have certain limits of malpractice, but also that the provider furnish the company with evidence of such insurance. Therefore, many providers are under the impression that they are not practicing bare.

As can be seen from the preceding example clauses, most providers are in effect practicing bare. Most providers have no protection from adverse results arising out of a Hold Harmless Clause in an agreement. Most malpractice insurance companies do not provide such coverage. If your malpractice insurance company does not provide coverage for such events, it is incumbent upon you and your associations to lobby the malpractice insurance carriers to provide such coverage. An additional rider, at an additional premium, for Hold Harmless coverage would help the practitioner sleep better at night.

The first question that the provider should ask is "Would I consider practicing without malpractice insurance?" If the answer to that question is "no," then the next question that the provider should ask is "Why am I assuming the risk under the Hold Harmless Clause?" If the provider cannot provide a lucent answer to that question (stating "I have no choice" is not a lucent answer), then the provider should not sign the managed care contract.

Nonetheless, if the provider has signed managed care contracts, then the provider should understand that he or she is practicing bare and should take steps to reduce his or her exposure. In effect, the provider should attempt to become "judgment proof." Such a step does present its own risks.

Ultimately, the first step for every physician who signs a managed care contract with a Hold Harmless agreement is to read the contract and then consult an attorney or other professional. Plaintiff attorneys are beginning to make inroads in suing managed care companies. The managed care attorneys foresaw such events and provided protection for the company in the contracts most providers have signed.

As plaintiffs become successful in suing and recovering from managed care companies, those companies are going to seek indemnity from the provider. Unless providers protect themselves, they are likely to become a collateral casualty of events. The current practice of medicine presents risks to the provider. The provider may not be able to insure against these risks and therefore should take defensive steps to avoid future problems.

[E] Staff Education and Training

The medical staff is an extension of the physician. As already discussed, the physician can become vicariously liable for staff transgressions. Furthermore, several federal regulations, including HIPAA and OSHA, have specific staff training requirements. Failure to provide the required training subjects the physician not only to the risk of employee transgression, but also to the risk of administrative discipline for failure to conduct proper training of staff.

[F] Elimination of Risky Treatments

One of the methods most often overlooked in malpractice risk management is an evaluation of the risk–reward ratio of treating certain patients or performing certain surgical procedures. Managed care has effectively reduced the reimbursement of treatments and surgeries across the board. In the past, the physician could demand a reasonable fee for the risk involved. Now, that fee is determined by someone other than the physician. Although the resource based value (RBV) includes a malpractice component, sometimes that component does not adequately reflect the risk of certain procedures or the increased risk of certain patients.

Therefore, physicians should evaluate their own practice and identify those procedures and those patient types that carry a high risk of malpractice for which the physician is not adequately reimbursed. Physicians then should tailor their practice so that they no longer provide those services. The revenue lost will be worth the risk of the malpractice suit and the collateral consequences.

This is simply the unintended consequence of insurance companies and other managers reducing the physicians' reimbursement. If the reward is high enough, people will take the risk. If the reward is reduced and the risk remains the same, fewer people will be willing to engage in that behavior—simple free market economics. A physician need not feel bad for turning away patients or dropping certain procedures from his or her practice. That is simply part of risk management.

Conclusion

Medical risk management is no longer just about medical malpractice; it has not been for some time now, despite the recent resurgence of liability fears. In fact, since most practicing physicians have malpractice insurance, a malpractice suit should be viewed as a mere inconvenience and the practitioner should realize that the lawsuit is mainly about someone else's money.

A shift in thought paradigm is needed. The medicolegal landscape has changed. The physician in practice today is faced with many legal challenges that have the potential to destroy the medical practice and the individual's personal assets. Therefore, every practice should have a qualified attorney on retainer. The legal risks are only going to increase!

Additional Readings

1. DeMatti, TF: Team players. New Medicare rules and expanded physician assistant roles. *Modern Physician,* October 1998.
2. Dunevitz, B: NCQA watchdog tactics assess health plan's performance. *MGMA Update,* January 1999.
3. Fenton, CF: Medical fraud and anti-trust compliance. In Marcinko, DE: *Profit Maximization for Physicians.* Anadem Publishing, Columbus, Ohio, 1998.
4. Hetico, HR, and Marcinko, DE: Reimbursement support services in medicine. In Marcinko, DE: *Profit Maximization for Physicians.* Anadem Publishing, Columbus, Ohio, 1998.
5. Moore, PL: Compliance must be done. *MGMA Update,* January 1999.
6. Warn, BA, and Woodcock, E: Operating policies and procedures for medical practice. *MGMA* no. 5052 (1999).

Websites

The following URL addresses have also been found to contain worthwhile medical risk management information:

- www.achpr.gov
- www.mgma.com
- www.NCQA.gov

Chapter 8

Sexual Harrassment Risks in Medical Practice

(He Said, She Said . . . There Is No Quid Pro Quo)

Vicki L. Buba

The medical workplace has changed enormously over the past several years as a result of—and in response to—sexual harassment issues. Consequently, all physician employers today must not only know the law, they must know how to investigate allegations—how to recognize and prevent harassment; how to handle claims; and, how to see to it that employees are trained and fully aware of every key aspect of the issue.

www.FedPubSeminars.com

The courts have defined sexual harassment as unwelcome sexual advances, requests for sexual favors, and other verbal or physical conduct of a sexual nature when:

1. Submission to such conduct is an explicit or implicit term or condition of employment;

2. Submission to such conduct is used as the basis for a favorable employment decision or the employee's rejection of such conduct is used as the basis for an adverse employment decision; or

3. Such conduct unreasonably interferes with an employee's work or creates an intimidating, hostile, or offensive working environment.[1]

This definition, although accurate from a legal perspective, offers little or no guidance to a physician or other employer who is trying to articulate to professional or nonprofessional employees what behavior is prohibited and what is acceptable. Unfortunately, there is no clear-cut line to provide an answer to the relevant question: what specific acts are classified as sexual harassment?

Of greater interest to many small employers, such as physicians and health-care professionals, is under what circumstances the doctor-employer can be held liable if an employee claims she has been sexually harassed.[2]

Preferential Treatment

The most easily recognized sexual harassment occurs when a doctor, medical office, or other supervisor offers an employee a raise or promotion in exchange for sexual favors or when a supervisor demotes or fires an employee who refuses a request for sexual favors. This type of harassment has been referred to as *quid pro quo harassment.*

Over the past decade, a great deal of publicity has been given to this type of behavior. As a result, most employers fully understand the perils of the office romance, and little commentary is necessary. Suffice it to say that it is never acceptable for any doctor or supervisor to offer an employee job-related rewards in exchange for sexual favors. If a supervisor engages in such behavior and the employee complains, it is highly likely that the employer will be liable for sexual harassment.

Hostile Medical Office Work Environment

Less obvious, and the basis for the majority of the sexual harassment suits brought today, is the area of sexual harassment referred to as "hostile work environment." A hostile work environment claim results from any conduct, verbal or physical, that embarrasses, degrades, offends, or shows hostility toward an individual or a group of individuals because of their gender. Harassing conduct may include gender-related slurs, sexual remarks, negative stereotyping, unwanted touching, or any other type of gender-related behavior that would be offensive to a reasonable person.

It is important to recognize that hostile work environment harassment is merely a subcategory of sexual harassment. It is unnecessary for a physician-employer to become caught up in terminology. Rather, it is important to understand the general characteristics of sexual harassment so that the harassing behavior can be eliminated from the work environment.

Any claim of sexual harassment necessarily involves behavior based on gender, but it does not necessarily involve sexual comments or sexual activity. The behavior may be directed toward a particular individual or a group of individuals. It may involve written or graphic material. It may be actions or comments that create a sexually charged atmosphere. It may be conduct by a supervisor or a coworker. Finally, it can be any type of gender-related behavior that creates an intimidating, hostile, or offensive work environment. The key question in deciding whether behavior is sexually harassing is whether the conduct is offensive and unwelcome and whether it has the purpose or effect of unreasonably interfering with an individual's work performance.

Unreasonable Interference With Work Performance

The most frequently asked question is where the threshold lies for behavior that reaches the level of unreasonable interference with work performance. In other words, what is offensive to the level of interfering, and what is merely annoying? The measure is twofold: how severe is the behavior, and how pervasive is it?

The United States Supreme Court has stated that the behavior must be "sufficiently severe or pervasive" so as to interfere with work performance, but what does "sufficiently" mean? It is actually a test of weight and can be viewed as a continuum of behavior. At one end of the continuum, a single episode may be "sufficient" if that single act is extremely severe. For example, if a doctor or supervisor forces sexual contact with a subordinate, such as genital fondling or sexual intercourse, that single event will likely be sufficient to constitute sexual harassment.

At the other end of the continuum is behavior that, taken in isolation, appears innocent or innocuous, such as a casual remark. Doctor Arni says to Employee Betty, "Nice dress—sexy." Obviously, the comment is inappropriate in the workplace, and potentially, Employee Betty might be offended or embarrassed by the comment, but if that single comment is the only event that occurs, it would not be sufficient to create a hostile work environment because it is unlikely that this single remark will interfere with Employee Betty's work performance.

Such is the analysis a court will employ in deciding whether behavior is sexually harassing. In the context of the continuum, the court will ask how severe the behavior was and how often it occurred. Behavior that is less severe but that occurs on a repetitive or frequent basis is likely to create a hostile work environment. Similarly, behavior that occurs on an infrequent basis but is exceptionally crude and offensive is likely to be sufficient to interfere with an employee's work performance and thus form the basis for a claim.

Two-Pronged Test for Offensive Behavior

One question that often arises is, How can anyone ever know for sure what behavior is offensive and what is not? After all, some language may highly offend a person of extreme sensibilities but may be everyday language to someone else.

To resolve this issue, courts have established a two-pronged test for offensive behavior. That test asks first whether the conduct was severe and pervasive enough to create a hostile and abusive work environment and then whether this victim subjectively perceived the environment to be hostile or abusive.[3] In other words, would a "reasonable" person be offended, and was this particular person offended? Both questions must be answered yes before the behavior will be classified as sexual harassment.

Examples of Sexual Harassment

Using the continuum approach and the two-pronged test, let's examine several examples of behavior and see which might be considered sexual harassment.

[A] Compliments

Simple compliments are part of every day's social interaction, but under certain circumstances they may create a hostile work environment. Consider the following examples:

> **Example 1:** "You look nice today. That dress really accents your dark hair."

This comment is simply a pleasant remark. Even if the employee to whom it was directed was offended or felt it was too personal, it would not rise to the level of sexual harassment since a reasonable person would not find it offensive.

> **Example 2:** "You look really nice today. With your dark hair, that color really makes you look sexy. You ought to be a model."

Obviously, this comment is more personal than the first. The overtone is that the employee to whom the remark was directed is sexually attractive. Thus, in deciding whether the comment is sexually harassing, a little more analysis is necessary.

The first question is whether a reasonable person would be uncomfortable or embarrassed by such remarks. The personal nature of this comment makes it more likely that a reasonable person would be offended, particularly if such comments were made on a repeated basis. This example illustrates the fluid nature of the continuum already described. The comment is not extremely severe, but certainly is inappropriate for a medical or other office environment. Consequently, if there were several occurrences of this or similar comments, the behavior would likely be determined to be sexually harassing.[4]

> **Example 3:** "Nice boobs! Are they real? Come on over here so I can really check out your tits."

This comment certainly falls further down the continuum as to the degree of severity. Such a comment is not only inappropriate but also highly offensive and would warrant disciplinary action. One occasion may not reach the level of interfering with work performance, but very few repetitions such as this would be necessary to reach the threshold for sexual harassment.

[B] Sexist Words

Often certain words are associated with one gender or another and, if used repeatedly, may form the basis for a sexual harassment claim.

Example 1: "You are such a bitch."

There is no question that the term *bitch* refers to a female. However, in today's society, this term has become so commonplace that it is often accepted in conversation. Consequently, use of this term, if there were no other events, would likely not be sufficient to constitute sexual harassment.

Example 2: "All women are c____s and don't deserve to be treated with respect."

Again, the referenced word refers to females only. However, the crudeness of the language places this event further along the continuum in terms of severity. This particular comment becomes even more offensive because it is combined with a stereotyping remark about women. For all of these reasons, it is likely that a few repetitions such as this would be sufficient to constitute sexual harassment and to create a hostile work environment. Accordingly, such language should be prohibited in the workplace.

Example 3: "Men are such idiots. I guess that's because they let their little head do all their thinking."

There are several problems with this remark. First, there is a not so subtle reference to the male anatomy. There is also the blanket assumption that not only are all men less intelligent than women, but that the reason for this anomaly is that men are more interested in sex than in intelligent pursuit.

Again, one comment such as this is probably not sufficient to form a claim. However, in combination with other behavior or similar behavior on a repeated basis, a claim might be asserted.

[C] Office Jokes

For decades, joke telling has been part of our social interaction, both on and off the job. Over the last several years, thanks in part to Bill Clinton, political jokes have taken a turn to include sexual overtones. What happens when these jokes are introduced into the working environment? The criterion remains the same: would a reasonable person be offended by the jokes, and was the complaining individual offended?

When an employee complains that office jokes are too "off-color," such that they are embarrassing and interfere with work performance, the defense is nearly always the same: "It was just a joke; I didn't mean anything." However, such a defense will not be effective.

Remember that the basic definition of sexual harassment is any conduct that has the purpose *or effect* of interfering with work performance. Motive, or lack thereof, is irrelevant. Jokes of a sexual nature that are offensive and embarrassing can create a hostile work environment, *even if the jokester harbored no intent to do so.*

Does this mean an employee cannot tell jokes at work? Of course not. It does mean that if any employee tells jokes that might offend, the employee had better be sure of his audience. Two friends kidding around does not mean that one of the friends can suddenly decide to complain of sexual harassment and prevail. However, if one of the parties does decide to complain, an employer may have problems defending the action if the jokes are of a sexual nature and do not belong in the workplace.

It is important to understand a few other aspects of office joke telling. The first is that offensive language and embarrassing jokes may create a hostile work environment, even if two people voluntarily engage in the conduct. The hostile work environment occurs when the off-color jokes are inadvertently overheard by others who find the jokes embarrassing or offensive. Of course, the solution to this potential problem is to keep all such joking out of the office, hospital, or work environment.

Another pitfall of sex jokes may be seen when an individual brings a cartoon to the office and gives it to a friend who finds it highly amusing. That person makes a copy and passes it on to a third person, who also finds it amusing, not offensive. This chain continues until eventually the cartoon comes into the hands of people who are not so amused. Depending on the crudeness (or severity) and the frequency with which such conduct occurs, a hostile work environment could evolve, even though it started as two friends engaging in what they perceived to be harmless fun.

[D] Touching

Touching is an area subject to various interpretations by different individuals. Some people simply do not like touching of any type. Others have difficulty talking to another without some touching. Like compliments, touching can be analyzed along a continuum to see if it is sexually harassing.

> **Example 1:** A dentist walks over and says "good job" and simultaneously pats the employee on the shoulder.

Such touching cannot rise to the level of sexual harassment because no reasonable person would consider such conduct offensive.

> **Example 2:** A female internist says, "Nice tie; you always wear such professional-looking clothes." The comment is combined with the woman fondling the tie and then rubbing the male employee's arm.

The comment sounds harmless, but combined with the touching described, it takes on a personal feeling and becomes more intrusive. Although not extremely severe, if such conduct occurs on a regular basis, it is likely to make the male employee uncomfortable and create a hostile work environment.

> **Example 3:** A chiropractor employer walks over and says, "You look tired; let me give you a massage."

This conduct definitely has a personal overtone and is inappropriate in the workplace. The problem is that even if the employee is uncomfortable with such touching, she may not feel comfortable telling her doctor employer to stop. Consequently, the conduct can recur, resulting in the employee feeling very oppressed or uncomfortable about what goes on in the workplace, and eventually she may complain of sexual harassment.

> **Example 4:** A male podiatrist says "good job" and pats the female employee on the rear.

Again, she may not feel comfortable telling the supervisor to stop. However, the personal nature of the conduct can create a hostile work environment if the behavior is repetitive.

[E] Invitations

Employees often ask if the state of current sexual harassment law means there can no longer be any romance or dating between persons who work together. Of course there can. Employees and even health-care supervisors and subordinates are still free to engage in consensual relationships. However, this area warrants a few pertinent comments.

[1] WHEN "YES" BECOMES "NO"

Two individuals may engage in a romantic relationship without any legal consequences. However, if one of the individuals becomes disenchanted, the rules change. Any further pursuit, which may be unwanted, can create a hostile work environment, regardless of what the previous relationship was like.

[2] A SENSE OF OBLIGATION

Often, when an employee asserts a claim of sexual harassment against a doctor supervisor, the defense will be "But it was mutual. She participated voluntarily." The employee will respond by saying "I didn't feel like I had any choice; he was my boss." This issue has come before the courts on many occasions, and the U.S. Supreme Court has resolved it by affirming that a plaintiff who voluntarily participates may still have a claim. The test is whether the conduct was unwelcome, not whether participation was voluntary.[5]

Obviously, a doctor who engages in office romance had better be sure the other party's participation is voluntary and not something that stems from a sense of fear or obligation. Under any circumstances, a supervisor who engages in such relationships in the workplace runs the risk of having a sexual harassment complaint filed against him.

[3] LISTENING FOR CLUES

Another word of advice, particularly to physicians, is to be perceptive in listening to the response to an invitation. An employee may feel nervous about refusing an invitation from a medical supervisor, but may still give hints as to her feelings.

For example, the doctor supervisor asks, "How about dinner Friday?" and the employee responds, "No thanks, I already have plans."

The following week, the doctor supervisor again asks, "How about dinner Friday?" and the employee responds, "I'd love to, but I'm visiting a sick friend."

The following week, the doctor supervisor again asks, "How about dinner Friday?" and the employee responds, "Sorry, I have to stay home and sort my sock drawer."

Consider what is going on. The employee has not said, "Please don't ask me out; I don't want to go out with you." However, the message should be just as clear as if she had.

[F] Demands or Threats

Demands for sexual favors, sometimes combined with threats if sexual favors are not forthcoming, often form the basis for sexual harassment complaints. If the demands or threats are made by supervisors, there is no question that such conduct is sexually harassing. However, similar behavior occurring between coworkers may also form the basis for a claim.

An employee who repeatedly invites another employee on dates sets up a hostile work environment if the second employee refuses. In some cases, the invitations may be combined with following the employee home or giving gifts to persuade the employee to change her mind. In extreme cases, it may be combined with threats against the invitee if she does not agree to some relationship.

As an employer-physician, if you learn of such a situation, it is imperative that it be stopped. If knowledge of the threats or persistent unwanted demands is ignored, you will be held liable if a claim is raised.

Gender-Based Animosity

A sexually hostile work environment often results from comments or actions that contain some sort of sexual connotation. However, this cause of action stems from actions that are based on gender. Consequently, sexual content is not required. Acts that fall into this category are easily recognized because they are generally based on negative stereotyping.

> **Example 1:** "Women are not as intelligent as men, so men make better physical therapy department managers."

Obviously untrue, this comment demonstrates a bias against women and, if often repeated, certainly is likely to interfere with a female's work performance. Notice that the characteristics of gender-based animosity are much like those of ordinary gender discrimination. Consequently, it would not be uncommon for a woman to bring both a hostile work environment claim and a discrimination claim. Since they both arise out of the same body of law, either claim could be viable.

> **Example 2:** "I don't understand why she works in this office. Women belong at home, taking care of the house and raising kids. They don't belong in the workplace."

Again, there is no reference to any sexual terms, but there definitely is an overtone of gender bias. These two examples are obvious ones. Consider the following example of gender bias that might not be so obvious.

> **Example 3:** "We have an opening for a computer medical technician. Since men tend to be better at wiring and configuring a computer, let's hire a man."

Obviously, gender has nothing to do with technical ability. Does this mean that if an employer hires a man, the decision will be challenged? Certainly, if the hiring is accompanied by statements like these. However, the best way to avoid lawsuits in this area is to refrain from making remarks and to utilize neutral testing procedures to screen candidates.

Same-Sex Harassment

Before 1998, courts around the country were split on the issue of whether sexual harassment claims could be asserted only if the behavior occurred between a male and a female. Some courts held that sexual harassment can occur only if the harasser and the victim are of different sexes. Other courts held that sexual harassment is illegal, even if both parties are of the same sex. Still other courts held that sexual harassment between two persons of the same sex can occur only if one of the parties is a homosexual.

In 1998, the U.S. Supreme Court settled the issue in its ruling in *Oncale v. Sundowner Offshore Services, Inc.* when it ruled that sexual harassment is behavior based on gender and it applies whether the parties are different sexes or the same sex.[6] The Court also said that the relevant question was whether there was a hostile work environment because of gender, and, therefore, the sexual orientation of the parties was not to be considered.

With this ruling, the Court expanded the body of law previously delineated as sexual harassment. The ruling affirmed that the test was whether the behavior was offensive and whether it was sufficiently severe or pervasive to be actionable. The Court emphasized that male-on-male horseplay is not prohibited. However, when it rises to the level of more serious acts, such as genital grabbing, threatened sexual acts, or severe language that offends or frightens the victim to the extent that it interferes with the victim's work performance, it is prohibited under the law governing sexual harassment.

Doctor-Employer Liability

A key question is under what circumstances the physician or other employer will be liable for sexual harassment in the workplace. The rules vary according to whether the harassing party is a supervisor or a nonsupervisor.

[A] Liability for Supervisor's Harassment

For many years, the courts held that when the harasser is also a supervisor, the employer will be absolutely liable. This liability is based on the premise that a doctor, or other employer, must have notice of the harassment in order to be liable and that since supervisors are agents of the employer, there is notice. In 1998, the U.S. Supreme Court clarified the employer's liability, and although the Court said that employers are not absolutely liable, the course prescribed for avoiding liability placed a high burden on the employer.

The Court outlined an affirmative defense that would permit the employer to avoid or limit liability. An affirmative defense exists when the employer exercised reasonable care to prevent and promptly correct harassing behavior and when the victim unreasonably failed to take advantage of any preventive or corrective opportunities to avoid harm.[7]

What does this mean in everyday language? It means the physician-employer must have a strong policy defining and prohibiting sexual harassment. It must be adequately disseminated to all employees, and it must include a reporting procedure. It is important that the policy specifically identify the individuals to whom an employee may address a complaint and also include alternate reporting procedures for cases when the harasser is the supervisor of the complaining individual.

It is not sufficient to merely have a policy in place and to disseminate it to employees. In addition to developing the policy, the physician-employer must be prepared to uniformly enforce the policy once it has been established.

[B] Reporting Procedure

It is also essential that the doctor-employer have some procedure in place for investigating sexual harassment complaints. As previously noted, the efficiency with which an employer investigates a complaint will play into the court's decision as to whether the employer is able to take advantage of the affirmative defense. This means that you should take all claims seriously. The result of an investigation may be a report back to the complaining individual that there is no evidence to substantiate the complaint but that all individuals involved, including the alleged harasser, have been warned that such behavior will not be tolerated and will be the subject of disciplinary action.

Disciplinary Actions

Many events may contribute to a sexual harassment claim, even though each of them standing alone may be insufficient to prevail in a court of law. However, because the threshold for a sexual harassment claim falls in a gray area, employers have the right to protect themselves by establishing rules that may be more stringent than those imposed by a court. Many doctors and employers adopt a "zero tolerance" policy. Such a policy means that when any employee engages in the behavior previously described, that employee will be disciplined, even for a single incident.

The important point to remember is that the discipline must be uniformly imposed. In other words, an employer cannot discipline one employee for telling off-color jokes and then ignore the same behavior by another employee because "he was only joking around." Disciplinary action may be something as simple as a verbal conversation explaining to the alleged harasser that these things do offend some people and the harasser should avoid such behavior in the future. Obviously, more serious violations may warrant more serious disciplinary action, up to and including termination of employment.

The bottom line is that doctor-employers must be able to show they have done everything within their power to prevent sexual harassment and that when complaints are made, they have immediately investigated and, when necessary, taken corrective action. This is the only way in which a doctor-employer may avoid liability for sexual harassment complaints.

Tangible Employment Action

If harassment results in a tangible employment action (e.g., discharge, demotion, or undesirable reassignment), and the harasser is a supervisor, the affirmative defense is not available.[8] A tangible employment action does not necessarily mean the employee has lost some economic benefit. It could also mean a loss of status, loss of promotion opportunities, or loss of anything perceived to be a benefit of the job.

Further, threats of loss of tangible benefits may form the basis for a hostile work environment claim, even if there is no follow-through with the threatened action.[9] An example of this would be when a doctor or supervisor continuously threatens to fire or demote a female employee because "as a woman, she's not smart enough to do the job." The threat itself is sufficient; no action is required.

Punitive Damages

Punitive damages are sums of money that are awarded to a plaintiff to punish the defendant. The sum of money awarded relates to the assets of the defendant and the need to punish that defendant, rather than to the economic loss of the plaintiff.

Until recently, many courts felt that although an employer could be held vicariously liable for damages resulting from a sexual harassment complaint, punitive damages would not be appropriate. However, the U.S. Supreme Court addressed the issue in 1999 and stated that punitive damages may be imposed if the conduct is "that of a managerial agent."[10] Punitive damages do not require a showing of egregious or outrageous discrimination. However, punitive damages will not be imposed when the decisions of the managerial agent are contrary to the employer's good faith efforts to comply with the laws governing sexual harassment.

The question becomes, who is a managerial agent? A court will look at all of the circumstances to determine if the individual is a "managerial agent." Questions a court will ask may include the following: What is the supervisory responsibility of the individual? How much power does the individual have to enforce company policies? How much authority does the individual have to hire and fire employees? and other similar questions. In a small medical office, an office manager who has merely a title and no real managerial duties will likely not be deemed to be a managerial agent. Conversely, a doctor in an office, even if he or she does not ordinarily hire and fire staff members, may likely have sufficient authority and power to be deemed a managerial agent of the group.

Financial and Economic Costs

There are positive reasons to consider your medical practice climate. Preventing discrimination and harassment boosts worker morale and productivity. But there are also costly negatives you want to avoid: discrimination and harassment lawsuits cost companies more and more each year. A study released in January 2002 by Jury Verdict Research, Inc., found the following:

- The national median jury award for employment-practice liability cases, which include discrimination and retaliation claims, rose 44 percent—from $151,000 to $218,000—between 1999 and 2000. The median award had stayed level at about $150,000 between 1997 and 1999.

- Of all discrimination types, age discrimination plaintiffs won the most money from 1994 to 2000.

- The overall median jury award in discrimination cases was $150,000 for the 7-year span.

The study also showed an increase in public awareness and jury sympathy for the plaintiffs in discrimination cases:

- In 2000, 62 percent of plaintiffs in sex discrimination cases (including sexual harassment) won their cases, compared with only 43 percent in 1994.

- Sixty-seven percent of race discrimination plaintiffs won their cases in 2000, compared with 50 percent in 1994.

A 1999 survey of 496 companies published by the Society for Human Resource Management found the following:

- Sexual harassment complaints increased at those companies by almost 140 percent between 1995 and 1998.
- Small businesses averaged nearly one claim per 100 employees in 1998—five times higher than the rate of one claim per 500 among large businesses.
- Only 51 percent of small businesses said that they offered sexual harassment prevention training, whereas 76 percent of large companies did.

These statistics suggest that whether your medical practice is large or small, you need to take harassment and discrimination prevention training seriously.

Commonsense Approach

This chapter does not begin to cover all of the examples of behavior that may constitute sexual harassment or a hostile work environment. It is, however, intended to illustrate that a physician-employer who wishes to avoid sexual harassment claims will be more successful if he or she exercises common sense in this area. A workplace, even a small doctor's office, should always be viewed as a professional environment. Employees should be viewed as just that. When an individual walks through the office door in the morning, that individual is not a female, not a Jew, not a black, but simply an employee there to do a job. An employer who makes attempts to enforce such an attitude will go far in eliminating sexual harassment in the workplace.

Endnotes

1. See *Meritor Savings Bank, F.S.B. v. Vinson*, 477 U.S. 57 (1986).
2. Laws prohibiting discrimination and sexual harassment apply equally to behavior of men and women. Throughout this chapter, references to "she" can be read as "he or she."
3. See *Harris v. Forklift Systems, Inc.*, 510 U.S. 17 (1993).
4. Of course, this assumes the second prong of the test has been satisfied and that this particular victim is offended or embarrassed.
5. See *Meritor*, 477 U.S. 57 (1986).
6. See *Oncale v. Sundowner Offshore Services, Inc.*, 523 U.S. 75 (1998).
7. *Faragher v. City of Boca Raton*, 524 U.S. 775 (1998).
8. Ibid.
9. *Burlington Industries, Inc., v. Ellerth*, 524 U.S. 742 (1998).
10. *Kolstead v. American Dental Association*, 527 U.S. 526 (1999).

Chapter 9

Medical Office Workplace Violence Risks

(Pondering the Unthinkable . . . Preventing and Planning for the Horrific)

W. Barry Nixon

Violence in the workplace is a serious safety and health issue. Its most extreme form, homicide, is the third leading cause of fatal occupational injury in the United States. According to the Bureau of Labor Statistics Census of Fatal Occupational Injuries (CFOI), there were 639 workplace homicides in 2001 in the United States, out of a total of 8,786 fatal work injuries. A total of 2,886 work-related fatalities resulted from the events of September 11th. Excluding these fatalities, the overall workplace fatality count was 5,900 for 2001.

www.OSHA-slc.gov

Medical office workplace violence is known to be a serious problem in many countries in the industrialized world, and research by the World Health Organization indicates that violence in the health-care workplace is actually a global phenomenon. Crossing borders, cultures, work settings, and occupational groups, violence in the health-care workplace is at very high level. The new research shows that more than half of the health sector personnel surveyed had experienced at least one incident of physical or psychological violence in the year previous to the study.[1]

Introduction to Medical Workplace Violence

An October 2003 survey of doctors conducted by the Health Policy and Economic Research Unit of the British Medical Association (BMA) also reported that half of all

151

doctors believe that violence is a problem in the workplace. Of the almost 1,000 doctors who responded to the survey, the key findings were the following:

- Violence is a problem in the workplace for almost half of doctors.
- One in three respondents had experienced some form of violence in the workplace in the last year; this was the case for both hospital doctors and general practitioners.
- The majority of violent incidents took place in the doctors' office or hospital ward. Among general practitioners the majority of incidents took place in the office or waiting room, and for hospital doctors, the most frequently cited location was the hospital ward.
- Among hospital doctors, those working in accident and emergency and psychiatry were more likely to experience patient violence.
- Among doctors who reported some experience of violence, almost all (95 percent) had been the victim of verbal abuse in the past year.
- The main cause of violence was perceived to be health-related problems or personal problems, dissatisfaction with the service provided, and/or drugs or alcohol.

Dr. Brian Patterson, newly elected chairman of the BMA's Northern Ireland Council, summed up the survey findings up by stating, "The findings of these surveys provide us with hard factual evidence of what we knew anecdotally to be the case—that violence in the medical workplace is widespread, all too frequent and on the increase."

Case Example

Interestingly enough, whereas the aforementioned overwhelming research reports the impact of patient violence, another research effort conducted by Australia's Crime, Violence and Injury Lead Program and Institute of Criminology revealed the following about health workers as perpetrators of violence: "In 59% of the responses on the survey nurses and doctors indicated that health workers themselves were perpetrators of aggressive response towards patients."[2]

Additionally, the following case example illustrates a horrific incident in which a medical center employee murdered a doctor.

> At the medical center the problem was work performance. Chen, 42, came to the University of Washington after two years at a residency program at the University of Mississippi. Prior to his arrival, he was a promising scientist, but he began to struggle in one of the nation's most renowned and demanding pathology programs. He became angry and difficult as he was told his work was below average, and engaged in shouting matches with his supervisors. When his supervisors recommended he consider moving to another program or undergo psychological counseling, he grew more upset.

Some pathology colleagues were so scared by Chen that they started locking their doors when he was around. "There was considerable concern and consternation on the part of the department faculty," says John Coombs, associate vice president for medical affairs and associate dean of the medical school. "And there was fear as well."

That increased when department officials learned that Chen was shopping for a gun. Medical residents saw yellow pages turned to gun shops, and even spotted a map to a gun shop on his computer screen. At a meeting in late May, he was asked by department officials and police if he was going to buy a gun, and he said he wanted one for protection. Officials warned Chen that it was illegal to carry a gun on the UW campus. Because Chen had no criminal record or ever made a threat against any specific individual, there was nothing more law enforcement or University officials could do. A UW policeman even saw Chen at a Bellevue gun shop but didn't report it until after the shooting.

Two weeks before his final work-day, Chen's background check was complete and he was cleared to pick up a .357 Glock semi-automatic pistol, which he had purchased for $479. Chen meticulously planned his suicide, and prepared letters to be sent after his death, including one to Haggitt, whom he apparently did not intend to kill. It is possible that Chen changed his mind and decided to kill Haggitt, or perhaps Haggitt tried to intercede and stop Chen's suicide. The medical examiner's report was inconclusive and we will never know what went on behind those locked doors.[3]

Health-Care Workplace Violence Defined

Having established the reality of violence as an issue in the health-care industry, we must define the meaning of workplace violence: "violent acts, including assaults and threats, that occur in, or are related to, the workplace and entail a substantial risk of physical or emotional harm to individuals, or damage to an organization's resources or capabilities." More specifically it includes the following:

- Actual violence that causes or is intended to cause injury or harm to a person or property
- Threatening remarks and/or behavior in which intent to harm is stated or implied or that indicates a lack of respect for the dignity and worth of an individual
- Verbal abuse
- Mobbing, bullying, emotional abuse
- Possession of a weapon while working or on company property

US workplace violence is governed by the Occupational Safety and Health Administration (OSHA), which is a division of the U.S. Department of Labor. Under OSHA's General Duty Clause, employers are required to provide a safe work environment for employees that is free of known hazards. Since workplace violence has been recognized as a "known hazard," the courts have said that conditions constitute a known hazard when they

- Create a "significant risk" to employees in other than "a freakish or utterly implausible concurrence of circumstances"
- Are known to the employer and are considered hazards in the employer's business or industry
- Are ones that the employer can reasonably be expected to prevent

One should be aware that workplace violence is unique as a workplace hazard because, unlike other hazards, it does not involve a work process, but instead an act committed by a person. Workplace violence is committed by a perpetrator, and the following can be perpetrators:

- An individual (stranger) who has no legitimate relationship with an employee or the employer, such as a robber of a convenience store
- An employee or ex-employee
- An individual who is or has been a client, customer, contractor, or vendor or has had a legitimate relationship with the employer
- An individual who has an intimate, family, or other relationship with an employee

Now that we have a common framework for what workplace violence involves, let's turn our attention to the core focus of this chapter: the financial risk management impact that it can have on organizations in the health-care industry.

Financial Risk Management Impact of Workplace Violence

Let's begin with some historical data on the cost of workplace violence.

- In 1995 the National Council of Compensation Insurance found $126 million in workers' compensation claims for workplace violence.[4]
- A study released by the Workplace Violence Research Institute in April 1995 showed that workplace violence actually resulted in a $36 billion annual loss.[5]
- According to the Bureau of Justice Statistics, about 500,000 victims of violent crime in the workplace lose an estimated 1.8 million workdays each year. This presents an astounding $55 million in lost wages for employees, not including days covered by sick and annual leave and a loss of productivity that has direct consequences for an employer's bottom line.[6]
- Lawsuits in the area have been impacting cost substantially. The average out-of-court settlement for this type of litigation approaches $500,000 and the average jury award is $3 million. A few awards have reached as high as $5.49 million.[7]

- For 6 to 18 weeks after an incident happens, there is a 50 percent decrease in productivity and a 20 to 40 percent turnover in employees.[8]
- A Bureau of Justice Statistics Special Report in January 2002 on violence in the workplace shows that nurses are second only to police officers in being physically assaulted on the job. For the period between 1993 and 1999, there were an average of 429,000 cases of violent victimizations per year. These were predominantly assaults reported by nurses.[9]
- Also, the Bureau of Labor Statistics reported a rate of 8.3 assaults per 10,000 hospital workers in 1999. This rate is much higher than the rate of nonfatal assaults for all private sector industries, which is 2 per 10,000 workers.[10]
- According to the 1997 *NIOSH Fact Sheet*—"Violence in the Workplace"—64 percent of all nonfatal assaults occurred in service industries, and of these over 38 percent occurred in health-care-related operations.[11]
- The *Fact Sheet* further reported that 48 percent of nonfatal assaults in the workplace are committed by health-care patients.[12]
- Nonfatal workplace assaults result in more than 876,000 lost workdays and $16 million in lost wages.
- Staff working in psychiatric and long-term care settings are at high risk. A stunning 50 percent of all long-term care staff and 46 to 100 percent of nurses, psychiatrists, and other therapists in psychiatric facilities experience at least one assault during their careers.[13]

The actual cost of workplace violence is very tough to pinpoint because, in most instances, appropriate financial data specific to workplace violence in a given organization are generally not kept.

Thus, at a macroeconomic level it is very hard to clearly track the cost. In addition, multiple variables are involved, including hard and soft cost. Probably the most difficult issue is that companies are reluctant to expose imperfections in their operations, safety procedures, or employee practices. Most firms that experience serious workplace violence incidents want to put a spin on the events to minimize the negative publicity and impact on the business. So the costs are buried in the shuffle to get the event behind them and present the aura of "all is well" and business as usual to avoid spooking their customers and shareholders. An example of a real cost that impacted a medical facility involved OSHA fining a Chicago psychiatric hospital $5,000 and imposing an abatement program to address violence after numerous violent attacks on staff by patients occurred. In contrast, the average cost for a fatal violent incident ranges from $250,000 to $1 million.

Most workplace violence experts agree that serious workplace violence incidents are generally preventable if a company has a progressive and comprehensive workplace violence prevention effort in place. However, even for a firm that practices due diligence, the stark reality is that we cannot predict who will explode, when or where it will happen, and the commensurate outcome. Potential perpetrators don't walk around with a neon sign saying "coming attractions today at 3:00 p.m. in the Medical Center cafeteria." Consequently, we must focus on preparing for an emergency situation, very much like we develop a disaster plan to deal with the unexpected. It is like throwing dice: the only certainty is that a set of numbers will come up, but knowing which numbers will be rolled is impossible. Workplace violence specialists advise that there are important steps organizations can take to improve the "predictability" of violence (see prevention measures later in the chapter); however, in the final analysis workplaces are faced with mitigating as many of the risks that they can identify and hoping they have done enough.

The development of your medical practice, hospital, office, or clinic risk mitigation plan should focus on protecting five key assets: facilities, technology, information, networks, and people. It starts with looking at what could damage any of these assets or seriously prevent the business operations from continuing. This fundamentally means you have to understand the risk and what you can do to prevent the situation from occurring and how to mitigate its effects if it does occur. The final stage involves business impact analysis, which examines the actual financial cost should an event occur that seriously impacts the business.

Assessing the Risk of Workplace Violence

Statistically speaking, for businesses in general, the odds of having a workplace homicide occur at the place of work are remote. In fact, you are more likely to get struck by lightning than to be a victim of workplace homicide. Now before you skip over the rest of the chapter because you consider the risk of homicide at work to be negligible, consider the following:

- During the 1990s, on average, 19 people were murdered at work each week, or close to 1,000 people on an annual basis. In the 21st century the numbers have been 677 (2000), 635 (2001), and 609 (2002).[14]
- The cost of a single homicide at work averages between $250,000 and $1 million when all costs are considered.[15]

This last-mentioned point raises a critical issue that often is overlooked because of the relatively low statistical risk of the occurrence of workplace homicide: the *impact* of such an occurrence. Once a homicide occurs in your workplace, it brings the whole enterprise into the spotlight. Unlike an industrial accident, which statistically has a higher incidence rate, a workplace homicide is newsworthy and will likely result in front page coverage by national newspapers, and in both morning and evening news. In addition, senior executives will be called in to address the press. This increased scrutiny and press coverage, which are generally not positive or desirable, could impact the actual performance of the company's stock and the market's perception of its performance.

A study released by Oxford University and the Sedgwick Group analyzed the impact of catastrophes on shareholder value. The study compared 15 companies that experienced a serious man-made disaster and followed the stock value and trading volume, with somewhat surprising results. A year after the event, some stock prices had actually increased, while other companies lost millions or went out of business entirely. The study reports that there are two elements to the catastrophic impact: "The first is the immediate estimate of the associated economic loss. The second hinges on management's ability to deal with the aftermath." A key factor in how effectively a company recovered was how management reacted. Crisis has a tendency to magnify your strengths and your weaknesses. A comprehensive crisis preparedness plan can help you react to crisis effectively so that you do not end up as a negative example in a similar study someday.

Thus, given a pragmatic assessment of the impact of such an event, it is prudent to not simply dismiss workplace homicide as an event unworthy of investing company resources in because of the low statistical probability. Just think about how much fun it will be explaining to your company president or CEO why you chose to ignore the threat of workplace violence when the company is under siege by the news media, government agencies, attorneys, and community and family members of the victim(s) because you dismissed it as a low risk.

Although this warning may be a bit sobering, the reality is that workplace homicides are only the tip of the iceberg, and a much larger risk lies in nonfatal workplace violence incidents. It has been estimated that annually there are 1.8 million nonfatal incidents reported, and many suspect this prevalence is underreported by approximately 50 percent.[16] Also, these numbers apply to incidents in which there was actually physical contact, including simple assaults (those not involving a weapon), aggravated assaults (those involving a weapon), robberies, thefts, rapes, sexual assaults, and so on. These numbers do not include arguments, threats, harassment, bullying, and intimidation, which are recognized as occurring more frequently. These often less sensational incidents that will never be reported in the media are of the greatest financial risk to the employer.

In addition, it should be noted that the workers who are most exposed to "at risk" behavior are those who have routine contact with the public, exchange money, or work alone or in small numbers late at night or in the early morning, or in high-crime areas. Moreover, the vast majority of murders and assaults in the workplace are committed by strangers.

Contributing Factors to Workplace Violence

In order to fully assess the risk involved with workplace violence, it is important to understand the contributing factors. Once these are known, you can target solutions that are aimed at minimizing or eliminating those factors.

First, it is important to recognize that the likelihood of a violent event occurring is heightened by the presence of these three variables:

1. A stressful event
2. An emotionally charged individual
3. An insensitive, uncaring, inflammatory environment

When these three variables collide, you have a very real and present possibility for violence to occur.

It is important to note that the first variable, a stressful event, is a wild card because what one person views as stressful another takes in stride. At the same time, some events we can clearly predict are likely to induce stress, such as a termination, a bad performance review, a criticism made in front of other people, or a disrespectful or demeaning mode of addressing someone.

Cary Cooper, professor of organizational psychology at the University of Manchester Institute of Science and Technology in northern England, believes the best way to understand and prevent workplace stress is to conduct a stress audit or risk assessment program. "Every organization is different and every job is different. The baseline has to be a systematic diagnosis of what is happening in [individual] companies now and how it can be improved [by interventions]. It is important to develop standards for workplace counseling or stress management training."[17]

Managers, too, must reexamine ingrained beliefs about stress. "It is not enough [for managers] simply to remove the negative [aspects of work]. They must look at the whole experience of the employee—what makes them happy and fulfilled at work as well as angry and frustrated," Cooper says. "They must reinforce the positives—giving regular feedback and showing staff they respect, value and trust them."

In the end, stress management comes down to good management: get it right and you will go a long way toward eliminating stress in the workplace. This should be of concern to U.S. managers, since it is estimated that "stress costs a staggering $300 billion annually to U.S. employers as unemployment rises and companies cut staff in what is euphemistically known as 'down sizing.'"[18]

The second of the three variables, an emotionally charged individual, has to do with the mental and emotional state of a person. If we are observant and knowledgeable regarding what to look for, we can often recognize the early warning signs. Once supervisors recognize the warning signs and are properly trained to intervene, escalation up the aggression scale can likely be interrupted.

The third variable, interestingly enough, focuses on the setting or environment that the person is subjected to. Within an organizational context this means that the organizational culture, management style, ways of treating employees, perceived fairness of the problem resolution processes, and so forth can have a great bearing on either escalating or deescalating potential hostile situations. This reality is generally overlooked by organizations that tend to find it convenient to focus all the attention and responsibility on the individual.

Although there are no clear-cut data that directly establish the cost impact of having a work environment that is perceived as being positive by employees, research does point out that there is a correlation between these positive environments and experiencing fewer incidents of violence.

Focusing on Prevention: The Zero Incidents Approach

In 1998 the Supreme Court determined in *Faragher v. City of Boca Raton* that companies must prevent—not simply react to—a hostile workplace. Thus, the concept of having "zero tolerance" for workplace violence, which focuses on "how the firm will react once violence has occurred," becomes an insufficient approach that needs to evolve to the more progressive approach of "zero incidents," which focuses on elimination of at-risk behaviors before an incident occurs.

"Zero incidents" is a comprehensive approach, process, and system characterized by an emphasis on prevention of violence and/or injury to employees. The focus is on identifying early individual and organizational warning signs by assessing facility risk, level of individual threat, and organizational violence-prone factors. The goal is to identify and eliminate or mitigate risk factors that are known to increase the likelihood of a violent incident occurring. In addition to focusing on zero incidents, this approach typically incorporates a zero tolerance for threats and acts of violence and subjects employees who violate the policy to disciplinary action up to and including termination.

The number one obstacle to developing a proactive preventative approach to reducing violence in the workplace is the reality that most medical directors, executives, and managers in organizations are in denial and believe that "it couldn't happen here." Results from a recent Gallup survey[19] indicated that many American businesses are turning a blind eye toward warning signs of workplace violence. "The warning signs are well known, but too many companies are burying their heads in the sand," said Frank Kenna III, president of the Marlin Company. Many people rationalize the fact that they're not confronting the issue. They say they don't want to overreact, and so they assume that any fears are unfounded and ignore the signs, hoping they'll go away. The survey reported that only 25 percent of respondents indicated they received any training in how to identify warning signs and what to do about them. Overcoming this mindset is the starting point to implementing a strong and effective effort to prevent workplace violence.

Establish a Workplace Violence Prevention Committee

Management must demonstrate a commitment by taking workplace violence seriously and appointing an influential manager to be responsible for the workplace violence prevention effort. This manager should establish a Workplace Violence Prevention Committee (also referred to as a Threat Management Committee). Participants on the committee should include representatives from Security, Human Resources, Occupational

Health and Safety, Legal, Finance, Risk Management, Public Relations, doctors, nurses, and the Union, if applicable. Smaller firms that do not have these specific dedicated resources should designate an Operations person to put together an appropriate team to address the issue using available resources.

[A] Focus on Eliminating At-Risk Behaviors

The committee should focus on creating a violence-free work environment by eliminating at-risk behaviors on both an individual and organization level. One of the key responsibilities of the committee should also be to establish a Workplace Violence Zero Incident Policy (see model policies at www.Workplaceviolence911.com/ModelPolicies). Note that a zero incidents focus is a proactive approach that targets prevention and goes beyond zero tolerance, which generally focuses more on reacting. An example of addressing an at-risk behavior in a medical center could be to have a procedure for flagging the charts of high-risk patients to give early alert to staff or remind them to check for weapons and to keep security on standby.

[B] Establish a Workplace Violence Prevention Policy

A cornerstone of your program is to establish a clear workplace violence prevention policy that will set the framework and provide guidance to managers, doctors, nurses, and employees. The focus should be on violence prevention, with the ultimate goal being zero incidents. In addition, the policy should make the concept of treating people in a respectful manner and maintaining their dignity a central theme that is integrated into the policy and its communication. (See www.Workplaceviolence911.com for information on the Ultimate Workplace Violence Prevention Policy.) Following is an excerpt from such a policy:

> It is the policy of Name of the Health-Care Organization to provide a safe and secure work environment for its employees, customers, vendors, contractors, and members of the public by taking a zero incidents approach toward workplace violence. The goal of this policy is prevention of violence and/or injury to employees by focusing on early identification of individual and organizational warning signs and assessing facility risks and individual threats. Name of the Health-Care Organization also has a zero tolerance for all acts or forms of violence in the workplace. All reported acts of physical violence, threatening statements, or harassing, intimidating, and disruptive behaviors will be taken seriously and will not be tolerated.
>
> An employee that makes threats, commits acts of violence, or violates the policy will be subject to disciplinary action up to and including termination.
>
> The Name of the Health-Care Organization is committed to working with its employees to maintain a workplace free from all forms of violence, threats of violence, harassment, intimidation, and other disruptive behavior.

All employees are charged with the responsibility for contributing to the maintenance of a safe and secure work environment.

All reports of physical and/or verbal violence made to management will be taken seriously, and appropriate action will be taken by management to resolve the situation. It is also our policy that no retaliation of any kind will be tolerated against an employee who, in good faith, reports an act of violence or violation of this policy. Retaliation is explicitly prohibited.

Organizations are also starting to incorporate directly into their workplace violence prevention policy statements that bullying behaviors are considered threatening behaviors because they cause emotional abuse and can lead to the creation of a hostile work environment and also create hostile feelings between employees.

Establish a process for record keeping to be able to track actual threats, incidents, close calls, and escalating conflicts for trends or patterns. Also evaluate interventions and programmatic efforts to evaluate their success and to maintain continuous improvement.

Assess the health-care organization's conflict resolution process and bolster it to ensure that it is an effective tool for fairly addressing employee concerns, conflicts, and problems. Track usage of the process (high usage is not necessarily a bad indicator, and many times indicates that people trust your process), and periodically assess how employees are feeling about it.

Translate your workplace violence policy and training into multiple languages based on languages spoken in your workplace and by your clientele. When employees are represented by a union, you should consider introducing workplace violence prevention initiatives to be jointly developed as a part of the next contract. You should work with the union to predetermine how cases, complaints, and situations will be handled and how processes will be used, and consider including mediation to provide an objective third party to negotiate outcomes.

[C] Formulate a No Weapons in the Workplace Policy

Incorporate a "No Weapons in the Workplace" provision into your workplace violence prevention policy, or establish a separate policy that clearly states that no weapons are allowed on the premises and that employees are prohibited from possessing a weapon while on duty. Medical centers and hospital emergency rooms should also conspicuously post signs clearly stating that all weapons are prohibited on the premises.

[D] Define the Nature of the Risk to the Company

The Workplace Violence Prevention Committee should also research the nature of risk to the health-care company associated with the health-care industry. Ask questions like the following:

- How does violence from the surrounding community have the potential to affect your workplace?

- What services that you offer have a history of being exposed to violence in the industry, such as trauma or acute psychiatric care? What kinds of incidents, types of facilities, geographic characteristics, and so forth can you point to?
- How frequently are assaultive incidents, threats, and instances of verbal abuse occurring, and where? Who is involved?

Where there are known hazards that exist within any business, industry, or geographic area, specific actions should be taken to mitigate and address the problems. This is essential, because these are the signs that indicate the greatest potential for violence to occur and also represent the highest potential liability.

To illustrate the point, say you have located a medical clinic in a low-cost area and crime data for the area indicate that there have been several rapes in parking lots at several warehouse facilities and another clinic near your location. It would be prudent to take precautionary steps to enhance security in and about your facility. This could include making sure you have sufficient lighting in the parking lot areas, providing escort service for employees leaving the building at night, asking for increased police patrols, and so forth. To ignore the crime data and not anticipate a potential problem puts you in a defensive position. If one of your employees is victimized on your property or while working, you will have to explain why you chose not to take any preventative actions.

[E] Conduct Facility Risk Assessments

Conduct periodic facility risk assessments to identify unsafe areas, hazards, or vulnerabilities in your physical facilities that could contribute to significant risk. For example, are there access doors that have broken locks, are effective access control processes in place and enforced, are there dimly lit stairwells, or is there an external entrance door that is regularly propped open?

[F] Conduct Organizational Violence Assessments

Conduct periodic organizational violence assessments to identify management practices, employee behaviors, and perceptions that are not conducive to creating a violence-free workplace, such as terminating employees via e-mail, harassment of employees, or incongruent policies. The assessment should closely review safety records for a history of violent incidents and "close calls." This information can help you determine trends, conditions, circumstances, and underlying causes of violence as well as identify cultural norms and behaviors. One such behavior is bullying, which often is endemic in a given firm and which can substantially contribute to undue stress or conflict. Studies are starting to show that bullying often precedes actual violence, so it should be considered a potential warning sign. Collect utilization data from the Employee Assistance Program and analyze the results. This type of information can be key in identifying risk factors on the organization level. Also conduct a "dignity and respect" audit of all human resource, security, safety, and operational policies to ensure they are designed to treat employees in a sensitive and respectful manner.

The preceding point is particularly important for designing termination, layoff, and discipline procedures that are sensitive to ensuring fair, respectful, and dignified treatment of employees. According to *The Disposable Worker: Living in a Job-Loss Economy*, a study published by the Center for Workforce Development at Rutgers University, the vast majority of employers are ignoring this advice. The study states that workers laid off from their jobs during the past 3 years received no advance notice, no severance pay, and no career counseling from their employer. This flies in the face of strong evidence that employers who are arrogant, abrupt, rude, stingy, or just plain gutless in their practices are courting aggression and violence. Dick Ault, Ph.D., a former FBI agent specializing in profiling, put it well by stating that special precautions should be taken when risk behaviors are present. His view that "you have to approach the firing of anyone with the utmost of dignity, even people who really don't deserve it," are words that employers should heed.

[G] Make an Individual Threat Assessment

Identify external experts experienced and thoroughly trained in how to professionally assess the violent nature of an individual and the likelihood of an employee becoming violent. It is important to have a resource on contract prior to the need for their services.

[H] Enhance Physical Security

Enhance physical security measures and establish workplace violence audit team(s) to conduct ongoing assessments of the effectiveness of security efforts. The following are some common security-sensitive areas:

- Emergency department
- Pharmacy
- Medical records department
- Mother/infant care
- Cashiers
- General outpatient clinics
- Specialized outpatient clinics (substance abuse, abortion, etc.)
- Animal research
- Mental health units

In addition, to harden targeted areas or improve control, use Security Prevention Through Environmental Design (SPTED)—engineering/architectural controls processes to follow when building or retrofitting facilities—to maximize crime prevention. For example, set up emergency rooms so that there are barriers, such as doors requiring key card access to the public areas where patients are being kept. Have intake personnel protected by bullet-resistant plastic barriers or an overly wide counter that cannot easily be reached over.

Provide nursing personnel with handheld alarms or noise devices and/or communication devices to be able to get help, such as cellular phones, pagers, whistles, and mobile alarms, to use while on duty. Establish processes for pinpointing their whereabouts using Global Positioning System technologies.

[I] Synchronize Your Personnel, Security, and Safety Policies

Synchronize your personnel, security, and safety policies to ensure that they create an integrated workplace violence prevention effort.

[J] Develop Crisis Response Procedures

Establish a Crisis Response Team (specially trained to deal with crisis) and develop crisis response procedures to deal with an incident. Select members based on preestablished criteria, which should include the ability to remain calm during a crisis or pressure situation, special skills related to handling crises or emergencies, and technical competency related to health care, knowledge of facilities, public relations, security, and so forth. The team should put a crisis communication and public relations plan in place before a crisis occurs. Additionally, preestablish a critical incident debriefing process and skilled counselors to be able to assist victims after an incident. Your Employee Assistance Program or an external network will be able to provide these support services.

Keep in mind that the speed at which you are able to address the needs of employees who have experienced a traumatic event will dictate how fast you are able to return work levels to normal operations. Within the following few days of an incident, reactions such as fear, anxiety, and exhaustion as well as anger may surface. In the long run, lack of confidence, depression, and the development of posttraumatic stress disorders (PSTDs) are possible outcomes.

[K] Establish Emergency Protocol with Police

Create an emergency protocol with police. This should include identifying who is the contact person when an incident needs to be reported. It is also important to identify a backup contact and also to preinform the contacts of who is responsible to contact them from your firm. You should also have them visit your site and learn your facility layout. In addition, you should make your address and building numbers clearly visible. Where there are multiple buildings, make address numbers clearly visible on the front and top of buildings.

[L] Enhance Hiring Procedures

Enhance hiring procedures to include health-care organization employment-screening processes focused on screening out violence-prone applicants before they are hired. Use critical behavior traits to identify behavior-based interview questions. Screening tools can include the following:

- Reference checks regarding previous employers
- Background checks, such as for a criminal background
- Verification of identity
- Driving record
- Credit history
- Drug testing
- Psychological assessments
- Critical behavior traits

See *Complete Hiring Guide to Screen for Violence Prone Individuals* for detailed coverage of enhanced hiring procedures, available at www.Workplaceviolence911.com.

[M] Promote Your Employee Assistance Program

Actively and regularly promote your Employee Assistance Program and train supervisors how to make an effective referral. If you are in a smaller organization that does not have an Employee Assistance Program, then establish a list of local service providers in your community to whom employees can be referred.

[N] Train Managers, Supervisors, Doctors, Nurses, and Employees

Provide ongoing training for managers, supervisors, doctors, nurses, and employees. Training should be provided in the following areas:

- Implementation of the Workplace Violence Prevention Policy
- How to identify early warning signs in patients, the public, and employees, and how to appropriately intervene
- Importance of reporting, taking threats seriously, and responding
- How to deescalate potentially hostile situations, such as by treating patients, the public, and employees in a respectful manner
- Effective ways to deal with domestic violence situations in the workplace
- If deemed appropriate for your setting, training in how to safely restrain patients

Focus on developing *core competencies* in effective conflict resolution, hostility/anger management, and emotional intelligence.

[O] Involve Health-Care Employees in the Prevention Effort

Make sure all employees know that workplace violence prevention is everybody's business, and help them understand the important role they can play in reducing violence. A truly effective prevention effort must maximize the participation of employees and their support. By encouraging the following practices, employers can enlist employee support, and they will contribute substantially to a successful effort to prevent violence at work:

- Reporting threats, suspicious activities, or violent actions, regardless of whether you personally believe the threat is serious
- Avoiding horseplay, practical jokes, harassment, or other risky behaviors that could lead to injury, create animosity or shame, or invoke angry reactions
- Treating all employees, customers, and contractors with dignity and respect; remembering that how we say something is just as important as what we say
- When feeling overly stressed, seeking help from the Employee Assistance Program or other support services designed to act as "relief valves" for frustrations or problems, such as church, family, and friends
- Actively following the firm's policy regarding workplace violence and the procedures for dealing with workplace threats and crises

Additional interventions that employers can use to focus on preventing workplace violence include the following:

- Publish a list of "who to call" and resources available to assist with issues
- Use external resources as appropriate for:
    - Individual threat assessments
    - Legal assessments
    - Facility risk assessment
    - Security protection firm
    - Employee Assistance Program support
    - Organizational threat assessment

Disastrous Planning Mistakes

One of the cruelest myths in crisis and medical workplace violence prevention planning is the belief that plans that are adopted, but not tested, will actually work as planned.

Another costly fallacy is for health-care organizations to focus solely on protecting their hard assets, such as facilities, technology, information, and networks, and to forget their people. You may test your alarm systems, system recovery processes, and backup information protections and then have your people improperly trained or not trained in what they need to do. Even worse, what they have been told to do causes confusion because it has never been tested to have the kinks worked out. You need to prepare your people for crisis because they will make the difference in how quickly and effectively you are able to return to normal business operations.

The third myth regarding crisis planning is the belief that you can effectively insure losses in a disaster. Ken Smith, former vice president of consulting operations for Sun-

Gard Planning Solutions in Wayne, Pennsylvania, and an expert in handling crisis claims, says that "settling claims after a disaster is not a pretty process."[20] Insurers trying to mitigate casualty losses often lock horns with executives trying to recover quickly.

The responsibility for addressing prevention of workplace violence typically is assigned to one of the following functions: human resources, security, safety, or risk management. Additionally, the controller has a very critical role and responsibility with regards to protecting the health-care organization's assets and business continuity. This role has come to light in more recent times as a result of the Y2K concerns and the tragic World Trade Center terrorist act. As a result, auditors and controllers have become more sensitized to the need to focus attention and resources on a company's preparedness for crisis or disaster.

According to Bob Sibik, former senior vice president for continuity services at Comdisco Inc., Rosemont, Illinois, "auditing firms now put more emphasis on contingency planning, and boards of directors feel more responsible about maintaining business operations." He further suggests that controllers should divide their disaster budgets into three parts: one part to cover prevention measures; one part for insurance to cover business interruption losses; and one part for recovery and continuity services. Although there appears to be an increased interest by outside auditors wanting to talk about disaster plans, it is still rare for them to require disclosure or to issue a qualified report if they don't like the plan, explains Tom Walters, assurance partner in the Minneapolis office of Grant Thornton, the public accounting firm.[21]

The Association of Certified Public Accountants' (AICPA) Statement of Position (SOP) 94-6—"Disclosure of Certain Significant Risks and Uncertainties"—requires auditors to address risks; however, disclosure is required only if it is "reasonably possible that the events" that would cause the impact will occur in the "near term." The very nature of crisis in general, and of workplace violence in particular, makes it statistically improbable in the near term, Walters points out. Thus, the reality is that contingency planning (which is what workplace violence prevention planning is about) is a balancing act—balancing the cost of prevention and recovery against the need to sustain operations. On the one hand, you don't want to spend more than you need to, but people who continue to think of contingency and recovery planning as discretionary spending are like ostriches with their heads in the ground. "It is only discretionary until trouble strikes."[22]

Analyzing the Business Impact of a Workplace Violence Incident

At the extreme end of the impact spectrum is what followed the first World Trade Center bombing (not the most recent incident that occurred on September 11, 2001). Three out of four private businesses that were shut down by the disaster for more than 4 days never recovered the financial loss, and many never reopened. "This accentuates the critical need for organizations to have crisis or disaster plans as a part of the internal control environment," notes Alan J. Griffith, vice president and controller of Aramark Corporation, Philadelphia.[23] "The controller needs to play an active role and see that key business operations will be up and running when a disaster occurs."

Based on this reality, it is highly likely that the financial impact of workplace violence has a disproportionate and potentially more devastating effect on smaller businesses. These are the businesses that are least likely to have the ability to absorb nonplanned incremental financial expenditures to be able to switch work to another site or alternative operation, and the lost or delay in revenue can have a critical effect on business survival. This means that small businesses have even more of a need to have workplace violence prevention and recovery plans in place than their larger brethren. However, in general, it is the large Fortune 1000 companies that have tended to implement active workplace violence prevention programs.

Having established the business need for a disaster plan that includes workplace violence prevention, let's now explore the cost of prevention versus the cost of recovery.

Cost of Implementing a Prevention Effort

The cost of setting up a comprehensive and effective workplace violence prevention program will vary substantially depending on a number of factors, including the size of the organization, the number of employees, the number of locations/facilities, the extent of the policies, the training, the existing infrastructure to support it, and the decisions made regarding use of internal and/or external resources. Determining whether internal or external training resources will be used has a significant impact on the cost, as does the choice of the training delivery method. Also very significant regarding establishing the cost of a workplace violence prevention initiative is whether certain training, like a "behavioral interviewing and conflict resolution skills" course, is charged to a general training fund as opposed to the programmatic effort. Additionally, one must decide which department pays for employment practices liability insurance or whether it will be allocated across departments. Since these decisions vary from organization to organization, I included all of them in the cost for the workplace violence prevention initiative to be sure not to understate the prospective cost, regardless of the choices an individual firm might make.

To illustrate the cost associated with implementing a comprehensive workplace violence prevention program, I have created a hypothetical medical center with 200 employees (7 managers, 25 doctors, 53 nurses, and 115 employees) with the following average salaries:

- Managers' salaries: $125,000, or $60.09 per hour
- Doctors' salaries: $190,000, or $91.34 per hour
- Nurses' salaries: $75,000, or $36.05 per hour
- Employees' salaries: $40,000, or $19.23 per hour

In addition, I have assumed that there are internal staff members in human resources, safety, security, and training as well as a consulting rate of $2,000 per day for external resources. Table 9.1 illustrates the costs of a prevention program.

The Hidden Cost of Conflict

According to research by Dana Mediation Institute, studies show that up to 42 percent of employees' time is spent engaging in or attempting to resolve conflict. Even if we take

Table 9.1 *Focus on Prevention: The Zero Incidents Approach*

Preventive Action	Cost
Programmatic Steps	
1. Establish a workplace violence prevention committee	$2,000
2. Focus on eliminating "at risk" behaviors	Internal staff
3. Establish a comprehensive workplace violence prevention policy	*$500
4. Establish a no weapons in the workplace policy	*
5. Define the nature of the risk to the company	Internal staff
6. Make facility risk assessments	$2,000
7. Make organizational violence assessments	$6,000
8. Make an individual threat assessment	$1,000
9. Enhance physical security	(Capital budget, $60,000)
10. Synchronize your personnel, security, and safety policies	$2,000
11. Develop crisis response procedures	$4,000
12. Establish emergency protocol with police	Internal staff
13. Enhance hiring procedures	$7,500
14. Promote your employee assistance program	Internal staff
15. Train managers, doctors, nurses, and employees	$24,000
16. Involve employees in the prevention effort	Internal staff
Programmatic steps subtotal	$49,000
Employment Practices Liability Insurance (assumes $100,000 deductible)	$35,000
Capital budget	$60,000
Grand Total	**$144,770**

* *Based on the assumption that you use the Ultimate Workplace Violence Prevention Policy software (available on www.Workplaceviolence911.com).*

a conservative approach to this number and assume the actual time spent dealing with conflict is half or a third of this amount, it still translates into a substantial cost impact. Although many of these costs are difficult to pinpoint and quantify, the Dana Mediation Institute has developed the following model that identifies the cost of conflict to an organization.[24]

[A] Wasted Time

The amount, and value, of time wasted by unnecessary conflict is probably the most easily quantified factor. Time is money. Employees are paid money for their time. And every conflict consumes time that could be otherwise spent doing productive work.

[B] Reduced Decision-Making Quality

Conflict erodes the quality of decisions in two ways:

1. Every solo decision maker requires information from others to make the best decision. When information providers are in conflict with the decision maker, the information supplied is inevitably distorted.
2. When two or more people share responsibility for a decision, conflict between them causes decisions to be made by the outcome of their power contest, not from their objective judgment of what is best for the organization.

[C] Loss of Skilled Employees

Every employee who is considering a move to "greener pastures" by seeking or accepting a job offer has a choice: stay or leave? How is that decision made? Certainly compensation, location, and new challenges are among the considerations. But so is the quality of relationships with people in the current job. When relationships are rewarding and satisfying, we naturally do not want to lose them. When chronic, stressful conflict is present, we naturally want to reduce it. That new job offer may look appealing because it is a way out of an unpleasant relationship that feels irresolvable. The higher salary can be just a convenient and socially acceptable excuse.

[D] Restructuring Cost

There is probably "one best way" for every job function to be performed. Industrial engineers are experts in designing organizations for maximum efficiency.

What happens when conflict between employees causes the ideal design to be altered to reduce their interdependency or otherwise accommodate the "human factor"? Inevitably, the result is lower efficiency.

[E] Sabotage, Theft, and Damage

It is our human nature to feel angry when we are in conflict. We may feel unappreciated, exploited, unfairly treated, or victimized by our coworkers, managers, or employer.

What do we do with that anger over weeks, months, or years of frustration? It is also human nature to feel impelled to "act out" anger in the form of retaliatory behavior. Of course, our personal ethics and integrity enable most of us to restrain the impulse to act out destructively. But others are not so restrained. And, there's a good chance that some of those people work where you do!

[F] Lowered Job Motivation

Employees' desire and sense of responsibility to perform their jobs to the best of their abilities are an intangible but precious resource in every organization. Every leader strives to inspire these qualities in his or her employees, to produce a high level of job motivation. Unresolved conflict wastefully drains that precious resource, like a hole drains water from a container that we are continually striving to fill.

[G] Lost Work Time

Nearly every employee has the right to sick days and other valid reasons for taking time off from work. We occasionally question ourselves, "Am I really sick enough to take the day off?" How does being entangled in a distressing conflict affect our answer to that question? Even the most responsible employee may understandably be nudged toward a "yes" answer. Less responsible employees, dreading the encounter awaiting them at the office while driving by the golf course on a sunny morning, may conclude, "This would be a great day to be sick!"

[H] Health Costs

Several of the foregoing factors defy precise measurement. The impact of conflict on a company's cost of providing health benefits for employees is perhaps the least measurable of the eight. But modern medicine now understands much about the impact of chronic stress on our immune system and our susceptibility to illness and injury. And conflict is nothing if not stressful. Although we cannot assign a number, it is no question that this contributes to the overall high cost of health care.

Cost of Recovery After an Incident

Now let's take a look at the commensurate cost associated with recovery after an incident has occurred. Table 9.2 presents some figures.

The significant cost differential between prevention and recovery is even further accentuated by the reality that there are "invisible" dollars lost by a company that has an unsafe workplace that we are unable to quantify, as some of the preceding points have discussed. This point is underscored by Dennis Johnson, a premier workplace violence prevention consultant, who adds: "What companies don't realize is that a good work environment costs less to run than a negative one."

Table 9.2 *Cost of Recovery*

Event	Cost
1. Incident debriefing with impacted employees (3 managers, 5 doctors, 10 nurses, and 27 employees working in impacted area)	$1,200
2. Center closed for 3½ days because of incident	$122,856
3. Revenue lost (assumes for 6 weeks after the incident there is a 25% productivity decline)	$1,724,694
4. Cleanup of incident area or crime scene	$2,000
5. Increase in annual health-care premiums because of increased use of psychological services (20% of employees need counseling for 3 months, 10% for 6 months, and 1% for 12 months)	$5,000
6. Lawsuit settlement (assumed out-of-court settlement at 60% of the average settlement of $500,000)	$300,000
7. Public relations campaign, marketing, communication strategy with stakeholders to counter negative press and restore confidence in company	$10,000
8. Replacement cost for 10% turnover of workforce, e.g., 25 managers and 75 employees (assumes 25% of salary replacement cost for managers and 10% for employees against national figures of 50-100% of salary for replacement cost)	$315,500
Total	**$2,481,250**

I have used conservative numbers in estimating the recovery cost; however, the following example illustrates a worst-case scenario.

Studies reveal a direct correlation between the prevalence of employee conflict and the amount of damage and theft of inventory and equipment. Covert sabotage of work processes often occurs when employees feel angry toward their employer. Much of the cost incurred by this factor is hidden from management's view, often excused as "accidental" or "inadvertent" errors. This cost is almost certainly greater than you realize.

> A former computer network administrator was found guilty in May 2000 of intentionally causing irreparable damage to his company's computer system. He created a "time bomb" program that permanently deleted all of the high tech manufacturing's sophisticated manufacturing programs. The damage, lost contracts and lost productivity totaled more than $10 million.
>
> Why did he do it? He got demoted after working for the company for about 10 years. He soon began developing the bomb, which he set off two weeks after he was terminated the following year.

The cost numbers clearly illustrate the significant difference in being proactive versus rolling the dice to gamble that "it won't happen here." Although the odds that it will not happen are clearly in your favor, if an incident does occur, your bet could cost the company significant dollars or, worse, cause its demise.

Assessment

To summarize, physicians, advisors, nurse-executives, administrators, and many managers view workplace violence as the sole responsibility of a deranged, psychopathic, or troubled employee, but the truth is that an outbreak of violence in an organization is often the result of chronic unresolved conflict that should have been noticed and properly managed. Despite our best attempts to place the blame on the individual's behavior, the organization is not blameless. Violence is the tragic aberration of an organization's culture, the culmination of personal frustration that has built to a crescendo because of perceived injustice, humiliation, loss of dignity, shaming, and perceived loss of value and control, which ultimately explodes into a desperate act.

Acts of health-care organization workplace violence can be reduced and many costs can be avoided with forethought, strategic planning, and progressive action. Attending to workplace conflict is not simply "soft hearted" or humanitarian; it is prudent business and risk reduction planning.

Yesterday, organizations that ignored the quality challenge didn't survive: recall American automobile manufacturers who faced the "quality invasion" of Japanese imports in the 1970s. Most companies responded well; hence Ford's slogan "Quality is Job 1!" Today, product and service quality management—such as total quality management, continuous improvement, and customer satisfaction programs—is an unquestioned requirement for business success.[25]

The competitive and leadership advantage of the 21st century for the industry may be strategic conflict management, and it may be the factor that determines who survives in the global competitive marketplace.[26]

Summary

This chapter has presented a comprehensive framework that can be used to intervene in the cycle that can build toward organization violence. The intent is to provide knowledge and tools to physician executives, practice management, and business and financial advisors so that they can understand the crucial role they can play in assisting an organization's effort to address workplace violence prevention and in mitigating avoidable cost impacts. The following lists a few more steps that can be taken:

- Install surveillance cameras at the entrance and inside of high-risk areas like the Emergency Department. The inside cameras should be very visible.
- Conspicuously post a sign by the entrance to high-risk areas stating that weapons of any kind are prohibited on the premises and that all entering are being photographed for security purposes.

- Install street-level cameras (similar to those at traffic signals that send tickets for running a light) to record license plate numbers.
- Install metal detectors and monitors that show pictures of the persons entering high-risks areas.
- Work with local police to establish a substation in or near the Emergency Department.
- Install cameras at the access door to where patients are being housed.
- Install panic buttons in high-risk areas, such as at the intake desk and in Emergency Department patient rooms, and give ER personnel mobile units to be able to alert security.
- Place curved mirrors at hallway intersections or concealed areas.
- Reconfigure all treatment rooms in high-risk areas to have two exits.

References

1. *Workplace Violence in Health Services,* Joint ILO/ICN/WHO/PSI research, 2002.
2. Sandra Marais, Violence in the workplace—The health sector, Conference on Workplace Trauma Solutions, March 24–26, 2004, Johannesburg.
3. Fatal Choices online at: www.Washington.edu, University of Washington, Seattle, WA.
4. National Council of Compensation Insurance, http://www.ncci.com.
5. Workplace Violence Research Institute, http://www.noworkvoilence.com.
6. U.S. Department of Justice, Office of Justice Programs, http://ojp.usdoj.gov.
7. Mable H. Smith, Legal considerations of workplace violence in healthcare environments, *Nursing Forum,* Vol. 36, No. 1, Philadelphia, Jan–Mar 2001. http://www.juryverdict.com.
8. Duane Fredickson, Detective, Minneapolis Police Department.
9. U.S. Department of Justice, Office of Justice Programs, http://ojp.usdoj.gov.
10. Bureau of Labor Statistics, http://www.bls.gov.
11. National Institute for Occupational Safety and Health, http://www.cdc.gov/niosh/homepage.html.
12. Ibid.
13. Carol A. Distasio, RN, BC, MPH, MSN, Protect yourself from violence in the workplace, *Nursing,* 32(6), p. 58-63, June, 2002.
14. *Fatal Occupational Injuries by Event or Exposure,* U.S. Department of Labor, Bureau of Labor Statistics, Census of Fatal Occupational Injuries, 1991–2002.
15. Bureau of Justice Statistics, http://www.ojp.usdoj.gov/bjs/.

16. Bureau of Justice Statistics, http://www.ojp.usdoj.gov/bjs/.

17. Helge Hoel, Kate Sparks, and Cary L. Cooper, University of Manchester Institute of Science and Technology, *The Cost of Violence/Stress at Work and the Benefits of a Violence/Stress-Free Working Environment,* Report Commissioned by the International Labor Organization (ILO), Geneva.

18. Steve James, Work stress taking larger financial toll, August 9, 2003, *Reuters.*

19. Steve Crabtree, American Confidence in Workplace Safety Holds Steady Despite Continued Violence, The Gallup Organization, November 15, 1999.

20. Richard H. Gamble, Apocalypse maybe, *Controller Magazine,* June 1998.

21. Ibid.

22. Ibid.

23. Ibid.

24. Dan Dana, Ph.D., Dana Mediation Institute, Inc., *The Dana Measure of the Financial Cost of Organizational Conflict: An Interpretive Guide,* 2001, www.mediationworks.com.

25. Ibid.

26. Ibid.

Additional Readings

1. Violence in the Workplace, *NIOSH Facts,* June 1997.

2. *Violence: Occupational Hazards in Hospitals,* DHHS (NIOSH) Publication No. 2002-101.

3. *Special Report on Violence in the Workplace,* Bureau of Justice Statistics, December 2001.

4. *Violence at Work: The Experience of UK Doctors,* Health Policy and Economic Research Unit, October 2003. (BMA the voice of doctors, www.bma.org)

5. *Workplace Violence in Health Services,* Joint ILO/ICN/WHO/PSI research, 2002.

6. Brochure published by the American Nurses Association, "Workplace Violence: Can You Close the Door on It?" December 1994.

7. Levin, PF, Hewitt, JB, and Misner, ST: Insights of nurses about assault in hospital-based emergency departments, *Journal of Nursing Scholarship,* Vol. 30, No. 3, p. 249, Indianapolis, 3rd Quarter 1998.

8. Colling, RL: *Security: Keeping the Health Care Environment Safe,* Joint Commission on Accreditation of Healthcare Organizations, 1996.

9. Marais, S, Van Der Spuy, E, and Rontsch, R: *Crime and Violence in the Workplace: Effect on Health Workers, Part II,* Crime, Violence and Injury Lead Programme, Medical Research Council and Institute of Criminology, University of Cape Town.

Chapter 10

Medical Malpractice and Tort Reform Risks

(Crisis or . . . Red Herring?)

Robert James Cimasi

Medical Malpractice is a term to signify bad or unskillful practice by a physician or other professional in which the health or welfare of the patient or client is injured. The failure of a professional to follow the accepted standards of practice of his or her profession is considered medical malpractice.

Medical malpractice in general is any act or failure to act by a member of the medical profession that results in harm, injury, distress, prolonged physical or mental suffering, or the termination of life to a patient while that patient is under the care of that medical professional. Usually harm must be proven to have occurred to constitute medical malpractice.

To prove a medical malpractice claim, the patient must prove the health care provider did not comply with an acceptable and reasonable standard of medical care in their specialty, and that this failure was the cause of the patient's harm.

www.Legal-Database.com

Malpractice Insurance History

Since the turn of the century, increased media attention has placed the political spotlight on medical malpractice and the issue of tort reform. In an effort to put these topics in context and consider the significant elements of the debate, this chapter presents a brief review and analysis of the current controversy, tracing the roots of the issue from the history of medical education to the development of the medical malpractice insurance industry and the origins of the tort reform movement; it also touches upon the effects of physician regulation and the increased incidence and costs of reported medical errors.

[A] The History of Medical Education and Practice

Medical education in the United States originated with several private schools that were not tied to established universities, each with its own unique set of entrance and graduation requirements. Harvard University and Johns Hopkins University were the only two university-based medical programs until the turn of the century. It was the Johns Hopkins program that set the foundation for national medical education by connecting science and medical research with clinical medicine.[1]

In 1904, the American Medical Association (AMA) founded the Council on Medical Education (CME), which created, for the first time, minimum national educational standards[2] for physician training. This standards board found that many schools did not meet the standards that they established. However, the council did not share the ratings of any of these medical schools "outside the medical fraternity."[3]

In 1910, the AMA commissioned the Carnegie Foundation for Advancement of Teaching to conduct a study of medical education and schools. Abraham Flexner conducted the inquiry (often referred to as the "Flexner Report"[4]) and reported that many of the proprietary medical schools were not meeting the AMA's goals. Flexner found an imbalance between the pursuit of science and education (with education lagging behind science). As the AMA gained more influence over the direction of medicine in the United States, increasing numbers of wealthy foundations and donors began to invest in leading university-affiliated medical schools that focused on medical education and either divested their research programs or subordinated them to their educational objectives. This trend continues today and is an illustration of the continuing development of accepted standards of care in the practice of medicine; these standards constitute the basis for the definition of medical error as a deviation from the norms of clinical care.[5]

Background

Malpractice, defined as "professional misconduct or unreasonable lack of skill,"[6] has always been a risk inherent in the practice of medicine. In fact, the earliest American malpractice case, for wrongful death, was in 1794.[7] Medical malpractice damages are typically awarded for economic or noneconomic damages. Economic damages compensate victims for actual monetary losses such as medical expenses, lost wages, and rehabilitation costs. Examples of noneconomic losses are pain and suffering, disfigurement, and loss of companionship.[8] In some instances, punitive damages may be awarded. Refer to section 10.03A for more information on punitive damages.

Generally, as medical technology improved (which some have correlated to an increased potential for errors), the population and volume of medical procedures also increased, and, as more people were able to afford medical care,[9] the amount of litigation increased.[10] Beginning in the 1970s, malpractice claims emerged as a growing problem. Eighty percent of malpractice suits that were filed between 1935 and 1975 were filed between 1970 and 1975,[11] and, more recently, the National Center for State Courts reported that tort filings in 30 states have actually declined since 1992.[12] Data from the same source for nine other states indicate an increase in medical malpractice filings in the past decade; however, the number of filings decreased from 1997 to 2000.[13] Of interest is that medical malpractice cases make up only 5 percent of total tort dispositions. It should be noted that when the filings are adjusted for changes in population, the rate per population remained constant throughout this period.[14]

Although damage awards are increasing, a 2002 *USA Today* report indicated that this increase is not primarily due to larger jury verdicts. Today malpractice verdicts and settlements over $1 million are approximately 1 in 12 claims. This has increased from 1 in 50 a decade ago. However, plaintiffs prevail in only about 1.3 percent of all claims filed, with approximately 61 percent of claims being dismissed or dropped, and 32 percent being settled with an average payout of only $300,000. In the end, only approximately 7 percent of claims ever go to trial.[15]

In the face of this rise in claims during the 1970s, malpractice insurance premiums increased. This may have been the result of carriers dropping out of the market, and the remaining insurance companies subsequently finding that they were able to raise their premiums, unopposed by market competition. Several states passed reform legislation in the mid-1970s while, during the same period, several physician-owned insurance companies were created in an effort to contain premiums.[16] After a brief respite, the 1980s brought new premium increases and an increase in large jury verdicts.[17] Although these factors received the bulk of media and public attention, there were, in fact, several other economic factors that significantly affected the rapid rise in premiums required by the insurance industry, such as stock market losses on insurance companies' investments. These factors will be briefly addressed later in this chapter.

Currently, in response to increases in malpractice insurance premiums, there have been reports that some physicians are moving out of states with high premiums, closing their medical practices altogether, taking early retirement, or choosing to "go naked," that is, practice without malpractice coverage.[18,19] Even as early as 1989, there were reports that there was a discernable trend in the relocation of some physicians, who, facing high insurance rates, moved to states perceived as having more favorable malpractice premiums, such as Indiana, which had capped damage awards in 1975.[20] Despite the enactment of laws restricting lawsuits and capping noneconomic pain and suffering awards, many Mississippi physicians are still unable to find malpractice insurance in the private market.[21] This trend of relocating to other states has been reported in the media as becoming more and more common in recent years. However, a March 2002 *USA Today* report indicated that there is little statistical evidence that more than a very small percentage of physicians have stopped doing high-risk procedures or relocated.[22] Malpractice premiums do not seem to influence where young physicians choose to establish their practices or where older physicians retire. In Nevada, an AMA-designated "crisis state," out of the 4,281 total physicians in the state in 2001,[23] only 35 physicians closed their practices, 12 retired, and 6 dropped obstetrics in the last year, while during the same period the state issued 335 new physician licenses.[24]

The 2002 *USA Today* report found that even though malpractice premiums were increasing, the percentage of a physician's revenue allocated to malpractice premiums was only 3.2 percent in 2002, compared to 12.4 percent for staff salaries, 11.6 percent for office expenses, and 1.9 percent for medical equipment.[25]

Figure 10.1 shows costs for malpractice insurance premiums as a percentage of medical practice expenses, based on the American Medical Association's own widely cited physician survey. After rising to a peak of 12.13 percent in 1987, they fell by almost 50 percent to a low of 6.21 percent in 1997. By 2000, the latest year reported by the AMA, malpractice premiums as a percentage of expenses had risen only slightly, to 7.46 percent. These data do not appear to support the rhetoric of a "crisis."

Data from the Medical Group Management Association (MGMA) on malpractice premiums as a percentage of total medical revenue parallel the AMA data, as illustrated in Figure 10.2.

Malpractice premiums as a percentage of total medical revenue fell from the late 1980s (3.65 percent in 1988) to a low of 1.61 percent in 1999 and rose to 2.20 percent in 2002. These data corroborate the AMA data findings, indicating that malpractice

Figure 10.1 *Malpractice Premiums as a Percentage of Medical Practice Expenses*

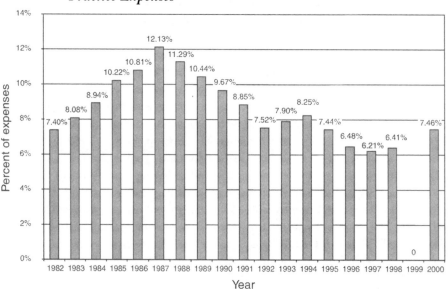

Source: AMA Socioeconomic Monitoring System Survey of Physicians 1987-2003.

Figure 10.2 *Malpractice Premiums as a Percentage of Medical Practice Revenue*

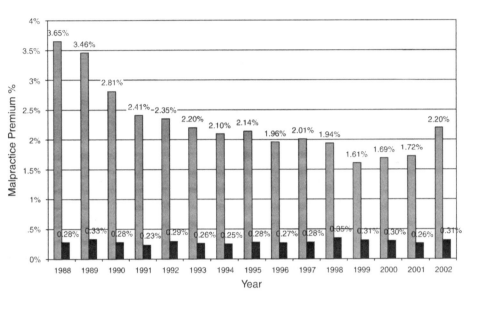

Source: MGMA Cost Surveys, 1988–2003.

premiums do not represent an overly large percentage of total medical revenue, and although up again slightly in the year 2003, are down significantly from their highs in the late 1980s. It is evident from the data presented in Figures 10.1 and 10.2 that the relative cost of malpractice premiums is significantly lower today than in the late 1980s and no higher than in the early to mid-1990s; this premium drop correlates to the increases in investment return. Figure 10.2 also charts other insurance costs as a percentage of total medical revenue, and these costs have been relatively stable.

Overall, the Consumer Federation of America reports that malpractice premiums account for only 0.59 percent of national health-care costs.[26]

There have also been widely publicized claims that fear of being sued has caused some physicians to practice "defensive medicine,"[27] that is, to order unnecessary tests and exams to make sure they "cover themselves" and are better able to defend against being sued for misdiagnosis or nondiagnosis. A recent report by the General Accounting Office (GAO) cautions against generalizing the limited existing survey indications that physicians, in certain specific circumstances, are practicing more defensive medicine in response to fear of litigation.[28] Defensive medicine has been declared as contradictory to the goals of managed care, which claims that this practice has resulted in many unnecessary treatments. Although defensive medicine practices may be seen by some to drive up insurance costs and charges, which are typically denied by managed care, many believe that, in fact, they may be in the best treatment interest of the patient in clinical terms. [29]

The Corporate Tort Reform Movement

[A] Tort Lawsuits

In simple terms, a tort is defined as a legal wrong, other than a breach of contract, that "causes harm for which courts will impose civil liability."[30] The tort system allows patients who are injured or wronged in some way to sue the wrongdoer, or *tortfeasor*. The wrongdoer is held accountable for his or her actions,[31] and the injured party is able to recover for damages incurred as a result of the tort. This system is also designed as a deterrent to provide an incentive for the prevention of torts. Although the vast majority of cases are settled out of court, an estimate of the 2001 direct costs of the U.S. tort system, made by Tillinghast-Towers Perrin, was $205.4 billion.[32]

Damages for a tort suit are generally classified as either compensatory damages or punitive damages.[33] Compensatory damages are damages that intend to compensate the injured party for present and future losses caused by the tortious act.[34] Compensatory damages awarded in personal injury suits often include: medical expenses incurred as a result of the injury; lost earnings and earning capacity; mental and physical pain and suffering; loss of enjoyment of life; and other "hedonic damages."[35] Punitive damages, sometimes referred to as "exemplary damages," are damages that are awarded to punish or deter serious misconduct, which is conduct that was committed "with a bad intent or bad state of mind such as malice."[36]

For years now, "tort reform" has been a commonly heard and greatly misunderstood phrase. *Black's Law Dictionary* defines tort reform as "a movement to reduce the amount of tort litigation, usually involving legislation that restricts tort remedies or that caps damages awards (esp. for punitive damages). Advocates of tort reform argue that it lowers insurance and healthcare costs and prevents windfalls, while opponents contend that it denies plaintiffs the recovery they deserve for their injuries."[37]

Even in the face of the news generated by the recent indictments of huge multinational corporations like Enron and Worldcom for financial fraud, the issue of tort reform has once again gained extraordinary media attention as well as intense legislative scrutiny and activity. The rising number of cases brought against corporations emphasizes the fact that the nation is becoming more litigious, and defendant corporations are more likely to lose a case now than in the past.[38] Although plaintiffs may be bringing more lawsuits against corporations, after the appeals process and legal fees, the bulk of the original jury awards appear to never actually reach the victims.[39]

Certain states and counties are believed to be more favorable legal venues for plaintiffs, which has been asserted as an inducement to some corporations to avoid expanding to those venues or areas with so-called "plaintiff-friendly" statutes. [40] The concern is that any actual loss of business employers could result in a loss of jobs and corporate taxes, which are detrimental to the citizens of these communities and the local economies. Additionally, in reaction to the perceived increase in the probability of corporations being sued and losing, insurance companies claim that they must raise premiums and/or retreat from underwriting. [41]

Tort reform proponents have alleged that the United States has the most expensive tort system in the world, with costs per citizen of about $721 per year. [42] Product liability suits against tobacco companies and vehicle manufacturers, and medical malpractice and negligence, generally top the list of the largest jury awards. [43] This may stem from the nature of these industries and the potential for physical injury from their products and services, as well as from the perceived importance of deterring future harm in these areas.

Some claim that the cost of the tort system amounts to "tort abuse" and may be out of hand. [44] As may be expected, they have suggested some possible solutions to the "problem" they have claimed. These solutions include tort reforms at the federal level, including class action reform, medical malpractice reform, a national settlement related to asbestos-related disease claims among others, as well as control of punitive damages. [45] At the state level, suggested changes to existing laws include modifying the joint and several liability of defendants (where defendants who are only minimally responsible for damages remain responsible for 100 percent of the liability); placing caps on noneconomic damages; and restricting punitive damages (which were originally enacted to punish defendants for particularly heinous conduct but have, in some cases, been perceived as no longer restricted to that level of wrongdoing). [46] Joint and several liability reform and noneconomic damage caps are popular strategies, often proposed for tort reform in the medical malpractice area.

[B] "Frivolous Lawsuits"

The tort reform movement often claims that "frivolous lawsuits" are driving up insurance and societal costs. However, the Harvard Medical Practice Study, published in 1990, found that only one in eight medical errors committed in New York hospitals resulted in a medical malpractice claim. [47] Also, it was found that, in Missouri, one in eight injured medical patients actually files a claim, and only 1/16 of claimants achieve any damage award. [48]

Rand Institute for Civil Justice in 1996 is cited as stating that "business cases account for 47% of all punitive damage awards. In contrast, 4.4% and 2% of punitive damage awards are due to product liability and medical malpractice cases respectively." [49] Proponents of the tort reform movement also claim that insurers have to settle frivolous lawsuits to "make them go away." However, insurers themselves insist that they do not settle "frivolous lawsuits." [50] At the same time, it appears rational to assume that plaintiffs' attorneys working on contingency would be very reluctant to take on a "frivolous case" because they must often invest tens of thousands of dollars, out of pocket, to prepare for a suit.[51]

The number of cases that actually go to trial is very low compared to the number of claims actually filed. For instance, almost 90 percent of medical malpractice claims against Texas physicians are closed with no monetary damages awards being paid out,[52] and over 70 percent of suits are won by physicians, are dismissed, or are dropped altogether.[53]

Proponents of tort reform often claim that noneconomic damages are frivolous and do not compensate plaintiffs for real injuries. However, noneconomic damages compensate plaintiffs for real harms, such as blindness, physical disfigurement, loss of fertility, loss of sexual function, loss of a limb, loss of mobility, and the loss of a child.[54] Children and the elderly, who do not have active work careers, are only able to recover for noneconomic damages for pain and suffering. It is very difficult for their families to recover economic damages because they have no earnings.[55]

Physician Self-Regulation

[A] The State Licensing Process

Most professions in which specific skills are required (e.g., real estate brokers, mental health counselors, cosmetologists, engineers) are governed by a licensing board. The state licensure of physicians imposes both barriers to entry into, and standards of practice upon, the practice of medicine. Medical societies were the first organizations to confer state licenses for physicians, beginning in 1781 with Massachusetts and New Hampshire. State licensure of physicians by state medical boards began in 1873, with the exception of a couple of earlier examples (New York in 1760 and New Jersey in 1772), and by 1895 nearly all the states had a board of medical examiners. In 1915 the National Board of Medical Examiners was founded to further standardize care.[56] Today, every U.S. state has a medical board that supervises the licensing of physicians.[57] These state agencies or boards are governed by members of the profession. A "police" function of the states is to ensure that only licensed professionals may provide services[58] and to impose disciplinary action on those persons who operate "unlicensed."

The approach and application of disciplinary actions by state licensing boards vary from state to state. Generally, there has been no established focus by these boards on preventing medical errors, and what little prevention has been undertaken has met with resistance by providers and health organizations.[59] This hesitancy to reprimand and sanction incompetent physicians sometimes results, in part, from state agency staffing and financial constraints (e.g., some states don't have the funding or staff resources to investigate and discipline physicians). It has been alleged that another possible cause of the lack of enforcement is that the boards are composed of physicians, who may be loathe to report or discipline their own kind.[60,61] Such intradisciplinary protection may stem from the culture of collegiality from medical school and residency, where students and beginning physicians, by necessity, "stick together" and do everything as a team in order to survive the ordeal.[62] According to the consumer advocacy group Public Citizen, the tendency is for most state licensing boards to protect their fellow physicians from the public and focus on attempting to rehabilitate rather than sanction or revoke the licensure of questionable physicians.[63] However, the disciplinary process is designed to rehabilitate, retrain, or as a last resort remove incompetent providers from practicing.[64] A 1990 Office of Inspector General study of disciplinary actions from 1985 to 1989 showed that disciplinary actions were hindered by limitations on agency authority, limitations on sharing information with other state agencies, requirements for a clear and convincing standard of proof, lack of standards to measure competent medical care, and lack of communication between state medical boards.[65] Refer to Section 10.04C for information on the large percentage of medical malpractice cases attributable to a relatively small number of physicians.

[B] Self-Regulation

The AMA has endorsed expert witness disciplinary programs, and several professional physician specialty associations have proceeded to institute programs to discipline their member physicians that provide what the association deems false or misleading expert witness testimony on behalf of plaintiffs in medical malpractice cases.[66] The AMA believes that medical testimony is similar to practicing medicine and should be subject to peer review.[67] For example, the American Association of Neurological Surgeons (AANS) recently disciplined a neurosurgeon acting as an expert witness in a malpractice case. AANS suspended Gary Lustgarten's AANS membership for 6 months after finding that Dr. Lustgarten misrepresented what they believed to be standards of care in the neurosurgery profession.[68] The North Carolina Medical Board revoked Dr. Lustgarten's medical license after finding that he engaged in unprofessional conduct by misstating the appropriate standard of care.[69] Plaintiff's attorneys claim that such programs intimidate physicians from serving as expert witnesses, and they note that there have been no disciplinary actions filed against these associations' members testifying on behalf of the defense.[70] However, the AANS has won every judicial challenge to its expert witness disciplinary program. The U.S. Court of Appeals for the Seventh Circuit found that professional associations have the right and the duty to use internal disciplinary measures to identify and sanction their members who give misleading testimony as expert witnesses.[71]

[C] Questionable Doctors: How Does the Public Know?

Often, physicians who have faced multiple malpractice suits, or who have been charged with malpractice, are not discharged or blocked from practicing medicine by the state or states in which they are licensed. The result is that such physicians continue to practice without public knowledge of the physician's history. However, a licensee has a property right in his or her license and so has a right to due process before the license can be restricted.[72] In 1999, the Quality of Health Care in America Committee of the Institute of Medicine issued a strategy for improving preventable medical errors by "developing a nationwide public mandatory reporting system and . . . develop[ing] . . . voluntary reporting systems."[73] In this report, *To Err Is Human: Building a Safer Health System,* the committee suggests the creation of a multilevel system whereby health-care providers, consumers, and the government would all have a part in preventing medical errors. The committee's goal is a 50 percent reduction in medical errors by 2004.[74] From this viewpoint, it is reasonable to conclude that success in achieving a significant drop in medical errors would directly correlate with a reduction in potential malpractice claims. Organized medicine criticized the report's recommendations because they believe that it might jeopardize patient confidentiality and effective peer review, increase liability, create incentives to hide errors, reduce patient confidence in the health-care system, and create inaccurate comparisons in safety for rural providers.[75]

[D] Is It Always Gross Negligence?

It is often stated that, as a society, we tend to hold our physicians in exalted stature on the one hand and to extremely high and demanding standards on the other. Physicians must often work with patients' lives in their hands, and so have an almost superhuman "godlike" status. Living up to such difficult standards and expectations is, in the best of circumstances, very problematic and is exacerbated by the complex and often imprecise art and science of medicine.

If it were to be determined that most medical errors are not intentional or grossly negligent but rather mistakes from systems or processes that break down (e.g., mislabeling drugs, falls, restraint-related injuries), designing a better system that makes mistakes less likely to occur may be the best approach to controlling medical errors and the resulting incidence of medical malpractice cases.[76] Regrettably, it is still significantly uncertain whether the rising incidence of reported medical errors should be attributed to intentional error or gross negligence, or to simple process mistakes. In the end, the definition of malpractice may be based to a significant degree on the fact that the "intention" of the medical error means little to the damaged patients or their family. An extreme illustration would be that monetary damages don't bring back the dead.

Several studies have shown that medical errors are a leading cause of death. The Institute of Medicine's (IOM) 1999 study reported that as many as 44,000 to 98,000 deaths may be directly linked to medical errors.[77] According to the IOM, this rate is higher than deaths due to car accidents, AIDS, and breast cancer.[78] Medical malpractice has also been reported to be the eighth leading cause of death.[79] An Auburn University study of 36 hospitals and nursing homes in Colorado and Georgia found that nearly one out of every five pharmaceutical doses administered in a typical hospital or skilled nursing facility was in error. Approximately 7 percent of these errors were potentially harmful.[80] A study published in *Pediatrics* magazine found that children with special medical needs had significantly higher rates of hospital-reported medical errors.[81] Another study, published in the *New England Journal of Medicine,* estimated that surgical teams leave surgical tools in 1,500 patients a year.[82] A review by the U.S. Agency for Healthcare Research and Quality of patient safety indicators showed that medical injuries in hospitals caused increased length of stay for patients, resulting in increased medical costs.[83] Postoperative sepsis had the highest mortality rate and highest associated cost of all medical injuries.[84] Indeed, deaths related to hospital infections are the fourth leading cause of mortality according to the U.S. Centers for Disease Control and Prevention. A *Chicago Tribune* investigation found that nearly three-quarters of these hospital infections were preventable.[85] However, some question the accuracy of these statistics. A study published in the *Journal of the American Medical Association* suggested that previous interpretations of medical error statistics were misleading.[86]

Over the last several years, the IOM report and others have increased public awareness of medical errors.[87] A recent study by the U.S. Agency for Healthcare Research on 18 types of hospital complications "sometimes caused by medical errors" found that "postoperative infections, surgical wounds accidentally opening and other often-preventable complications lead to more than 32,000 U.S. hospital deaths and more than $9 billion in extra costs annually."[88]

Harvard business professor Regina Herzlinger has asked "why McDonald's can turn out millions of perfect French fries every day, while some hospitals still amputate the wrong legs."[89] Leading hospitals, including Boston's Children's Hospital, affiliated with Harvard University; Duke University Medical Center; and New York Mount Sinai Hospital,[90] are facing a flood of publicity regarding recent medical errors, some resulting in death. Teaching hospitals face the problem that while they have an enormous amount of expertise, they also draw the most complex cases from around the country, even the world.[91] Their status as teaching hospitals is a double-edged sword: although they train tomorrow's physicians and nurses, each student must go through a learning process in order to become a top physician. Unfortunately, this learning process entails performing supervised medical procedures on human beings in order to become an independent physician. It has been observed that this may be the derivation of the phrase "*practice* of medicine."

A 2002 study by Lamb et al. found that when errors did occur, most hospitals disclosed harm at least some of the time, but were more likely to disclose nonpreventable harms than preventable harms.[92] The researchers found that about one-third of hospitals had board-approved disclosure policies. Even though two-thirds of the hospitals reviewed did not have formal policies, they were either in development of a policy or still had a routine practice to inform patients and/or families when a patient had been harmed.[93]

It should be acknowledged that medical errors made in hospitals may stem from a number of sources apart from physicians. A 2003 CNN report found higher death rates at hospitals that did not require a certain level of education for nurses.[94] According to a study by the University of Pennsylvania that reviewed data from 168 Pennsylvania hospitals, surgery patients' rates of death were higher when the number of nurses with at least a bachelor's degree was low.[95] Lower staffing of nurses also contributes to death rates. [96]

Medicine has been found to be one of the most stressful professions. Not only are physicians often responsible for life and death decisions, but their training and continuing practice can be emotionally, mentally, and physically draining, which can increase the probability for medical errors. In 2002, the Accreditation Council for Graduate Medical Education voted to limit the number of hours a resident physician works to 80 hours per week to reduce medical errors, as well as for other considerations.[97] Because of the significant pressures inherent in medicine and the career's demands on their social, physical, emotional, and mental lives, physicians have higher rates of drug abuse (in fact, drug and alcohol abuse are among the most common reasons for disciplinary action)[98] and suicide (physicians are about two to three times as likely to commit suicide than the population at large).[99]

As mentioned previously, the practice of medicine may be considered to be both a science and an art. Because of this, medicine requires physicians to make difficult medical decisions based on a combination of their knowledge, their experience, consultations with other physicians, and the patient's and family's wishes. Because we, as a society, require physicians to make clinical decisions that are inherently dangerous, the question arises as to whether we must also provide "societal protections" for these decisions.

The Medical Malpractice Crisis

[A] Allegations of Greed: The Traditional Physician and Insurance Company–Based Arguments

A common argument made by insurance companies and businesses is that "greedy" juries[100] are awarding larger verdicts because of litigious plaintiffs[101] and "ruthless" lawyers.[102,103]

Although the GAO reported that jury awards are rare,[104] *Jury Verdict Research* reports that the average jury award was up 79 percent in 1999 from 1993.[105] However, opponents of tort reform claim that malpractice awards are rarely excessive. The median malpractice payout in 2000 was only $125,000.[106] At the same time, managed care companies have limited the amount of time physicians spend with patients and have discouraged physicians from making referrals or ordering more diagnostic tests, while reimbursement levels from HMOs to physicians are falling, and medical errors appear to be common.[107]

[B] The Proposed Tort Reform Solution: The Traditional Argument's Answers, Including Tort Reform

Tort reform advocates, including physician and insurance company lobbies alike, have suggested placing monetary caps, typically $250,000 (often modeled after California's Medical Injury Compensation Reform Act [MICRA] caps), on pain and suffering awards to plaintiffs. (Refer to Table 10.1, "Selected states' Medical Malpractice Liability Reform Measures" appended, for information on the various states' caps.) This would reduce the amount of money insurance companies would have to pay out. Many states, like California, have caps already in place.[108,109] In mid-September 2003, Texas passed a $750,000 cap on damages ($250,000 per defendant).[110] In response to this cap, the largest insurance carrier in the state announced it would cut its medical malpractice premiums by 12 percent.[111] This reaction has generally been the exception rather than the rule. Bob White, president of First Professional Insurance Company, the largest malpractice insurer in Florida, said, "No responsible insurer can cut its rates after a [medical malpractice tort reform] bill passes."[112] At the federal level, in 2003, a House bill on economic caps passed, but S.11 (The Patient's First Act of 2003) did not pass in the Senate.[113] A recent Bush administration U.S. Health and Human Services (HHS) report alleged that the legal system was to blame for rising medical malpractice premiums.[114] Critics maintain that key numbers in the report are "dubious or old." Several key sources have direct financial ties to the insurance industry.[115]

The argument has been made that caps on damages violate either the federal or state constitutions. The question is whether legislatures have the authority to establish caps or whether that should be left to the judicial branch of government. Supreme courts in several states, such as Illinois and Ohio, have found that caps violated the state constitution. Caps may also violate the Equal Protection Clause of the Fourteen Amendment to the U.S. Constitution.[116] Opponents of caps suggest that caps discriminate against children, women, seniors, and minorities because a larger percentage of payouts to members of these groups are made up of noneconomic damages. In states with caps on noneconomic damages, children, women, seniors, and minorities usually receive less compensation than white males with the same injuries.[117] Evidence from California suggests that as a result of caps on noneconomic damages, the provable losses for many seniors, low-income workers, at-home moms, and parents of infants who die at birth are often not enough to persuade an attorney to take their case.[118] Opponents also suggest that caps on noneconomic damages also negatively impact the permanently injured.[119] Critics contend that the caps have not kept up with inflation.[120] For example, California's 1975 cap on noneconomic damages is worth only $40,389 in 2002 dollars. Conversely, in 2002 dollars, a patient would need to recover $1,547,461 in order to have the same medical purchasing power as $250,000 in 1975 dollars.[121]

Some have rejected the theory that putting a cap on noneconomic awards slows the rise of malpractice insurance premiums.[122] According to a *Business Week* commentary, states like Arizona and Vermont have premiums that remain low despite no caps.[123]

Table 10.1 *Selected States' Medical Malpractice Liability Reform Measures*[i,ii,iii,iv,v,vi]

State	Year of Cap	Noneconomic Damages Cap	Punitive Damages	Economic Damages Cap	Other Actions
Alabama[192]	1987	$1,000,000 cap on total damages only for wrongful death.	$1,000,000 cap on total damages only for wrongful death.	$1,000,000 cap on total damages only for wrongful death.	1987 caps on noneconomic damages of $400,000 and $250,000 cap on punitive damages both ruled unconstitutional.
Alaska[192]	1997	$400,000 or $8,000 times life expectancy. For severe injury $1,000,000 or $25,000 times life expectancy.	$500,000 or 3 times compensatory damages. For malicious actions $7,000,000 or 4 times compensatory damages.	None	50% of punitive damages to state fund.
Arizona[192]		None	None	None	Attorneys' fees may be reviewed by court upon request.
Arkansas	2003	None	$1,000,000	State cannot use joint and several liability.	Must be filed in county in which act occurred (venue reform).
California	1975	$250,000		No cap. Defendants are jointly and severally liable for any economic damages.	MICRA (Medical Injury Compensation Reform Act) also modifies collateral source rules, and includes required periodic payments of future damages. Limits on attorneys' fees.[192]

State	Year			Total damages against hospital or physician limited to $1,000,000. Permissible wrongful death damages of $250,000	
Colorado[192]	1988–1990	$250,000. Total damages against hospital or physician limited to $1,000,000. Permissible wrongful death damages of $250,000	Not to exceed actual damages award. Court may increase to 3 times actual damages. Total damages against hospital or physician limited to $1,000,000. Permissible wrongful death damages of $250,000	Total damages against hospital or physician limited to $1,000,000. Permissible wrongful death damages of $250,000	
Connecticut[192]		None	None	None	Limits on attorneys' fees.
Delaware[192]	1976	See punitive damages.	Only if malicious intent or wanton conduct established.	None	Limits on attorneys' fees.
District of Columbia[192]			None	None	None
Florida	2003	$500,000 for physician liability; $750,000 for medical facility liability.	Damages over 3 times economic damages presumed excessive (1997).[192]	None	Limits on attorneys' fees.[192]
Georgia[192]	1992	See punitive damages.	$250,000 cap unless for intentional harm.	None	
Hawaii[192]	1986	See punitive damages.	$375,000 pain and suffering exclusive of mental anguish, disfigurement, and loss of enjoyment and consortium.	None	Attorneys' fees must be approved by court.[192]
Idaho	2003	$250,000 to wrongful death or personal injury; not applicable to willful or reckless conduct or felonies. Cap adjusted annually starting in July 2004 for average state wage increase.	None[192]	None	

continues

Table 10.1 *Selected States' Medical Malpractice Liability Reform Measures*[i,ii,iii,iv,v,vi]   *(continued)*

State	Year of Cap	Noneconomic Damages Cap	Punitive Damages	Economic Damages Cap	Other Actions
Illinois[192]	1985	Cap overturned in *Best v. Taylor Machine Works* in 1997.	None for medical malpractice.	None	Limits on attorneys' fees.
Indiana[192]	1998	Total cap of $250,000 per provider and $1,250,000 total cap for providers and State Patient Compensation Fund.	Total cap of $250,000 per provider and $1,250,000 total cap for providers and State Patient Compensation Fund.	Total cap of $250,000 per provider and $1,250,000 total cap for providers and State Patient Compensation Fund.	Limits on attorneys' fees.
Iowa[192]		None	None	None	Court may review attorneys'-fees.
Kansas[192]	1988	$250,000 cap on damages to each party for all defendants.	Lesser of $5,000,000 or highest gross income for last 5 years determined by judge and $0 for wrongful death (1994).	None	
Kentucky[192]		None	None	None	
Louisiana[192]		Total cap of $100,000 for qualified health-care providers.	Not recoverable except under specified conditions. Total cap of $100,000 for qualified health-care providers.	Total cap of $100,000 for qualified health-care providers.	
Maine[192]	1999	$150,000 limit for wrongful death.	$75,000 limit for wrongful death.	None	Limits on attorneys' fees.
Maryland	2000	Soft/adjustable cap of 3 times the economic loss found in the case (up to $1 million).	None[192]	None	Court will review attorneys' fees when disputed.[192]

Massachusetts[192]	1986	$500,000 unless impairment of bodily function, disfigurement, or other special circumstances.	None	None	Limits on attorneys' fees.
Michigan[192]	1986	$280,000 cap ($500,000 cap for specialty circumstances) set in 1994 and inflation adjusted annually.	None	None	Limits on attorneys' fees.
Minnesota[192]	1986	None	None	None	None
Mississippi	2002	$500,000	None[192]	A defendant who is less than 30% at fault is liable only for his share of damages. If a defendant more than 30% at fault, can be held liable for up to 50% of the damages.	Cases only filed in county where incident occurred; statue of limitations shortened to 2 years for suing nursing homes.
Missouri	1986	None currently	None[192]	None	$350,000 noneconomic cap, limited venue shopping and limiting frivolous lawsuits vetoed by governor 2003. An older $557,000 inflation adjusted cap thrown out in appeals in 2004.
Montana[192]	1995	$250,000	None	None	None
Nebraska[192]	1986	$1,000,000 cap on total damages against health-care providers qualifying for state excess insurance.	Punitive, vindictive, and exemplary damages prohibited. $1,000,000 cap on total damages against health-care providers qualifying for state excess insurance.	$1,000,000 cap on total damages against health-care providers qualifying for state excess insurance.	Court review of attorneys' fees for reasonableness.

continues

Table 10.1 *Selected States' Medical Malpractice Liability Reform Measures*[i,ii,iii,iv,v,vi] *(continued)*

State	Year of Cap	Noneconomic Damages Cap	Punitive Damages	Economic Damages Cap	Other Actions
Nevada	2002	$325,000, physician liability limited to $50,000 for government and nonprofit trauma centers.	$300,000 or 3 times compensatory damages only for fraud, oppression, or malice (1996).[192]	None, but joint and several liability of defendants applies to economic damages.	Prohibits insurers from using financial losses from investments as reason for increasing physicians' premiums.
New Hampshire[192]	1977	$150,000 cap on wrongful death damages limited to surviving spouse.	$150,000 cap on wrongful death damages limited to surviving spouse.	$150,000 cap on wrongful death damages limited to surviving spouse.	Attorneys' fees subject to court approval. Older caps on noneconomic damages found unconstitutional by NH Supreme Court in *Carson v. Maurer* (1980).
New Jersey[192]	1997	None	Greater of $350,000 of five times the compensatory damages.	None	Limits on attorneys' fees.[192] Proposed state subsidies of of insurance premiums.
New Mexico[192]	1976	$600,000 cap on total damages excluding punitive and medical costs. Providers not liable for above $100,000.	Providers not liable for above $100,000.	Providers not liable for above $100,000.	
New York[192]		None	None	None	Limits on attorneys' fees.
North Carolina[192]	1995	None	$250,000 or 3 times compensatory damages.	None	
North Dakota[192]	1995	$500,000		Damages above $250,000 subject to court review.	
Ohio	2003	$350,000 (loss of limb or organ function, $500,000).		None	

State	Year				
Oklahoma[192]	1998	None	$100,000 cap for reckless disregard; $500,000, 2 times compensatory damages, or benefit derived for intentional or malicious acts.	None	Limits on attorneys' fees.
Oregon[192]	1987	$500,000 cap for wrongful death only.	Punitive damages only allowed where malice is shown.	None	Limits on attorneys' fees. OR Supreme Court ruled noneconomic damages cap unconstitutional except in wrongful deaths in *Lakin v. Senco Products* (1999)
Pennsylvania	2002	None	Cap of twice the actual damages.	None[192]	Proposed state subsidies of $200 million to help physicians pay for insurance over 3 years; 2002 passed venue shopping act that requires filing in the county where incident occurred.
Rhode Island[192]	1997	$100,000 minimum recovery for wrongful death.	Not recoverable against executor or administrator of estate. $100,000 minimum recovery for wrongful death.	$100,000 minimum recovery for wrongful death.	
South Carolina[192]		None	None	None	
South Dakota[192]	1997	$500,000	$1,000,000 cap on total damages found unconstitutional in *Knowles v. U.S.* (1996).		
Tennessee[192]		None	None	None	Limits on attorneys' fees.

continues

Table 10.1 Selected States' Medical Malpractice Liability Reform Measures[i,ii,iii,iv,v,vi] (continued)

State	Year of Cap	Noneconomic Damages Cap	Punitive Damages	Economic Damages Cap	Other Actions
Texas	2003	$250,000 per defendant, $750,000 possible total.	Lesser of 2 times economic + noneconomic damages. Capped at $750,000 (minimum $200,000) (1977).[192]	No cap. Defendants responsible only for their share of liability.	
Utah[192]	1986	$250,000	None	None	Limits on attorneys' fees.
Vermont[192]		None	None	None	
Virginia[192]	1976–1983	$1,500,000 total damages cap for injury or death with annual $50,000 increases.	$350,000	$1,500,000 total damages cap for injury or death with annual $50,000 increases.	
Washington[192]		None	None	None	Court will assess attorneys' fees for reasonableness. Caps on damages struck down in *Sofie v. Fibreboard Corp.* (1989).
West Virginia	2003	$250,000 except in wrongful death or bodily impairment cases ($500,000).	$250,000 except in wrongful death or bodily impairment cases ($500,000).	None	
Wisconsin	1975	$350,000 ($500,000 for minor's wrongful death). As of 4/1/03, new noneconomic damage cap was raised to $410,000.	$350,000 ($500,000 for minor's wrongful death). As of 4/1/03, new noneconomic damage cap was raised to $410,000.	$350,000 ($500,000 for minor's wrongful death). As of 4/1/03, new noneconomic damage cap was raised to $410,000.	Limits on attorneys' fees.[192]

				Limits on attorneys' fees. Limits on damages prohibited by constitution.
Wyoming[192]	"	None	None	None

i "State medical liability laws table." National Conference of State Legislatures, 2002 (www.ncsl.org/programs/insur/medliability.pdf, accessed 10/3/03).

ii "Medical Malpractice." Insurance Information Institute, http://www.iii.org/media/hottopics/insurance/medicalmal/. Accessed September 16, 2003.

iii "One size doesn't fit all with malpractice limits." Toland, B. Post-Gazette Harrisburg Bureau, September 23, 2003. http://www.post-gazette.com/pg/pp/03266/225026.stm. Accessed September 26, 2003.

iv "How the new tort reform law affects you." Ohio State Medical Association, www.osma.org/news/How-the-new-tort-reform-law-affects-you.cfm (accessed August 11, 2003).

v "Liability premium increases may offer opportunities for change." Bulletin of the American College of Surgeons, Vol 87, No. 2, p. 22-24.

vi American Medical Association, Advocacy Resource Center, (June 17, 2003). http://www.ama-assn.org/ama/pub/category/7470.html. Accessed 10/14/03.

Furthermore, Weiss Ratings, an independent insurance rating agency, reported, in June 2003, that insurers have not passed on savings from diminished claims loss generated by caps on noneconomic damages to physicians by lowering malpractice insurance premiums. Although caps on noneconomic damages may reduce increases in damage awards, they have not resulted in significant decreases in malpractice insurance premiums, which is ostensibly the cause of the malpractice "crisis." In states with caps, physicians experienced a 48.2 percent increase in median malpractice premiums from 1991 to 2002, whereas in states without caps physicians experienced an increase in premiums of only 35.9 percent.[124] This provides some evidence that in states without caps on noneconomic damages premium rates increased more than in states with caps—just the opposite of what was intended. This effect occurred despite the fact that the median payout in states with caps increased by only 83.3 percent compared to an increase of 127.9 percent in states without caps.[125]

The HHS report cited California's noneconomic damages caps as a model for national tort reform. It should be noted that a Medical Liability Monitor survey stated that while premium rate hikes in states with caps have been smaller over the past 2 years as compared to those without caps, the difference is not as large as believed.[126] However, Medical Liability Monitor reported that, in 2001, malpractice premiums in California, with a cap on noneconomic damages, were 8 percent higher than the average for states without caps on noneconomic damages.[127] California premiums increased 190 percent in the first 12 years after the enactment of caps on noneconomic damages. Premiums in California stabilized only after the passage of Proposition 103, insurance industry reform. Nonetheless, premiums in California have again increased 37 percent since 1998, compared to a national average increase of 5.7 percent.

In fact, many advocates of tort reform have admitted that tort reform, in and of itself, will not necessarily lead to decreases in medical malpractice premiums. Sherman Joyce, president of the American Tort Reform Association (ATRA), stated that "we wouldn't tell you or anyone that the reason to pass tort reform would be to reduce insurance rates." Note that ATRA "was formed in 1986 to represent hundreds of U.S. and foreign corporations in their bid to overhaul civil liability laws at the state and national levels" and that, in 1995, ATRA received $5.5 million from "Big Tobacco" companies, which represented over half of their budget that year.[128] Insurance industry representatives have declined to promise that tort reform will lead to decreased malpractice premiums.[129]

In their recent research on malpractice and caps on noneconomic damages, the American Academy of Actuaries (AAA) observed that "such reforms may not assure immediate rate reductions, particularly given the size of some increases being implemented currently, as the actual effect, including whether or not the reforms are confirmed by the courts, will not be immediately known." AAA also stated that "poorly crafted tort reforms could actually increase losses and, therefore, rates."[130]

An important consideration is that the capping of noneconomic damages does not control payments for economic damages, such as medical bills, lost wages, and other tangible losses. Medical costs are reportedly increasing by approximately 15 to 20 percent a year, which, in turn, drives up the economic damages component of malpractice awards and settlements. A September 2002 study conducted by the Congressional Budget Office estimates that, because malpractice insurance premiums represent a relatively small percentage of overall health-care costs, a nationwide cap on noneconomic damages would result in a savings of only 0.4 percent on overall health insurance premiums for the general public.[131] For more detail on the differing state caps, refer to Table 10.1, which lists states with damage caps and the amount of those caps.

Another method suggested for providing a limit of financial risk to insurers is to establish a statute of limitations on claims made by plaintiffs, currently in place in many states, such as Missouri.[132] However, courts in 18 states have found statutes of limitations on malpractice claims unconstitutional.[133] Other methods of tort reform called for by proponents would enable or enhance the ability of defendants to countersue claimants who file frivolous lawsuits.[134] According to Dr. John Stanely, president of the Metropolitan Medical Society of Kansas City, the cost to have a frivolous malpractice claim dismissed from the court system is about $25,000.[135] Another way to lower malpractice premiums would be to create compensation programs outside of the courts to handle malpractice cases.[136] As discussed previously, a more proactive and preventative approach to preventing lawsuits by lowering medical malpractice awards (and therefore premiums) would include building rapport with patients; reducing medical errors; and establishing "honesty policies" for full disclosure of errors.[137] For example, the Copic Cos, a Denver malpractice insurer, encourages its physicians to immediately report incidents of medical errors or complications, and, within 72 hours, the insurer then offers to cover lost wages or medical costs resulting from any injury arising from the incident.[138]

[C] Patient Legal Protections: Checks and Balances on Abuse: Nontraditional Market-Based and Consumer Advocate-Based Arguments

Consumer advocates seem to agree that sufficient legal remedies must remain in the system to protect the legitimate interests of patients who have been damaged and their families, and they note that insurance rates have historically fluctuated as a natural part of the economy.[139] For example, when the economy was strong in the late 1990s and the stock market was performing well, rates of reinsurance, required for risk management for smaller insurance companies, were comparatively low, prompting new insurance companies to enter the market.[140,141] New competition encouraged existing insurance companies to compete for market share and lower their premiums.[142,143] Reserves are the amounts set aside by insurers to pay anticipated damage claims.[144] The Weiss Ratings study reported that medical malpractice insurers consistently underreserved since 1997.[145] This was confirmed by the American Academy of Actuaries (AAA), which stated that insurance companies miscalculated the amount of money needed to be in reserve. Thus when the economy is performing poorly, having insufficient reserves would cause an increase in insurance premiums.[146]

The argument supports the contention that insurers underreserved and insurance rates were artificially low over the past decade.[147,148,149] While the economy was prosperous, insurance companies invested in the stock and bond market to increase their profits. Stocks represent a growing percentage of cash and invested assets for members of the Physician Insurers Association of America, more than doubling between 1995 and 1999, from 7.0 to 14.2 percent, and falling to 11.5 percent by 2001.[150] Investment income as a percentage of premiums declined from 46.5 to 31.4 percent between 1995 and 2001 as premiums have risen and investment income has fallen or remained steady.[151]

The argument related to the effect of underreserving and reliance on financial markets contends that because of economic performance, insurance companies lowered rates when the economy was doing well[152,153] and are now raising rates as a result of current economic performance, not in solely a causal correlation to malpractice claims loss. Victor Schwartz, general counsel to the American Tort Reform Association, said, "Insurance was cheaper in the 1990s because insurance companies knew they could take a doctor's premium and invest it, and $50,000 would be worth $200,000 five years later when the claim came in. An insurance company today can't do that."

In the early 21st century, the U.S. economy began a downturn, returns from the stock market dropped precipitously, and there were several conspicuous investigations into large corporations for financial wrongdoings.[154] All these were indications of the disruption to the investment marketplace that resulted in insurance companies experiencing significant drops in value and return on their investment portfolios.[155,156] Reinsurance also became more difficult and more expensive to secure because the reinsurance industry suffered financial losses in the same manner.[157] The AAA confirmed that pretax investment income as a percentage of earned premium decreased from approximately 45 percent in 1995 to 30 percent in 2001 and that in 2002 the ratio fell to 18 percent. Because investment income is used to supplement funds derived from premiums to cover losses, such poor investment performance then requires raising premiums.[158] These factors have led to significant vulnerability in insurer stability.

Weiss Safety Ratings reported, in June 2003, that 34.4 percent of medical malpractice insurers are vulnerable to financial difficulties, compared to only 23.9 percent of property and casualty insurers.[159]

In addition to financial vulnerability, an August 2003 GAO report found many of the new entrants to the insurance industry who entered the market during the period of prosperous market conditions were then forced to leave the market or declare bankruptcy when the market experienced a severe downturn.[160] Notably, even established firms, such as the St. Paul Cos., the largest U.S. medical malpractice insurer, began exiting the market in 2003, citing unpredictable losses.[161] The reasons cited included that "real" premium rates were now catching up after years of artificially low premium rates the insurance companies had been charging physicians based on anticipated premium investment returns. As might be expected, within the context of supply and demand, the diminished supply of malpractice insurers in the market has been cited as a contributing factor in increasing premium rates.[162]

Another factor that has been discussed is that medical malpractice insurance has a long "tail," meaning that there is usually a significant time lag between a malpractice act resulting in a cause of action and the liability exposure for damage awards to plaintiffs. It takes an average of 2 years from the time that an incident occurs before the claim is reported to the insurer and another 2½ years before the average claim is closed.[163] Because of this delayed timing issue, insurance companies may now be faced with larger liabilities from prior periods, at the same time that the recent economic downturn is limiting their ability to fund payment of the claims.

Consumer groups contend that only a small percentage of physicians account for the majority of the medical malpractice claims, and these physicians are not being reprimanded publicly.[164] In 1988, a national computer database (the National Practitioner Databank [NPD]) was created through the Department of Health and Human Services to track questionable physicians. This database, however, was not made publicly accessible,[165] but rather was reserved for medical professionals and hospitals.[166] However, a website launched by the group Public Citizen (founded in part by consumer advocate Ralph Nader) is linked to a site created by Dr. Sidney Wolfe, which allows patients to search for physicians disciplined by 41 states and the District of Columbia. Aptly named www.questionabledoctors.org, the site makes state-maintained physician disciplinary data public nationally for the first time, enabling consumers to identify disciplined physicians by state, and what action was taken.[167] Dr. Sidney Wolfe's Questionable Doctors site does not include data related to malpractice claims against physicians. Currently, at least six states, California, Florida, Idaho, Massachusetts, Oregon, and Washington, make such information publicly available to consumers, and links to descriptions of these data are available at www.healthcarechoices.com.

Although the NPD does include malpractice claims information, this information is not publicly accessible to consumers. In a study prepared for the Missouri Association of Trial Lawyers, it was noted that NPD data report that 4.8 percent of physicians are responsible for over half (51 percent) of medical malpractice claims and that 1.7 percent of physicians account for a staggering 27.5 percent of all claims.[168] In fact, over the past 12 years, according to the report, only 5.1 percent of U.S. physicians accounted for 54.2 percent of payouts.[169]

Consideration of these facts has served as the basis for those who assert that "tort reform" must include efforts to prevent torts, not simply to prevent redress afterwards.

[D] Other Approaches to Controlling Premiums: Nontraditional Answers

Several other solutions for the current "crisis" have been proposed. They include reforming the peer review process so that it effectively reprimands, sanctions, or removes those physicians who account for a significant number of the claims;[170] increasing regulatory scrutiny and control over insurers' investment policies and premium rate setting; providing significantly more publicly available information on medical errors, malpractice claims, and physicians impairment to consumers; and stopping the practice of "venue shopping," that is, picking counties/cities that are historically favorable to plaintiffs. Of course, another solution is for physicians and payors who provide reimbursement (based in part on costs of providing those services) to simply accept that malpractice premium costs are subject to cyclical variation and that the lower premiums of the 1990s represented a "break" because of prosperous markets. Since these do not now exist, they must now play catch-up with higher premiums.

Conclusion

[A] Summary

The national debate over the medical malpractice "crisis" has become a highly contentious and polarized topic, in which a growing number of "red herring" issues have appeared to seize the agenda. What may be needed to resolve conflict among the various interested parties is the introduction of a disinterested, third-party arbiter to develop and present an independent analysis utilizing a rational methodology based on the types of information presented in this chapter. (Refer to the "Medical Malpractice Insurance and Tort Reform Bibliography" appended after Table 10.1 for a listing of resources.)

As with many controversial issues, there appears to be truth to portions of the arguments made by both proponents and opponents to the recent legislative tort reform initiatives, as well as elements of partisan political arguments in each. Neither side could successfully argue that it is in the best interest of patients, or society overall, to have malpractice insurance rates at a level that would effectively prohibit physicians from practicing in certain geographic areas or within certain medical specialties. At the same time, neither side could successfully argue that there is not a legitimate need for society both to maintain controls on the quality and safety of medical care and to provide available avenues of redress and adequate recovery of damages for patients who have been damaged because of negligence.

Some areas of potential compromise might be the issue of "venue shopping" by attorneys, while at the same time addressing the lack of self-policing of errant physicians by the medical profession. Agreement might be achieved in restricting the ability of plaintiffs to select legal venues for no other reason than that they have been historically favorable to large jury awards, while still respecting the rights of plaintiffs to seek redress before a jury of their peers. At the same time, the lack of self-policing of impaired or malpractice-prone practitioners could be partially addressed by providing greater public access to the National Practitioner Databank so that patients could make informed decisions about physicians to whom they entrust their care and often their lives.

Perhaps tort reform opponents should ask themselves, "If physicians were to reasonably police themselves and control medical errors, do patients and society at large benefit by having the cost of limitless malpractice awards impair the funding and limit the hope of the life-sustaining promise of evolving medical technology?"

Perhaps tort reform proponents should, in turn, ask themselves, "If limits are placed on the ability of plaintiffs to seek legal redress and receive full compensation for their injuries, to whom will the savings from the diminished damage awards, if any, accrue?" Specifically, if malpractice insurance tort reform results in an amount of funds from malpractice insurers not being paid to plaintiff claimants, will the insurers be required to pass these "savings" directly to physicians by way of reduced insurance premiums? Note that, as described in Section 10.04D, insurers and tort reformers have both stated that caps will not necessarily lead to lower premiums. It is the rise in malpractice premiums that is the gravamen of the crisis. If tort reform doesn't lead to lower malpractice premiums, it might exacerbate the crisis by reducing the rights of damaged patients to the recovery of damages without serving its ostensible purpose of solving the "malpractice crisis," that is, onerous insurance premiums.

[B] Changes in the Technology and Practice of Medicine

The issues of the medical malpractice crisis and tort reform should be considered within the context of the dynamic changes in the health-care delivery system. The last two decades have seen the accelerated transformation of U.S. health-care service sector *professions* into a service *industry* enterprise, whereby professional health services have been "unitized, protocolized, and homogenized," many believe, in order to facilitate their "sale" as if they were just any other market commodity, such as soy beans or pork bellies. These changes have accelerated the "corporatization" of medicine, as demonstrated by the increase in for-profit health care in hospitals, outpatient technical component providers, and health insurance payors. During this period, the intensified attention of the general media; the explosion of available information on the Internet; and the rise of direct-to-patient advertising by pharmaceutical, medical device, and provider entities have acted to inflate patients' expectations of the knowledge and abilities of physicians and the public's perception of the seemingly limitless advances of health-care technology and the invincible capabilities of medicine.

Within this sometimes surreal environment, and despite the technological advances in medicine, physicians have often been seen as resistant to standardizing care through the use of now available technology, which holds the promise of preventing many medical errors with practice protocols and algorithms that assist in the detection and prevention of medical errors. Such standardization is seen to represent a restriction of the latitude of physicians' professional judgment, and an affront to the traditional role of physicians. However, technological solutions for medical error prevention are increasingly being successfully employed, along with more sophisticated care mapping, disease management, and other clinical practice protocols and best practices, to avoid unnecessary medical variation and related error.

The rise of managed care has also acted to control medical utilization levels during this period, restricting physicians' referrals to specialists, limiting the use of diagnostic testing, and pressuring physicians (through reimbursement mechanisms) to curtail time spent with patients. Physicians have not been overly successful in resisting the efforts of managed care payors to control these types of essentially clinical decisions, which many believe would assist in controlling errors and subsequently limiting medical practice liability.

[C] The Perfect Storm

The confluence of many of the factors and trends affecting both the medical profession and insurance industries over the last 2 decades has resulted in what may be called "The Perfect Storm" for medical errors and physician malpractice premiums. Increasingly complex procedures have met with overblown patient expectations. Meanwhile, the value and return from malpractice insurance companies' investments have plummeted. Both managed care insurers and providers appear to be looking for scapegoats in an environment of rising health-care costs and insurance premiums. The resulting milieu is the "perfect storm" of rising health-care and health insurance costs; rising medical malpractice premiums; intense, and often inaccurate and inflammatory, media coverage; and strident accusations of blame from all sides.

When so many different forces come together at once, it is not enough to remove any one factor and to leave the crisis, or storm, largely intact. Multivariate problems, such as the issues of medical malpractice and tort reform, require the gathering of facts and empirical data with the independent and unbiased application of accepted analytical methodology, in order to arrive at a rational strategy and plan of action that might bring lasting relief to the problem. Although many studies have addressed aspects of the overall problem, the polarization of the parties involved has effectively prevented, to date, an unbiased, coordinated study and approach to the perceived "crisis."

Perhaps there has never been a better time than now for reasoned debate and rational discourse on these topics, informed by historical perspective, based on empirical fact and established, scientific methodology, and free from the strident polemic, accusatory condemnation, and assessment of blame that is pervasive in the present rhetoric. As to whether the current issues of medical malpractice and tort reform truly represent a "crisis" or are only a "red herring," perhaps it is now time for both opponents and proponents of these issues to reflect on the words of the Indian philosopher, Dandemis (aka Lao Kiun): "Do not condemn the judgment of another because it differs from your own. You may both be wrong."

References

1. Kirk SA and Reid WJ: *Science and Social Work: A Critical Appraisal* (New York: Columbia University Press, 2002), Chapter 1, pp. 2–3.
2. Ibid.
3. Ibid.
4. Abraham Flexner: *Medical Education in the United States and Canada: A Report to the Carnegie Foundation for the Advancement of Teaching,* 1910.

5. Kirk and Reid: *Science and Social Work*, pp. 2–3.

6. *Black's Law Dictionary*, 5th edition (St. Paul, MN: West Publishing, 1979), p. 864.

7. Furrow BR, Greaney TL, Johnson SH, Jost TS, and Schwartz RL: *Health Law: Cases, Materials and Problems*, 3rd edition (St. Paul, MN: West Publishing, 2000), p. 308.

8. Cornell, EV: *Addressing the Medical Malpractice Insurance Crisis*, Washington D.C.: National Governors Association Center for Best Practices, (December 5, 2002), p. 5.

9. Ibid., p. 310.

10. Furrow et al.: *Health Law*, p. 309.

11. Ibid., p. 310.

12. Tort and Contract Caseloads in State Trial Courts, Examining the Work of State Courts, Williamsburg, VA: National Center for State Courts, 2002, p. 24.

13. Ibid., p. 27.

14. Ibid., p. 28.

15. Special Report: Hype outraces facts in malpractice debate; Degree of crisis varies among specialties and from state to state, *USA Today*, (March 5, 2002), p. A.01.

16. Furrow et al.: *Health Law*, p. 310.

17. Ibid.

18. VandeWater J.: A looming health care crisis. http://www.stltoday.com/stltoday/news/stories.nsf/DocID/3E284D525D947ED186256DA, (accessed 9/22/03).

19. Berenseon RA, Kuo S, and May JH: Medical malpractice liability crisis meets markets: Stress in unexpected places. http://www.hschange.com/CONTENT/605/, (accessed 9/30/03).

20. Frey W: Physicians seek out states with favorable malpractice statutes, *Health Week News*, (October 23, 1989), p. 12.

21. As Physicians Still Uninsured Despite Tort Reforms in Miss, Congress Daily, Washington D.C.: National Journal Group, Inc., (9/22/03).

22. Special Report, p. A.01.

23. Pasko T: *Physician characteristics and distribution in the U.S.*, Chicago, IL: American Medical Association, 2003, p. 44.

24. Putting a face on malpractice insurance debate; Doctors, lawyers represented by patients are too often left out, *USA Today*, (March 5, 2003), p. D.07.

25. Special Report, p. A.01.

26. American Trial Lawyers Association, *Fact Sheet: Medical Malpractice Fibs and Facts.* http://www.atla.org/ConsumerMediaResources/Tier3/press_room/ FACTS/medmal/medmalfibsfacts.aspx, accessed 10/16/03.

27. The medical malpractice insurance crisis hoax, *Multinational Monitor*, March 2003, pp. 9–12.

28. Implications of Rising Premiums on Access to Health Care, Washington D.C.: U.S. General Accounting Office, GAO-03-836, 8/03, p. 6.

29. Medical malpractice insurance crisis hoax, pp. 9–12.

30. Dobbs DB: *The Law of Torts* (St. Paul, MN: West Publishing, 2000), p. 1.

31. Justice for the injured: Defending the civil justice system from the corporate "tort deform" movement, *Multinational Monitor,* March 2003, pp. 23–26.

32. U.S. Congressional Budget Office, *The Economics of U.S. Tort Liability: A Primer,* October 2003, pp. viii, 10. Washington, DC: U.S. Government Printing Office.

33. Dobbs: *The Law of Torts*, p. 1047.

34. Ibid., pp. 1047–1053.

35. Ibid., pp. 1047–1053.

36. Ibid., pp. 1062–1063.

37. BA Garner, ed.: *Black's Law Dictionary*, 7th edition (St. Paul, MN: West Publishing, 1999).

38. Dial D, Germano T, Hartwig R, Hudgins JM, and Woollams: "Tort excess: The necessity for reform from a policy, legal and risk management perspective." http://server.iii.org/yy_obj_data/binary/727182_1_0/tortreform.pdf. Link from http://www.economypage.com, accessed 9/22/03.

39. Ibid.

40. Ibid.

41. Ibid.

42. Ibid.

43. Ibid.

44. Ibid.

45. Ibid.

46. Ibid.

47. Ibid.

48. What malpractice crisis? www.bizjournals.com/bizoutlook/?jst=b_ol_lk, accessed 9/9/03.

49. American Trial Lawyers Association, "The real frivolous lawsuits in America: Businesses suing businesses." www.atla.org/homepage/bizvsbiz.aspx?print=1, accessed 6/5/03.

50. American Trial Lawyers Association, *Fact Sheet.*

51. Special Report, p. A.01.

52. Searching for solutions to escalating malpractice costs, *Medical Economics Magazine,* May 24, 2002. www.findarticles.com/cf_0/m3229/10_79/ 87149501/article, accessed 9/9/03.

53. Why premiums are soaring again, *Medical Economics Magazine,* July 9, 2001. www.findarticles.com/cf_0/m3229/13_78/77035508/p1, accessed 9/9/03.

54. American Trial Lawyers Association, *Fact Sheet.*

55. Mexican teenager buried; parents considering legal action over death, *USA Today,* March 5, 2003, p. A.02.

56. Sigerist, Henry E: The history of medical licensure, *Journal of the American Medical Association,* Vol. 104 (March 30, 1935), pp. 1057–1060. [reprint]

57. Furrow et al.: *Health Law,* pp. 76–356.

58. Ibid.

59. Institute of Medicine, *To Err Is Human: Building a Safer Health System,* November 1999. www.nationalacademies.org.

60. Cooper H: Medical boards are said to be lax on doctors, *Wall Street Journal,* Wednesday, January 13, 1993.

61. Boodman SG and Davis P: Virginia doctor's misconduct left trail of broken lives. Medical system failed to protect patients, *Washington Post,* September 28, 2003.

62. Ibid.

63. Ibid.

64. Furrow et al.: *Health Law,* 2nd edition, p. 75, 1997.

65. Ibid, p. 76.

66. Expert witness watchdog, *Modern Physician,* August 1, 2003.

67. American Medical Association, Physician loses license over expert testimony, August 19, 2002. www.ama-assn.org/amednews/2002/08/19/prsc0819.htm, accessed 10/27/03.

68. Expert witness watchdog.

69. American Medical Association, Physician loses license.

70. Expert witness watchdog.

71. Court rules for AANS in Austin case, *AANS Bulletin,* Vol. 10, no. 3 (Fall 2001).

72. Furrow et al.: *Health Law,* 2nd edition, p. 76, 1997.

73. Institute of Medicine, *To Err Is Human.*

74. Ibid.

75. "Health Law" 2nd ed. by Furrow, Barry R., et al: St. Paul, MN: West Group, 1997, p. 76.

76. Institute of Medicine, *To Err Is Human.* www.nationalacademies.org.

77. Ibid.

78. Ibid.

79. The Medical Malpractice Crisis, By Kelly M Pyrek. http://www. surgicenteronline.com/articles/2c1feat1.html, accessed 9/21/03.

80. Medication Errors Observed in 36 Health Care Facilities, *Arch Intern Med.,* Vol. 162, no. 16 (9/9/02), p. 1897–1903.

81. Hospital-Reported Medical Errors in Children, *Pediatrics,* Vol. 111, no. 3 (3/03), p. 617–621.

82. Danger in the O.R.? The Associated Press, 1/16/03.

83. Excess length of stay, charges, and mortality attributable to medical injuries during hospitalization, Zhan C, Miller MR. *Journal of the American Medical Association,* Vol. 290 No. 14 (October 8, 2003), p. 1868–1874.

84. Ibid.

85. Infection Epidemic Carves Deadly Path, *Chicago Tribune,* (7/21/02).

86. Estimating Hospital Deaths Due to Medical Errors, *JAMA,* Vol. 286, no. 4 (7/25/01).

87. New Push After Transplant Tragedy—Hospitals Search for Ways to Prevent Errors, Help Doctors Learn From Others, DoctorQuality, www. doctorquality.com/www/products/rpm/resources/news_022003.htm, (accessed 10/1/03).

88. Med complications may cost $9B per year, Yahoo! News, Oct. 7, 2003 (news.yahoo.com/news?tmpl=story2&cid=534&u=/ap/2003100//ap_on_he_me/costly_complications&printer=1, accessed 10/8/03).

89. Focused Factories, HospitalConnect.com, 7/1/02.

90. Leading hospitals under fire for errors, Associated Press, *New York Times.* http://www.nytimes.com/aponline/national/AP-Hospital-Errors.html? pagewanted..., accessed September 29, 2003.

91. Ibid.

92. Hospital disclosure practices: results of a national survey, Lamb, EM, Studdert, DM, Bohmer, RMJ, Berwick, DM, and Brennan, TA: *Health Affairs,* Vol 22 No. 2, (March–April 2003), p. 73–83.

93. Ibid.

94. Study: Nursing education, death rates linked, CNN.com, Sept. 24, 2003, http://cnn.health.printthis.clickability.com/pt/cpt?action..., (accessed 9/21/03).

95. Ibid.

96. Ibid.

97. Hospital Accreditor Will Strictly Limit Hours Worked by Residents, The Cutting Edge Newsletter for the OR Professional, June 17, 2002. http://www. orsoftware.com/cuttingedge/view_newsletter.asp?NID=25, accessed 10/2/03.

98. Medical boards are said to be lax on doctors, Cooper, H. *Wall Street Journal*, Wednesday, January 13, 1993.

99. Physician suicide in North Carolina, Revicki DA and May HJ. *Southern Medical Journal*, 78, No. 10 (October 1985), p. 1205–7.

100. Future looks bleak as malpractice premiums continue upward spiral: insurers increasing rates to make up for past mistakes, rise in jury awards, www.findarticles.com/cf_0/m0KGX/1_24/83037164/print.jhtml, (accessed 9/9/03).

101. Back on the tort reform merry-go-round, *Modern Healthcare*, (July 15, 2002). www.modernhealthcare.com/articleID=2184, (accessed 9/9/03).

102. Why premiums are soaring again, *Medical Economics Magazine*, (July 9, 2001), www.findarticles.com/cf_0/m3229/13_78/77035508/p1..., (accessed 9/9/03).

103. Malpractice Reform is dead; long live malpractice reform, Scott, Jeanne Schulte. *Healthcare Financial Management*, (September 2003) p. 32–34.

104. What malpractice crisis? www.bizjournals.com/bizoutlook/?jst=b_ol_lk, (accessed 9/9/03).

105. Future looks bleak as malpractice premiums continue upward spiral: insurers increasing rates to make up for past mistakes, rise in jury awards, www.findarticles.com/cf_0/m0KGX/1_24/83037164/print.jhtml, (accessed 9/9/03).

106. Fact Sheet: Medical Malpractice Fibs and Facts, American Trial Lawyers Association, http://www.atla.org/ConsumerMediaResources/Tier3/press_room/ FACTS/medmal/medmalfibsfacts.aspx, (accessed 10/16/03).

107. Why premiums are soaring again, *Medical Economics Magazine*, (July 9, 2001), www.findarticles.com/cf_0/m3229/13_78/77035508/p1...., (accessed 9/9/03).

108. Ibid.

109. What's behind the current malpractice insurance crisis: industry experts explain why premiums are currently soaring, www.findarticles.com/cf_0/m0LMB/9_21/94595455/print.jhtml, (accessed 9/9/03).

110. Texans approve $750,000 limit on damage awards, Modern Healthcare Daily Dose, 9/16/03. www.modernhealthcare.com.

111. Texas carrier to cut med mal rates by 12% following vote on cap, Page, L. *Modern Physician*, September 15, 2003.

112. Fact Sheet: Insurers and Lobbyists Admit Tort "Reform" won't heal the med mal liability system, and it won't reduce premiums..., American Trial Lawyers Association, www.atla.org/ConsumerMediaResources/Tier3/press_room/FACTS/medmal/inslobyadmit.aspx, (accessed 10/16/03).

113. Malpractice Reform is dead; long live malpractice reform, Scott, Jeanne Schulte. Healthcare Financial Management, (September 2003) p. 32–34.

114. Confronting the New Health Care Crisis, Department of Health and Human Services, 7/24/02, p. 1.

115. Fact Sheet: Medical Malpractice Fibs and Facts, American Trial Lawyers Association, http://www.atla.org/ConsumerMediaResources/Tier3/press_room/FACTS/medmal/medmalfibsfacts.aspx, (accessed 10/16/03).

116. Alaska's Tort Reform Legislation Still Mired in Uncertainty, American Medical Association, 10/14/02, www.ama-assn.org/sci-pubs/amnews/pick_02/ prca1014.htm, (accessed 10/15/03).

117. Fact Sheet: Medical Malpractice Fibs and Facts, American Trial Lawyers Association, http://www.atla.org/ConsumerMediaResources/Tier3/press_room/FACTS/medmal/medmalfibsfacts.aspx, (accessed 10/16/03).

118. California's awards cap lowered premiums, but some patients paid cost, *USA Today,* 3/5/03, p. A.02.

119. Fact Sheet: Medical Malpractice Fibs and Facts, American Trial Lawyers Association, http://www.atla.org/ConsumerMediaResources/Tier3/press_room/FACTS/medmal/medmalfibsfacts.aspx, (accessed 10/16/03).

120. California's awards cap lowered premiums, but some patients paid cost, *USA Today,* 3/5/03, p. A.02.

121. Fact Sheet: Medical Malpractice Fibs and Facts, American Trial Lawyers Association, http://www.atla.org/ConsumerMediaResources/Tier3/press_room/FACTS/medmal/medmalfibsfacts.aspx, (accessed 10/16/03).

122. A second opinion on the malpractice plague. A Commentary, Woellert, L. *Business Week,* March 3, 2003, p. 99-100.

123. Ibid.

124. Medical Malpractice Caps Fail to Prevent Premium Increases, According to Weiss Ratings Study, Weiss Rating Inc., 6/2/03, www.weissratings.com/News/Ins_General/20020602pc.htm, (accessed 10/15/03).

125. Ibid.

126. A second opinion on the malpractice plague. A Commentary, Woellert, L. *Business Week,* March 3, 2003, p. 99–100.

127. Fact Sheet: Medical Malpractice Fibs and Facts, American Trial Lawyers Association, http://www.atla.org/ConsumerMediaResources/Tier3/press_room/FACTS/medmal/medmalfibsfacts.aspx, (accessed 10/16/03).

128. Corporate Astroturf and civil justice: The Corporations behind, Citizens Against Lawsuit Abuse, *Multinational Monitor,* Mar. 2003, p. 18.

129. Fact Sheet: Medical Malpractice Fibs and Facts, American Trial Lawyers Association, http://www.atla.org/ConsumerMediaResources/Tier3/press_room/FACTS/medmal/medmalfibsfacts.aspx, (accessed 10/16/03).

130. Ohio Medical Malpractice Commission: Statement of James Hurley, ACAS, MAAA, Chairperson, Medical Malpractice Subcommittee, American Academy of Actuaries, American Academy of Actuaries, June 11, 2003 (www.actuary.org).

131. Congressional budget office cost estimate, H.R. 4600, U.S. Congressional Budget Office, Sept. 25, 2002, p. 6.

132. Ten things you should know about medical malpractice and insurance premiums, Missouri Association of Trial Attorneys, www.matanet.org, (accessed 9/9/03).

133. The Unconstitutionality of Medical Malpractice Limitations, American Trial Lawyers Association, www.atla.org/ConsumerMediaResources/Tier3/press_room/FACTS/medmal/One%20Pagers/medmal%20constitutionality%20factsheet.aspx, (accessed 10/16/03).

134. Docs return fire: countersuing in frivolous malpractice cases, *Modern Physician,* (September 2003), p. 6.

135. Plaintiffs say malpractice no prescription for riches, Twiddy, D and Brown, MS. *The Business Journal of Kansas City,* August 22, 2003, http://www.bizjournals.com/industries/health_care/physician_practices/2003/08/25/kansas..., (accessed August 25, 2003).

136. Special Report: Hype outraces facts in malpractice debate; Degree of crisis varies among specialties and from state to state, *USA Today,* 3/5/03, p. A.01.

137. Why premiums are soaring again, *Medical Economics Magazine,* (July 9, 2001), www.findarticles.com/cf_0/m3229/13_78/77035508/p1..., (accessed 9/9/03).

138. Insurer, hospitals try apologies for errors; Institutions see lawsuits, claims diminish under such policies, *USA Today,* 3/5/03, p. B.05.

139. Groups blame malpractice crisis on medical errors, *OB/GYN News,* (Feb. 15, 2003), www.findarticles.com/cf_0/m0CYD/4_38/98165950/print.jhtml, (accessed 9/9/03).

140. Future looks bleak as malpractice premiums continue upward spiral: insurers increasing rates to make up for past mistakes, rise in jury awards, www.findarticles.com/cf_0/m0KGX/1_24/83037164/print.jhtml, (accessed 9/9/03).

141. Medical malpractice: implications of rising premiums on access to healthcare, United States General Accounting Office, (August 2003), p. 1–57.

142. Future looks bleak as malpractice premiums continue upward spiral: insurers increasing rates to make up for past mistakes, rise in jury awards, www.findarticles.com/cf_0/m0KGX/1_24/83037164/print.jhtml, (accessed 9/9/03).

143. Medical malpractice: implications of rising premiums on access to healthcare, United States General Accounting Office, (August 2003), p. 1–57.

144. Statement of the Physician Insurers Association of America, Physician Insurers of America, 2/11/03, p. 8.

145. Medical Malpractice Caps Fail to Prevent Premium Increases, According to Weiss Ratings Study, Weiss Ratings, Inc. 6/2/03, www.weissratings.com/News/Ins-General/20030602pc.htm, (accessed 10/15/03).

146. Ohio Medical Malpractice Commission: Statement of James Hurley, ACAS, MAAA, Chairperson, Medical Malpractice Subcommittee, American Academy of Actuaries, American Academy of Actuaries, June 11, 2003 (www.actuary.org).

147. Why premiums are soaring again, *Medical Economics Magazine,* (July 9, 2001), www.findarticles.com/cf_0/m3229/13_78/77035508/p1..., (accessed 9/9/03).

148. Future looks bleak as malpractice premiums continue upward spiral: insurers increasing rates to make up for past mistakes, rise in jury awards, www.findarticles.com/cf_0/m0KGX/1_24/83037164/print.jhtm, (accessed 9/9/03).

149. What's behind the current malpractice insurance crisis: industry experts explain why premiums are currently soaring, www.findarticles.com/cf_0/m0LMB/9_21/94595455/print.jhtml, (accessed 9/9/03).

150. Statement of the Physician Insurers Association of America, Physician Insurers of America, 2/11/03, p. 9.

151. Ibid, p. 8.

152. Why premiums are soaring again, *Medical Economics Magazine,* (July 9, 2001), www.findarticles.com/cf_0/m3229/13_78/77035508/p1..., (accessed 9/9/03).

153. Malpractice Reform is dead; long live malpractice reform, Scott, Jeanne Schulte. Healthcare Financial Management, (September 2003) p. 32–34.

154. What's behind the current malpractice insurance crisis: industry experts explain why premiums are currently soaring, www.findarticles.com/cf_0/m0LMB/9_21/94595455/print.jhtml, (accessed 9/9/03).

155. Back on the tort reform merry-go-round, *Modern Healthcare,* (July 15, 2002). www.modernhealthcare.com/articleID=2184, (accessed 9/9/03).

156. Medical malpractice: implications of rising premiums on access to healthcare, United States General Accounting Office, (August 2003), p. 1–57.

157. Ibid.

158. Ohio Medical Malpractice Commission: Statement of James Hurley, ACAS, MAAA, Chairperson, Medical Malpractice Subcommittee, American Academy of Actuaries, American Academy of Actuaries, June 11, 2003 (www.actuary.org).

159. Medical Malpractice Caps Fail to Prevent Premium Increases, According to Weiss Ratings Study, Weiss Ratings, Inc. 6/2/03, www.weissratings.com/News/Ins-General/20030602pc.htm, (accessed 10/15/03).

160. Medical malpractice: implications of rising premiums on access to healthcare, United States General Accounting Office, (August 2003), p. 1–57.

161. Ohio Medical Malpractice Commission: Statement of James Hurley, ACAS, MAAA, Chairperson, Medical Malpractice Subcommittee, American Academy of Actuaries, American Academy of Actuaries, June 11, 2003 (www.actuary.org).

162. Medical Malpractice, Insurance Information Institute, http://www.iii.org/media/hottopics/insurance/medicalmal/, (accessed September 16, 2003).

163. Statement of the Physician Insurers Association of America, Physician Insurers of America, 2/11/03, p. 4.

164. Groups blame malpractice crisis on medical errors, *OB/GYN News,* (Feb. 15, 2003), www.findarticles.com/cf_0/m0CYD/4_38/98165950/print.jhtml, (accessed 9/9/03).

165. US to set up computer data bank to track bad doctors and dentists, *Detroit Free Press,* Saturday, December 31, 1988.

166. US sets up physicians' data bank. Repository of compiled disciplinary, malpractice records, Cimons, M. *New York Times,* Saturday, December 31, 1988.

167. Questionable Doctors website. http://www.questionabledoctors.org.

168. Ten things you should know about medical malpractice and insurance premiums, Missouri Association of Trial Attorneys, www.matanet.org, (accessed 9/9/03).

169. Groups blame malpractice crisis on medical errors, *OB/GYN News,* (Feb 15, 2003), www.findarticles.com/cf_0/m0CYD/4_38/98165950/print.jhtml, (accessed 9/9/03).

170. Ibid.

Chapter 11

The Capitation Liability Theory

David Edward Marcinko
Charles F. Fenton, III

A physician owned mutual insurance company is a non-profit insurance company owned by its policyholders and structured for their benefit. A mutual insurer established under, and subject to, state insurance laws, is organized to provide the highest quality resources for its insureds at competitive rates. Each of its policyholders, be they physician/surgeon, dentist, hospital, managed care organization, or licensed healthcare facility, is able to participate in the operations of the company by establishing a Board of Directors.

AMA Council of Medical Services

Professional malpractice liability insurance protection is a major fixed operational expense in any at-risk medical practice. In most practices, liability insurance costs often represent one of the largest single line-item expenses, often falling second only to staff payroll expenses. Current management literature is replete with information extolling the business virtues of fixed-rate or capitated reimbursement models of medicine. These include the increased patient volume, consistent cash flow, improved collection patterns, and fixed operational costs of this new payment structure. Managed care business detractors, on the other hand, identify potential negatives, such as increased administrative costs, financial conflicts of interest, performance quotas, and skewed medical liability risk. Managed care business detractors have induced a shift in the focus of most practices over the past decade from being a profit center to a cost driver, and they have greatly influenced the liability purchasing decisions of some medical practices as declining reimbursement rates have made cost containment and efficiency an imperative.

The Liability Insurance Industry

To contain these liability overhead expense costs, the physician-executive should understand the dynamics of the insurance industry selling process. Insurance is generally sold through one of three agency avenues:

- Direct insurance agents serving as employees of a single insurance company
- Captive insurance agents representing only one insurance company
- Independent insurance agents representing multiple insurance companies

An agency relationship is defined as the permission to solicit, create, modify, or terminate a property and casualty malpractice insurance policy. Under this Law of Agency, the agent and insurer are one and the same, and the acts and knowledge of the agent are deemed to be acts and knowledge of the insurer, regardless of whether the insurer has actually authorized the agent to do business. The insurer is bound by acts of its agent if a relationship has been established through express, implied, or apparent authority.

Direct and captive insurance agents have little incentive to promote any company other than the one they represent. Independent agents bring a different set of complexities to the arena. For example, they often receive bonuses or incentives or are held to production quotas as a requirement of employment. Commission structures are the most important incentives at work on the selling side of the process, since different companies pay varying percentages of total premium dollars sold. This can work against the doctor, because the agent has an incentive to sell the highest-priced product to earn the greatest commission. Upon request, however, a reputable insurance brokerage house will provide in writing a detailed market comparison that demonstrates the major options available to the practitioner. This is because, in contrast to agents, an insurance broker is an independent contractor who examines the malpractice needs of the client and then shops for coverage to best fill those needs. Moreover, group insurance purchasing usually nets a better deal than a practitioner could negotiate individually. Thus, if capitated medicine, as demonstrated by many managed care organizations (MCOs), continues, the potential for reduced operational costs through lower medical malpractice premiums could be significant.

This is the major thrust of the capitation liability theory (CLT). Moreover, it suggests that a fixed-rate reimbursement system reduces the incidence of malpractice because it reduces the total number of patient–physician encounters and the acuity of those encounters, particularly for invasive procedures such as surgery and for procedural specialists. Consequently, some providers in the current health-care context may be paying too much for professional liability protection, and others too little.

However, a 2003 study by Mercer University School of Medicine in Georgia showed that 2 to 4 percent of doctors were planning to leave the state that year because of high malpractice premiums. Alan Dever, lead investigator of the study, also reported the following:

- Thirteen percent of doctors had difficulty finding malpractice insurance.

- Twenty percent had changed insurance during the past year.
- Eleven percent had stopped providing emergency room coverage because of malpractice insurance.
- One in five family practitioners reported plans to stop providing high-risk procedures.

The Liability Premium-Setting Process

Most liability insurance companies and their associated underwriters and actuarial advisors have limited interest in the nuisances of patient care and tend to focus on economic factors such as income–loss ratios, market forces, and trend analysis as a basis for a continuing line of insurance coverage. Their bottom line concern is financial and typically considers only those factors that can be altered to realize projected growth, profitability, and return on capital projections. Carriers have considerable latitude in how they function as a business, whom they insure, how they align their members, in what manner they allocate reserves, and how they manage cost and income factors and determine market variations for the purpose of setting premium levels. If their cost trend is downward and their profit trend is upward, efficiency is confirmed. To this end, underwriters and actuaries strive to make the premium pricing process a scientific discipline, but ultimately the process is still a decidedly heuristic one.

As the liability premium-pricing process arrives at the bottom line of corporate fiscal responsibility, the stability of the individual company and national market forces determine premium structure on a comprehensive basis. Managed care entities may be national in scope, but the delivery of health-care services is a local business. The potential negative effect of national pooling on individual premium pricing is significant because the capitation liability theory (defined shortly) is confirmed. Unfortunately, liability underwriters are reluctant and even secretive about sharing confidential experience data. These professionals are skilled at data collection, information management, and manipulation and trend analysis to justify and defend their own charges. Challenging such cost projects and making a case for premium reductions is not easy but can be addressed with adequate knowledge, information, and persistence, as described in the following paragraphs.

The Capitation Liability Theory

The capitation liability theory (CLT) considers four primary areas of potential significance in malpractice liability management and premium costs. The "litigation equation" includes (a) patient communication factors, (b) provider health-care delivery systems and reimbursement factors, (c) payer factors, and (d) revised liability legislation and patient encounter data factors.

Patient communication factors include reduced economic and financial fear, consideration of cultural barriers, improved medical awareness through continuing education, concern for geographic access, focused primary and specialty care availability, management information systems, and the frequency and duration of utilization.

Provider reimbursement factors and health-care delivery systems include both soft and hard varieties. Soft provider factors include increased patient availability to services, accessibility to timely appointments, office and quality care satisfaction surveys, communication assessments, known fixed costs, and technical information interchanges. Hard factors include managed operational procedures, reduced illness severities, defined treatment options, reduced clinical variations, outcomes measurements and quality monitoring, performance quotas, aligned financial incentives, and predictable reimbursements.

Payer factors include practitioner screening and shifting, quality assessment, behavioral modification and team care, provider discipline, complaint management, cost and call economic considerations, and adequate capitalization rates.

Liability factors include allegation frequency and severity, standards of care, defensibility, risk management, premium pricing, loss adjustment, settlement losses, and administrative costs.

To fully understand capitation liability theory, all four parts of the litigation equation must be recognized. These factors, when integrated with underwriter data and experience, determine the level of liability risk and the ultimate cost of malpractice coverage. If capitated medical care is deemed to involve less risk than is seen in the indemnity environment, the cost of liability coverage should gradually decrease as the percentage of capitated manager care increases in a particular office setting. In actual terms, the CLT suggests that capitated insurance and patient care risk are inversely, but not necessarily proportionally, related, since experiential data will determine the percentages.

Premium Structures and Models

Collectively, liability claim managers suggest that financial issues are a secondary, albeit precipitating, factor in 15 to 25 percent of all malpractice allegations. Adjudicators further state that aggressive attempts to collect account balances, deductibles, co-payments, and noncovered services are a significant causative factor in litigious individuals. The liability factor is compounded if the medical outcome is less than desirable. The theory also does not discount the significance of contingency legal arrangements prevalent in the litigation process. Correspondingly, the following four reimbursement structures and models can be reviewed in light of this information.

The *fee-for-service reimbursement model* was the bedrock of health-care financing until recently and was the dominant model of paying for medical services. This insurance-driven and technology-motivated approach was powered by utilization and consumption with limited concern for the total cost of care or economic consequences. While indemnity providers continue to be forgiving in the management of patient indebtedness, the incidence of financial hardship and subsequent litigation is believed to be the most frequent in this system. A recent review of provider-owned insurance carriers generally supports this conclusion.

Conversely, a *capitated model reimbursement system* views the patients and the services they require as a cost driver to be debited against a fixed rate or constant reimbursement scheme. Utilization is controlled, referrals are managed, and technology is limited, but new behavioral problems are created, such as stress, frustration, and liability. However, patient indebtedness and personal financial hardship are substantially reduced, and so is a precipitating liability factor.

The *quasi-socialistic model* is powered by entrepreneurs who believe that health care is immune to market forces such as competition or accountability. Reformer-change agents suggest that consumer needs and social welfare in general will prosper through structured business systems with quantifiable and measurable processes. This top-down management structure embraces the general public opinion that affordable health care is a right and that managed markets are the best model for this philosophy. Although results remain uncertain, the market trend is irreversible.

A *mixed model or transitional reimbursement system* represents the best, or perhaps the worst, of both payment options and is a major administrative challenge for the health-care provider. Services may be classified as a profit or debit depending on the payer arrangement, and all care must be taken with equal concern for quality, medical necessity, and appropriateness. Gatekeepers manage the capitated care, control referrals, and provide care for at-risk financial reimbursement, with the ultimate payer intent of a 50/50 provider mix of primary care and specialists. Frustration is significant for all participants, but the number of malpractice allegations is believed to be reduced.

A preliminary evaluation of these four reimbursement methodologies suggests that the level of malpractice risk and associated litigation is decreasing as the volume of capitated managed care increases.

[A] Insurance Legislation Implications

In response to the liability crisis of the early 1980s, the current malpractice insurance market has evolved as a result of legislative action with the introduction in 1986 of the Liability Risk Retention Act (LRRA). This act turned a hard market for malpractice insurance soft, as legislative action expanded the definition of liability and preempted state regulations that restricted small groups from underwriting for commercial insurance buyers engaged in similar or related business activities.

The LRRA permitted risk retention groups (RRGs) and purchasing groups (PGs) to qualify as insurance companies and to retain certain layers of risk while transferring higher layers to reinsurers. In essence, the LRRA flipped the insurance industry upside down and returned the decision-making process and control back to the consumer.

The fundamental difference between RRGs and PGs is that RRGs retain risks and PGs do not. In enacting the LRRA, Congress provided two ways for insurance buyers to obtain liability coverage. These included becoming owners of their own liability insurance company (RRG) or becoming members of a PG that purchased insurance from a commercial carrier, usually at a substantial discount. The homogeneity requirement states that both RRGs and PGs must be engaged in a similar or related business, but there are no group size requirements, a significant marketing factor. PGs can evolve into RRGs if growth, profitability, and actuarial data are favorable. The advantages can be summarized by the following benefits:

- Tailor-made coverage
- Favorite premium rates
- Better policy terms
- Ownership of the loss experience
- Segregation of loss data
- Reward for good experiences
- Risk management and loss prevention programs
- Long-term commitments from insurers

As the health-care delivery system is transformed by consolidations, mergers, and acquisitions, so is the liability need of the individual, group, or institutional provider. Traditional insurance solutions are no longer suitable for the medicine of the new millennium as hospitals are combined into larger systems, and large systems are merged into even larger organizations with ownership of, or in partnership with, physicians and alternative treatment centers. Risk factors and pricing models of the past become inappropriate for contemporary providers who function within a corporatized structure.

As these larger organizations develop, their malpractice insurance needs change, and so must the companies that supply those needs. Larger groups can afford to take on attrition, or frequency risks, internal to their own capital base and organization structure. As systems grow, groups become increasingly interested in risk layering, reinsurance, and loss-sensitive pricing options.

Larger systems can institute and provide their own internal risk prevention, quality monitoring, and incident management processes. Medical malpractice premium pricing ceases to be a one-dimensional market, even in the same geographic community or specialty provider class. Regulatory management and capitated reimbursement price controls are thus redefining the industry at all levels, and liability pricing and pricing flexibility are no exception.

In fact, according to a *Physicians & Surgeons Update*, "claims trends in the medical liability market have remained essentially unchanged" for 5 years running, and no rate change is anticipated for the coming year, with all physician and surgeon liability policies extended to twelve-month terms.[1] Moreover, the frequency and severity of average indemnity payments are not necessarily reflective of the entire medical liability industry or specialty underwriters. The significance of risk-based, capitated reimbursement systems in the stability of the current professional liability market is not identifiable from current data, but they are believed to be a factor. Additionally, liability data from the several closed-panel capitated reimbursement systems suggest support for the stability trend. As interesting as this may be, staff model HMOs, which are a shrinking type of delivery option, are not necessarily reflective of other vertically integrated and at-risk delivery systems more prevalent in the emerging health-care marketplace.

Therefore, the following six processes can be used to support reduced professional liability costs in an ever-evolving reimbursement system:

- Knowledge of the local medical malpractice market environment and the provider's position in it
- Clarity on how and by whom medical service payment is provided, as well as payment mix, percentages, and trends
- Reluctance to accept quoted liability rates as the only possible option, since further inquiries, comparisons, evaluations, and alternatives may be available
- Implementation of a data-tracking system with risk management and risk education
- Features, technology-driven proprietary information, and specific data for each medical specialty
- Familiarity with the concept of class coverage or multiple coverage for a given exposure incident; a single policy covering all entities is always less expensive than multiple policies covering multiple entities
- Dissemination of risk and the transfer of professional liability to corporate medicine (i.e., PPMCs, IPAs) enterprise systems and managed care structures, thereby layering risk and coverage

Consequently, doing nothing to reduce professional liability costs in an increasingly integrated delivery system environment with capitated reimbursement is a guaranteed financial drain on the medical office's net income after expenses.

[B] Indemnification Concerns

An indemnification or hold harmless clause in a managed care contract is quite specific about the legal relationship between the medical provider (agent, servant, or employee) and the managed care entity, should a medical malpractice issue occur. In the strongest possible language, most MCOs will attempt to shield or indemnify themselves from the actions of their providers, according to the vicarious liability concept of respondent superior under the normal laws of agency.[2] Furthermore, according to attorney Richard W. Boone, JD, of Vienna, Virginia, "what we are really recognizing is that although there may be two entities being sued, there is really a single vent." It then makes legal and economic sense to know in advance which entity will be providing the defense and indemnification and price the capitated contract accordingly. Applying this advice may necessitate additional negotiations, but it does suggest another reason to rethink risk-based reimbursement and liability protection in a managed care environment.

Liability Coverage Forms

Over the past decade, medical liability has been one of the most profitable and exciting segments of the insurance industry, producing returns averaging 30 percent over the 5 years from 1989 to 1993 and well above the financial sector industry average. Specialists, underwriters, provider-owned mutual companies, or health-care associations now underwrite about 70 percent of the U.S. medical malpractice market, with 73 percent being claims-made policies.

Under traditional insurance policies, an occurrence form was maintained even if a negligence claim was made several years later, and a claims-made form developed to prevent the stacking of claims. By definition, occurrence is the repeated stacking of risk exposures, and a loss that occurs during two or more policy periods means that two or more sets of policy limits apply on top of each other. By contrast, a claims-made policy covers claims that are first made during the policy period. Other features of the claims-made form are that it reduces the time medical records must be kept for future claims and that it is more inflation proof than occurrence coverage. Most other provisions of the two forms are identical, and the only real difference is what triggers the coverage. Occurrence coverage applies to the injury that occurs during the policy period, whereas the claims-made form states that insurance applies only if a claim is made during the policy period. Another departure from the occurrence form is that the claims-made agreement states that insurance does not apply if the claim occurred before the retroactive date or after the policy period. Usually, when an occurrence policy is renewed by a claims-made policy, the retroactive date is the effective date of the claims-made policy, thus eliminating overlapping coverage. Once established, the retroactive date may be advanced only with the written consent of the insured doctor, and after being informed of the right to buy a supplemental extended reporting (SERP), or tail coverage, policy. Otherwise, a gap would result if the coverage were to be renewed on an occurrence form or if the coverage were permanently terminated. Once in effect, SERPs of unlimited duration cannot be canceled and can be purchased for an endorsement charge of about 200 percent of the annual coverage premium. SERPs effectively then become the transitional opposite of the retroactive date, since they exclude coverage for earlier occurrences because other insurance applied. It is also important to note that claims-made policies are initially less costly because the SERP is purchased later, whereas tail coverage is initially included with an occurrence policy, making it more costly.

More recently, however, health care has become a claims-made market of change with intensified financial challenges and consolidation driven primarily by the evolving managed care industry and the risk-shifting capitated reimbursement environment. The capitation liability theory can be considered one result of this paradigm shift.

The Contrary Viewpoint

The paradigm shift in health-care reimbursement may signal a decrease in medical liability risk; or it may actually increase the risk. Errors of commission, which may be more likely in a fee-based system, are easier to prove than errors of limited treatment and omission. Nevertheless, the changes in health-care reimbursement may actually be setting the stage for increased medical liability costs in the new millennium, as described in the following three models.

[A] Pure At-Risk Capitation Model

Under the *pure at-risk capitation model*, the health-care provider receives a sum-certain each period in return for treating a certain pool of patients. The provider must provide care to all patients that request it during the specified time period. The fewer patients that the provider treats, and the fewer treatments rendered per patient, the lower the cost per patient and the greater the profit during that time period. Obviously, this model creates a powerful incentive for the provider to treat fewer patients and to provide fewer services to each patient. The incentive is to undertreat. Under this scenario, the number of liability claims made is likely to decrease because fewer patients are treated and fewer at-risk procedures are performed. However, the likelihood is great that the claims that are presented will result in a larger payout because, by undertreating a patient, one gives the adverse condition significant time to worsen until definitive treatment is undertaken, and damages will be much greater.

For example, if an MCO limits the provider's ability to provide mammogram screenings, far fewer women will be diagnosed with the earlier stages of breast cancer. By the time a woman falls within the age parameters of the MCO to be eligible for the mammogram, a small surgical lesion may have progressed to a large metastasized lesion. The eventual liability would become much greater. This model is more common with primary care provider (PCP) medical groups. In the current trend, PCPs are seeing more patients whereas the specialists are seeing fewer patients. The gatekeeper concept, and the plans that require the PCP group to pay specialists, all seek to encourage treatment by PCPs and to limit referrals. The incentive for this outcome is the real or perceived increased cost of specialist treatment. Not only are PCPs seeing more patients, they are also treating more conditions and performing more procedures that, a decade ago, were more often under the purview of a specialist. The result is that PCPs may end up treating conditions and performing procedures for which they are not suited by training or experience. As PCPs venture into these areas, the likelihood of incompetence, patient injury, and liability claims increases.

In this model, specialists also see more patients that are likely to increase the specialist's risks. The patient may have had previous treatment by the PCP and the specialist's treatment may be more advanced. In the past, the chances were that a specialist may have initiated conservative treatment, but now he or she gives more advanced treatment and thus increases his or her risk. Not only may the prior treatment by the PCP have been ineffective, but the patient may actually be worse. Consequently, a sicker patient increases the risk for the specialist. Finally, the pure at-risk capitation model may increase risks for greater injuries and greater awards/settlements.

[B] Reduced Fee-for-Service Model

Under the *reduced fee-for-service model,* the provider receives a fee for every patient treated and a fee for every procedure performed. The provider can increase revenue by increasing the number of patients treated and the amount of procedures performed. Under this scenario, there is no decreased liability risk, or it may actually increase, for several reasons.

First, more patients are treated and more procedures are performed. Each individual patient encounter carries with it a degree of risk. By increasing the number of encounters, one increases the risk. It would appear that the risk would increase arithmetically, but in fact it has the potential to increase exponentially because the provider only has a certain amount of time in which to provide the service. In the current environment, the provider must squeeze more encounters into the same time period than he or she did a decade ago. The increased workload may increase the provider's stress and fatigue. With increased stress and fatigue, mistakes are more likely. Therefore, the increased liability risk is due not only to the increased number of patients, but also to the increased fatigue levels, which may result in medical error. Under this model, there is also the possibility of undertreatment. The provider may determine that the reimbursement for certain procedures is unreasonably low and may avoid such procedures. To the extent that the provider performs a lesser procedure, the possibility of liability increases.

[C] Hybrid Capitation/Reduced Fee-for-Service Model

This hybrid model is commonly employed with a group of specialists, as opposed to primary care physicians. An entire group of specialists will be capitated with a fixed dollar amount (risk pool). The allocation to the individual specialist will be based on a function of the allowed rate of all procedures performed by the individual, compared with the allowed rate of all procedures by the group. Although the entire group of specialists is capitated such that the MCO's liability is limited, each individual provider still acts on a (reduced) fee-for-service basis. Unless there are disincentives, this forces each provider to compete for a smaller share of the monetary disbursement. By performing more services and procedures, the individual provider can increase the share of the total allocated capitation. However, by increasing the number of services performed in aggregate, he or she reduces the total reimbursement per service or procedure.

Unlike the pure at-risk capitation model, which gives incentive to reduce the number of services and procedures, this hybrid capitated/fee-for-service model actually creates incentives, up to the point of diminishing marginal (marginal cost greater than marginal benefit) returns, for the individual to increase the number of services. The increase in services will continue until the individual perceives that the per-procedure reimbursement has fallen to levels that make the addition or continuation of certain services and procedures unprofitable.

This model has several advantages for the MCO. First and foremost, the MCO's liability is limited and definite. Second, specialists will individually seek to increase the number of patients treated. Consequently, MCO patients have access to needed specialist care. Finally, this model also has the potential to have the same drawbacks as both the at-risk capitated model and the reduced fee-for-service model. There is incentive both for undertreatment in certain instances, and for increased patient encounters in other instances.

Miscellaneous Liability Factors

The current managed care environment also poses several other threats that may increase the number and severity of claims. These factors relate mostly to the depersonalization of modern medicine and create forces that can increase the likelihood of a lawsuit.

Unlike in prior decades, there is a significant decrease in patient loyalty. Patients are driven by MCO plans, and providers are driven by costs and revenues.

Patients perceive physician services to be interchangeable and medically equivalent. Currently, most have no loyalty to any one individual provider. Patients select PCPs based on the list in an insurance book. When they change plans (either by employer substitution or by change of employer), they often are required to select a new PCP from a new list of options. Patients consider the PCP to be the "insurance company's doctor," and the idea of "my personal doctor" departs with bygone days. Loyalty to medical specialists is especially strained because in the past patients often chose specialists based on reputation. Now, it is just as likely that the patient will be referred to an unknown specialist and have no input into the selection process. This factor, combined with less time for the specialist to develop patient rapport, leads to the patient viewing the specialist more impersonally, when considering whether to file a malpractice claim.

Additionally, with patients changing MCO plans and being subjected to different medical provider panels, there is the increased likelihood that one provider may start a treatment plan and may not finish it. With patients switching providers, the provider will lose control of the patient. Subsequent treating physicians may find fault with the prior treatment and cause the patient to seek redress. This also may increase the likelihood of claims.

Current Trends

Since there are numerous methods of managed care provider reimbursement, it is impossible to determine with certainty that the incidence of liability claims will increase or decrease over time. Recent trends do demonstrate a decrease in claim frequency, with an increase in claim severity. For example, in a 2003 study done at Brigham and Women's Hospital and at Harvard School of Public Health, and published in the *New England Journal of Medicine,* Dr. Donald Berwick, of the Institute for Healthcare Improvement, noted that surgical tools such as sponges, clamps, and retractors are still left in about 1,500 patients each year. If the number of claims decreases but the severity of those claims rises, then there will be no net change in medical malpractice claims experience, and hence no change in insurance premiums.

In a 2002–2003 Political Action Committee report demonstrating the extent of the current malpractice insurance crisis, the AMA reported that 12 states are in "crisis" and about 30 more are problematic, based on anecdotal reports of premium increases and practice abandonment. Especially hard-hit states were Florida, Georgia, Mississippi, New Jersey, New York, Ohio, Oregon, Pennsylvania, Texas, Washington, and West Virginia. See Table 11.1.

More stable states were Colorado, California, Hawaii, Indiana, Louisiana, New Mexico, Rhode Island, and Wisconsin, presumably because of caps on economic damages.

Specialty-Specific Insurers

One way to keep malpractice liability premiums low may be through specialty-specific carriers, using RRGs, as member physicians perform underwriting tasks, rate setting, and strategic operations. They also provide additional services, such as providing risk and practice management experts, and are less likely to settle lawsuits. First prominent in the 1970s, when they controlled more than 60 percent of the medical malpractice market share and $6.1 billion in net premiums, their power dwindled in the 1990s. They are making a comeback today.

But there is a downside to physician-owned insurers. These include limited experience, reserve requirements, financial backing, and sparse track record. Nevertheless, there are more than 51 specific submarkets, and 40 so-called bed pan mutuals, that now

Table 11.1 *Top Five Medical Malpractice Payments**

State	Physicians	Claims	Total	Median
Maine	3,588	413	$ 18,947,319	$262,482
Illinois	35,943	6,639	271,050,075	250,000
Massachusetts	28,886	2,709	120,874,822	250,000
Alabama	9,877	592	34,839,809	200,000
Connecticut	13,279	1,463	72,233,556	200,000

**Source: Modern Physician,* July 2003.*

serve orthopedic surgeons in Pennsylvania (Positive Mutual Risk Retention Group, Inc.), ophthalmologists in San Francisco (Ophthalmic Mutual Insurance Company), podiatrists in Tennessee (Podiatry Insurance Company of America), general practitioners in Illinois (Illinois State Medical Inter-Insurance Exchange), internists in New Jersey (MIIX Advantage Insurance Corporation), optometrists (Optometric Insurance of America), and chiropractors (Nationwide Chiropractors) across the country.

The Physician Insurers Association of America in Rockville, Maryland, which represents many of these RRGs, reports a membership combined ratio (a measurement of company viability) of 141, compared to an industry average of 154. Actuaries suggest the figure should be closer to 125.

The top five physician-owned medical malpractice mutual companies are MLMIC Group, Doctors Company Insurance Group, Pro Assurance Group, Healthcare Indemnity, Inc., and the NORCAL Group. Laggards include neurosurgeons and ob/gyns. A related innovation may be a tracking company, or system of medical providers, that monitors and follows the unhappy patients who are the most likely to sue.

Conclusion

Liability underwriters and actuarial advisors are risk-adverse by education and training. They react slowly, cautiously, and incrementally to shifting risk factors, especially toward trends that suggest reduced underwriter income and liability premiums. Physicians and medical group administrators must therefore develop their own strategies for evaluating liability risk factors, and they may lead the trend toward reduced operational expenses through managed liability costs. This is accomplished by exploring the advantages of LLRAs, as presented in this chapter.

Acknowledgments

The author thanks Dr. G. Stephen Gill, MBA, MHS, for technical assistance in the production of this paper.

References

1. American Association of Family Physicians: www.aafp.org.
2. American College Emergency Physicians: www.empractice@acep.org.
3. Leimberg, SR: *Tools and Techniques of Insurance Planning*. National Underwriter, Cincinnati, 1997.
4. Vaughn, E: *Fundamentals of Risk and Insurance*. Wiley & Sons, New York, 1995.

Additional Readings

1. Addressing the medical malpractice insurance crisis. NGA Center for Best Practices Issue Brief, Health Policy Studies Division, December 5, 2002.
2. AMA/specialty society medical liability project. *Professional Liability Update,* April, 1991.
3. Bellandi, D: A win for docs in California: Effort to raise caps on malpractice awards fails. *Modern Healthcare,* p. 42, *30*(19):30-34, 2000.
4. Woellert, L: A Second opinion on the malpractice plague. *Business Week,* March 3, 2003, pp. 98, 100.

Websites

The following URL addresses have also been found to contain worthwhile malpractice and professional liability insurance information:

- *America's Medical Liability Crisis: A National View.* American Medical Association: www.ama-assn.org/amal/pub/upload/mm/399/mlrmap.pdf.
- Analysis: Cause of rises in medical malpractice insurance rates. News Library.com http://nl.newsbank.com/nlsearch/we/Archives?p_action=doc&p_docid=0F9079 4791FEC...(accessed 2/5/03).
- Are insurer investments in good shape? Association of Trial Lawyers of America. Association of Trial Lawyers of America website: www.atla.org/ ConsumerMediaResources/Tier3/press_room/FACTS/medmal/medmal.aspx (accessed 10/16/03).

Endnotes

1. St. Paul Medical Services.
2. See www.law.cornell for further information on the law of agency.

Chapter 12

Medical Malpractice Trial Risks

(A Necessary Evil . . . or Simply Evil?)

Jay S. Grife

rimum non nocere.[1] This Latin phrase is one of the earliest commands students of medicine receive and provides an ethical foundation for their mission to heal the sick. It asks little in objective terms but demands an immense measure of dedication and knowledge from those who practice their profession. Yet, it is roughly estimated that one of every five practicing health-care professionals will confront the enigmatic process of medical malpractice within a 12-month span. Although most health-care practitioners will never see the inside of a courtroom, the sequelae of the event itself can scar the psyche forever. What can be done when the inevitable happens, and what can you as a practicing doctor do to confront the process?

"Even among the sciences, medicine occupies a special position. Its practitioners come into direct and intimate contact with people in their daily lives; they are present at the critical transitional moments of existence. For many people, they are the only contact with a world that otherwise stands at a forbidding distance. Often in pain, fearful of death, the sick have a special thirst for reassurance and vulnerability to belief."[2] When this trust is violated, or when patients think it is violated, American jurisprudence offers several remedies, with the core being civil litigation. Patients seek the counsel of an attorney for many reasons: an untoward result of treatment or surgery; an outstanding invoice being mailed to a less-than-happy patient who decides that the doctor's treatment did not measure up to expectations; a physician's wife, employed as the office manager, charging a patient $85 to complete a medical leave authorization form; or simply a perceived lack of concern on the part of the doctor or his or her personnel. Compound any of these scenarios with well-meaning friends and family, and the proverbial prescription for litigation has been filled.

This discussion suggests way to prevent such events from happening. All of these ways are based on honest communication.

In the United States, a trial is thought to be the most common manner in which disputes are resolved. Contrary to what we see on television, very few cases actually make it to trial; most are either dismissed or resolved through mediation or arbitration. The U.S. Department of Justice recently reported that only about 3 percent of all civil cases are resolved by a trial. The vast majority of civil lawsuits, and in particular medical malpractice cases, are settled or dismissed before any of the litigants see a courtroom.

Dear Doctor, You Have Been Served a Lawsuit

Don't run to the nearest bridge or fly into an explosive tantrum. Don't throw your hands up in the air and blame the world. It is estimated that one in every two health-care professionals will be the recipient of such news at some time during his or her professional career.

[A] First Steps

When such an event happens, it is best to finish the day and, when things are subdued, sit down and slowly assess what has happened. If you read and believe the complaint that the plaintiff's lawyer has served you, you will probably conclude that not only are you negligent but that you border upon the criminal.

At this point, take the patient or plaintiff's medical records and make exact copies of every single document. Copy your computer files that reference this patient onto a portable medium of your choosing. Put the originals in an envelope and seal it. *Do not make any changes to the medical records or to the computer data.* Your patient's medical records are your best evidence, and in the world of medical-legal jurisprudence, an inference of truth and fact immediately attaches to them that can be permanently shattered by any changes, well meaning or otherwise.

[B] Call Your Medical Malpractice Insurance Company

Contact your medical malpractice insurance company. Speak to a representative in the claims department, advise him or her of the current situation, and follow his or her instructions for reporting the claim. Your cooperation with your carrier is essential if you are to conform to most policies and ensure that you do not do anything to waive your coverage. At some time in the immediate future, your insurer will assign your case to a defense attorney, who will become your constant companion for the next several years. It is this person who will undertake the investigation of your case and the study of your patient's allegations. At times your lawyer will appear to be your therapist or knight in shining armor, and at other times may even seem to be working against your best interests. None of this is factual. Your lawyer is an expert assigned to investigate your case and to provide you with the best defense and advice available, all the time looking through the lens of objectivity. Remember, your view is tinted with emotion and the passion that you have done nothing wrong. But make no mistake about it; it is your lawyer who will tell you when you should hold them and when you should fold them.

[C] Secure Personal Counsel

Personal counsel is an attorney with extensive experience in the management of medical negligence cases and one that does so on a daily basis. Personal counsel should be an attorney who has been researched by you and/or your associates so that you feel comfortable knowing that this person has the understanding and skill necessary to represent your interests. It is a lawyer whom you may retain *independent of* counsel assigned by your insurance carrier. In the vast majority of cases, personal counsel is an attorney whom you will retain to represent your interests at your cost. The essential difference to appreciate is that counsel assigned to you by your insurance company will be retained and reimbursed by your insurer, but personal counsel is an attorney of your choosing whom you agree to retain and compensate.

Is this necessary? If you are a health-care professional who has no insurance coverage, chances are your decision to go bare will necessitate the retaining of personal counsel. Of course, those who have adeptly concealed their personal assets so as to be judgment-proof might not deem it necessary, but in that event the doctor must be ready to accept the possibility of an adverse financial judgment and the necessity of a bankruptcy proceeding if legally applicable. While those doctors going bare might consider the fact that they have no insurance to be the best insurance against a plaintiff's lawyer filing suit, it takes only one compassionate plaintiff's lawyer to upset that apple cart.

Those doctors who have malpractice insurance have a different type of decision to make in retaining personal counsel. The malpractice insurance company has assigned an attorney to you and will be compensating that attorney for his or her efforts in defending you. That same attorney and/or his or her law firm may have numerous other doctors they are representing who maintain coverage with the same insurance company. Some view this as a conflict of interest. Is the assigned attorney representing your interests or that of the insurance company? Despite the best efforts of the assigned defense counsel, it is not out of the question for that counsel to appreciate the financial realities of the situation. Once your case is over, new business is dependent upon the insurance company and not you. So the dilemma of the personal counsel comes down to whether you deem it prudent to retain and compensate an attorney to solely and without question represent your interests, even at the expense of your assigned counsel and the insurance company. The decision is an individual one, but also a necessary one. In those cases in which I have been retained as personal counsel, my job has been to review the case and decide whether the plaintiff's case has merit, and I may decide it does, even if my client, the defendant-doctor, is at risk of an adverse judgment greater than the amount of insurance coverage available. If this is a possibility, it becomes my job to ensure that my client does not face that eventuality, and my exclusive duty is to the doctor who has retained me.

The Trial Players

In every civil trial, besides counsel for the respective parties, there is a plaintiff (patient) and a defendant (doctor). Although it is not mandatory that the plaintiff be represented by an attorney, an unrepresented plaintiff who is *Pro Se* most likely will find the course difficult to traverse. The plaintiff is the aggrieved party, or accuser who files a complaint, and the defendant is the party against whom a complaint is lodged, or the accused. Some cases may involve multiple plaintiffs, multiple defendants, or both. Regardless of the numbers of parties involved, there must be *de facto* two opposing sides to a lawsuit. Often those respective sides make for interesting bedfellows, such as where several of the named defendants each perceive the other as being at fault. In those cases, the finger pointing often is directed away from the plaintiff and toward the other defendant(s) in the case. At those times, the mentality can often shift toward a Darwinian one of survival, leaving the plaintiff the sole benefactor.

In addition to the parties and their respective counsel, witnesses, both lay and expert, form the main body of testimony that will be elicited and heard by the judge and jury. The respective parties both present their witnesses in a procedural order as determined by the venue of the litigation. Both lay and expert witnesses serve to tell the story of the parties to the court. In a medical malpractice case, lay witnesses generally explain the facts of specific events they have witnessed, or more likely, how the plaintiff has been affected by the alleged negligence. The parties may also call a special kind of witness, called a medical expert, to testify on their behalf. An expert witness is simply a witness with experience in a particular field, whose testimony will aide the lay jury in understanding the medical aspects of the case. Often the expert witness can be the trump card necessary for that party to prevail, but all too often medical experts tend to "cancel each other out," leaving a jury to decide based upon the remaining evidence presented.

In most medical malpractice cases, the plaintiff must present expert testimony from a health-care practitioner that the defendant fell below the standard of care required and caused injury to the patient. These are the two essential prongs that, when conjoined, equate to negligence in legal terminology, liability being a breach in the standard of care and causation being that the negligence caused the plaintiff damages. It is essential to understand that a plaintiff cannot prevail in litigation if only one of these two prongs has been left unsatisfied. For example, if a physician failed to diagnose cancer in a terminally ill patient, the fact that the diagnosis was not made can be deemed negligent but the negligence in the failure to diagnose did not damage the patient in that she was terminal when she initially presented. It is this two-pronged test that delineates legal negligence from commonly expressed negligence or a bad result from the care and treatment provided.

In rare instances, and in ever diminishing jurisdictions, expert testimony is not required in medical negligence matters. In those instances, the legal doctrine of *Res Ipsa Loquitur*, or "the thing speaks for itself," often will prevail. Normally, in a medical malpractice case, a plaintiff is required to establish (1) a breach in the standard of care or an act or omission by the defendant that was not in keeping with the degree of skill and learning ordinarily used under the same or similar circumstances by members of the defendant's profession; and (2) causation, or evidence that such negligence or omission caused the plaintiff's injury. However, the doctrine of *Res Ipsa Loquitur* precludes the need for direct proof of negligence through medical testimony and allows cases submitted under the doctrine to proceed to the jury even in the absence of testimony as to negligence, because a jury is permitted to draw an inference of negligence from the specific act itself. The classic example of such an incident would be leaving a surgical instrument inside a patient's body, or operating upon the wrong limb.

The judge and jury are the final participants in a trial. The judge presides over the trial and makes rulings regarding the law and its application to the case. Only the judge is permitted to rule upon issues of law. The jury members are called the triers, or judges, of fact in that they listen to the evidence and determine the facts, based upon their collective wisdom. For example, when two parties tell different versions of an event, the jury must decide which side it believes is true. In cases where there is no jury, the judge decides both the law and the facts.

Burden of Proof

In all civil trials, the plaintiff, as the accuser, has the burden of proving his or her case. Much like a criminal defendant, a civil defendant has no burden of proof and is presumed "innocent" of any claim as alleged by the plaintiff. As a result, if the plaintiff presents insufficient evidence to support his or her claim, the defendant's counsel will likely seek a directed verdict pursuant to the prevailing law from the judge. Should the judge conclude that the plaintiff has failed to establish those elements of medical negligence as required, the judge will order the verdict directed in favor of the defendant-doctor. In other words, the defendant wins without having to present his or her case. The burden the plaintiff carries in a civil arena is that he or she must prove his or her case by what is called a preponderance of the evidence. In other words, the plaintiff must prove it is more likely than not that the facts as presented prove the case. The burden is distinct from that in criminal law, where beyond a reasonable doubt is necessary. The best way to visualize this burden is to imagine a set of scales. If the scales are even, or tipped in favor of the defendant, then the plaintiff has not carried his or her burden, and loses. In order to prevail, the plaintiff must tip the scales in his or her favor. And it can be tipped by no more than 50.1 to 49.9 percent.

To succeed in a case of alleged medical malpractice, a plaintiff-patient must present evidence that the defendant-doctor was negligent, and the plaintiff does this by proving that the treatment provided was below the *applicable standard of care*. This phrase is often misapplied and misunderstood, but in essence it means that the health-care provider failed to use the degree of care and skill that a reasonably prudent practitioner under similar circumstances would have used in treating a patient. Although the standard of care has a fairly universal legal meaning, it has variances throughout the different states. In some jurisdictions a national standard of care is the accepted norm, and in others it can be a locality rule. The difference is of vital significance because when expert testimony is sought, that expert must be knowledgeable and able to testify as to the standard of care pursuant to that jurisdiction, regardless of whether it be local or otherwise. In those minority areas where the locality rule remains in effect, often an expert must be from that specific community or have discussed the standard of care with a local doctor so as to be sufficiently versed in it.[3] In addition, the standard of care, even though established by the medical community at large, is constantly evolving. Care that violates the standard of care today may not necessarily violate the standard of care several years ago. This distinction is an important one, since most cases take several years to reach trial readiness. Of critical importance is to appreciate that even when the public at large often will equate a bad result as negligence, legally it may not be a violation of the standard of care.

For the plaintiff to succeed in tipping those scales in his or her favor, expert medical testimony is required to establish a violation of the standard of care in virtually all medical malpractice cases. A plaintiff that fails to present the required expert medical testimony in a medical malpractice case, but for those instances where *Res Ipsa Loquitur* is applicable, will lose. As noted previously, the plaintiff must also produce expert medical testimony as to a violation of the standard of care and that the alleged negligence caused the injury.

Finally, it is an unfortunate reality that the jury often does not have the medical knowledge necessary to appreciate the nuances of medicine and the clinical judgment afforded doctors. That is not to say that juries do not do their utmost to reach a reasoned verdict, but medicine can be a difficult proposition for the trained individual, let alone a layman. In a case several years ago in California, a jury listened to the evidence in a medical malpractice case for several weeks. Following a plaintiff's verdict, several of the jurors agreed to discuss their deliberations with the parties' counsels. When asked for a reason that the jury found for the plaintiff against the physician, one specific juror admitted it was because of the expert medical testimony. When probed further, the juror stated that he believed the plaintiff's medical expert to be most credible and knowledgeable because whereas the defendant's expert had charged $500 per hour to testify in court, the plaintiff's expert had charged $650 per hour.

Types of Trials

There are two types of trials available to the parties, trial by jury or a bench trial exclusively by the judge. In a trial by jury, the judge determines the law and the jury determines the facts. In a bench trial, the judge wears both the hats of being the judge of law and the judge of fact. The U.S. Constitution guarantees a trial by jury. If a party does not request a jury trial, that right may be deemed forfeit; by the same token, both sides must agree to waive a jury trial.

So why would anyone choose to have a case heard by a judge as opposed to a jury, or vice versa? The reasons are mainly based on preconceived notions about judge and juror biases. Generally, most litigants favor a jury over a judge because the decision is put into the hands of many rather than in the hands of one.[4] Plaintiffs usually like juries because lay individuals are believed to be more sympathetic, and a plaintiff can appeal to the emotions of a jury. Conversely, defendants usually prefer bench trials because a judge is thought to be more objective in deciding a case. Requesting a bench trial can also result in a much quicker trial date. Since court dockets in most large cities are becoming increasingly congested, the time difference between a jury trial date and a bench trial date can be literally years.

None of the perceptions about the benefits of a jury trial or a bench trial applies to all situations—every case is different. There is at least some empirical evidence that some of the commonly held conceptions about bench and jury trials are actually misconceptions. For example, although it is almost universally believed that juries tend to favor plaintiffs and award much higher monetary amounts, a recent study by the Department of Justice[5] suggests that *judges* favor plaintiffs and return higher verdicts. Still, jury trials outnumber bench trials by about two to one.

Discovery Process

In that most medical negligence cases are fact driven, the topic of discovery demands a specific and integral role in the trial process. Discovery simply is the methodology used in American jurisprudence for each side to discover all of the evidence that is available in the case and to have that documentation analyzed. Although specific states have rules that may limit discovery, the purpose is to prevent trial by ambush.[6]

According to the Federal Rules of Civil Procedure, discovery can include written interrogatories or questions; requests for production; depositions, either oral or through written statements; requests for examination; requests for inspection of evidence; requests for admission; and, finally, independent, or as plaintiffs' lawyers commonly label them, compulsory medical examinations.

The scope of the these discovery methods is generally a book in itself, so suffice it to say that discovery is the process whereby each party exchanges information so that the merit of their respective cases can be evaluated. Lawyers will use this evidence in developing the theory of their case and the order in which that evidence will be presented to the trier (judge) of fact. Although discovery is often viewed as a mundane part of the process, in reality it is the very topic that often proves dispositive in the ultimate outcome of the case, whether it be tried, settled, or rejected.

Depositions

One of the discovery methods listed does deserve specific discussion because the deposition, or oral statement under oath, is such a vital piece of the puzzle. In general, either party may depose any other person, but a deponent usually has some relevance to the case, whether it be as a fact witness, an expert witness, or a before-and-after witness (a person who can testify as to the state of affairs of a person before and after the incident in question).

Depositions are taken to gain an insight into what information will be necessary to prosecute or defend a case. Even more important is that the oral deposition provides the respective lawyer with a chance to evaluate that person's reactions to stress, to personally see the temperament of the witness, to view the witness's demeanor, and to analyze how that person responds to spontaneous events. The format is typically oral and in question-and-answer dialogue, although recent technology has permitted depositions via telephone conference, videoconference, and Internet medium exchanges. Depositions can be taken in a written question format, but often this type has limited value because the deponent will not be asked any follow-up questions and a statement cannot be investigated further.

There are lists of do's and don'ts that lawyers provide their clients, but the fundamental character of the deposition is for the deponent to tell the truth. Although it is rare that a trial sees the Perry Mason moment, these do in fact happen and when they do, the result is often exactly what viewers of that classical television series see. As a rule, in light of the attorney client privilege, I insist upon knowing whatever skeletons are in my client's closet, past or present. It is of ultimate importance that clients confide the truth to their lawyer so that any adverse issue can be addressed through cognizant decision, rather than surprise. In a recent case, my client was being deposed and admitted to me that she was a lesbian. Her sexual preferences did not matter, but the fact that she disclosed a misdemeanor arrest for marijuana did. I advised her to tell the truth about both issues and explained why this was important. During her deposition, when the homophobic defense counsel abrasively probed her sexuality, she readily admitted her own sexual preference. That was fine, but the defense lawyer continued to "push her buttons" until she finally screamed at him to "shut the f... up." The die was cast because the next line of questioning involved her arrest record as to the marijuana. When my client denied any other arrests but for the drugs, it was simple for the defense counsel to show her documentation of four earlier felony arrests, including one for fraud, which ultimately cost her the case. The important fact to remember is that we all have a past and that being truthful as to its content can often dictate a successful outcome of a case.

Motions *In Limine*

Motions *in limine* are one of the many weapons lawyers use to limit the jurors hearing evidence that is deemed to be irrelevant or too prejudicial to a party. A lawyer must be tactical in this area so that the jury never can appreciate that information is being withheld, thereby creating doubt as to the honesty of that lawyer. A typical example and one that I confront often is whether to permit the jury to know that, in addition to being a lawyer, I am also a doctor. In every case I must gauge the advisability of disclosing to the jury that I am also a doctor or simply use a motion *in limine* to prevent that fact from being disclosed. Can you imagine the impact upon the jury if the fact that I am a doctor were withheld and a witness, expert or lay, through intention or true neglect, testified something to the fact of "come on now, you are a doctor, you know it's true"? The jury might interpret this as a conspiracy to have a special "hired gun" doing that party's bidding rather than as a simple advocate of the truth. Or the jury may interpret this as part of a game plan to protect one of my own physician colleagues despite the apparent negligence.

Jury Selection

The selection process for a jury begins with what is called the jury pool. A number of citizens are selected as potential jurors, usually several times the number of jurors needed for a trial. From this pool of potential jurors, the jury panel is selected.

The size of the jury panel varies by state and locale. Most juries consist of about 6 to 12 individuals on a panel. In addition, 1 or more alternate jurors may also be selected. Alternate jurors sit with the jury and hear evidence just as all the other jurors do. In some states, they also sit in on jury deliberations, though they are not allowed to participate. If for some reason a member of the selected jury is unable to continue with the trial or deliberations, the alternate juror fills in. The number of alternate jurors varies, and determining that number is usually left to the discretion of the judge. Generally, the longer the trial, the more alternate jurors are sworn in.

Before any potential juror appears at the courthouse for a trial, usually a questionnaire form is mailed for the individual to complete and return to the court. Such forms generally request demographic information such as name, age, occupation, educational background, participation as a party or witness in previous litigation, previous jury service, and so forth. Attorneys for the parties are able to obtain and review these questionnaires in advance of the trial date.

On the day of trial, when the potential jurors arrive at the courthouse, the judge typically asks some generic questions about their ability to serve. The judge may ask whether any potential juror has a problem staying for the duration of the trial, or whether the potential jurors know any of the parties or their attorneys. The purpose of these questions is for the judge to determine which, if any, of the potential jurors will be excused immediately from service.

Many juries tend to be composed of citizens with little or no college education. One of the possible reasons for this result is that many professionals, especially medical professionals, request to be excused from jury service, citing their professional commitments as justification. Ironically, professionals are usually the first to complain when juries who lack any representatives with advanced education hear their own cases. Once the judge is finished with the preliminary screening of the jury pool, voir dire begins.

[A] Voir Dire: Questioning of the Jurors

Voir dire literally means "to speak the truth." It is the term used to represent the preliminary questioning of potential jurors. The purpose of voir dire is to uncover any prejudice or bias in potential jurors. Plaintiffs' attorneys in medical malpractice cases will try to determine if the potential jurors have any strong connection to a health-care provider that might make the juror favor the defendant-doctor. Similarly, medical malpractice defense attorneys will try to uncover any bad experiences the potential jurors may have had with a health-care practitioner, which may make the juror biased in favor of the patient. The judge, the attorneys, or both can conduct the questioning. Most jurisdictions allow the attorneys to conduct voir dire. The key to successful voir dire is not to change an avowed racist into a liberal but to discover that juror's attitudes and position as to issues, and thereafter appropriately respond to that disclosure.

Voir dire is such an important aspect of the trial process that often studies conclude that the trial is over when voir dire ends. Attorneys will spend a great deal of time in voir dire preparation to detect juror bias, adverse attitudes and thoughts, and prejudice, be it overt or covert. This is simply a human exercise using intuition, gut feelings, and common sense, and in which the input from a plaintiff or defendant often has as much influence as that of counsel. In some cases, jury specialists and consultants such as psychologists are retained to provide expertise in the process. These experts often provide invaluable insight into the process, but as any consultant worth her salt will admit, it is an inexact science. The essence of the process is to identify those potential jurors who tend to exhibit a positive identity toward your case facts or those who react adversely, while at the same time not being so blatant as to tip your hand to the opposition.

Beyond trying to eliminate bias against their clients, attorneys often use the voir dire process to try to "educate" the jury and to develop a rapport in their favor. They also use voir dire to begin placing before the potential jurors the theories of the complaint and defense so as to try to gauge their reactions. Skillful attorneys will tacitly use the questioning process of voir dire to prepare the jury to find in favor of their clients.

[B] Challenges of Jurors

When the attorneys and/or the judge have finished voir dire of the potential jurors, challenges may be made to remove potential jurors from serving on the sworn jury panel. Attorneys use the challenge phase of jury selection to remove jurors who may favor the other side's case. To remove potential jurors, two types of challenges may be made to "strike" the individual from the jury.

The first type of challenge is a challenge for cause. A "for cause" challenge is one in which the attorneys are required to state and present reasons for removing the potential juror. The rationale given is usually that the challenged juror cannot hear the case fairly for one reason or another. For example, a juror may have stated that he or she will not abide by a judge's instructions because he or she does not think they are fair. Such a situation is a clear reason for having the juror removed for cause. The number of for-cause challenges are unlimited, and the judge decides whether to excuse the challenged potential juror. Other challenges for cause may be based on a claim of juror bias. In practice, however, very few for cause challenges based on alleged bias are sustained. In the famous Attica prison riot trial in New York, Ernie Goodman, counsel for one of the alleged rioting prisoners, was fortunate enough to have law students who used questionnaires, canvassed the neighborhoods of potential jurors, and provided insight into what make of automobile was in the driveways and whether any bumper stickers were attached. That information, along with the typical television habits of the potential jurors and the complexion of the neighborhood, helped Goodman ferret out most of the racial predisposition. Discovering that persons living in a certain neighborhood were more prone to racial bigotry served Goodman well during the voir dire process. The process is inexact and a juror can fool the system.

The second type of challenge is a peremptory challenge (*peremptory*, meaning absolute, not *pre*emptory). Each party is given a certain number of peremptory challenges by which to remove any potential juror from the panel. In civil trials, each side generally has two or more peremptory challenges.

No reason is needed to strike a potential juror when using a peremptory challenge, and the individual is automatically excused. The only exception is that the strike must be race and gender neutral. If a pattern of strikes suggests that peremptory challenges were used to remove potential jurors because of their race or gender, the entire process must be restarted. Volumes of law journal articles have been written about race- and gender-based peremptory challenges, and an extensive discussion is beyond the scope of this chapter. Suffice it to say that objecting to peremptory challenges because they are race or gender based is the exception rather than the rule. In most cases, the number of challenges allowed is too small to show any pattern.

Challenging a juror can often be a tactical decision that often has far-reaching consequences. Certainly it seems simple enough to strike a juror who has voiced concerns that doctors are all quacks, but caution must be exercised so that the opinion of that one potential juryperson will not poison the attitudes of the remaining jury panel. It could be catastrophic for an attorney to continue questioning and to elicit responses from that potential juror so that persons in the courtroom can all listen to it. On those occasions, counsel may request that the court permit the examination of that juror "in camera," or outside the hearing of the remaining jury panel. In this manner, an attorney can more freely delve into the prospective biases that the juror may harbor and, if necessary, establish a for-cause strike rather than a peremptory strike.

[C] Jury Selection Logistics

Ordinarily, the court fills the jury box with potential jury panel members by randomly selecting names from the pool of potential jurors. When a potential juror is removed by a challenge, that juror is replaced with another member of the jury pool. Each newly selected potential juror is questioned and then, if appropriate, challenged. When each side has exhausted all of its challenges, the jury selection is complete.

The time to conduct jury selection varies. Supposedly, in the "old days," jury questioning would take many days. In our current heavily congested court system, however, most judges limit the voir dire process to just a few hours.

[D] Preliminary Instructions to the Jury

Once the jury is selected, the judge will swear in those selected and give the jury preliminary instructions. These instructions usually involve statements of the law and the case, such as the basic allegations in the lawsuit, which side carries the burden of proof, and the presentation of evidence. The judge will also instruct the jury regarding more general issues, such as note taking, limitations on discussing the case, and breaks in the trial. Of course, in a bench trial, no preliminary instructions are necessary. After the judge gives the jury preliminary instructions, the formal presentation of the case begins with opening statements.

Opening Statements

The opening statement phase of a civil trial is when the case really begins. Some lawyers very firmly believe that cases are won or lost during opening statements and voir dire. In this phase, attorneys provide a road map of the trial by telling their client's side of the story, while at the same time trying to convince the jury to find in their client's favor. Lawyers will use this opportunity to build upon the rapport developed during voir dire so that the jury will appreciate the theory of the case in factual terms.

Arguments are not allowed during opening statements. Rather, attorneys are only allowed to state what the evidence will show. Most attorneys find this to be a distinction without much of a difference. For example, the statement "Dr. Smith crippled Mrs. Jones by performing unnecessary surgery" could be considered argument and may not be allowed during opening statements. Stating "the evidence will show that Dr. Smith crippled Mrs. Jones when he performed unnecessary surgery," however, is not considered argument because the attorney is merely stating what he believes the evidence will show.

Depending on the complexity of the case, attorneys may use exhibits during opening statements. Such exhibits are not considered evidence but are only illustrative of what each side intends to prove. Some attorneys may even use very technical computerized presentations during opening statements. Any such "props" are fair game as long as the information presented can be described fairly as "what the evidence will show."

The time length for opening statements varies from jurisdiction to jurisdiction and from case to case. Cases that take several weeks to try may involve half-day-long or longer opening statements. Cases that take a few days to try—which is probably most cases—involve an hour or so per side for opening statements.

During the voir dire process and again during the opening statement, jurors will take a measure of the attorney's credibility and use this later in the decision-making process to see whether that attorney really did establish those points of fact as promised. Gaining the trust of the jury can often trump the factual evidence elicited during the trial. It is important to remember that the jury has the role as trier of the facts, and it is the attorney who presents these to the jury throughout the trial process.

Presentation of Evidence

[A] Order of Evidence Presentation

Since the plaintiff has the burden of proof, the plaintiff presents his or her case first. The presentation of the plaintiff's case is called the plaintiff's case-in-chief and includes what are called the essential elements of the complaint. These elements are what the law requires every plaintiff to prove in order to prevail in the case. It is the minimum amount of evidence necessary for the court to permit the case to proceed. For example, and in very general terms, in a medical malpractice or tort case, the plaintiff must prove that there was a duty owed by the defendant to the plaintiff, that the defendant breached that duty or standard of care, that the breach in the standard of care proximally or directly caused damage or injury to the plaintiff, and that the extent of damages sustained by the plaintiff was thus and so. A failure to present evidence on any one essential element produces a failure of the plaintiff to carry his or her burden. When the plaintiff finishes presenting his or her evidence, the defendant has the opportunity to make a motion for what is called a directed verdict.

When a defendant moves for a directed verdict, he or she is asking the judge to enter a judgment in his or her favor because the plaintiff has failed to present evidence essential to the elements of the plaintiff's case. If the plaintiff has in fact failed to present evidence on a crucial aspect of the case, the judge will enter a verdict in favor of the defense. The case is over, and the defendant need not present his or her case.

If, however, the plaintiff has presented sufficient evidence, regardless of how weak that evidence may be, then a directed verdict motion will be denied. The judge will not substitute his or her judgment for that of the jury in determining whether evidence is strong enough for the plaintiff to win. In that situation, the defendant will have to present his or her case-in-chief.

Following the defendant's case-in-chief, the formal presentation of evidence is usually concluded, unless the plaintiff wants to present rebuttal evidence. Rebuttal evidence is evidence that may be presented to address any new issues raised by the defense that were not previously addressed by or disclosed to the plaintiff. The decision of whether to allow rebuttal evidence lies with the judge. In some cases, the defendant's "response" to rebuttal evidence may even be allowed.

[B] Witnesses

After the attorneys finish telling the jurors what the evidence will show in opening statements, the formal presentation of evidence begins. Trial evidence is presented primarily by calling witnesses to testify on the client's behalf. The party calling the witness first asks questions during what is called direct examination, or "direct." The opposing party then gets an opportunity to ask questions of the witness during cross-examination, or "cross."

Questions on cross must be limited in scope to those asked on direct. Issues not raised during the direct examination may not be raised exclusively during cross. Cross-examination is not required but is generally a part of the witness examination. In some instances, an opposing party may have no questions at all, either for tactical reasons or because the witness testified to unimportant or uncontested issues. During cross-examination, the attorney will try to show how that witness's testimony should not be given the authority for which it was elicited. Television is a wonderful medium for showing how cross-examination is used to discredit, weaken, impeach, and undermine a witness's testimony, but a good attorney will often use this time to simultaneously curry favorable opinions from the witness toward that attorney's client's position. Through the strategic use of leading questions, which are questions that call for a yes or no response, attorneys can often use the opponent's witness to limit issues, if not actually help their own cause.

Following cross-examination, the party calling the witness has an opportunity to conduct redirect examination, or "redirect," and following any redirect, re-cross-examination may take place. Each subsequent examination, however, is limited in scope by the subject matter of the previous examination. Lawyers use redirect to rehabilitate their own witness, who may have been weakening during cross-examination. The idea is that as each round of questioning is concluded, the focus gets narrower and narrower. Consequently, if no questions were asked on cross, redirect is not allowed. After recross, the process is usually concluded, although on rare occasions a judge may allow further direct and cross if circumstances so warrant.

[C] Exhibits

Exhibits are tangible pieces of evidence that are relevant to the case. Medical records, photographs, and diagrams are common examples of exhibits that may be used during a civil trial. Basically, any tangible object may be used as an exhibit if it will aid the trier of fact in understanding the issues of the case.

The introduction of exhibits at trial is done primarily through witnesses. In order for an exhibit to be introduced into evidence, a witness must testify that the exhibit to be introduced is authentic, true, and accurate, and it must be relevant to an issue in the case. Such testimony is called foundation testimony. Before any exhibit can be introduced into evidence, a foundation must be laid.

Not all exhibits are introduced into evidence. For example, a skeletal model of the skull may be offered as an exhibit in a neurosurgery injury case because it might aid the jury in understanding the case. The skull model, however, may not be relevant to any issue in the case, and therefore cannot be introduced into evidence. Such an exhibit is called a demonstrative exhibit.

In contemporary trial presentations, parties are using computer-generated exhibits to assist in the telling of their stories. Studies have often conflicted but in general conclude that juries retain only 10 percent of the oral evidence that they hear, 20 percent of the visual evidence, but almost 70 percent of evidence that combines the two aspects into a common presentation. PowerPoint and Excel[7] presentations provide a mechanism whereby a party can present visual explanations of what a lawyer is orally describing to a jury so that the picture adds the thousand extra words to that said in court. A day-in-the-life video is a short ten-minute or so presentation that plaintiff's counsel uses to show the tragedy of the plaintiff's daily travails to the jury. Overhead projections and computer-generated graphics can vividly exclaim the importance of the evidence. The impact of this type of demonstrative evidence should not be underestimated, because despite the lofty cost for the preparation of these types of exhibits, the impact can be dispositive.

In a case from Mississippi, a plaintiff claimed that since the defendant's orthopedic ankle surgery, she was essentially disabled from doing those activities that she deemed essential. For three years, discovery and depositions tested those claims, and she always maintained them under oath and before God. The weekend or so prior to trial, defense counsel contacted the plaintiff's lawyer and asked that she come over to view video surveillance that would be used at trial. Sure enough, there was the plaintiff parking in a handicapped parking space, walking into the gym in a workout uniform, and thereafter, doing aerobics. When confronted, her explanation was that she could do this only at times when she had taken sufficient doses of pain medication and that was the case in the surveillance videos. It took the jury only 20 minutes to decide otherwise.

[D] Objections

During the course of witness testimony or the attempted introduction of an exhibit into evidence, an attorney may state an objection. The main purpose of an objection is to prevent the presentation of certain information to a jury. Information that is not relevant or otherwise prohibited from being presented to a jury is objectionable. It is important to know that the conduct of a trial is not a wide-open search for the truth. Rather, it is a decision-making process in which the parties present their cases according to rules of evidence and procedure.

For routine objections, the attorneys will make brief statements in open court in support of or in opposition to an objection. The judge will then issue a ruling out loud from the bench. In some situations, however, an attorney may object to potentially damaging testimony that he or she wants to keep from the jury, in which case arguing the objection in open court may reveal the damaging information. In such an instance, the attorneys may ask to approach the bench for a "sidebar." Each attorney then approaches the judge's bench and discreetly argues the objection out of the jury's earshot. If the objection involves a major issue that requires extensive argument, the judge will excuse the jury from the courtroom so the attorneys can present their arguments out loud and on the record.

If evidence is excluded and an attorney feels the judge's ruling was incorrect, the attorney may make what is called an offer of proof. In this instance, the excluded evidence is presented on the record but out of the presence of the jury. In this way, the evidence is preserved if the party decides to appeal the decision. An offer of proof is rare, but it is effective if an appeal is contemplated.

Summation

When each side has concluded its case, closing arguments begin. As with opening statements, the time length allowed varies from case to case and court to court. Unlike opening statements, summation provides the attorneys with a final opportunity to convince those jurors who may be in limbo as to the merits of their case. In addition, skillful counsel will focus upon those jurors who they think are aligned with their position and provide these jurors with the ammunition or evidence necessary to convince other potentially undecided jurors during deliberations. It is the lawyers' final occasion to argue all of the elements of their case, from proving liability to maximizing damages. Conversely, defense counsel will use this opportunity to debunk the plaintiff's case and argue for a defense verdict.

The court does limit exactly what an attorney can argue in closing, but latitude is generally the name of the game. Counsel may draw inferences from the evidence, and although these inferences may be less than factual, if they are grounded in the truth, they are not improper. Courts often advise the attorneys that the final summation is meant as a time to convince the jury of the truth of their argument.[8] Lawyers do this through a skilled recitation of the evidence, but there is one "Golden Rule": Lawyers for the patient are not permitted to ask the jurors to put themselves in the place of the plaintiff and to ask the jurors to decide the matter at hand based upon that perception. Similarly, it is improper for defense counsel to ask the jurors to be the defendant. Lawyers are skilled orators who use their abilities to persuade a jury to accept their version of the facts. Yet fairness and objectivity are the goals that the court should strive to maintain, and most lawyers work within those parameters.

Final Instructions

Following closing arguments, the judge usually excuses the jury so that the attorneys can argue over final instructions: the instructions on the law the judge gives to the jury to guide them in reaching a decision. Only instructions of law that are supported by evidence in the case are given, and that is what the attorneys argue about. Each side will try to persuade the judge to read an instruction to the jury that is favorable to its case.

As noted previously, the jury, as the fact finders, will determine what they believe to be the true version of the facts presented at the trial. The jury will then apply those facts to the law as provided in the final instructions. For example, a final instruction may read as follows:

"In order for the plaintiff to prevail, the plaintiff must prove that A, B, and C occurred. If you find the plaintiff has proven each of these elements, your verdict must be for the plaintiff. If you find the plaintiff-patient has failed to prove even one of these elements, your verdict must be for the defendant doctor." As with preliminary instructions, final instructions are omitted in a bench trial.

When the judge has decided which final instructions he or she is going to give, the jury is brought back into the courtroom and the final instructions are read. The judge also instructs the jury on the logistics of reaching a decision, such as choosing a foreman and taking breaks. The jury then retires to the jury room to deliberate.

Jury Deliberations

During jury deliberations, the jury members are allowed to discuss the case among themselves. If they have followed the judge's preliminary instructions, this will be the first time they discuss the case. Jury research shows that the process of reaching a decision varies widely from jury to jury, as does the time to reach a decision. Like many aspects of the trial process, a lot of conceptions exist about jury deliberations. If the jury deliberates for a relatively short period of time, it is believed they will return a verdict in favor of the defense. This conception comes from the belief that even if the jury quickly decided in favor of the plaintiff, it usually takes a long time to calculate damages. This conception, however, has proven to be a misconception in many cases.

While the jury is deliberating, the parties and their attorneys usually leave the courthouse and wait at a more comfortable location (usually a nearby restaurant, because, for some reason, most jury trials conclude at the end of the day). When the jury returns with a verdict, the parties are contacted to return to the courtroom.

If the jury is unable to reach a verdict, then the jury is considered to be a hung jury. The remedy in the case of a hung jury is a new trial. Because most judges, parties, and plaintiffs' attorneys would rather crawl across a room full of broken glass than retry a case, judges will pressure the jury to keep deliberating until they are able to reach a decision. If that fails, the judge declares a mistrial, and a new case is eventually scheduled.

The Verdict

When the jury returns to the courtroom to announce its verdict, the collective hearts of the parties and their attorneys can probably generate a registration on a Richter scale. It is the moment of truth, the climax of the entire trial process. After the verdict is read, either party may poll the jury to "verify" that each juror supports the decision, though a polling of the jury is always done, if at all, by the losing party.

Once the jury is polled, the losing party can also ask the judge to overturn the jury decision, called a motion for judgment notwithstanding the verdict, or JNOV (judgment *non obstante veredicto*). A motion for JNOV is only granted if the judge, in hindsight, believes the case should not have been submitted to a jury because there was no evidence that a reasonable person would have credited on an essential element of the plaintiff's case. The judge has the discretion to enter a JNOV, but such discretion is rarely invoked. In most situations, judges are very hesitant to substitute their own judgment for that of the jurors. Once the judge enters a verdict, the trial is over. In a 2002 case involving a professional football player, the jury returned a $5.2 million verdict in favor of the player, but the trial judge, stating at that late date that the plaintiff had failed to prove his case, awarded the defendant a JNOV. As is often the case in that situation, the parties compromised the jury verdict so that neither side was happy with the result.

A medical malpractice trial is nearly always a roller coaster ride of emotions. When the opposing side is putting on its case, you can feel as though you are being pummeled over the head with a baseball bat, and defeat is inevitable. Moments later, your attorney can perform a stunning cross-examination, and victory seems certain. Such is life in our adversarial system, where two parties present the case in a punch, counterpunch format. When the verdict is finally entered, regardless of the outcome, most parties are relieved that it is over. All have a more thorough understanding as to why 97 percent of civil cases never make it this far.

Preventing and Reducing Incidents of Malpractice

As a practicing medical professional, it is important to realize that although you can accept your position in a malpractice case as a passive victim, there are numerous methods at your disposal to protect you, your practice, and your family from potential litigation. Certainly there is no one approach currently available that would guarantee that a health care practitioner might never become involved in malpractice litigation. Despite this lack of assurance, there are alternatives that might well determine whether a potential case is successful.

[A] Honesty

At each and every risk management conference, the universal principle promoted by insurance carriers and the foundation that cements a successful doctor-patient relationship is honesty. The ability to honestly communicate with a patient is of such fundamental importance that it is often taken for granted. It is a simple truism that we as human beings want to be told the truth and be told it in such a way that it is beyond reproach. As Paul Starr wrote, patients are often marginalized when they seek the care and treatment of a physician and look up toward that person for those words of reassurance and certainty. In no way am I suggesting that doctors should simply tell the patient the truth that the patient wants to hear. The communication should be one that displays a sense of reality, credibility, compassion, and earnestness. *It can't be stressed to any degree more than this.*

All too often, clients whom I interview ask me why their doctor did not tell them the truth. It might not be presented in such a straightforward manner, but it often is as simple as that. On numerous occasions, clients have told me that "if only my doctor had told me the truth, I would never have sued him," or "why didn't my doctor tell me that there was a problem following surgery?" or "why did my doctor not tell me that the nerve in my arm was cut by mistake?" or "if only my doctor had fessed up." Patients want to know the truth, and despite any hesitance that you might harbor, tell them the truth. Patients are human beings like doctors. They make mistakes, as do doctors. Car mechanics often don't fix a problem the first time they try, and plumbers often return to fix a leak in a pipe they just soldered closed. Patients know and understand this, so don't sell them short.

I know that at first blush you are sitting there saying to yourself that there is no way I can tell the patient what really happened because, if I do, he or she will think I am admitting I was negligent, run to a lawyer, and sue me. I only wish that I could statistically recount to you the times when I did exactly as I have advised and told the truth. I will say it again and again. Look the patients in the eyes and simply explain to them what happened, why it happened, and what you plan to do to help them overcome the complications that they perceive. Candor is a must, yet it must be dosed with a touch of caution. While not admitting liability per se, don't sugarcoat it so as to appear condescending. Speak up in a timely manner, because avoidance can readily be misconstrued. It is not a contest of wills but a willingness to provide people with the reality of their condition and the assurance that you as their physician care, will listen, and will work with them to resolve the crisis.

Of course, there are those instances when a patient will not take your news cordially. If that is the case, then that patient probably would have jumped in the car, run and looked in the yellow pages, consulted a lawyer, and filed a lawsuit regardless of what you might have said. Tell the truth and the truth will set you free.

[B] Medical Records

Not only are the patient's medical records a legal document, but these documents remain the central focus of any competent medical malpractice investigation. The records should honestly and in detail reflect the care and treatment provided to that patient based upon the presenting circumstances. Self-serving statements about what the patient did to cause the current complications not only wave a red flag; they hoist it high. This can't be emphasized beyond underscoring the fact that the medical records create the very nature of one's credibility.

In a recent case, the defendant-doctor's notes stated that postoperative problems were caused by chasing after a cat that escaped, in the house. The records stated that the patient came into the office the following day with tree bark and dirt all over the operative bandages. The doctor wrote that her patient told her that she had to climb a tree in the patient's yard to rescue the cat. The problem faced was that the patient/plaintiff denied the entire episode ever happened. While admitting she did have a pet cat run out of the house, she steadfastly denied climbing tress or running to catch the animal. The case in question settled within a few weeks after the doctor's deposition after the doctor stated that her notes were truthful and accurate—simply because I showed the doctor pictures of the patient's home and yard and, as you might have surmised, there were not any trees to be found.

The proverbial SOAP (subjective, objective, assessment, and plan) method of charting still reflects a professionalism that is imperative when case records are reviewed. Medical records should be typewritten or computer generated if at all possible. Each entry should be dated and endorsed by the treating doctor. Notes that are handwritten need to be legible. Despite any situation that you may encounter and even under the most careful of conditions, do not, I repeat do not, ever modify or alter your medical chart. Scientific advancements in time dating of paper and ink make alterations the easiest way to ensure a plaintiff's success. Any record can be changed to modify an error, but you should simply draw a line through the errant portion, note the correction, and date both entries. Not only does this ensure the integrity of your medical chart, but it also presents a reviewer with the image of a conscientious and honest practitioner.

Conclusion

As hard as it might be to accept, every trial lawyer will tell you that despite the jury's most earnest efforts, there are those cases you should win and those cases you should lose that turn out exactly the opposite. Despite the best efforts of all concerned, sometimes the decision is not the proper one. During a recent jury trial, the defendant was a well-known hospital affiliated with the community's largest church. In fact, the name of the hospital reflected the church's denomination. During voir dire, the plaintiff's lawyer was specific in asking the jury panel about their religious affiliations, their membership in church-related groups, and almost every other conceivable situation that might have a root in jury prejudice in support of the hospital. The judge provided unlimited voir dire, and there were numerous in camera examinations of prospective jurors. The jury was selected, and the case was set to begin that following Monday morning. With a packed courtroom, and with the judge and parties all present, the jury were escorted into their respective seats. Juror number two, a middle-aged female, took out a pink Bible, put it between her hands, and prayed during the entire trial. I think you can appreciate the significance, and the regrettable outcome, for the plaintiff, whose 7-week-old child died during an anesthesia-related incident at the hospital.

Acknowledgments

All examples are from actual cases, but the settings and details of the parties were modified to protect confidentiality and privacy.

Additional Readings

1. American Medical Association: Tort reform be damned: We've got a better plan. *Medical Economics*, February 1, 1988, p. 206.
2. American Tort Reform Association: Summary of 1990 tort reform enactments. *Professional liability update*, February 1991.
3. Another questionable malpractice insurer is making the rounds. *Medical Economics*, October 1, 1990, p. 126.
4. Brandon, KA: An easy way to keep track of your insurance. *Medical Economics*, January 2, 1989, pp. 59–66.
5. Buba, DJ: Anatomy of a civil trial. In Marcinko, DE (Editor): *Financial Planning for Physicians*. Aspen Publishing, New York, 2003.
6. Physicians still uninsured despite tort reforms in Mississippi. *Congress Daily/A.M.*, September 22, 2003.

Websites

The following URL addresses have also been found to contain worthwhile malpractice and professional liability insurance information:

- A looming healthcare crisis. VandeWater, Judith. STLToday.com http://www.stltoday.com/stltoday/news/stories.nsf?DocID/EDA. (accessed 9/22/03), p. 3.
- Alaska's tort reform legislation still mired in uncertainty. Albert, Tanya. amednews.com www.ama-assn.org/sci-pubs/amnews.pick_02/prca1014.htm (accessed Oct. 14, 2002).

Endnotes

1. First, no harm to the patient.
2. Paul Starr, *The Social Transformation of American Medicine*, Basic Books, 1982, pp. 4–5.
3. Idaho is an example of such a jurisdiction.
4. The actual number of jurors can vary from state to state in civil trials.
5. See Civil Jury Cases and Verdicts in Large Counties, Civil Justice Survey of State Courts at: www.usdoj.gov/bjs/abstract/cjcavilc.htm.
6. It is interesting to note that in New York State, the identity and/or deposition of a medical expert is not disclosed until the time of trial, so in this setting, ambush can be a tactical weapon.
7. Microsoft incorporated.
8. *O'Barr vs. United States*, 105 p. 938 (Oklahoma 1910).

Chapter 13

Financial and Operative Risks of Divorce

(Keeping It Civil and Equitable . . . Not Going Broke)

Anju D. Jessani

sWhen one partner has a closed mind and is divorcing the other, they are in love with their negative feelings. So they put their negative feelings in charge of the door to their mind. And when you try to reason with them, you're telling them that their negative feelings are wrong. That causes their negative feelings to lock the door even tighter.

Homer McDondal, BS, M.Ed.

The medical professional is in service to others. Unfortunately, a divorce may occur that is not even discussed with a trusted advisor or financial planner. Perhaps this is because the topic may be viewed as too delicate. Nevertheless, the truth is that much financial damage is done by this lack of disclosure.

Domestic and Spousal Issues

The statistics are overwhelming: one in two marriages ends in divorce. As Barbara Dafoe Whitehead writes in her book *The Divorce Culture*, "Divorce is now part of everyday American Life. It is embodied in our laws and institutions, our manners and mores, our movies and television shows, our novels and children's storybooks, and our closest and most important relationships."

Divorce can be devastating in many ways. It has created both economic and emotional disadvantages for many children. Nationally, over 1 million children are affected each year by the divorce of their parents. As Whitehead illustrates, divorce figures prominently in the altered fortunes of middle-class families. It has reduced both the levels of parental time and money invested in children. The various studies suggest that divorce carries multiple risks and losses for children, including loss of income, loss of ties to father, loss of residential stability, and loss of social resources. For families in which money is tight during the marriage, separation and divorce are even more financially difficult. Adding an additional residence with its prerequisite overhead to an already tight budget is obviously a daunting task. The income that used to support one home and lifestyle is now split between two homes and two lifestyles.

There has been a great deal of controversy in trying to quantify how much the standard of living declines following divorce for women. Adding to the complexity of the issue was the proclamation of Lenore Weitzman in her book *The Divorce Revolution*, published in 1985, that after a divorce women and children suffer an average 73 percent decline in the standard of living, while divorced men's standard increases by 42 percent. Seven years later it was revealed that her conclusions were based on faulty computer calculations, and her numbers actually yielded a milder 27 percent drop for women and children, and a 10 percent increase for men. More recently, Sanford Braver, Ph.D., of the University of Arizona, has shown that when these numbers are adjusted for taxes and expenses fathers usually have during parenting time, mothers and fathers fare about equally 1 year after divorce.

Whatever the statistics regarding standard of living, the reality is that within most marriages the husband more frequently takes responsibility for understanding and managing the finances. Additionally, women are more likely to remain in the marital home following a separation, thus inheriting a large fixed expense that may prove be an excessive, albeit short-term, burden to them. At the time the decision is made to separate or divorce, many women do not have an understanding of how to manage their household budget, or how to manage their assets and liabilities.

An issue many divorcing physicians face is that the other spouse (in the past the wife) may have concentrated his or her energies on managing the home, while the physician concentrated on earning and managing the finances. The problems of physicians' spouses are often compounded in divorce; not only do they not understand their personal finances, but their absence from the work force has made them financially dependant on the other. At what probably will be the most emotionally taxing time in their lives, they are forced to play catch-up.

Taking a more active role in their own financial planning during the marriage may help the spouse of a physician avoid some of the financial pitfalls of separation and divorce. There are many resources available for this. Barbara Stanny provides an excellent overview and reading bibliography on how people can get smart about money in her book *Prince Charming Isn't Coming*.

Although one can hardly plan for such an event as divorce, there are certain steps to take that may lessen the financial impact of divorce. One of the tools is the *prenuptial agreement (PNA)*.

Prenuptial Agreements

A *prenuptial agreement* is a contract between prospective spouses. Most prenuptial agreements contain provisions limiting the distribution of marital property and alimony in the event of divorce and limiting the distribution of property to a spouse in the event of death. It is important to note that most states specifically prohibit provisions regarding child support.

With more people getting married later for the first time, often with substantial assets, and people getting married for the second+ time(s) with children from previous marriages, the prevalence of PNAs is increasing. It is particularly important in the case of a female physician, especially if she has been married before, has substantial assets, owns a closely held business, marries a spouse with substantial debt, has agreed to pay for the medical or professional education of a soon-to-be spouse, or has children from a previous marriage.

Some couples feel that discussing what happens if the marriage fails hinders the romance and shows a lack of commitment toward the marriage. However, at the end of the marriage, few couples agree on how to split their assets, or on what a fair amount of support would be. Whether parties choose to have a prenuptial agreement, communicating about financial issues strengthens the trust and starts the marriage off on the right foot. Whether or not to sign a prenuptial agreement finally comes down to a decision that the couple will have to make together. Parties don't need to have the prenuptial agreement to have the discussion and information sharing that is part of the prenuptial agreement process.

Wills, insurance policies, pension plans, IRAs, and other assets from prior marriages should also be addressed, updated, and changed if needed, along with beneficiary designations, as part of the process of prenuptial agreement planning.

Because of past uncertainty over whether courts could enforce prenuptial agreements, a uniform treatment of prenuptial agreements was sought through the Uniform Premarital Agreement Act (UPAA). The UPAA was approved by the National Conference on Uniform State Laws in 1983 and has been adopted in whole or in part by approximately half the states. Although the standards for enforcing prenuptial agreements vary from state to state, in almost all states, four conditions are imposed:

- Each party must make complete disclosure to the other of his or her assets, liabilities, sources of income, and any other facts likely to affect his or her financial position.
- Each party must be represented by separate and independent legal counsel (or must make a voluntary and well-considered decision to waive such independent legal counsel).
- The terms of the agreement must be "fair" at the time the agreement is entered into, a standard with respect to which even reasonable people may differ.

- Finally, the agreement may be set aside by the courts if enforcement of the agreement would impoverish either party and thereby create a risk that either party (or any minor children of either party) would require public assistance.

The value of a PNA is much like other legal contracts, and it can be challenged for myriad reasons. In looking at the validity of PNAs, the courts have sometimes overturned agreements signed under duress, such as the night before the wedding, even when both parties have had legal counsel. So it makes sense to take the time to put together the PNA in an orderly fashion.

Since divorce may affect an existing medical practice in many ways, including a forced sale, a PNA may well complement a properly drawn up buy/sell agreement and practice equity-sharing agreement.

Often, the couple may go through prenuptial planning to discuss financial issues that are emotionally difficult to bring up on their own, but they may choose not to have a formal document drawn up. In some cases, this decision is based on the understanding that in most states, premarital assets, if kept separate from marital property, remain separate property and are not subject to distribution at the time of divorce. In other cases, a trust or a will may serve the same function as the intent of a prenuptial agreement.

An additional point to note for men or women marrying a party who is divorced and has child and/or spousal support payments is that the earnings from income-producing assets may be included in the paying party's income for the purposes of calculating support. Therefore, it would make sense to keep your incoming-producing assets such as bonds in your own name, so that that income is not perceived as belonging to the paying party, thus increasing his or her support payments.

The Decision to Divorce

Sanford Braver, Ph.D., has conducted research on who leaves whom; the wife was identified as the initiator in approximately two-thirds of his samples. In Braver's research on divorcing parents, the top two ranked factors for both men and women in initiating a divorce were gradual growing apart and losing a sense of closeness, and serious differences in lifestyle and/or values. For men, the third ranked factor was severe and intense fighting or frequent conflict, while the third ranked factor for women was not feeling loved or appreciated by their spouse. Contrary to popular wisdom, extramarital affairs and abuse rank much lower in factors for divorce.

The level of commitment both in training and in practice that is required of a physician can weigh heavily on a marriage for the very reasons Braver illustrates. It is understandable that both the physician and his or her spouse may have a hard time maintaining a sense of closeness with the excessive time demands of a busy practice and being constantly on call. Spouses may feel that they are less important to their physician spouse than his or her job. Additionally, if the physician sees his or her role as breadwinner as more important than a spouse's role, the power imbalance that the situation creates can lead to marital discord.

As difficult as marriage is, it remains the condition or goal of the vast majority of Americans. Married couples that seek a stable marriage may want to take a careful look at the research conducted by University of Washington psychologist John M. Gottman, Ph.D. He researched 140 newlyweds over a 6-year period. To his surprise, he found that the marriages that did work all had one thing in common: the husband was willing to give in to the wife! Unfortunately, despite Gottman's research, couples continue to divorce. We don't appear to be able to live with people very well, but we are not very good at living alone either.

Despite the rhetoric about people rushing into divorce, research shows that people who initiate the breakup have usually contemplated the possibility of divorce for more than a year before they take a strong stand. Especially for abandoned spouses, the emotional upheaval of divorce can be overwhelming and disorienting because they are not even aware of the impending doom. Then, at one of the most emotionally vulnerable points in their life, parties are forced to make important financial decisions and parenting decisions that could impact the rest of their lives. It is a good idea to seek emotional support from a professional during this time of crisis to deal with the anger, grief, hurt, and guilt that is normal to experience at this period of loss. Many people find that joining a support group and hearing other people's stories helps. Names of support groups in various areas are made available through local newspapers, churches, and synagogues and on the Web at www.divorcesource.com.

[A] Divorce Mediation

Divorce usually requires a division of all assets and liabilities, including investments, pensions and business holdings, custody and parenting time decisions, establishment of child and sometime spousal support, planning for educational funding, and tax, insurance, and estate planning. Many of the decisions divorcing parties make are best made in a collaborative manner. Therefore, you and your spouse may want to consider mediation.

Mediation is a court-approved process in which a trained neutral person, called a mediator, encourages and facilitates the resolution of a dispute between two or more parties. The mediator does not replace the services of attorneys but supplements their role to first an advisory position, and later as someone who assists couples in processing divorce complaints through the court system. Mediators include attorneys, mental health practitioners, accountants, and other professionals with special training and experience in the practice of family and divorce mediation.

On average, even with attorney costs for each party, the cost of a mediated divorce is about one-third the cost of a litigated divorce. Additionally, as Jessica Pearson and Nancy Thoennes found in their Denver study of 120 mediated and 120 litigated cases, the parents in the mediated cases were more pleased with and more likely to follow their agreements than the parents who went to court. Other benefits of mediation include the following:

- Mediation is not adversarial. The nature of the legal system requires the participants to be adversarial. Many people in disputes are not adversaries. Rather, they may want to problem-solve because they understand the importance of maintaining their ongoing relationship.
- Mediation is private. In many states divorce records and divorce proceedings are open to outsiders. Resolving the conflict in the confines of the mediator's office limits the information available to the public to what the parties agree will be included in their divorce judgment.
- Mediation is faster. Since all discussions are held face-to-face, resolving the dispute takes less time in mediation than resolving it through intermediaries.

The mediator usually meets with clients in anywhere from three to eight sessions. At the end of the process, the mediator will draft a Memorandum of Understanding (MOU), which summarizes in plain English what the clients agreed to and, where appropriate, why they made the agreement. The spouses take the MOU to their respective separate attorneys for review, advice, and incorporation into their formal legal agreement, and it is ultimately filed with the court as part of the divorce decree.

Successful mediators come from many different backgrounds. As the Mediation Information and Resource Center (MIRC, www.mediate.com) indicates, competence depends partly on the context of the dispute and the parties' expectations. It also depends on whether the mediator has the right mix of acquired skills, training, education, experience, and natural abilities to help resolve the specific dispute. Important skills and abilities include neutrality, the ability to communicate, the ability to listen and understand, and the ability to define and clarify issues.

To learn more about the mediation process and/or acquire a list of Advanced Practitioner Level mediators (those with the highest level of training and experience), you can contact the Association for Conflict Resolution at (202) 667-9700, or on the Web at www.acresolution.org. The site also provides a list of state mediation organizations, some of which may have their own accreditation procedures. A mediator's accreditation will help ensure that the mediator has the education, experience, skills, and ethical standards necessary to help address the conflict, and that the mediator has a commitment to the process and the practice of mediation.

Recommended reading for parties contemplating mediation is John Haynes's textbook for mediators, *The Fundamentals of Family Mediation*, as well as Sam Marguelies's book, *Getting Divorced Without Ruining Your Life*.

[B] Choosing a Divorce Attorney

Whether you choose to mediate or litigate, you will still require the services of an attorney. As a medical professional or the spouse of a medical professional, you will probably have more at stake in your divorce than the average person getting divorced. Selecting the wrong lawyer can cost you untold aggravation and expense. You are paying the bills, and you will have to live with the results.

Start with a list of lawyers provided by relatives and friends; the best source for professional service providers comes from satisfied clients. You can call your local bar association and chamber of commerce for additional names. It is recommended that you interview at least three law firms before choosing an attorney. Many attorneys provide free initial consultations or will ask for only a nominal fee. Explain when you are setting up the initial consultation that you wish to obtain a sound evaluation of your legal situation and to see if you are comfortable about working together. Bring all pertinent written information with you, such as last year's tax return, bank account and brokerage statements, mortgage statements, and recent credit card bills.

The following tips on how to choose a divorce lawyer are from the late Elaine Majewski, an advocate for divorce reform:

1. **Qualifications.** Ask attorneys to describe their legal training, how long they have practiced family law, how many family law cases they have handled, and what proportion of their time is spent on family and divorce matters. If the answer is less than 30 percent, this attorney may not spend sufficient time in this practice area to stay abreast of new developments and current case law.

2. **Attorney's Philosophy.** Ask attorneys about their views on child custody, visitation/parenting time, child support, and related matters. What are their feelings about shared custody? Inquire about their outside activities and professional associations, since these facts will tell you a lot about their views. Will the lawyer first seek to resolve the matter amicably in lieu of the traditional adversarial approach? Seek to work with any attorney who is receptive to your ideas and desires. Tell attorneys that you will meet them at their office, since you can learn much about their outlook from the awards they have received, the photographs they display, and the books they read.

3. **Fees.** Inquire how much they charge, in what increment of billable time, who will actually do the work, and whether a flat or mixed fee arrangement can be worked out. Be aware that novices often charge less for an hour, but they may require more time to handle a problem. What are the specifics of the retainer arrangement, as well as costs for travel, meals, administrative assistance, and so on? Is this attorney willing to submit an itemized bill each month?

4. **Point of View.** Once you have presented the facts, the attorney should be able to point out the strengths and weaknesses of your case, assess your probability of achieving your goals, give you an estimate of how long your matter will take to resolve, and make an estimate of the approximate legal fees he or she would anticipate. Some lawyers neglect to give honest appraisals, and clients are then misled and spend large sums of money on losing causes. Ask the lawyer to also estimate what the minimum and maximum fee might be.

5. **Work Style.** Will attorneys return phone calls within 24 hours? In their absence, how will your inquiries be answered? How are you charged for these inquiries? Does the attorney utilize e-mail? Will the attorney agree to keep you apprised of all developments in your case and make no offers or agreements without first consult-

ing you? Make sure that the attorney will be available to you and that you are comfortable with his or her work style and manner.

6. **Handling Your Case.** Be sure that the lawyer of your choice will be working on your matter. People often go to prestigious firms expecting their problem to be handled by the lawyer they contacted initially, only to be surprised that the case has been turned over to a junior associate. To avoid this, state in the retainer agreement that the matter is to be handled by the lawyer of your choice.

7. **Referrals to Others.** Does your attorney work with or refer clients to mediators, mental health professionals, tax professionals, appraisers, and others when appropriate? Does he or she get a fee or any type of remuneration for these referrals? (Attorneys should not be in a position to gain financially from these referrals.)

It is important to leave the interview feeling that the lawyer is open and responsible to your needs and that the case would be prepared and handled property. Majewski offers the following clues to look for at the initial interview:

- Were you received at the appointed hour or kept waiting?
- Did the attorney present an outward appearance of neatness and good grooming?
- Did the attorney discuss the fee arrangement with you up-front?
- Was the lawyer a clock watcher?
- Did the attorney leave the room frequently during the interview or permit phone calls?

Majewski also suggests that you may want to observe attorneys in a courtroom setting to see how they handle themselves. Find out when the attorney will be in court and sit in and observe. You can look up the attorney's rating at Martindale-Hubbell. Inquire if you can speak to previous clients; references will help you learn more about an attorney. If you do not feel comfortable with a lawyer you interview, shop around.

[C] Some Do's and Don'ts and Pitfalls as You Prepare to Separate

Marriage involves a legal contract; therefore, the legal system must be involved when changing the status of the contract. Use the legal system for division of property, custody and parenting time arrangements, and child and spousal support. Do not use the legal system to:

- Punish an ex-spouse
- Get even for years of problems
- Resolve who was bad or good, right or wrong, etc.
- Show the children "who really loves them"
- Maintain control over an ex-spouse
- Get something from an ex-spouse that you didn't get in marriage

Carol Ann Wilson, CFP©, president of the Institute of Certified Divorce Planners suggests that the first financial agenda for the medical professional when contemplating divorce is to continue paying bills and the mortgage payment and to maintain joint accounts even if the couple is no longer living in the same house. Insurance policies should not be canceled, credit card debt should not be increased, and no money should be transferred. Moreover, couples should register accounts in both names with bilateral signatures required to make withdrawals or investments. Duplicate copies should be forwarded to each party.

According to Esther M. Berger, CFP©, be prepared to deal with the following "dirty trick" financial tactics, regardless of which spouse you may be:

- Your wife asks her HMO to delay paying part of her salary, bonus, or yearly withholding until after the divorce, making her income appear low in order to pay you less than you are entitled.
- Your husband funnels savings into his own account weeks before filing for divorce.
- Your wife's medical convention trips to the Caribbean are visits to an offshore bank that you knew nothing about.
- You discover that your husband has generously gifted joint assets to friends, family members, and medical colleagues so the assets can't be split during a property settlement.
- To your wife's amazement, her almost worthless stock options in a PPMC suddenly become worth a bundle six months after the divorce.

An Overview of Family and Divorce Law

Which state you live in will determine grounds for filing, child custody and parenting time options, how property is divided, and guidelines for child and spousal support. As a result, a New York divorce decided by the courts may look very different from a California divorce, even though the circumstances of the parties may be quite similar.

Almost every state offers some form of uncontested divorce. In New Jersey this means the parties have lived separate and apart for at least 18 consecutive months; in New York the parties must have lived separate and apart pursuant to a written agreement for a period of 12 months; California offers grounds of "irreconcilable differences." You should check your state statute for the grounds that apply to your case. In most states, no matter what the grounds, fault has no impact on how assets are divided, how custody is decided, or how alimony is established.

We will take a look at each of these major components you need to decide as you face a divorce:

- Custody options and parenting time issues
- Child support and other financial issues related to the children
- Distribution of marital assets and liabilities

- Spousal support or alimony and related tax issues
- Other tax considerations of separation and divorce

[A] Custody Options and Parenting Time Issues

The standard most courts look to for custody in adversarial situations is the "best interests of the child." However, no matter what the custody arrangement, both parents usually do have rights with the child. Additionally, most states offer some form of joint custody as an option, and joint custody is a presumption in approximately one-third of states. James Cooke, president of the Joint Custody Association, Los Angeles, offers the following custody definitions:

- **Sole Custody.** This is an award of custody to one parent with parenting/visitation rights to the noncustodial parent. The custodial parent retains exclusive authority and control regarding the education, medical care, religion, discipline, and financial support of the child or children.

- **Joint Legal Custody.** Both parents retain and share responsibility and authority for the care and control of the child or children. The sharing of that responsibility can traverse an entire spectrum, from casual cooperation to specifically delineated times and functions. In its broadest interpretation, joint legal custody has encompassed nearly all major responsibilities and opportunities that are relegated to custodians (e.g., medical care, schooling, religion), except for day-to-day residence.

- **Joint Physical and Legal Custody.** This is joint legal custody plus the allocation of significant periods of time for the child or children with each parent. Variations for sharing physical custody can include freedom of movement between two homes, school year versus summer vacation with exchange weekends and nights, workday versus weekends, with special vacation periods, and so forth.

- **Split Custody.** This awards one or more of the children to one parent and the other child or remaining children to the alternate parent. Parents and courts considering the split custody alternative will wish to weigh carefully the wisdom and necessity of ensuring that the children do or do not have significant time together with their siblings.

Beyond negotiation of the types of custody, divorcing parties need to focus on the parenting time needs of their children. Perhaps the most frequent mistake seen in couples returning to court for postdivorce litigation is no specific parenting schedule. At the time of the divorce, sometimes one or both parents state that they don't need a schedule—they can work the schedule out, and both parents are free to see the children anytime they want. This doesn't give the children much assurance. Most children need the security of knowing where they are going to be and with whom. Holidays can become complete chaos, with both parties wanting the children at the same time; right after Thanksgiving and Christmas, family courts are clogged with unhappy parents upset because they assumed they were going to have their children over the holidays and were disappointed. Sometimes, the parenting schedule breaks down completely when the first of the parties starts dating.

Furthermore, divorcing parents should work out a schedule with clear pickup and drop-off times and locations. Getting copies of their children's school schedules is essential so that the couple can account for all the children's holidays, including teachers' conventions and winter and spring break. As the children get older, you also have to take into account after-school activities and athletic schedules. Once the parties have a schedule, they can always adjust it to meet each other's needs. However, it is important that clients commit to schedules that are workable; if they know they have to work late most weekdays, scheduling a Wednesday midweek visitation may not make sense.

Divorcing parents should try to determine at what age (if any) they or the children can elect to change the arrangements. Finally, it is helpful for parties to establish a venue, such as mediation, for resolving inevitable conflict that will come up in coparenting their children after their divorce.

When it comes to decisions regarding the children, there are only win/win and lose/lose options; there are no win/lose situations. Should a parent win something that is unfair to the other parent, the parties are likely to wind up back in court at some later date, with the child ultimately being exposed to harmful parental conflict, in addition to the financial and emotional cost to both parents. Half of divorced couples with children go back into litigation after their divorce is final. Working out a comprehensive and fair divorce agreement is a cooperative endeavor and may seem daunting when the parties are in the throes of mourning the loss of the marriage and possibly experiencing a great deal of anger; however, it's worth the up-front time and effort in terms of future returns and savings.

[B] Child Support and Other Financial Issues Related to the Children

Parents have a legal and moral obligation to provide their children with the necessities of life. Child support is mandated by law. Most states have a variation of the following formula: 17 percent of net income for one child, 25 percent of net income for two children, 29 percent of net income for three children, 31 percent of net income for four children, and 35 percent of net income for five or more children. If physical custody is shared for long or frequent periods of time, depending on the financial circumstances of the parents, the needs of the children, and the time spend with each parent, support payments may or may not be required and may be subject to state guidelines. Always check the formula and guidelines for your state.

In most instances, child support is paid to the custodial parent and not the children. Child support covers food, clothing, and shelter for the child. Additional expenses that are usually not included in the basic child support obligation include medical insurance, child-care needs, and private school tuition if appropriate. Some states provide for these expenses to be shared, whereas other states suggest that the parents pay for these expenses based on their percentage of income. As opposed to alimony, child support is not taxed as income to the recipient and is not deductible to the payer.

A frequent question is: When does child support end? With the ratification of the 26th amendment to the Constitution granting 18-year-olds the right to vote in 1971, many states reduced the age of majority from 21 to 18. According to the law, most college students are now adults. Some states, adhering strictly to the law, limit parental obligation for support to the age of minority. Other states authorize child support during higher education up to a certain age. A third group of states have ambiguous statutes.

The child support guidelines were enacted because many women with children were falling into poverty because of inadequate levels of support. The federal legislation requires the states to develop a formula for determining child support in the hope that the formula raises the level of support and makes support more uniform. The Child Support Enforcement Amendments of 1984 require state child support enforcement agencies to initiate wage withholding when the parent obligated to pay support falls behind in an amount equal to 30 days of support.

Related to the issue of postmajority child support is the issue of whether parents are required to pay for their children's college education. Some courts refuse to authorize college expenses based on the argument that if the marriage had continued, the parents would be under no requirement to pay for college. Some states provide that both (divorced) parents are responsible for providing a college or other postsecondary education for their child, depending on their ability to pay at that time and the child's aptitude, opportunities, and inclinations. Some states will actually specify a dollar limit for educational expenses, such as the cost of the state university. It is therefore important to look to your state's statute. Additionally, you should know that even though states may lack the power to order college expenses, the court may look to your divorce order to establish an enforceable obligation.

[C] Distribution of Marital Assets and Liabilities

In the United States, a few states, influenced by their French or Spanish heritage, have the continental system of community property (50-50), which essentially means that property or assets acquired by either husband or wife during the marriage, except for gifts from third parties, belong equally to the husband or wife. Community property does not mean that each asset is divided 50-50, but rather that the net value of the assets received by each spouse must be equal. Thus, it is not uncommon for one spouse to be awarded the family residence, with the other spouse receiving the family business and investment real estate. Community property states include Arizona, California, Idaho, Louisiana, Nevada, New Mexico, Texas, and Washington.

The majority of states base their marital law on British common law and provide for equitable rather than equal distribution. In equitable-distribution states the court determines a fair and reasonable distribution, which may be more or less than 50 percent of any asset to either party. The equitable-distribution laws vary from state to state. Each state has its own criteria for determining what is an equitable, fair, and just division of assets. You should check what the criteria are for your state. Relevant factors may include:

- The duration of the marriage
- The age and physical and emotional health of the parties
- The income or property brought to the marriage by each party
- The standard of living established during the marriage
- Any written agreement made by the parties before or during the marriage concerning an arrangement of property distribution
- The economic circumstances of each party at the time the division of property becomes effective
- The income and earning capacity of each party, including education, background, training, and so forth
- The contribution by each party to the education, training, or earning power of the other
- The contribution of each party to the acquisition, dissipation, preservation, depreciation, or appreciation of the amount or value of the marital property, as well as the contribution of a party as a homemaker
- The tax consequences of the proposed distribution to each party
- The present value of the property
- The need of a parent who has physical custody of a child to own or occupy the marital residence and to use or own the household effects
- The debts and liabilities of the parties
- The need for creation, now or in the future, of a trust fund to secure reasonably foreseeable medical or educational costs for a spouse or children
- Loss of inheritance rights upon dissolution as of date of dissolution
- Loss of pension rights upon dissolution as of date of dissolution
- Any award of maintenance
- The amount of each person's separate property
- Any other factors which the court may deem relevant

A few states provide that whoever has title to the property is the owner. Although this was the prevalent system throughout the United States in the first half of the twentieth century, most states realized that this system was fraught with problems and changed to the community-property or equitable-distribution process of division. In both community-property and equitable-distribution states, it does not matter who holds title to the asset or property acquired during the marriage. The property may have been acquired by either husband or wife during the marriage and may be in either party's name.

In both community-property and equitable-distribution states, marital property usually does not include property provided for in a written agreement such as a Prenuptial Agreement. It also does not include "separate property," which is defined as property acquired before marriage, or property acquired by bequest, devise, descent, or gift from a party other than the spouse; it also does not include compensation for personal injuries. However, the increase in the value of separate property may or may not be considered marital property in some states, and in other states it is only considered marital property to the extent that the appreciation is due in part to the direct or indirect contributions or efforts of the other spouse.

It is important to note that the enhanced earning capacity from an educational degree or license earned during the marriage may be considered a marital asset in some states, giving the other spouse the right to a percentage of the enhanced earnings. In other states, the other spouse may only be entitled to be reimbursed for the costs of acquiring the degree or license.

Businesses and professional practices, real estate, 401(k) plans, and other qualified plans, individual retirement accounts, pension plans, bank accounts, brokerage accounts, whole life insurance policies, business interests, stock options, automobiles, profit-sharing plans, income tax refunds, and other assets acquired during the marriage are considered marital assets. Some assets may have tax ramifications. The parties must factor in tax consequences of the gain or loss, as well as the impact of depreciation, in determining the true value of an item.

[1] BUSINESSES AND PROFESSIONAL PRACTICES

Certified public accountants and business appraisers are hired to determine the value of a business or professional medical practice. The accountant or appraiser who is hired reviews the books and records of the practice and prepares a written report. Usually judges will look to provide the other spouse with an offset of the value of the practice.

[2] PENSION PLANS (DEFINED BENEFIT PLANS)

Pension plans usually specify the monthly benefit the retiree will receive upon retirement at a specified age. If there are no other assets to offset the present value of a pension plan as determined by an actuary, the other spouse may receive a percentage of each future pension check, or at some other designated time as allowed by the pension plan, based on the numbers of years the spouses lived together as husband and wife and the total number of years the employed spouse has been participating in the pension plan.

The laws governing pensions are different for private corporate physicians than they are for government and military health-care workers. Private corporate employees are usually covered under the Federal Retirement Equity Act of 1984, which created what is known as the "Qualified Domestic Relations Order," or "QDRO" (pronounced "quadro"). The QDRO is a court order to designate how a specific retirement plan will be divided, to whom it will be paid, and requires the employer to comply with the terms of the order. If you or your spouse is a government or military employee, you and your attorney should seek to understand the nuances of the specific plan.

[3] 401(K) PLANS AND OTHER QUALIFIED PLANS (DEFINED CONTRIBUTION PLANS), AND INDIVIDUAL RETIREMENT ACCOUNTS (IRAS)

If there are no other assets to offset the net value of a 401(k) plan, other qualified plan, or IRA, the other spouse may receive a percentage of these accounts. This distribution usually occurs concurrent with the divorce. He or she will be able to defer taxes on the distribution by placing the funds in a rollover IRA account. Please note that although there is usually an additional 10 percent penalty for early liquidation of these accounts, the early distribution tax does not apply for receipts from 401(k) plans and other qualified plans paid to an alternate payee through a QDRO.

[4] REAL ESTATE OR MARITAL RESIDENCE

There are some financial pitfalls that must be considered in dealing with the marital residence. For physicians, ignoring these could be a financial disaster since it is not unusual for a doctor to have a significant part of his or her net worth tied up in home ownership.

The Taxpayer Relief Act of 1997 provided new rules for home sales. The act provides for a couple to exclude $500,000 in capital gains and for an individual to exclude $250,000 in capital gains, every 2 years. Additionally, it states that to qualify for these exclusions, this home must have been your primary residence for 2 of the past 5 years. (As a medical professional, if you have an office at home, any portion that qualified for the home office tax deduction does not qualify for this tax-free profit.)

There are special rules in the Taxpayer Relief Act for divorcing couples regarding home sales. Divorcing couples should be entitled to a partial exclusion of taxes, even if they don't meet the 2-year time test. For example, if a divorcing couple had a $375,000 gain during their 18 months of home ownership ($500,000 × 75 percent), they could exclude the whole gain. Additionally, a taxpayer is treated as using his or her home as a principal residence during any period that the taxpayer's spouse or former spouse is granted use of the residence under a divorce or separation agreement.

Where minor children are involved, it is common for the custodial parent to be allowed to live in the residence with the children for a specified period of time after the dissolution of marriage is finalized. During that period of time, the spouse who lives in the home is usually required to make all mortgage, property tax, and homeowner insurance payments when due. The house may be sold when: there are no children living at the property, the youngest child attains the age of majority, or any date as otherwise agreed on by the parties or specified by the court, with the proceeds to be divided based on the agreement in the divorce settlement. In this situation, the parties will still be entitled to take the $500,000 joint exclusion after the divorce.

If there is a large gain on the house at the time of the divorce, a pitfall to avoid is transferring the entire house to one of the parties in the divorce settlement. If that spouse subsequently were to sell the house and have to report the entire gain on his or her separate return, only $250,000 of the gain (from the time of the original purchase of the house) would escape taxation.

[D] Spousal Support or Alimony and Related Tax Issues

During the divorce process, no one word seems to incite riot as easily as *alimony* (also known as spousal support or maintenance). Issues such as closure, dependency, and deservedness come into play. However, once you separate the emotions and stereotypes from the actual mechanics, alimony can offer some couples financial advantages. As attorney Steve Abel states in *The Friendly Divorcebook*, "allowing your feelings to take over on the matter may prevent you from saving a great deal of money. Maintenance might save money by means of smart tax planning, just at a time you both need it."

Publication 504 issued by the Department of the Treasury provides information for divorced or separated individuals, including the federal rules regarding alimony. "Alimony is a payment to or for a spouse or former spouse under a divorce or separation instrument. . . . Alimony is deductible by the payer and must be included in the spouse's or former spouse's income."

The crux of the benefits of alimony relates to taxes. We have a progressive tax system in the United States. People who earn more are taxed at a higher percentage than those who earn less. By shifting earnings to the lower taxpayer, both parties can benefit. An illustration may help. Let's say that a doctor husband has $80,000 in taxable income and the wife has $20,000 in taxable income. Assuming each party is filing as head of household, the husband will owe about $17,476 in federal taxes and the wife will owe $3,004 in federal taxes. Together, they will owe $20,480. Now let's shift $20,000 of the husband's income to the wife; the husband's taxable income would now be $60,000, and he would owe $11,976 in taxes, while the wife's taxable income would now be $40,000 and she would owe $6,476 in taxes. Together they would owe $18,452—a savings of $2,028 in taxes. As the differences in income become larger, the savings also become larger.

If you have children, most courts are looking for child support by that state's child support guidelines in your divorce agreement. It is therefore wise to calculate the child support guidelines, and not to muddy the waters by calling child support "alimony." However, there may still be situations where the higher-paying spouse intends to provide support beyond the child support guidelines or plans to make periodic payments to the other spouse. It may benefit the parties to structure these payments as alimony.

To be alimony, a payment must meet certain requirements:

- The payment is made pursuant to a divorce or separation instrument; it cannot be a verbal agreement.
- The instrument does not designate the payment as not alimony.
- Alimony does not include child support or payments pursuant to equitable distribution.
- The parties should live in separate households (there are some exceptions).
- The parties must file separate tax returns and also live in separate households.
- The payment must be in cash (or check, etc.); transfer of services or property is not permitted.

- There is no liability to make payment after the death of the recipient spouse.
- Alimony cannot terminate or drop by more than $15,000 from the prior year in the first 3 calendar years of payment. There is the potential to have to recapture if this does occur, unless the drop is due to death or to the remarriage of the person receiving payments.
- There must be no contingency related to payment of alimony based on an event impacting your child or children, such as leaving school or the children becoming employed.

There is always some risk involved with actually getting payments over a period of time versus getting a lump sum payment up-front. The factors that often lead to these risks include additional expenses from a new marriage or new family, cohabitation (although some agreements specifically have clauses addressing this issue), inability to pay as a result of incapacitation through illness, payment withheld as punishment, and refusal to pay.

To avoid some of these risks, another way to receive alimony is through a so-called *alimony substitution trust.* In this vehicle, liquid investments such as stocks and bonds are placed in trust with a custodian with generated interest and dividends sufficient to pay each month's agreed alimony stipend. Stipulations are made in the trust provisions to sell portions of the portfolio if sufficient cash is not generated by the portfolio's investments. Some professionals feel this arrangement is a better vehicle for periodic alimony payments than the goodwill of the payer spouse because it avoids the "check is in the mail" syndrome.

Although many people believe that alimony is assumed, it is not as common as you may think it to be. Only one out of six divorce cases even considers it as an option. Temporary spousal support is more common and occurs at the time of separation, mostly to help the receiving spouse get on his or her feet again. Either it is agreed upon or an order is issued. However, if your marriage is a long-term marriage in the eyes of the court (this usually means over 20 years) and your spouse's income is less than one-third of your income, you may be expected to pay alimony. Although few states have alimony guidelines as they do for child support, most have statutory criteria for an award of alimony.

Some of the factors that may be part of your state's criteria may include:

- Parental responsibility
- Income available to either party through investments or any assets held by that party
- The tax treatment and consequences to both parties of any alimony award including the designation of all or a portion of the awarded alimony
- The actual need and ability of the parties to pay
- The duration of the marriage
- The age and physical and emotional health of the parties
- The standard of living established in the marriage and the likelihood that each party can maintain a reasonably comparable standard of living

- The earning capacities, educational levels, vocational skills, and employability of the parties
- The length of absence from the job market and custodial responsibilities for children of the party seeking maintenance
- The time and expense necessary to acquire sufficient education or training to enable the party seeking maintenance to find appropriate employment, the availability of the training and employment, and the opportunity for future acquisitions of capital assets and income
- The history of the financial or nonfinancial contributions to the marriage by each party, including contributions to the care and education of the children and interruption of personal careers or educational opportunities
- The equitable distribution of property ordered and any payout on equitable distribution, directly or indirectly, from current income, to the extent that this consideration is reasonable, just, and fair
- Any other factors that the court may deem relevant

Most alimony falls under the category of "rehabilitative alimony" in that it is paid until the spouse is reasonably able to support himself or herself. In cases where the spouse has not worked during a long-term marriage, that spouse may be awarded "lifetime alimony," which ceases upon the death of either party or the remarriage of the person receiving the support.

Some states also provide for "reimbursement alimony," which is intended to reimburse one party who supported the other party through an advanced education. It is assumed that the supporting party anticipated participation in the fruits of the earning capacity generated by the education. Basically, some states attempt to reimburse the person who did not go to school for an advanced degree because he or she will not benefit from the increased salary or earnings of the person who received the degree.

In the past the wife was almost always the recipient, but the courts no longer view gender as a consideration. In most states marital conduct is also not a consideration. The decision is based purely on the economic consequences of each spouse. If an agreement between spouses is reached out of court, the court will give it significant consideration.

Other Tax Considerations of Separation and Divorce

[A] Filing Status

As previously mentioned, child support is not taxed as income to the recipient and is not deductible to the payer, whereas alimony is usually taxed as income to the recipient and is deductible to the payer. The tax laws impose other rules for separated or divorced individuals. If you are in the process of going through a divorce, it would be wise to read through the IRS publications related to separation and divorce, as well as to consult with your tax advisor, so that you are in the best position to negotiate these monetary aspects of your divorce.

Your filing status for your tax return is your status on the last day of the year for the year you are filing. If you and your spouse are living apart but are not legally separated, or if your divorce decree is not final, you may file a joint tax return. You should know that married filing separately currently results in the highest tax rate; it pays if both parties can cooperate—better to share the savings than pay more to the IRS out of spite. You are considered single if you are unmarried or separated from your spouse either by a divorce or a court-approved separate maintenance decree and if you don't qualify as a head of household.

Because the head of household tax rate is lower than the single tax rate, you may want to see if you can qualify for this status. You can qualify as a head of household only if you were unmarried on the last day of the most recent year of filing your tax return or separated for over 6 months, and have at least one dependent child, and pay more than half the cost of keeping a home for yourself and this dependent, and this was the dependent's main home for more than half the year. In a family with two or more children, with proper tax planning, both parents could qualify as head of household if the parents structure their parenting time so that each parent has physical custody of at least one child. If your taxable income is $95,000, you would save nearly $2,000 in taxes by filing as head of household rather than single, and nearly $3,500 as head of household rather than married filing separately. Head of household status and exemptions for dependents are separate issues.

The Economic Growth and Tax Relief Reconciliation Act of 2001 promised to deliver tax savings to Americans in the coming years. The new law adds several measures to alleviate the marriage penalty, which had caused the combined tax liability of a married couple filing jointly to be greater than the sum of their tax liabilities computed as if they were two unmarried filers; however, this does not go into effect until 2005.

[B] Exemptions for Dependents

Only one parent can claim a child on his or her tax return. The parent who had custody of the child for the greater part of the year is generally treated as the parent who provided more than half the child's support and is usually allowed to claim the exemption for a child. Noncustodial parents can still claim the child exemption if the custodial parent signs a statement (using Form 8332) agreeing not to claim the child's exemption and attaches this statement to their return, or attaches a copy of certain pages of their divorce decree or separation agreement addressing exemptions. There are separate rules for divorce agreements made prior to 1985.

Generally, you can deduct $3,050 (as of 2003) for each exemption for a dependent you can claim on your tax return. If you are at a 35.5 percent tax bracket, each deduction results in a net saving of $1,083.

High-income earners should be aware that there is an exemption phaseout as gross adjusted income exceeds certain thresholds. As of 2003, these are $209,250 for married filing jointly, $174,400 for heads of household, $139,500 for singles, and $104,625 for married filing separately. You must reduce the dollar amount of your exemption by 2 percent for each $2,500, or $1,250 if you are married filing separately.

[C] Child Tax Credit

Additionally, the IRS provides a child tax credit for each qualifying dependent under age 17 (see Exemptions for Dependents). The parent who claims the exemption for the child is also entitled to claim the child tax credit. A tax credit is a dollar-for-dollar reduction in your tax liability. Each dollar in tax credit results in a dollar offset against your income tax. Under the Economic Growth and Tax Relief Reconciliation Act of 2001, the child tax credit, which was $500 in 2000, is increased to $1,000 as follows:

Calendar Year	Maximum Credit Amount Per Child
2001–2004	$600
2005–2008	$700
2009	$800
2010 and after	$1,000

High-income earners should be aware that there is a phaseout of the child tax credit as gross adjusted income exceeds certain thresholds. These are $110,000 for married filing jointly, $75,000 for head of household or single, and $55,000 for married filing separately. For every additional $1,000 income, you lose $50 of the credit. With a joint return over $119,000, the child tax credit is completely eliminated.

Low-income earners should be aware that the new tax law makes the child tax credit refundable to the extent of 10 percent of the taxpayer's earned income in excess of $10,000 for tax years 2001 through 2004, and 15 percent after 2005. In plain English, this means that the IRS will refund money, even if you have no tax liability, so long as your income exceeds $10,000.

[D] Child-Care Tax Credit

If you paid someone to care for your child under age 13, or other qualifying person, so you could work or look for work and you have physical custody of a child, you may also be able to take the credit for child and dependent care. If you are divorced or separated and you have physical custody of the child, you can treat your child as a qualifying person, even if you cannot claim the child's exemption.

If you are the noncustodial parent, you cannot treat your child as a qualifying person even if you can claim the child's exemption.

The maximum child-care expense allowed is 35 percent of $3,000 for one dependent, and $6,000 for two or more dependents. The credit percentage is reduced in steps to 20 percent as gross adjusted income increases from $15,000 to over $43,000. As an example, if your income is $50,000, your maximum child-care tax credit will be $600 for one child, and $1,200 for two children. Again, a credit is a dollar-for-dollar reduction in your tax liability.

[E] Education Credits

The hope credit ($1,500 per child for the first 2 years of college) and the lifetime learning credit (up to $1,000 per return for all years of postsecondary education) follow the same rule as the under-age-16 child tax credit. The parent who claims the exemption may also claim these education credits. The education credits have income tests associated with them of a maximum of $50,000 for a single or head of household return and $100,000 for a joint return.

[F] Earned Income Credit (EIC)

The earned income credit (EIC) is a tax credit for certain people who have earned income under a specified threshold. There are different thresholds for people without children, people with one child, and people with two or more children. As with the child-care tax credit, you must have custody of a child for he or she to be considered a qualified child.

[G] Child's Investment Income

If your dependent child has unearned income of more than $750, he or she will have a tax liability on these earnings. The custodial parent or parents may choose to include this income on their return rather than file a return for the child. The IRS specifically states not to use the return of the noncustodial parent. Note that if your child's interests, dividends, and other investment income total more than $1,400, part of that income may be taxed at the parent's tax rate instead of the child's tax rate.

[H] The Jobs and Growth Tax Relief Reconciliation Act of 2003

The Jobs and Growth Tax Relief Reconciliation Act (JGTRRA) of 2003 presents a significant opportunity for physicians and their financial advisors to rebalance an integrated personal financial plan, going forward. The typical taxpayer will save about $671, according to the U.S. Tax Policy Center. The most important provisions of the new law include the elimination of the marriage penalty and changes in the child tax credit.

[1] ELIMINATION OF THE MARRIAGE PENALTY

One of the questions most frequently asked by the medical professional revolves around the filing of a joint tax return versus the filing of a separate return. This question comes up because of the so-called marriage penalty that was built into the standard deduction and into the tax rates for married couples filing a joint return. Fortunately, the marriage penalty has been eliminated for dual-income married couples, effective January 1, 2003. The basic standard deduction amount is twice the standard deduction for single individuals in 2003 and 2004, and will be raised from the current $7,950 to $9,500. Those who itemize their deductions on their income taxes won't see any effect, but the majority of couples who take the standard deduction will save $155.

But, for physicians living in either community property or common law states, extra care in the documentation of income and deductions ("ownership") is a must. In community property states most items of both income and deduction will be split 50-50. However, each community property state has its own rules as to how income from separate property (property owned by one spouse or the other, not jointly, such as inherited property) is treated. For common law states, income is traced to ownership and deductions claimed by one spouse must be paid from that spouse's separate funds.

[2] PHYSICIAN RESIDENTS AND YOUNG CHILDREN

Effective January 1, 2003, the child tax credit was increased from $600 to $1000.

Parents who took the child tax credit on their 2002 returns got "advanced payment" checks in the summer of 2003 for up to $400 per child to reflect the new, higher credit. This functioned much like the advance payment rebate checks 2 years ago, when taxpayers received up to $300 each in the mail. The $1,000 credit will last for 2 years before shrinking to $700 in 2005 through 2008. In 2009, the credit will rise to $800 before returning to $1,000 in 2010.

[3] STAYING INFORMED

Knowing the new rules of JGTRRA will benefit the medical professional, and all taxpaying citizens. To stay informed of further JGTRRA changes, visit the site www.irs.ustreas.gov for tax tables and updates. To download a complete copy of the JGTRRA bill, visit www.taxplanet.com.

Older Divorcing Medical Professionals

Although marriages are more apt to break up around the 7-year mark, not on a silver anniversary, divorce has become more common, and therefore divorce among older people has also become more common. When divorce does occur in later years, it can present more complicated financial issues when compared with earlier breakups, says Gregg Parish with the College for Financial Planning.

If, for example, a party dies or becomes incapacitated during the divorce, the surviving spouse will retain complete control of the finances. A common situation, Parish says, is when a couple owns a home in joint tenancy with rights of survival. Thus, if one spouse dies, the other automatically inherits the house. Parish recommends that older couples in the throes of separation change the ownership to tenants in common, in which each party is considered to own half the property.

Another area older physicians going through a divorce should be especially cautious about is inheritances or gifts from their own parents. Your parents may want to stop or delay distribution of their estate to you to reduce the chances that the property will become mixed into marital property. Or the recipient might put any gifts or inheritances into a separate account or trust.

Alimony is more prevalent among this age group of divorced couples. It is not uncommon to find a woman who may not have employable skills and who must rely on her former spouse for support. As is the case for child support payments in younger parties, steps should be taken to ensure continuation of funds to the recipient if the obligated party dies before the recipient; this can be done through instruments such as life insurance.

For most older divorcing couples, after their house and their pension, their next most valuable asset is their Social Security rights. Each party vests in the other's Social Security account after 10 years of marriage. That means that even a nonworking spouse can usually collect 50 percent of the benefits of the earning spouse; alternatively, the spouse with lower earnings can either collect benefits based on his or her own earnings, or collect 50 percent of the benefits his or her spouse is entitled to. This collection does not impact how much the higher-earning spouse can collect. You can learn more about Social Security benefits and rules by contacting the Social Security Administration at 1-800-772-1213.

What is often missed in the analysis of divorce is the inequity in Social Security benefits for the nonworking spouse or lower-earning spouse after separation or divorce. The issue of Social Security benefits can easily be addressed in the divorce agreement by stipulating that the parties will equalize Social Security benefits with the higher-earning spouse providing to the lower-earning spouse one-half the difference between the payments provided by the Social Security Administration to each of them. Since Social Security benefits are taxable, it is further recommended that these payments be regarded as alimony, and therefore will be taxable to the recipient.

Another divorce area often overlooked, given today's older physician population, is elder-care obligations. For example, if a doctor is involved in the care and financial assistance of an older family member, this must be placed on the table at the divorce resolution planning discussions. America is aging, and 25 percent of its population is 60 or older. Every 7 seconds someone turns 50. It is not unusual to live many miles from aging parents.

Imagine the impact if an in-law is in a long-term care facility that is dependent upon the financial help of the children, who now get divorced. What happens to the elder person's ability to meet his or her financial obligations and stay in the current facility? How can quality care be coordinated? Who will monitor the ongoing health and mental and physical issues? When does the aging parent need in-home care? Assisted living arrangements? A skilled nursing facility? Yet, the generation of medical professionals between the ages of 40 and 60 are dealing with aging parents at the same time their children are entering college. This double financial squeeze has created a new set of elder-care issues.

Most cities and local government agencies are addressing this issue, and many non-profit organizations are attempting to fill the gap in this growing societal issue. The following information resources are helpful in this regard: Medicare.gov; Medicaid.gov; careguide.com; seniorhousing.net; senior.net, www.caregiver911.com; www.n4aorg; www.nafcares.org; financialroadmap.com.

Additional Readings

Braver, Sanford, with O'Connell, Diane: *Divorced Dads: Shattering the Myths.* Penguin Putnam, New York, 1998.

Bunn, R, Jessani, A, and Williamson, J: Planning for home sales in a divorce and some pitfalls to avoid, *National Public Accountant,* May 1999, Vol. 44, pp. 14–38.

Ellman, IM, Kurtz, P, and Bartlett, K: *Family Law, Cases Text, Problems.* Michie Company, Charlottesville, VA, 1991.

Haynes, John: *The Fundamentals of Family Mediation.* State University of New York Press, Albany, NY, 1994.

Jessani, AD: Ten common parenting-related mistakes in drafting divorce agreements, *American Journal of Family Law,* Summer 2000, Vol. 14, pp. 102–107.

Stanny, Barbara: *Prince Charming Isn't Coming.* Penguin, New York, 1997.

Trafford, Abigail: *Crazy Time: Surviving Divorce and Building a New Life.* Harper-Collins, New York, 1992.

Wilson, CA: Five errors financial planners commonly make when working with divorcing clients, JFP, October 2000.

Divorce Websites

- www.mediators.com
- www.mediationnow.com
- www.divorceinfo.com
- www.divorcewithoutwar.com
- www.divorcesource.com
- www.divorcenet.com
- www.yourdivorceadvisor.com

- www.split-up.com
- www.StopYourDivorce.com

Additional Websites

- www.seniors.gov
- www.seniornet.com
- www.eldernet.com
- www.ageofreason.com
- www.thirdage.com
- www.seniorhealth.about.com
- www.thegeezerbrigade.com
- www.aarp.com
- www.4seniors.com
- www.oldtime.com
- www.eapage.com

Chapter 14

Asset Protection Principles

(What Is at Risk . . . How to Protect It!)

Edward J. Rappaport
J. Christopher Miller

Once upon a time, I had a lot of physicians as clients. Now, the only physicians I have as clients are those who invented some product and have a royalty stream, or who made a lot of money selling their practice. HMOs and large corporate practices have driven down the compensation being paid to most physicians to where they can no longer afford my services. This is a dramatic turnaround in only about 5 years. Truth is, most physicians can't afford the sophisticated asset protection structures which work very well, and which are now designed to give effective protection to upwards of at least $5 million in net assets. Instead, today physicians are often burned when placed into "cheapie" trusts, limited partnerships, or the like. Physicians also seem to be particularly susceptible to losing their money to offshore trust and investment schemes. Many would be much better off with umbrella liability policies or litigation expense policies than the structures they have now.

Jay D. Adkisson, J.D., Molnar Adkisson Consulting, LLP

This chapter demonstrates how avoiding risk and handling your assets in certain ways can minimize your chances of losing assets to creditors. Asset protection receives attention from professionals in all spheres who have accumulated wealth. Investments made in the 1990s multiplied from the booming economy, but in the first years of the twenty-first century they have shrunk even more quickly than they had grown. The blame for such catastrophic losses falls partly on the bursting of Wall Street's speculative bubble and partly on a loss of confidence in the accuracy of financial accounting and auditing. No sector of the investment world has been left untouched. Unforeseeable events, such as the terrorist attacks of September 2001, divorce, and the collapse of Enron, one of the largest corporations in America, as well as

Worldcom, Global Crossing, Ltd, and HealthSouth, have launched a renewed, if not frantic, interest in wealth preservation.

The first step in constructing a solid asset protection plan is to assemble an experienced and professional advisory team that can be trusted to stay current on the swift changes in this area. Together, you will be able to plan and execute a course of action customized to your needs and objectives.

Getting Started

Strong asset protection depends substantially on timing. The sooner you act to protect your assets, the greater the odds of your success. Many asset protection strategies construct barriers between assets and creditors, and if those barriers are built when creditors are closing in, courts may not respect them. If, on the other hand, such asset protection tools are used when your financial outlook is healthy, they can prove to be an effective deterrent against the reach of creditors.

Appreciating the Risks

Physicians and medical professionals share a unique disadvantage when it comes to asset protection. They are constantly haunted by the prospect of being sued for malpractice. Most have solid malpractice insurance coverage in force, but if that pool runs dry, the courts may look to the professional individually to compensate patients for any injuries suffered while under the professional's care. Malpractice insurance itself may not be sufficient to completely protect a physician against professional liability claims. As verdicts increase in size, policy limits may become inadequate. Alternatively, insurance companies have a strong incentive to deny coverage by arguing that a claim falls outside the scope of coverage. Preparing for these possibilities will leave you much more financially sound than if you do not plan ahead before such a calamity arises.

Aside from the professional risks you take merely by agreeing to examine and treat a patient, dangers to your assets surround you. As discomforting as it may sound, your family and neighbors are in fact potential adversaries. Unfortunately, your position as a medical professional in today's society subjects you to elevated risks of a nasty lawsuit if you are negligent in your personal conduct.

An accident while driving to the hospital in response to a call, or a simple slip-and-fall incident on your home's sidewalk, will more likely find its way into a courtroom because plaintiffs (and their lawyers) perceive you as a deep pocket.

Alternatively, there may come a time when your marriage fails, and you are faced with equitably dividing property between you and your spouse. Asset protection strategies act differently in the context of a divorce, and family-oriented claims need to be treated differently in the scope of creating a plan. In the event that a claim arises from outside your professional activities, or if you find yourself swallowed by consumer debts, several asset protection methods will help you prevent your assets from slipping away.

Asset Protection Tools

[A] Good Record Keeping

The best defense against any claim is a complete and accurate record of the facts. In particular, medical malpractice claims will frequently be stalled or thwarted by a consistent written description of the symptoms you observe and the treatments you prescribe. Extensive record keeping will not only help formulate a defense against a claim, but it will also (and perhaps more importantly) create the appearance that you are careful and highly competent in all of your affairs. Members of a jury may not be able to discern whether the medical judgments you made in a particular case were good or bad, since they do not have the years of education and training that you have undergone. They can, however, sense whether your practice is honed and organized. If your records are thorough and consistent, jurors will assume that you dedicate as much attention to the substantive aspects of your work as you do to the tedium of record keeping. If you are active in the management of your office, you should keep track of its operations and establish logs for your employees to complete as they perform their daily tasks. Not all information, however, ought to be written down.

[B] Insurance

If caution and good record keeping do not save you from incurring a liability, the first defense against having an adverse effect on your net worth is to insure yourself against the loss. Insurance is the easiest way to avoid risk because you are paying someone else to bear that risk. Insurance companies derive their profit from pooling the risks of many policyholders, and thus provide a valuable service to society.

The best piece of advice anyone can share with someone about to commit to an insurance policy is to compare insurance policies before signing up. Just like you should comparison-shop for a new car, you should ask around at several agencies before allowing an agent to submit your application. Rates for comparable policies vary widely, and policies may differ significantly in the size and scope of coverage they offer. Research the typical attributes of a policy, such as its deductible and the extent of its exclusions. Find out whether the insurance carrier is financially secure and whether its investments are liquid. Deciding which combination is right for you demands careful consideration and a trusted advisor.

[1] MALPRACTICE INSURANCE

With respect to the scope of malpractice coverage, many liability insurance policies will deny coverage if an intentional tort is alleged. One example of an intentional tort is intentional infliction of emotional distress, which doctors may need to defend against if they misdiagnose a patient while having a financial interest in the treatment of the diagnosis. Battery is another intentional tort with which doctors are often charged. *Battery* can be defined as any injurious contact without consent.

The necessity of obtaining informed consent from each patient is becoming increasingly important as a defense against such claims. Intentional torts are to be distinguished from torts of negligence, which are usually covered under most liability insurance policies. Negligence claims arise out of mistakes usually attributable to carelessness. Make sure your insurance policy extends to intentional torts to prevent these kinds of cases from being denied coverage by your insurance company.

[2] LIFE INSURANCE AND DISABILITY INSURANCE

The most valuable asset owned by most physicians is not their home or their stock portfolio; rather, it is their future income potential. You can protect against its loss by ensuring that its full value is replaced if you are unable to continue working into the future. Life and disability insurance are the tools used to protect this value. An easily overlooked factor to consider when buying life insurance is the amount of debt you have outstanding. Be sure to provide enough proceeds for your spouse and children to satisfy any obligations you have assumed, such as the mortgage on your home or continued payments on automobiles or boats, as well as enough money to support them until they can find other sources of income. If you are an insurable candidate, think twice before turning down additional coverage, because sometime later, you might lose that status and be unable to increase your insurance posture.

[3] GENERAL LIABILITY INSURANCE

When consulting with an insurance agent, inquire about umbrella-type general liability policies. In addition to protecting you from the plaintiff adopting a shotgun approach to litigation, the general liability insurer bears a burden to defend covered claims as well as to indemnify against losses. That is, the insurer pays the fees and expenses incurred while the claim is being litigated. Because of this duty, consider the legal fees and expenses you would save in addition to the possible damage awards when considering the purchase of an umbrella policy.

[4] NATURAL DISASTER INSURANCE

Finally, protect against the loss of accumulated assets by insuring them against the wrath of Mother Nature. Most homeowners' policies do not cover damages arising from floods or earthquakes. If a home, or any other real property, is in an area subject to floods or earthquakes, consider the value of purchasing insurance that covers such catastrophes. Take the time to review your homeowners' policy, making sure that it will repair or replace your roof if damaged by hail and will apply in the event of high winds, rather than only in tornadoes. The key to the maintenance of any type of insurance is to anticipate all of the possible calamities and then to decide whether you can afford to lose the assets exposed to those calamities.

[C] Layered Organizations

[1] PRACTICE FORMAT

Considering the format and corporate structure of your health-care practice is another way to limit personal liability and protect your assets. The most successful means of reducing the risk from professional conduct is the creation of a layered organization. Your practice should operate through an entity (or set of entities) that limits the liability of its owners. A series of subsidiary organizations operating under an umbrella entity may limit your personal liability after a colleague suffers liability in a claim, or if the practice is found liable for a breach of contract.

Traditionally, layering of a physician's business structure involved the use of a professional corporation governing an office whose stockholders were either the physicians themselves or other professional corporations embodying each practicing physician. Nowadays, the new and different forms of business entities do not require the formalities attendant to a corporation, but still benefit from statutory limits on the liability of their owners. Such entities include **limited liability companies** (LLCs) and **limited liability partnerships** (LLPs). Layering these types of organizations on top of one another can provide the same protection from claims by creditors without incurring the double income taxation of more traditional corporations. Many new organizational formats are designed to make asset protection easier, although sorting through the alphabet soup created by these new entity types can be difficult.

[2] A COMPARISON OF BUSINESS ENTITY TYPES

Generally speaking, a **corporation** consists of one or more shareholders that appoint one or more directors, who in turn manage the corporation and its actions. Shareholders are held responsible for the liabilities of the corporation only to the extent they have value in their shares. More specifically, the shareholders' personal risks are limited by the interest they have in the corporation, which equals the investment they made when buying or subscribing for the shares, plus any corporate earnings that have not yet been distributed as dividends. Except for special circumstances discussed later in this section, the personal assets of each shareholder are not at risk when a corporation suffers losses or is presented with a liability.

A **limited liability company** (LLC) is very similar to a corporation in its role as a barrier between the personal assets of its owners and its liabilities. An LLC can also be owned entirely by one person (or by another entity) or by more than one person, which makes it a convenient format for a medical professional looking to protect himself or herself from professional liabilities. LLCs also offer increased flexibility for tax planning and management purposes. Certain single-member LLCs can be entities that are disregarded for tax purposes, but for state law purposes, still provide a layer of insulation between the owner's assets and the LLC's operational debts.

A **limited liability partnership** (LLP) is much like an LLC, except that because it is a form of partnership, there must be more than one partner. You would likely use an LLP instead of an LLC if you wanted cohesiveness among several people or bodies but wanted to minimize subjecting each partner to the risks carried by other partners. An LLP has several advantages over a general partnership because, as its name suggests, the liability of each of the partners is limited to the value of the partner's interests in the partnership. That is, a partner in an LLP would not risk personal assets to the same degree as a partner in a general partnership. In a general partnership, any liabilities that the partnership incurs flow back to the partners, and each partner is jointly and severally liable for those general partnership debts.

The difference between an LLP and a **limited partnership** (LP) is rather subtle. Both types of entities are improvements over a general partnership from an asset protection standpoint in that not every partner puts the partner's assets on the line when partnership liabilities arise. The difference between the two is that, in a limited partnership (LP), there must be at least one general partner who risks paying for liabilities of the limited partnership beyond the general partner's interest in the partnership. In other words, the general partner exposes personal assets to creditors of the partnership. In a LLP, every partner can absorb the benefit of limited liability.

The following are business entity types and their identifiers:

- General partnership
- Limited partnership (LP)
- Corporation (Inc. or Corp.)
- Limited liability company (LLC)
- Limited liability partnership (LLP)
- Professional corporation (PC)
- Professional limited liability company (PLLC)

The asset protection traits of the LLC and the LLP are about to be tested through litigation arising from the Enron collapse. Many of the entities giving rise to the debts that brought that corporation to its knees were LLCs and LLPs.

Arthur Andersen, the largely defunct accounting group that allowed the Enron financial statements to escape the impact of those debts, was itself a limited liability entity. As Enron's shareholders and employees seek redress, they are sure to challenge the ability of partners in an LLP or members in an LLC to avoid the debts incurred by those entities. If the courts elect to find exceptions to the current rules regarding the liability shelter provided by these entities, the value of these entities as asset protection devices may diminish significantly.

[3] AN IDEAL APPROACH

A modern structure of a practice might be a LLP in which several LLCs are general partners. The LLP would be the umbrella organization in which all of the pratice's operations take place. Each of the general partner LLCs might be wholly owned and managed by an individual practicing medical professional, and each general partner LLC would have a voice in the management of the LLP. Each of the LLCs would also be insulated from liability.

In this hypothetical organization, the LLP would be at the forefront of each litigation proceeding and would be the primary operational entity to which patients remit payments and from which distributions are made to the various LLCs. The LLCs would employ the physician and distribute the earnings received from the LLP to the doctors individually. To be effective in insulating the LLCs, the LLP would need to make distributions of its profits promptly and regularly, so those profits are not exposed to the claims of plaintiffs. Also, the operational entity would not own the building in which the office is housed. Instead, a holding company of some form would be created, and a lease would be signed between the holding company and the LLP to prevent the building from exposure to seizure by creditors.

On the other hand, the operating LLP cannot be merely a phantom. It must have some working capital of its own to be respected as a litigable party. It must also have its own incidents of business, such as a checking account and letterhead, and the functional differences between the LLP, the holding company, and the LLCs should be respected in practice to ensure the success of the shields created by layering the organization.

The benefit of layering an organization derives from the fact that courts treat corporations, LLPs, and LLCs as individual legal entities. Certain claims against the entity must first exhaust the assets of the entity before attaching to the assets of the entity's owners. In summation, it is a good idea to minimize the quantities of assets held by the businesses conducting the operations of your practice, but to not allow those quantities to be so small as to make reasonable the argument that the LLP is merely a shell that carries no weight.

As stated previously, the owners of LLPs and LLCs, as opposed to partners in a general partnership, will not be liable for more than their investment and their share of the profits unless a claimant can pierce the veil of the entity. Although this rule, like any statement of the law, is subject to change in the future, courts now allow plaintiffs and creditors to pierce the veil only when the alternative would sanction fraud or promote injustice, and only when the entity and its owners have perfectly aligned interests. In other words, treating each part of the layered organization as a separately functioning entity makes it more difficult for plaintiffs to reach the assets of the owners. Because the owners of the LLP in the sample model are LLCs, plaintiffs would need to pierce two veils and show two alignments of interest before getting to the assets of the physicians themselves.

Layering an organization, however, does not protect an individual from direct *tort liability* if the individual is negligent or has committed fraud. In cases of potential professional tort liability, such as a malpractice claim, the professional is personally liable for any claims arising from his or her negligent conduct. Layering a business organization will not protect against malpractice claims or other tortuous wrongdoing. The layering of a business organization is instead meant to prevent claims based in contract and vicarious claims against colleagues' negligent or intentional acts (i.e., harassment or discrimination claims) from reaching the personal assets of a physician. For these sources of liability, treating each layer as serving a different function in the business, and dealing with each entity as a separate business, could prove quite effective in protecting the assets of the owners of the business.

[D] Qualified Retirement Plans

Current tax laws encourage both employers and employees to create and regularly contribute to retirement plans for use at a later stage in life. Qualified retirement plans may be initiated by individuals in the form of an individual retirement account (IRA), or initiated in employer-sponsored plans meeting the requirements of Internal Revenue Code section ("I.R.C") 401(k), from which 401(k) plans get their name.

In general, employer-sponsored retirement plan assets are protected from the claims of creditors under the provisions of the Employee Retirement Income and Security Act (ERISA). Thus, you should contribute as much as possible to retirement plans during your career in practice. Under ERISA, contributions made to a qualified retirement plan are treated as being withheld from the employee. Although the employee holds the promise of future payments from the plan assets, he or she may not make use of those funds or have any of the other benefits of present ownership of those funds. Because of the restricted nature of the employees' access to plan assets, the creditors of the employees are likewise prevented from seizing those assets while they are in the plan.

There are several exceptions to this general rule of protection, however, and nobody should rely on retirement plans to protect him or her from all types of creditors. For example, several states consider the value of an employee's retirement plan contributions when deciding how to split the assets of a couple during a divorce. Because of the variety of rules applied by different states and the speed with which those rules change in this field, you should consult with an expert in the area of deferred compensation before relying heavily on retirement plans for protection of your assets. Retirement plans that provide for distribution of the proceeds at death also lose their protection from creditors at death, which may be the worst possible time if an accident takes a person's life and simultaneously gives rise to claims against his or her estate. Consult with the plan administrator to establish a structured retirement plan providing the most protection for the retirement assets, but not negatively impacting the ability to enjoy those assets when they become available.

The general rule for individual retirement accounts is not the same as the rule applied to employer-sponsored plans. Contrary to popular belief and to the surprise of many, IRAs are *not* protected under ERISA, and thus may be exposed to creditors' claims unless state law provides creditor protection. The good news is that the laws of many states protect IRAs from creditors' claims much like ERISA shields employer plans from creditors. For example, in Georgia, IRAs are exempted from the claims of creditors by statute, and in the event of bankruptcy, IRAs are not considered available assets for liquidation. Claims for alimony and child support, however, are given an exception to this rule, proving once again that no tool of asset protection should be relied upon exclusively.

The theory supporting the protective value of retirement assets is that the nominal owner does not actually own the assets. In most cases, a brokerage or investment company will serve as a custodian of the IRA for the investor, holding the account for the benefit of that investor and agreeing to comply with the complex rules governing the administration of retirement accounts. The benefits are relatively temporary, however, in that once a person has reached retirement age, the custodial relationship does not give the custodian sufficient power to withhold assets from the investor if the investor wishes to dissolve or "cash out" the IRA, and this right of immediate access to the funds may give creditors the right to demand the same access, again depending upon relevant state law. This result not only allows creditors to seize the assets held in a custodial IRA but also imposes adverse tax consequences on the investor because of the early termination of the IRA.

A relatively new development in this area is the enactment of the Roth IRA. A Roth IRA is an IRA in which the participant receives no income tax deduction for a contribution to the Roth IRA. In addition to growing in value tax-exempt, the distributions to a participant from a Roth IRA are tax-free. The ability of the Roth IRA to escape the claims of creditors is currently unclear because of its recent appearance, but logically it should be, and thus far has been, treated just as a traditional IRA is treated.

[E] Joint Ownership of Assets

A common means of protecting assets from the reach of creditors is to transfer property into a spouse's name. Assuming that the spouse is not also at substantial risk of being the target of lawsuits because of the spouse's profession or lifestyle, it is a moderately effective means of accomplishing that goal. Creditors with valid judgments against an individual may only attach and seize those assets owned by that individual. Anything worth doing is worth doing right, however, and there are several pointers to structuring asset ownership in a way that maximizes its protective value.

A small number of states, such as Hawaii, Pennsylvania, and Florida, have statutes that automatically protect property jointly owned by spouses from creditors of either spouse, but often not from creditors of both spouses together. Property that benefits from this characterization is held in as a "tenancy by the entirety," and this prevents only one spouse from transferring away property that the married couple obtained together.

Again, variation in state law determines just how beneficial the formation of a "tenancy by the entirety" can be from an asset protection standpoint. The reason for this protection comes from a public interest in the preservation of marital assets, such that one spouse's indiscretion may not harm the position of the other spouse. The most significant limits to the advantage provided by the tenancies of the entirety are, first, that the creditors with claims against both spouses may seize such jointly held property, and, second, that upon the first death between the spouses, the property flows directly to the surviving spouse alone, who then no longer has the benefit of the creditor protection. Moreover, in April of 2002, the U.S. Supreme Court sharply curtailed the benefit provided by tenancies by the entirety by ruling that it does not shield an asset from the federal authorities, even if the tax liability was incurred only by one spouse.[1]

Some states in the South and West are community property states, and a resident or a former resident of a community property state may determine the true protective value of holding assets in a proper form. Under the community property theory, all property acquired by either spouse during the residency (or in some states prior to or during the residency) will be considered jointly owned property even if titled to an individual spouse. Merely by moving to one of these community property states, a person can automatically shift assets, thus reducing the quantity of assets subject to the creditors of the wealthier spouse.

For most of the nation, a good rule of thumb is to make sure that your largest assets, such as your personal residence, are not jointly owned with rights of survivorship. Although joint tenancy with rights of survivorship may ease some burdens associated with probating a decedent's estate, this form of ownership is the least favorable type when viewed through the asset protection prism. These assets, if they are held in some common ownership structure (as opposed to outright ownership by one spouse or the other), should be held as tenants in common. Tenancy in common is best described as a situation in which each spouse owns a one-half undivided share in the property but does not have the automatic right to full ownership at the death of the other spouse. Three advantages flow from this form of ownership:

- **Neither spouse owns the property exclusively.** A creditor seizing the interest of one spouse would not have a valuable asset because it could not evict the remaining spouse, so creditors will attack these assets only as a last resort to satisfy their claims.

- **If either spouse were to die, only half of the property would be subject to estate tax.** Joint ownership of property as tenants in common also helps in the estate planning arena by facilitating the process of equalizing the assets held by each spouse. The same logic applies to property held jointly by medical professionals who are not married to each other. If property is owned jointly among siblings or business associates, the owners should make sure that the deed names them as tenants in common. Otherwise, each successive death among the owners will trigger an increasing estate tax burden, leaving the last living owner to pay estate tax on the full value of the property, notwithstanding the estate tax paid by the other owners.

- **A dying spouse has the ability to control how his or her interest is distributed.** In many simple wills, all property of a spouse is given by bequest to the surviving spouse. Such a bequest could include partial ownership interests in real estate. If the surviving spouse is concerned about asset protection, this additional property would not be beneficial because it would easily be sacrificed to the survivor's creditors. One way of avoiding this result is to build an estate plan in which each spouse bequests the partial interest owned by that spouse to a trust. At the first death between the two spouses, the trust will hold the partial ownership interest for the benefit of the surviving spouse. The trust holding the partial residence interest preserves the deterrent faced by creditors of the surviving spouse because seizure of the surviving spouse's interest would not terminate the spouse's right to use the land provided for in the trust.

Assets should be held in a way that protects them from creditors for the long term. The form of asset holdings should thus be a significant part of the discussions held with professional advisors, so that the protection lasts beyond your death or that of your spouse. Structure the protected assets so that they do not flow back to you if your spouse should pass away. In this manner, integrated asset protection, estate planning, and financial planning unite to protect the family's interests by extending the benefits of creditor protection for the long term.

Following are forms of joint ownership:

- Tenancy by the entirety
- Tenancy in common
- Community property
- Joint tenancy with rights of survivorship (JTWROS)

[F] Gifting

One easy asset protection tool you can use to ensure that your children inherit your legacy is to begin giving assets to them early, before your future creditors claim them. Gifting should be used much more frequently than it is, but the obvious disadvantage of gifting property to children is that the donor no longer has the use of or control over the property. More emphatically, you must commit to the permanent loss of the property, so you must be absolutely sure that you will not ever need the gifted assets. This risk is especially significant when planning for future possibilities of creditor invasion.

Gifting is an effective protection against creditors, and a number of different methods are available to effect this intent, without always subjecting the assets to the whims of descendants not ready to handle money. First, small outright gifts to multiple beneficiaries may be made annually. This has the effect of reducing the quantity of assets subject to creditors' claims, but it also entrusts the donee receiving those gifts with control over those assets.

Outright gifts (i.e., those not made to a trust) made to any individual other than a donor's spouse are subject to gift taxation if they exceed $11,000 in a calendar year.

Amounts less than $11,000 are exempted from gift tax under I.R.C. § 2503(b), also known as the annual exclusion. Spouses may combine their exclusions to provide up to $22,000 in benefits to their children or other beneficiaries, but it is important to consult with a tax professional before making sizable gifts.

Although it does not prevent the imposition of gift tax, one alternative to outright gifting is to gift property in trust. This option involves giving your property to a trustee, who holds the property for the benefit of the intended beneficiary, and who bears a fiduciary duty to obey the instructions set forth in the document establishing the trust, otherwise known as the trust instrument. The trust instrument may include spendthrift provisions, which prohibit the trustee from distributing assets to certain beneficiaries except for specific uses and at particular times. The vital point here is that the trust separates creditors from the assets.

[G] Self-Settled Trusts

In almost all states, if you retain control or the benefit of assets held in a trust you create, the law treats the gift as illusory and will ignore the creation of the trust, allowing creditors to reach the property. Control of a trust is determined by several factors, including the power to exchange trust assets and the ability to withdraw money.

If the reality of the situation is that the trust was created merely as a smokescreen, and the assets are still within your reach, courts will reach through the formalities and treat the property as held solely in the donor's hands.

If that is the case, then how can a trust be considered an asset protection tool? The protection found in a self-settled trust lies in the ability of third parties, such as your children, to benefit from the assets of the trust without exposing them to claims of their creditors. If, after your death, a trust you create instructs the trustee to hold assets for the benefit of your children and to distribute assets to them only at the trustee's discretion to meet the actual needs of your children, then those assets will for the most part be inaccessible to the claims of any creditors of your children. Once a child has the right to request those assets from the trustee, however, that spendthrift protection falls away, and the trust assets become part of the child's assets in a debtor-creditor dispute.

A gift in trust can be made without saddling the beneficiary with the responsibility of managing the money wisely, and the beneficiary may still gain the benefits of the appreciation and income derived from the gift. The gift in trust is most useful when beneficiaries are too young to effectively manage the assets, or perhaps too immature to invest the money wisely. To educate the beneficiaries in money management, trust provisions often allow the income and principal of the trust to be distributed to the beneficiaries in stages. These stages often are delayed until the beneficiaries have reached adulthood, and they are intended to ease the transition from beneficiary to owner. Although you would like your children or grandchildren to turn a gift into something more valuable, trial and error plays a significant role in money management. Giving small, incremental gifts to the beneficiaries over time creates the opportunity for beneficiaries to learn the lessons of finance with smaller quantities of money, preserving the remainder of the trust property for a later distribution. Long-term asset protection means more than just protection from creditors. It means protecting the beneficiaries from themselves as well.

In addition to the stages of distribution, many trusts give the trustee the power to distribute assets to beneficiaries or on behalf of beneficiaries for specific purposes. In this way, a trust that delays distribution of money until after a child reaches the age of 25 years may still pay for the beneficiary's college and postgraduate education. The trustee may also be allowed to pay for such specific events as weddings and home purchases. This power must be discretionary, however, to preserve the asset protection features of the trust, and the beneficiary may refuse the distributed proceeds, though such an occurrence is extremely rare.

If a creditor can point to gifts made just prior to the effective date of the creditor's judgment, the creditor may be able to persuade a court to forcibly return the gifted property to the ownership of the donor and subject it to the claims of the creditors.

Complex Asset Protection Tools

The following methods of asset protection are significantly more sophisticated than those just described, and they will often require a substantial investment of time and money. They are also much more effective at sheltering large quantities of assets from creditors. A working knowledge of their availability will help you know to what degree you might wish to carry out your asset protection efforts.

Complex asset protection tools are aimed at deterrence rather than bulletproof shelter. They make the seizure of assets more difficult than it would otherwise be, and thus render those assets less attractive to creditors. Although asset protection specialists now practice each method with regular frequency, there are exceptions to almost every rule. Your likelihood of success depends in large part on the factual circumstances surrounding the inception of your asset protection plan. The primary object should be to steer clear of transfers that could be characterized as fraudulent conveyances. You should discuss the following ideas at length with your advisory team before making any moves with respect to these tools.

[A] Avoiding Fraudulent Conveyances

As a general rule, courts respect the efforts of people to preserve their assets. Courts balk, however, if such efforts seem fraudulent or are taken when there is potential liability to creditors or plaintiffs. The courts then label such efforts unethical, void, or even criminal. If you skipped to this portion of the text because you see trouble on the horizon, or are already involved in litigation, it is too late to act and a rescue attempt using the suggestions in this chapter will not patch existing problems. Despite your best intentions, you could be committing a fraud.

Fraudulent conveyances are transfers made by a debtor with the intent to hinder, delay, or defraud creditors. In the absence of concrete evidence of intent, such as a "smoking gun" memorandum, or the availability of testimony, courts look to a number of factors in deciding whether a debtor has the requisite intent. Among these factors are familial relationships between the debtor and the person receiving the conveyance, the proximity of the debtor to litigation, and whether the debtor received fair value in exchange for the transfer.

There is no bright line rule to help determine whether a conveyance will be deemed fraudulent because courts use such factors and arbitrarily weigh them to decide the existence of intent. This makes predicting the outcome of any particular fraudulent conveyance case difficult or impossible. There does, however, seem to be a spectrum along which some landmarks may be plotted. For instance, a physician with a thriving practice, a happy marriage, and a healthy financial balance sheet will not likely be charged with fraudulent conveyance, even if he or she does not receive full value in exchange for a transfer. On the other hand, a defendant in the midst of litigation making a transfer that leaves him or her without sufficient assets to pay a reasonable estimate of the damages will probably be making a fraudulent conveyance.

One of the key factors in determining the fraudulent nature of a conveyance is whether the transfer leaves the transferor unable to pay his or her debts, or with fewer assets than potential liabilities. In other words, if a transfer makes a person insolvent, or if the person is already insolvent, the transfer will likely be ruled a fraudulent conveyance. Thus, a doctor with a $7 million net worth who has recently become liable for a claim worth $3 million ought not to convey any amount close to $4 million at the risk of being punished for conveying the property fraudulently.

The punishment for a debtor found to have made a fraudulent conveyance is harsh. Creditors' remedies vary from state to state, but creditors are often given the option of voiding the transfer and taking back any property that was given. The debtor, however, may not undo the transfer in the same way. Additionally, the debtor will likely be forced to pay all of the creditor's expenses incurred in revoking the fraudulent conveyance. This rule of law leaves more power in the hands of creditors and makes it wiser to avoid making fraudulent conveyances at all costs than to risk the potential for punishment.

[B] Relocation

Relocation to another state that has passed debtor-friendly laws is a drastic step, but nevertheless a popular one. Some of the friendlier states include Florida, Arizona, and Nevada. These states have enacted laws that create special rights of ownership for debtors when creditors attempt to collect on judgments. Several states make joint ownership of property between spouses into an effective asset protection device. Again, however, proposed legislation after the Enron debacle may hamper your ability to use relocation as a means to defeat the claims of creditors.

Another debtor-friendly rule of law pertains to a debtor's ownership of the cash value of life insurance. Some life insurance policies accrue a cash surrender value, against which the policyholder may withdraw an advance on the death benefit payable, or for which the policyholder may exchange the policy. The cash surrender value turns the insurance policy into a liquid asset, which creditors could seize and then exchange for money. Florida and some other states offer their residents protection against creditors for the cash value of life insurance policies by declaring the surrender value exempt from garnishment upon an adverse judgment. This convenient legal feature makes the purchase of selected life insurance policies an even more attractive asset protection tool because creditors will choose not to seize the policy in an effort to recover the debt.

[C] Homestead Exemption

Florida also offers a generous homestead exemption. A homestead exemption is an asset protection shelter created by statute that prevents one parcel of real estate and its improvements from being attached and levied upon by creditors. By investing money in luxurious homes on large tracts of land in rural areas of Florida, many wealthy individuals are prudently protecting their estates from the reach of creditors.

> **Example:** Dr. David Mackenzie, a Florida resident and domiciliary, invests $4 million of his earned cash into a home with acreage in Florida. The home fully qualifies for the homestead exemption. If Dr. Mackenzie later declares bankruptcy, his home will be exempt from the liquidation of his assets. After the liquidation, all of his debts will be discharged by the bankruptcy court. Although Dr. Mackenzie may have lost his nonexempt assets, he will still own a $4 million asset free and clear of outstanding creditors, with which he may rebuild his accustomed lifestyle.

Another effective use of the homestead exemption is to backstop an incorrect form of jointly owned property. Although tenancies by the entirety and joint tenancies with rights of survivorship automatically leave the surviving spouse with the full ownership of property, the surviving spouse often may use the homestead exemption to preserve a primary residence against creditors' claims.

[D] Irrevocable Life Insurance Trusts

An irrevocable life insurance trust (ILIT) is a specialized trust instrument designed primarily to reduce estate taxes or to enable a client with significant nonliquid assets to generate liquidity to pay estate taxes without increasing the total estate tax liability. The client creating an ILIT transfers to the ILIT a preexisting life insurance policy on his or her life, or enough money to pay the premiums on a new life insurance policy. If the client survives 3 years beyond the contribution of an existing policy to the trust, or if the policy is purchased by a trust, the proceeds of the insurance policy payable on the client's death will not constitute part of his or her taxable estate. An ILIT is also helpful in protecting the cash value of policies from creditors in states where the cash value of life insurance is not protected from creditors' claims.

The primary drawback of the ILIT is that it is not revocable. The money spent on the premiums is not returnable to the creator of the trust, and the proceeds of the insurance policy owned by the trust must flow into the trust at the death of the person on whose life the policy was purchased. Even though the ILIT is not revocable, it may nevertheless be drafted with great flexibility. For example, terms such as *grantor's spouse* may be defined broadly as "the person to whom Grantor is married at the time of Grantor's death." As with any irrevocable document, care must go into its structure and textual references so that the document will have relevance and utility long after its creation.

ILITs also provide creditor protection to beneficiaries because the trust assets are not necessarily immediately available to them. If the ILIT is properly drafted, creditors will not be able to capitalize on an influx of money to the beneficiaries, as they would if the insurance proceeds were paid directly to the beneficiaries. Rather, as with spendthrift trusts created by a third party, the ILIT will serve as a barrier between creditors and beneficiaries, ensuring that the proceeds are spent for the benefit of the beneficiaries, rather than being ceded to their creditors. In favorable comparison to retirement assets, the ILIT can even protect a beneficiary from prioritized claimants, such as a beneficiary's former spouse.

Moreover, an irrevocable trust may prove to be a much more palatable alternative than a prenuptial agreement from the beneficiary's standpoint, particularly in a first marriage situation. In this regard, ILITs and other irrevocable trusts provide creditor protection in a number of ways to both the creator and the beneficiaries.

[E] Family Limited Partnerships

Family limited partnerships (FLPs) are business entities specializing in the management and prudent investment of family assets. They are used for the same reasons that professional business offices use layered organizations. As with other complex asset protection tools, FLPs do not necessarily make it impossible for a creditor to access an asset; instead they place obstacles between some claims of creditors and the valuable assets of the family. An FLP will often keep potential claims against individuals from endangering the assets held by the partnership by deterring creditors from pursuing the assets. A family limited partnership is a business and must be treated as a separate functioning entity, or the partnership will not be respected by the courts and the protections it offers will be unavailable. The creation and proper funding of an FLP are highly technical maneuvers with serious income tax and estate tax implications.

It is also distinctly possible that the law regarding liability limits in FLPs will change along with the law governing LLPs and LLCs. It is imperative to consult with an expert in asset planning before embarking on this course of action.

A modern alternative to the FLP, allowed in a growing number of jurisdictions, is a family limited liability company. With respect to the family LLC's asset protection capabilities, the structure of an LLC is similar enough to that of a partnership to indicate that creditors will not wish to seize interests in the LLC, but this analysis will limit itself to the context of a family limited partnership.

Family limited partnerships are different from general partnerships in that some, but not all, of the partners are insulated from liability for losses of the partnership. In a general partnership, all of the partners share liability for losses of the partnership. In a limited partnership, at least one partner is appointed as general partner, and that general partner is fully liable for losses of the partnership. In exchange for this disadvantageous position, the general partner has the power to manage the assets of the partnership.

Limited partners are passive owners and have very limited powers under the laws of most states. Additionally, limited partnerships are almost always governed by an agreement among the partners containing provisions that further limit the rights of the limited partners. One caveat must be raised, however, about the characterization of general partners as opposed to limited partners. If limited partners are proven to be making decisions about the operations of the partnership, they may be treated as general partners and may be forced to share the liability for losses with the general partner.

In a typical limited partnership agreement, a limited partner may have the power to assign, or transfer, all or part of the economic value of his or her partnership interest to another person with the prior consent of the general partner. The person receiving that assigned interest, called an "assignee," often receives the right to receive the distributions that would otherwise have been delivered to the transferor, but the assignee does not become a limited partner. As a result, the assignee is unable to exert much power within the partnership or redeem his or her interest in exchange for partnership assets. Even worse for the assignee, the tax attributes of a family limited partnership often require that the assignee pay income tax on a share of the limited partnership's income. Unless distributions are issued to the assignee by the general partner, the assignee will actual experience a negative cash flow upon gaining possession of the limited partnership interest.

Forming an FLP requires a significant amount of advance planning and legal advice. FLPs are not appropriate for all situations, and the Internal Revenue Service has in recent years devoted increased attention to the practice. If successful, however, an FLP can be used to discount the value of assets and thus reduce estate tax liabilities, as well as provide a formidable barrier to the reach of creditors.

> **Example:** Jack and Jill each contribute assets to form a family limited partnership, and in exchange, each receives a limited partnership interest. Jack and Jill also form an LLC to serve as a third partner, which will act as the general partner, and thus the lightning rod for any partnership liability. Jack and Jill then assign portions of their limited partnership interests to their three lovely children, Peter, Paul, and Mary, who each become assignees in the family limited partnership.

The family members receive only economic interests in the partnership distributions. Their economic interest entitles them to receive distributions granted by the general partner, but does not give them any of the powers and rights of a limited partner, whose rights are restricted anyway.

Creditors of both the limited partners and the assignees are not able to force their way into the partnership in the capacity of a limited partner. Instead, courts will allow creditors to step into the shoes of a limited partner, or assignee, by means of a charging order.

A charging order gives the creditor an assignment interest similar to that of any other assignee. However, it is only an economic interest in the distributions of the partnership. The creditor (or, for that matter, any other assignee) does not have any right to immediate payment because distributions are determined by the general partner according to the terms of the partnership agreement, or by statute.

Family limited partnerships are particularly effective in some states, such as Georgia, because a creditor levying on the partnership interest does not have the power to force dissolution of the partnership. In some other states, a limited partner (as opposed to an assignee) may have the ability to force the partnership to exchange its interest in the partnership for a pro rata share of the partnership assets by requesting a redemption. Thus, choosing the appropriate jurisdiction in which to form the family limited partnership is very important.

Another disadvantage faced by the creditor seeking to take over a partnership interest from a limited partner (or an assignee) is that the general partner has the ability to make or withhold distributions of cash to the creditor. Since partners are taxed on income realized by the partnership, regardless of whether that income is actually distributed to partners, the general partner's control over distributions places the creditor in peril of realizing income without receiving any cash with which to pay the tax generated by his or her share of the FLP's income.

Finally, the partnership agreement may provide that the existing partners have a right to purchase the assigned partnership interest from the creditor (or assignee) at the fair market value of the partnership interest. Since the fair market value of an assigned partnership interest is usually less than the value of that partner's percentage share of the partnership's assets, the creditor may be forced to settle for less than the value it had expected to realize from the assigned partnership interest. These significant drawbacks to the remedy of a charging order usually deter creditors from attempts to become an assignee of a partnership interest. Instead, creditors will often negotiate a reduced payment schedule or turn to other nonexempt assets of the debtor.

Family limited partnerships are also very useful in segregating separate property from marital property in the context of a divorce. If a spouse enters the marriage with a partnership interest, that partnership interest will usually not be blended into the marital estate for purposes of dividing property in a divorce. This attribute enables newlyweds to shelter family assets without the awkwardness of negotiating a prenuptial agreement.

When properly constructed and implemented, FLPs have the potential to significantly reduce the taxable estate of the partners contributing assets. It is vital that only an experienced practitioner well versed in the statutes and case law governing their operation implement the family limited partnership.

[F] Asset Protection Trusts

The transfer of assets to a specifically designed asset protection trust is a technique designed to deter creditors from seeking assets by putting those assets in a trust governed by laws that both protect the trust from certain claims of creditors and still permit the creator of the trust to receive discretionary distributions of principal and income from the trust. Laws that permit this type of trust, which flout the common law rule against creditor protection through self-settled trusts, exist only in Alaska, Nevada, Delaware, Rhode Island, and certain foreign countries. States pass such laws with the intent to attract investment capital, and as a result, often impose certain restrictions on the trustee and the investments made with the trust assets.

The difference between the asset protection trusts discussed in this section and the self-settled trusts introduced previously is that specialized asset protection trusts may provide creditor protection benefits to the person who contributed the assets to the trust without forbidding the trustee from distributing trust assets back to the creator of the trust.

An asset protection trust generally provides that a trustee has exclusive control over the trust management, and also that the trustee be permitted to distribute or withhold the trust income and principal, in accord with the instructions contained in the trust instrument. Often, the trustee is advised, but not directed, through the language in the trust not to distribute assets when the grantor or beneficiary is insolvent or involved in collection proceedings. This type of provision, called an "antiduress clause," shelters the trust proceeds from exposure to the creditors during the time when creditor protection is needed most.

The most important requirement of the asset protection trust is that it be established in a jurisdiction with laws that provide that judgments against the trust's grantor will not be enforced against the trust assets. In 1997, Delaware and Alaska each established laws providing some protection for certain trusts established in those states, and states like Nevada and Rhode Island have jumped on the bandwagon since then. The legislation was motivated by each state's desire to bring banking and investment business into the state.

In addition to the four states that now permit self-settled trusts to offer some sort of creditor protection, offshore jurisdictions such as the Cook Islands, the Cayman Islands, and the Bahamas offer exotic asset protection alternatives. Such offshore alternatives have advantages and disadvantages when compared with domestic trusts and are addressed separately.

[1] DOMESTIC ASSET PROTECTION TRUSTS

Domestic asset protection trusts (DAPTs) are created by accomplishing transfers to a trustee, which qualify for protections under the codified statutes of each state. The states have shrewdly drafted those statutes to maximize the in-state benefit realizable from the trusts. In Alaska, for example, the trust merits protection only if it is closely connected to Alaska: both a trustee and some trust assets must be located there, and the trust must answer several other requirements contained in the statute. If all of these requirements are met, the Alaska courts will assert jurisdiction over lawsuits attempting to seize the property, and the courts will apply Alaska law.

Alaska law validates and will enforce trusts that give a trustee the power to distribute assets, at the trustee's exclusive discretion, to a person who transferred property into the trust. The Alaska statute furthermore refuses to permit judgments of any creditor to impact property that was placed in a qualifying trust, unless one of several exceptions applies. Among the exceptions are fraudulent conveyances and trusts requiring the trustee to distribute assets to the grantor. Additionally, the law forbids most suits alleging that a transfer into the trust was fraudulent unless those suits are brought within 4 years of the transfer into the trust. This means that a qualifying trust properly funded at least 4 years before the grantor faces potential liability stands a good chance of being protected under the Alaska statute because a creditor may not raise the argument that the transfer into the trust was a fraudulent conveyance.

Delaware's statute regarding asset protection trusts is very similar to the law in Alaska. Delaware also requires that a trust be closely connected with the state of Delaware before extending its influence to the assets held by that trust, but once qualified, the trust may provide both optional distributions to the grantor creating the trust, and trustee discretion in making those distributions. The 4-year rule against lawsuits alleging fraudulent conveyance is carried over as well, but the statutes are not identical in their requirements. Delaware, for example, provides a more extensive list of rights that trust creators may retain without allowing creditor access. All four jurisdictions, however (Alaska, Delaware, Nevada, and Rhode Island), allow the trust created to be a potential distributee of income and principal of the trust at the discretion of the trustee. The two pioneer states in this field, Delaware and Alaska, also differ in the way they treat claims among family members, such as judgments for child support and alimony. The choice of selecting Delaware law, Alaska law, or another more recently enacting jurisdiction for the establishment of an asset protection trust is one that must be made with great care.

If an attorney successfully drafts a trust that may be interpreted only under the laws of a jurisdiction with an asset protection trust statute in effect, several advantages fall to the grantor. For example, the laws regarding trusts in Alaska and Delaware allow trusts to last indefinitely, whereas in most other jurisdictions, a trust's lifetime is limited. In addition, neither state applies an income tax to income realized by trusts. Thus, it may be possible to escape state income tax on trust income by creating a trust to which only Delaware or Alaska law applies.

On the other hand, the creator of a domestic asset protection trust runs the risk that a court will object to the constitutionality of the statutes that make them possible, leaving the grantor with a trust vulnerable to the claims of its creditors. Several academic arguments have been raised that the Delaware and Alaska statutes violate the Full Faith and Credit Clause of the U.S. Constitution, which requires states to enforce judgments of sister states. Additionally, the Supremacy Clause may enable federal bankruptcy courts to overrule the statutory language of the states and reach into asset protection trusts to satisfy creditors in a bankruptcy proceeding. To date, the Supreme Court has yet to rule on these issues, so that the validity of these statutes is neither certain nor implausible. A medical professional interested in creating one of these trusts should adopt a cautious approach and be ready to initiate a backup plan in the event that the trusts are invalidated.

Assuming that domestic asset protection trusts work as intended, they present the opportunity for individuals to transfer property to a trustee subject to the laws of the United States, and thus are liable for breaches of fiduciary duties. This provides a level of comfort that would not be available to creators of offshore trusts. Domestic trusts furthermore are generally less expensive to create and maintain than foreign asset protection trusts.

[2] FOREIGN ASSET PROTECTION TRUSTS

Offshore trusts are trusts established under the laws of a foreign jurisdiction, with foreign trustees, and using assets transferred outside the United States. The laws of the United States thus do not apply to the administration of those trusts, and the assets within offshore trusts are not subject to the jurisdiction of any U.S. court. Although the foreign venue may make it more difficult to pursue claims against trustees who mismanage money, the difficulty in pursuing claims is also faced by creditors, who must fight a legal battle in a foreign land to reach the assets of the trust. That can be very expensive, not just because the creditor will need to hire lawyers who can practice there, but also because the procedural laws of these jurisdictions make it very difficult to sue. Some jurisdictions require that a sizable bond be posted before a suit may be filed. Once in court, the rules of law in the foreign nation also apply to the trust, and several popular nations follow a rule of law allowing much more protection from creditors than would be available in the United States. Trusts created that provide the grantor with benefits at the discretion of the trustee are often insulated from creditors' attempts to seize them. Many jurisdictions do not enforce the fraudulent conveyance doctrine. A few nations even bestow upon the grantor some control over the size and timing of distributions by enforcing antiduress provisions. These provisions in an offshore trust advise the trustee to follow the directions of the grantor when the grantor is giving directions using his independent free will. If a court or a creditor is forcing the grantor to ask the trustee for money, however, the trustee has the power to refuse to comply with the request.

Tactics such as the use of antiduress provisions inspire disfavor by the U.S. courts no longer having jurisdiction over the assets. In a now famous ruling by the Ninth Circuit Court of Appeals in California, Denyse and Michael Anderson were held in contempt of court and sentenced to time in jail because they did not prove that their assets held in an offshore trust were impossible to reach.[2] That court stopped short of declaring the trust invalid, but its hostility to the trust's creation may be reflective of how other courts might view offshore trusts. Although the Andersons served a sentence for angering the court, the lack of U.S. courts to assert jurisdiction made it impossible for the creditor to access the assets. Ultimately, the asset protection device succeeded. Now that the contempt sentence has been served and the Andersons are back to their usual shenanigans, it is arguable that the benefits were worth the price paid. On the other hand, any assets that may later be repatriated to the United States will be subject to creditors' claims immediately upon arrival. The outcome in *Anderson* is therefore a mixed blessing.

Several asset protection specialists point to the extreme facts of the *Anderson* case and dismiss the notion that offshore trusts are a dangerous strategy. The Andersons were found guilty of managing a Ponzi-type pyramid scheme, and the court was attempting to recover the proceeds for the investors. Such facts would not arise in a case of medical malpractice, for example, because the patient would not have been the traceable source of the full amount of the damages.

Another demonstration of disfavor given offshore trusts was given by a bankruptcy court in the case of *In re: Stephan Jay Lawrence*.[3] Mr. Lawrence was an options trader who had moved several million dollars into an offshore trust just before a $20 million award was granted against him. When he later attempted to have the debt discharged in a bankruptcy proceeding, the bankruptcy court refused to grant the discharge because it viewed Mr. Lawrence as undeserving. In Mr. Lawrence's case, the asset protection trust effectively protected his assets, but the court ruled that he could not protect his assets under foreign law and protect himself under U.S. law as well, because that was not consistent with the spirit of the Bankruptcy Code. The court then ordered Mr. Lawrence to repatriate the assets in the offshore trust. In rehearing the case a year later, the same bankruptcy court held Mr. Lawrence in civil contempt of court and sentenced him with heavy daily fines and incarceration.[4] The court refused to believe Mr. Lawrence's testimony that he did not have the power to comply with the order. It specifically denied Mr. Lawrence the argument that compliance was impossible because, said the court, Mr. Lawrence himself had created the impossibility. On appeal, both the District Court and the Eleventh Circuit Court of Appeals affirmed the decision of the Bankruptcy Court, reasoning that the actions of Mr. Lawrence were entirely voluntary, and denied him the benefits of a true discharge available to most debtors in bankruptcy.[5]

The common thread in cases like *Anderson* and *Lawrence* is the courts' hostility to transfers they determine to be fraudulent conveyances. Without the taint of fraud, the creation of an offshore trust would stand a greater chance of being supported.

Offshore trusts were once used to hide assets from the Internal Revenue Service, such that the income they generated would avoid tax, although all foreign income of U.S. citizens is, and always has been, part of their taxable income. In response to this fraud, the IRS now requires that each offshore trust created by a U.S. citizen be registered and provide continuous reporting to the U.S. government. This requirement substantially increases the cost of creating and maintaining an offshore trust.

Both domestic and foreign jurisdictions giving shelter to trust assets against creditors' claims provide an opportunity to place sizable quantities of assets into a trust, while still having the potential to receive the funds at the discretion of the trustee. The asset protection trust is a very effective tool against creditors, notwithstanding the court rulings that have frowned on them so.

[3] ASSET PROTECTION TRUSTS AND DIVORCE

One area in which asset protection trusts are not typically successful is in the context of a divorce. In an equitable division of marital property, courts will frequently rule that assets placed into an asset protection trust are marital assets and subject to the jurisdiction of the court. The court will then shortchange the spouse contributing to the asset protection trust, or order that spouse to terminate the trust and split the income and principal with the divorcing spouse. Two recent examples of the latter type of ruling, in New York, have created the precedent that asset protection trusts are ineffective against spouses in a divorce. In most other contexts, however, the asset protection trust remains a viable solution to the challenges of creating an asset protection strategy.

Timing Is Everything

It merits repeating: timing is everything! Each method of asset protection introduced in this chapter works best if completed before danger of creditors appears on the horizon. Advance planning is key to the success of an asset protection strategy, and these ideas are intended to inspire present action rather than provide an escape route for medical professionals already nearing financial difficulty. Much like the diversification of assets in an investment portfolio, the methods are frequently used in concert with one another as redundant strategies to ensure effectiveness. Sanguine asset protection planners will employ several of them collectively because they all provide a unique approach to the challenge of asset protection. The tools in this chapter are also qualified with the intent that they be used with the consultation and advisement of professionals, since there are loopholes and pitfalls that make asset protection into a legal and financial planning sub-specialty itself.

The complex forms of asset protection are primarily used because they require creditors to expend additional time, effort, and money; for this reason, they are often more effective than the simple ones and are used frequently by physicians and couples of high net worth. Implemented properly and at the proper time, complex asset protection tools have proven highly effective at sheltering millions of dollars from the hands of creditors and plaintiffs, to the betterment of the people who use them wisely.

Additional Readings

1. *Federal Trade Commission v. Affordable Media, L.L.C.,* 179 F.3d 1228 (9th Cir. 1999).
2. 227 B.R. 907 (Bankr. S.D. Fla. 1998).
3. *Stephan Jay Lawrence,* 238 B.R. 498 (Bankr. S.D. Fla. 1999).
4. *Lawrence v. Goldberg,* F.3d (11th Cir. 2002).

Endnotes

1. See United States v. Craft, ___ U.S. ___ (Apr. 17, 2002).
2. See *Federal Trade Commission v. Affordable Media, L.L.C.*, 179 F.3d 1228 (9th Cir. 1999).
3. 227 B.R. 907 (Bankr. S.D. Fla. 1998).
4. See *In re: Stephan Jay Lawrence*, 238 B.R. 498 (Bankr. S.D. Fla. 1999).
5. See *Lawrence v. Goldberg*, ___ F.3d ___, (11th Cir. 2002).

Chapter 15

Selecting Insurance Agents and Risk Management Advisors

(Understanding Hidden Agendas . . . Wisely Choosing Consultants)

David Edward Marcinko
Hope Rachel Hetico
Rachel Pentin-Maki

Insurance is becoming more complex, and many people including physicians and businesses lack the time and expertise to buy insurance without the advice of an agent. Insurance agents who are knowledgeable about their products and sell multiple lines of insurance remain in demand. Additionally, agents who take advantage of direct mail and Internet resources to advertise and promote their products can reduce the time it takes to develop sales leads, allowing them to concentrate on following up on potential clients. Most physicians, individuals and businesses consider insurance a necessity, regardless of economic conditions.   www.BVLS.Gov

H iring the right insurance agent and/or medical risk management professional enables the physician to have a solid foundation on which to build a medical practice business entity, a comprehensive and integrated financial plan, and an economically successful life. Furthermore, the insurance agent may plug up risky need gaps that the physician may not even know exist. Hiring a good insurance agent or medical risk management consultant also leverages time.

Insurance Company Selection

The physician may have heard of Standard & Poor's, Moody's, and A.M. Best, possibly as a result of doing research for an investment. These are companies that monitor the strengths and weaknesses of the thousands of insurance companies that conduct business in the United States (and around the world). For example, a company that specializes in selling life insurance will be rated according to its ability to pay outstanding death benefit obligations. A property and casualty company, on the other hand, is rated on its ability to pay claims associated with property damages or losses. Independently, these rating services assign a rating to the insurance carrier based on their in-depth research.

[A] Financial Ratings

What do the financial strength ratings mean? It depends on the rating service. From our earlier example, Standard & Poor's rates companies from AAA (extremely strong) to CC (extremely weak). Within those ratings they may also assign a subrating of a plus (+) or a minus (–), which reflects the company's strength or weakness within the corresponding strength rating. Table 15.1 gives a summary of the three rating companies just mentioned. The categories are grouped to reflect the similar ratings classes for each company, but they may not show the actual wording used by the rating service.

How important is the financial strength of an insurance company? Well, how important is it for a patient to be treated in one of the best-rated hospitals in America? The answer to these questions will likely vary with each physician-consumer or patient. If someone is shopping for the least expensive insurance product, he or she may be will-

Table 15.1 *Financial Ratings*

	A.M. Best	*Standard & Poor's*	*Moody's*
Superior/Excellent	A++/A+/A/A-	AAA/AA+/AA/AA-	Aaa/Aa 1-3
Strong		A+/A/A-	
Very Good/Good	B++/B+/B/B-	BBB+/BBB/BBB-	A 1-3/Baa 1-3
Fair/Moderate	C++/C+	BB+/BB/BB-	Ba 1-3
Marginal			
Weak/Vulnerable	C/C-	B+/B/B-	B 1-3
		CCC+/CCC/CCC-	
Poor/Very Poor	D	CC	Caa/Ca/C
Extremely Weak			
State Supervision	E	R	
Regulatory Action			
Liquidation	F		

ing to overlook a poor financial strength rating in order to get the least expensive price. On the other hand, if a physician-consumer wants a company that has an exceptional financial strength rating, he or she should be willing to pay a little more for the security of knowing the company has a good chance of being there to pay any future claims. For many doctors it is worth a few extra dollars to get a little more peace of mind.

[B] Bankruptcy

What would happen if an insurance company went bankrupt? Although a relatively rare occurrence, the bankruptcy of an insurance company is still a very real and frightening possibility. Most cases of insolvency can be blamed on one of three circumstances: poor business decisions, corruption, or catastrophe.

Poor business decisions refers to how well a company invests its assets. As in any business, a few bad economic cycles, coupled with mismanagement, can force an insurance company to declare bankruptcy. According to the National Organization of Life and Health Insurers Guaranty Associations (NOLHGA), only two companies were declared insolvent in 2000 due to poor investment related business decisions, and only one in 2001.

Unfortunately, corruption and embezzlement may occur. A recent case involved the loss of $950 million dollars, included nine insurance companies, and spread through six southern states. This loss occurred when a company that was supposed to invest money for the nine insurers, instead transferred it into a variety of untraceable accounts. As a result over 100,000 policyholders were affected.

Catastrophes cannot be controlled or predicted. In the property and casualty industry one natural disaster can wipe out a small company. According to the National Conference of Insurance Guaranty Funds, Hurricane Andrew caused twelve insolvencies alone.

So now that we know the improbable can happen, what happens to the policyholder? The good news is that it is highly likely that a policyholder would receive insurance coverage, thanks to the state guaranty laws.

Every state has a "guaranty fund" or "guaranty association" created by law. This law assures that any insurance company bankruptcy will be "insured," much like the FDIC insures the potential insolvency of banks. Also similar to the FDIC, state guaranty funds will only protect a consumer's insurance interests up to a specified monetary limit, usually $300,000 for auto, home, and life policies. NOLHGA estimates that upwards of 90 percent of all insurance policyholders affected by a bankruptcy will be fully protected.

In many instances, a financially stable insurance company may take advantage of an industry bankruptcy and purchase all or part of the financially troubled company, for a bargain price. The acquiring insurance company would then assume financial responsibility for the insolvent company's policyholders.

What should the medical professionals do if their insurance carrier becomes insolvent? Usually no action is needed. Policyholders are usually contacted by the company, state guaranty association or insurance department.

[C] Lawsuits

It seems we live in an age where lawsuits are very common and a natural cost of doing business—and unfortunately the insurance industry is no exception. Lawsuits against insurance companies have lately involved misleading sales practices and improper compliance procedures.

The good news is that the industry is working at improving their reputation and increasing their collective commitment to compliance and sales practices. Not only are most companies more active in regulating themselves through various internal and external safeguards, but also the states' insurance departments and court systems have taken a more active role in protecting the consumer in recent years.

Introduction to Insurance Agent Selection

More than half the nation's 3.25 million insurance agents are independent. That means they are not regularly audited or reviewed by the companies whose products they sell. And state regulators don't have the resources to chase after any more than the most outrageous agents. Unfortunately, it's the bad agents that have been in the news a lot in the past few years. Among the misdeeds, according to insurance and financial journalist Liz Pulliam Weston, a publisher for MSN.com, are the following.

[A] Affinity Fraud

In April 2003, a Kansas insurance agent pleaded guilty to fraud charges after convincing at least 10 investors, including members of his church, to invest nearly $200,000 with him. The agent used the money to pay personal expenses, including payments in a bankruptcy plan. Targeting members of a religious, social, recreational, or ethnic group is known as "affinity fraud."

[B] Promissory Note Scams

Hundreds of insurance agents were caught up in enforcement actions by 28 states, the Securities and Exchange Commission, and the North American Securities Administrators Association in recent years for selling so-called promissory notes to investors. Typically touted as low-risk and conservative, the investments were actually high-risk and often fraudulent. Regulators estimate that investors lost hundreds of millions of dollars.

[C] Illegal Investment Sales

Arizona regulators accused nine insurance agents last year of selling unregistered securities, including promissory notes, viatical settlement policies, and interests in ATM machines. Investor losses were estimated at more than $12 million. The Arizona Corporation Commission's Securities Division suggested the sweep was prompted by growing concerns about crossover abuses in the insurance and securities industries. In another action, Florida regulators levied similar charges against eight insurance agents who sold "certificates of grantor" contracts issued by a company that promised returns of 9.25 to 15 percent for 1- to 10-year investments. A related SEC filing charged that money from new investors was used to pay bogus returns to earlier investors in a classic Ponzi scheme. Investors lost an estimated $17 million.

These examples don't include more routine insurance frauds, such as selling phony policies or pocketing policyholders' premiums. And they don't even touch on sales of legal but unsuitable investments, such as saddling elderly physicians and investors with high-risk, high-cost annuities.

Why Do Regulators Target Insurance Agents?

[A] Insurance Agents Have a Built-In Customer Base (Book of Business)

Scam artists have figured out that many agents have large, loyal customer bases and that these agents can be lured to tap these customers when the commissions being offered are high enough. Insurance agents typically know details about their customers' financial lives that allow them to tailor their sales pitches, and they may have built up trust and rapport with these clients over many years.

[B] Many Physicians and Investors Are Looking for Yield and Safety

At the same time, the incomes and wealth of the most vulnerable people, senior citizens and mature doctors, have climbed in recent years. Because of the huge drop in interest rates since 2000, lower yields on legitimate investments have left many seniors and mature doctors vulnerable to pitches for "safe, high-return" alternatives. Unfortunately, the vast majority of insurance agents lack training in evaluating investments. That is apparently why so many couldn't figure out that "safe return" and "high return" are mutually exclusive. Regulators and insurance insiders say that such a lack of financial sophistication means the agent is sometimes a victim along with the client. Many of the agents involved in the promissory notes scams, regulators say, believed the investments were legitimate and lost their own money as well as that of their customers. So how can you avoid getting scammed? The easiest course is not to buy investments from an insurance agent. If approached about an investment, keep these things in mind:

- **Don't buy investments from someone who isn't licensed to sell them.** Fraudsters often erroneously claim their investments aren't really securities. At the very least, your agent should have securities licenses if he or she is selling anything but insurance, and the investment itself should be registered with the SEC or your state's securities regulator. As the role of financial planning increases, many insurance agents are choosing to gain the proper licensing and certification to sell securities and other financial products. This includes passing an additional examination. Before agents can qualify as securities representatives, they must pass the General Securities Registered Representative Examination (Series 7 exam), administered by the National Association of Securities Dealers (NASD).

- **Call your state insurance and securities regulators.** Describe the investment to them and ask if they've heard of it. Regulators won't have heard of every new scam, of course, but you might avoid getting bitten by one that's been around a while.

- **Ask what the agent will get paid, and how that compensation compares to the other products he or she sells.** A reputable agent will talk to you about his or her commissions. Evasiveness on this issue should be a warning sign. When insurance agents or stockbrokers deliberately try to bury their fees, commissions, or expenses, it is known as "hiding the weenie."

- **Make sure your agent has some credentials.** If your agent is offering financial-planning advice, and you're not getting a second opinion from an independent advisor, then make sure your agent has some designations to show that he or she has done more than study a sales brochure. A CLU (Chartered Life Underwriter) is good, and so is a CFP© (Certified Financial Planner©) designation. Both require extensive study and rigorous testing in all facets of financial planning, not just insurance.

- **Demand to know the downside.** Agents know that dwelling on an investment's drawbacks can kill a sale, so they might not even bring up negatives, even when they're supposed to. So you have to ask, and keep asking until you get answers that make sense. Every investment has its risks and its drawbacks. Know those specifics before you invest.

- **Look for the deep-pocketed third party.** Any investment should be backed by a bank, brokerage, or insurance company. Of course, this won't eliminate all possibility of fraud, since well-known banks and brokerages can be scammed, too. But at least you'll have somebody with deep pockets to sue.

Hiring the Right Insurance Agent

In addition to what has already been said, there are a number of issues to keep in mind when considering an insurance advisor:

- **Titles:** Beware of misleading titles. There are many "agents" using fancy titles. Don't be afraid to ask about what the titles (or sometimes just initials) mean and how they were earned or awarded. Most meaningful designations are awarded following the completion of a series of courses and exams. There are, however, some that are used after the agent merely pays a fee and joins an organization. In particular, if someone claims to be a financial planner, ask if he or she is "certified." The industry tries to police the misrepresentation of unauthorized titles. This helps protect clients from getting important advice from someone who really isn't qualified. The Certified Financial Planner Board of Standards maintains a website to allow consumers to check on any CFP® licensee status. Their URL is www. cfp-board.org. So does the iMBA for the niche specific Certified Medical Planner® designation (www.MedicalBusinessAdvisors.com).

- **Experience:** Ask the prospective agent or broker about his or her background. How long has he or she been in the insurance or financial services industry? If someone was a car salesman three months ago, it's reasonable to consider getting a second opinion on any recommendation. This would be especially true if the deal sounded too good to be true.

- **Education:** Agents and brokers are both encouraged and required to continue their insurance and financial-planning education, not only to keep their various state insurance licenses, but also to maintain certain designations. For example, to maintain the right to use the designations of Chartered Life Underwriter (CLU), Chartered Financial Consultant (ChFC), Certified Financial Planner (CFP®), and Certified Medical Planner© (CMP©), the bearer must periodically report that the required number of "continuing education" course hours have been completed.

[A] Brokers Versus Agents

Simply put, a broker is a representative of the consumer. A broker is supposed to have the best interest of his or her client in mind when making a recommendation for insurance protection. Brokers normally have a number of different companies and products to choose from to meet their clients' needs.

A traditional agent represents the company for which he or she works, although he or she should also have the best interests of the client in mind. Many property and casualty (P&C) insurance companies still have what are referred to as "captive" agents who are usually restricted to which company's products they can offer for sale to clients. As a whole, the life insurance industry is moving away from having a large number of captive agents. Most insurance transactions today are conducted by agents with no real allegiance to a particular company. The exception is possibly the few agents that seem to gravitate to the companies that pay the most commissions.

[B] Commissions

It would be impossible to cover all of the variations of compensation schedules and payment arrangements within the insurance industry. There are, however, a few general rules that may be worth thinking about.

Some insurance companies have begun providing a base salary to their agents with incentive bonuses for superior performance. This is intended to remove the perceived evil of a commission-oriented recommendation. This cutting-edge concept has not yet been embraced by a large percentage of the career insurance industry. The top insurance professionals normally prefer a pure commission structure for the unlimited potential income.

Another attempt by life insurance companies to keep the size of the commission from influencing any recommendation for coverage is that of "levelized" commissions. Here, rather than the insurance company paying 80 to 110 percent of the first-year premium as a commission, the agent receives a level 10 to 15 percent for the first 10 policy years. Although this is common practice in P&C companies, it has not been universally accepted by life insurance companies.

As a general rule, agents are paid a lower commission in exchange for the insurance company providing office space, training, resource equipment, administrative help, and so on. Although this has been the preferred manner of distribution for many large insurance companies in the past, many companies are beginning to abandon this structure in favor of the less costly brokerage distribution system.

Brokers are truly independent salespeople. Unlike agents, they will usually receive a larger commission because of their anticipated expense of being independent. They must pay for office space, administrative support, and equipment from their commissions.

[C] The State Corporation Commission Insurance Department

What do the various states' insurance departments do? The states' insurance departments have the primary responsibility of providing protection for policyholders in the event of the insolvency of an insurance company. Beyond that, they have a number of other responsibilities:

- Regulating the licensing of and the continuing education of insurance professionals. As discussed earlier, insurance brokers and agents are typically required to continue their education. Each state insurance department sets those requirements that must be met in order for agents or brokers to keep their licenses.

- Protecting the consumer from fraud and deceptive sales practices. State insurance departments have the job of protecting consumers from being harmed by insurance companies and their representatives. This includes policing the business practices of those insurance companies that are incorporated within their boundaries, along with keeping a watchful eye on how insurance products are presented to consumers by insurance professionals.

- Approving of products sold by an insurance company. When a company wants to begin sales in a state, it must begin with having each product for sale approved by the state insurance department. This includes the insurance contract and any application or supplemental forms related to each product. Getting a product approved in all 50 states can be quite a project because many state insurance departments have different agendas and requirements. And simply because a product is "approved for sale" in a particular state does not mean it is a quality product.

- Punishing companies and insurance professionals, including revoking licenses and assessing fines. It is also not uncommon for insurance companies to be fined for the unfair sales practices of their representatives. Agents and brokers can also be individually held responsible for breaking the insurance regulations of a particular state. Such punishment can include removal of state licenses.

Insurance Agent Titles and Credentials

In insurance there is no magic license that shows the world that a particular insurance agent is a good one, and nobody likes to pay insurance premiums. Inadequate coverage, however, can completely devastate a family by quickly wiping out a lifetime of asset accumulation. Buying and maintaining the right amount and type of coverage from solid insurance companies at a reasonable price eliminates these risks in a very efficient manner. Unfortunately, an essential and relatively simple concept like this risk transfer has evolved into an subject that makes many people downright queasy. The saying goes "insurance is sold by agents, not bought by consumers." Nevertheless, there are two basic types of agents (personal and property).

[A] The Life Insurance Agent

Life insurance agents specialize in selling policies that pay beneficiaries when a policyholder dies. As we have seen, depending on the policyholder's circumstances, a cash-value policy can be designed to provide retirement income, funds for the education of children, or other benefits. At other times a term policy may be more helpful. There are many other policy variations. Some life insurance agents also sell annuities that promise a retirement income. Health insurance agents sell health insurance policies that cover the costs of medical care and loss of income due to illness or injury. They may also sell dental insurance and short- and long-term disability insurance policies.

[B] The Property and Casualty Agent

Some insurance agents sell property and casualty (P&C) insurance. P&C agents sell policies that protect doctors and their practices from financial loss resulting from automobile accidents, fire, theft, storms, and other events that can damage property. For private practitioners, property and casualty insurance can also cover injured workers' compensation, product liability claims, or medical malpractice claims.

A good P&C agent is needed to protect your home and medical practice. The P&C agent should have an array of carriers with which the business can be placed. One should not hesitate to place different types of coverages with different insurers. Most insurance companies will offer a discount if you place multiple coverages with them. However, this may not be as beneficial as insuring each need with a specialist.

There is a plethora of insurance designations that are narrow in scope and drift away from life and P&C insurance, are irrelevant to most physician families' needs, or are thin on quality content. These include CEBS (Certified Employee Benefits Specialist), RHU (Registered Health Underwriter), CIMC (Certified Investment Management Counselor), CMFC (Certified Mutual Fund Consultant), CIC (Certified Insurance Counselor), and a host of others.

Credentials and verification can be obtained from:

The American College
270 Bryn Mawr Ave
Bryn Mawr, PA 19010-2195
http://www.amercoll.edu

Following are the more meritorious insurance credentials:

- **CLU: Chartered Life Underwriter.** This preeminent life insurance credential is conferred by the American College, in Bryn Mawr, Pennsylvania.

- **ChFC: Chartered Financial Consultant.** This broad educational credential is granted by the American College. It covers most aspects of financial planning, but the majority of its holders are or were in the insurance business.

- **CFP:© Certified Financial Planner©.** Currently, to become licensed to use the marks, one must complete an accredited educational course, subscribe to a code of ethics, show 3 years of full-time experience in addition to an undergraduate degree, and pass a comprehensive 2-day, 10-hour examination. Topics, in addition to insurance, include taxation, investing, retirement, and estate planning. A state insurance license is still required. Maintaining the license requires adherence to the Code of Ethics and Practice Standards and fulfillment of the continuing education requirements. The continuing education requirement includes an ethics course once every 2 years.

- **CMP:© Certified Medical Planner©.** The Certified Medical Planner (CMP©) mark is a rigorous designation, first chartered in 2003 and awarded to advisors who have successfully completed all requirements, including insurance planning coursework, put forth by the Institute of Medical Business Advisors, Inc (www.MedicalBusinessAdvisors.com). Topics include all those in the CLU and CFP© tracks, as well as medical practice and risk management material for additional health-care specificity. A state insurance license is still required. It is an ideal complement to the CLU or CFP© designation for those insurance agents and/or financial planners interested in the burgeoning health-care advisory space.

- **MBA: Masters of Business Administration.** This is an academic degree that may or may not have any bearing on one's ability to render sound insurance advice. Typically, the MBA with a subspecialty in finance or insurance would add considerable value to the risk management experience. A concentration in marketing, technology, human resources, or project management would not. Certainly, the MBA with a specific medical risk management background, perhaps as a former physician, or in conjunction with an MHA (Master's in Healthcare Administration), would be very helpful in risk management or in consulting for the busy medical group, especially in the environment of managed care. Similarly, the MSFS (Master's of Science in Financial Services) is an academic degree that integrates the financial planning disciplines, but is not medically focused.

For more information about life insurance credentials, contact:

- The National Alliance for Insurance Education and Research, P.O. Box 27027, Austin, TX 78755.
- LIMRA International, P.O. Box 203, Hartford, CT 06141.
- Independent Insurance Agents of America, 127 S. Peyton St., Alexandria, VA 22314. Internet: http://www.iiaa.org.
- Insurance Vocational Education Student Training (InVEST), 127 S. Peyton St., Alexandria, VA 22314.
- National Association of Professional Insurance Agents, 400 N. Washington St., Alexandria, VA 22314.

For more information about health insurance credentials, contact:

- National Association of Health Underwriters, 2000 N. 14th St., Suite 450, Arlington, VA 22201. Internet: http://www.nahu.org.
- Health Insurance Association of America, 555 13th St. NW, Suite 600 East, Washington, DC 20004. Internet: http://www.hiaa.org.

For more information on property and casualty insurance credentials, contact:

- Insurance Information Institute, 110 William St., New York, NY 10038. Internet: http://www.iii.org.

For more information on fee-only, unbiased insurance advisors who sell no products and accept no commissions, contact:

Glenn S. Daily
234 E. 84th Street
New York, NY 10028-2902
212-249-9882
www.GlennDaily.com

Medical Risk Management Societies and Specialists

[A] Societies and Sources of Information and Products

The American Board of Quality Assurance and Utilization Review Physicians (ABQAURP) was established in 1977 and has evolved to become the nation's largest organization of interdisciplinary risk management, case management, peer review, and workers' comp administration professionals. Following is its address:

ABQAURP
2120 Range Rd.
Clearwater, FL 33765-2125
Phone: (727) 298-8777
Fax: (727) 449-0555
abqaurp@abqaurp.org
ewhite@abqaurp.org for information

Employers from all facets of the health-care industry recognize the value of the ABQAURP credential when seeking qualified health-care professionals to meet their consulting needs. Credentialed persons are distinguished by their level of skill in analysis and review and in the multifaceted health-care quality and management field. The ABQAURP credential offers opportunity, fellowship, networking, and the prestige associated with recognition of its receivers as experts in the field. Each year, ABQAURP provides live conferences at geographically convenient locations throughout the United States, as well as independent study options.

Other medical risk management associations include:

- American Society for Healthcare Risk Management (ASHRM)
  http://www.ashrm.org
- Health Forum—Statistics and Data
  http://www.ahadatasource.com
- *Hospital Statistics* [publication]
  http://www.ahastatistics.org

Further information about Health Insurance Portability and Accountability Act (HIPAA)-compliant, Electronic Medical Record (EMR) products and related Information Technology (IT) security and health-care outsourcing are available from:

[1] Dr. Ahmad Hashem, PhD
Global Healthcare Industry Manager
Microsoft Corporation
One Microsoft Way
Redmond, WA 98052-6399

Phone: (425) 705-9724
Fax: (425) 936-7329
Health-care technology information: http://www.microsoft.com/healthcare/
Practice management software guide: http://www.aafp.org/practice/techguide/

[2] Richard D. Helppie
CEO and Founder
Superior Consultant Company, Inc. (NASD-SUPC)
17570 West 12 Mile Road
Southfield, MI 48076
Phone: (248) 386-8300
Fax: (248) 386-8301
www.SuperiorConsultant.com

[3] Mary Rittle
Vice President
TASCware Inc.
950 North Point Parkway, Suite 350
Alpharetta, GA 30005
Phone: (770) 751-1200
www.TASCware.com

All of these companies provide software, Application Service Providers (ASPs), and related health-care products, with security features such as:

- Authorization: Captures physician referrals
- Precertification: Information including authorization
- Prescriptions: Captures previous and current medications
- Diagnostic tests: Input test results and comments
- Medical record captures
- Antepartum forms and reports
- Scanning: Reports, X-rays, video clips, and voice recognition (hardware)
- Mobility: Tablet PCs to check patient information from an Internet connection

Other medical practice, risk management, IT, and managed care textbook resources are available from:

[1] Dr. Peter R. Kongstvedt, FACP
Managed Care: What It Is and How It Works (2nd edition)
Essentials of Managed Healthcare (4th edition)
Jones and Bartlett Publishers, June 2003
40 Tall Pine Drive
Sudbury, MA 01776
Phone: (978) 443-5000
Fax: (978) 443-8000
www.jbpub.com

[2] Institute of Medical Business Advisors, Inc.
The Business of Medical Practice: (Advanced Profit Maximizing Techniques for Savvy Doctors) Marcinko, DE (Editor), 2nd edition, 2004.
Springer Publications, Inc.
536 Broadway
New York, NY 10012-3955
Phone: (212) 431-4370
Fax: (212) 941-7842
http://www.springerjournals.com/store/page1311_7.html

[B] Business and Medical Risk Management Degree Programs

Another way to reengineer your practice into a business, and integrate risk management concepts with insurance planning, is through education. Online master's degree programs for medical professionals, like those offered at Regis University [(303) 964-5447], the University of Tennessee [(423) 974-1768], Washington University (Olin) in St. Louis [(888-273-6820)], and the University of Wisconsin [(608) 263-4889], may help. More traditional MBA programs are the following:

Auburn University, Auburn, Alabama
www.pemba.business.auburn.edu

University of South Florida, Tampa
www.coba.usf.edu/programs/docs

University of Tennessee, Knoxville
www.pemba.utk.edu

University of Colorado, Denver
www.colorado.edu/execed

University of California, Irvine
www.gsm.uci.edu/programs/index.asp

University of Massachusetts, Amherst
www.intra.som.umass.edu/mba/acpe/?doc_id=1325

University of St. Thomas, Minneapolis
www.stthomas.edu/chma

Carnegie Mellon University, Pittsburgh
www.heinz.cmu.edu/mmm

Tulane University, New Orleans
www.hsm.tulane.edu

University Southern California, Los Angeles
www.marshall.use.edu/web/execdev.cfm

Oregon Health & Services University, Portland
www.ohsu.edu

University of Utah, Salt Lake City
www.uuhsc.utah.edu/medinfo

The Role of Advisor/Agent Teamwork

The major insurance and risk management players have been assembled. Will the team function together well enough to win the game? Getting all of the players on your advisory team to function well together may seem like a daunting task. In reality it should be the easiest part of the process.

After taking the time to select insurance agents and risk managers, you now should have a team composed of competent ethical professionals, such as financial and medical planners, accountants, and attorneys, who have shown they communicate effectively. It is likely that, if these people are as good as they seem, they may already know each other and may have worked with each other. Moreover, good advisors want to learn more. They feed off good interaction with other advisors because it makes them better able to identify and address issues with their clients.

This is not to say that merely hiring people adept in their particular field is all that is necessary for the development of good teamwork. The sports world is full of teams with loads of individual talent but no championship rings. There are steps that can be taken to help foster an appropriate level of teamwork.

1. Designate the quarterback. Only the CFP© financial planner or fully licensed CMP© medical planner has the professional mandate to coordinate a doctor-client's insurance, business, and financial affairs from the big-picture perspective. The planner, however, must hand the ball off to the other players to get the job done properly.

2. Make sure the players know about each other.

3. Define everyone's role and communicate your wishes to all the advisors.

4. Meet as a group on occasion.

5. Tolerate no arguments.

6. Make the advisors clarify confusing issues.

7. Always remember, and remind if necessary, that the doctor-client is the boss.

The core of the team is the certified financial and/or medical planner. From time to time, however, other people will be needed. Bankers, actuaries, MBAs, and real estate agents are the most common. To assemble these other players, one should get feedback from the core advisors. All other things being equal, an independent provider is usually better, the exception being the banker.

The easiest way to handle this issue is to get consensus agreement from the core team members as to the amount and types of insurance coverage. Once that is accomplished, appropriate agents can be contacted. In addition to the usual questioning regarding competence and a background check, the agent should be made aware that the core team will be reviewing all proposals. Proposals should include what is known as a ledger statement.

Acknowledgments

The author thanks Daniel B. Moisand, CFP©, and Gary A. Cook, MSFS, CLU, ChFC, LUTCF, RHU, CMP®, CFP©, for technical assistance in the preparation of this chapter.

Index

page numbers followed by t denote tables

A

AAA (American Academy of Actuaries) research on caps and noneconomic damages, 198
AANS (American Association of Neurological Surgeons)
  expert witness disciplinary program, 185
  expert witness testimony, 128
ABQAURP (American Board of Quality Assurance and Utilization Review Physicians), 312
"Acknowledgment of Receipt," 100
Activities of daily living (ADLs), and long-term care (LTC) insurance, 39–40
Actuarial Sciences, 1–2
Adkisson, Jay D., 277
Adkisson, Molnar, 277
Advance Beneficiary Notices (ABNs), 95
Affinity fraud, insurance agents, 304
AICPA (American Institute of Certified Public Accountants) Statement of Position (SOP), 167
Alimony and related tax issues
  alimony defined, 266
  alimony substitution trust, 267
  criteria for an award of alimony, 267–268
  "rehabilitative alimony," 268
  "reimbursement alimony," 268
  requirements for alimony, 266–267
Alternate jurors, 237
A.M. Best, 50–51, 51t, 301, 302t
  Annual Historical Dividend Report, 12
American Academy of Actuaries (AAA), research on caps and noneconomic damages, 198
American Association of Neurological Surgeons (AANS)
  expert witness disciplinary program, 185
  expert witness testimony, 128

American Board of Quality Assurance and Utilization Review Physicians (ABQAURP), 312
American Institute of Certified Public Accountants (AICPA) Statement of Position (SOP), 167
American Medical Association (AMA)
  Council on Medical Education (CME), 178
  the malpractice insurance crisis, 226
  on restrictive agreements, 77
American Society for Healthcare Risk Management (ASHRM), 312
Americans With Disabilities Act, 103
American Tort Reform Association (ATRA), 198
Anderson case, 297–298
Annual renewable (ART) life insurance, 6
Annuities
  deferred
    fixed deferred, 34
    variable deferred, 34–35
  immediate fixed annuity, 35–36
  immediate variable annuity, 36
  qualified, 36
  taxation of
    nonqualified annuity, 37
    qualified annuity, 36–37
    wealth transfer issues, 37
  Tax Sheltered Annuities [403(b)], 36
Antitrust rules, 117–118
Applicable standard of care, 234
Application for insurance, 27–28
Application Service Providers (ASPs), 313
Arizona Corporation Commission's Securities Division, 304–305
Arthur Anderson, 282
"As applied for/other than as applied for," 30
ASHRM (American Society for Healthcare Risk Management), 312
Asset protection principles. *See also* Marital assets, divorce
  appreciating the risks, 278–279

Asset protection principles *(continued)*
  complex tools
    asset protection trusts, 294–295
      and divorce, 299
      domestic asset protection trusts (DAPTs), 295–297
      foreign asset protection trusts, 297–298
    avoiding fraudulent conveyances, 289–290
    family limited partnerships (FLPs), 292–294
    homestead exemption, 291
    irrevocable life insurance trusts (ILIT), 291–292
    relocation to state with debtor-friendly laws, 290–291
  gifting, 287–288
  good record keeping, 279
  insurance
    comparing policies, 279
    general liability, 280
    life and disability, 280
    malpractice, 280
    natural disaster, 280–281
  joint ownership of assets
    community property, 286
    joint tenancy with rights of survivorship (JTWRO), 286
    "tenancy by the entirety," 285–286
    tenancy in common, advantages, 286–287
    transfer of property into spouse's name, 285
  layered organizations
    comparison of business entity types
      corporation, 281
      limited liability companies (LLCs), 281–283
      limited liability partnerships (LLPs), 281–283
      limited partnership (LP), 281
    ideal approach, 283–284
    practice format, 281
    tort liability and, 284
  losses in the investment world, 277–278
  qualified retirement plans, 284–285
  self-settled trusts, 288–289
  timing is everything, 299
Assignees, family limited partnerships, 293–294
Association for Conflict Resolution, 256
Assumption of risk, 5
ATRA (American Tort Reform Association), 198
At-risk capitation model, 223–224
Attica prison riot trial, 239
Attorney
  choosing a divorce attorney, 256–258
  retaining a personal counsel, 231–232
Audit, risk of, 130–131
Auditors, addressing risks, 167
Ault, Dick, 163

Australia, Crime, Violence and Injury Lead Program and Institute of Criminology, health workers as perpetrators of violence, 152
Automobile insurance
  liability coverage
    bodily injury, 47
    personal injury, 48
    property damage, 48
  physical damage coverage
    collision, 48
    comprehensive, 48
  repairs after the accidents, 49
  umbrella liability insurance, 49–50
  uninsured-underinsured motorists coverage, 49
Auxiliary personnel, rules of compliance, 93–94
Avoidance of risk, 4–5

B

Balanced Budget Act (1997), health-care fraud, 112
Bankruptcy, insurance companies, 51–52, 303
Battery, defined, 280
Behavior-based traits, screening out violence-prone applicants, 164–165
Bell-shaped normalization curve, risk management, 131
Bench trial, 235
Berger, Esther M., 259
Berwick, Donald, 226
Billing for medical services, 85–86
  rules of compliance, 92
Black-out period, Social Security, 3
Boat insurance, 47
Boone, Richard W., 221
Braver, Sanford, 252, 254
British Medical Association (BMA), violence in the workplace, 151–152
Brokers *vs.* agents, 307
Burden of proof, 233–234
Bureau of Economic Affairs (BEA), 4
Bureau of Justice Statistics
  assaults on hospital workers, 155
  financial impact of workplace violence, 154
Bureau of Labor Statistics Census of Fatal Occupational Injuries (CFOI), 151
Business practice litigation risks, 119
Business related insurance
  business owner policy, 68–69
  executive bonus plan (162 plan), 64
  key person insurance, 61–62
  nonqualified salary continuation, 65
  practice continuation funding or buy-sell agreement, 62–64
    forms of agreements, 63
    keys to a successful agreement, 62
    trusteed agreement, 63–64

professional liability insurance, 69
split-dollar plans
concept of, 66
employee-owned method, 67
employer-owned method, 66–67
summary, 67–68
types of policies to be careful of, 69–70
workers' compensation, 68
Buy-sell agreement, 62–64
forms of agreements, 63
keys to a successful agreement, 62
trusteed agreement, 63–64

C

California
medical malpractice liability reform measures, 189, 190t
medical malpractice premiums, 198
monetary caps on noneconomic damages, 198–199
Capitation liability theory (CLT)
business virtues of, 215
captive insurance agents, 216
conclusion, 227
contrary viewpoint
hybrid capitation/reduced fee-for-service model, 224–225
pure at-risk capitation model, 223–224
reduced fee-for-service model, 224
current trends, 225–226
detractors of, 215
direct insurance agents, 216
dynamics of the liability insurance industry, 216–217
indemnification or hold harmless clause, 221
independent insurance agents, 216
insurance legislation implications
Liability Risk Retention Act (LRRA), 219–220
processes to support reduced liability costs, 221
purchasing groups, 219–220
risk retention groups (RRGs), 219–220
significance of risk-based, capitated systems, 220–221
liability coverage forms
claims-made, 222
occurrence, 222
litigation equation
health-care delivery system and reimbursement factors, 218
liability factors, 218, 225
patient communication factors, 218
payer factors, 218
physicians relocating to other states because of high malpractice premiums, 216–217
premium-setting process, 217
reimbursement models
capitated, 219
fee-for-service, 218–219
mixed model or transitional system, 219
quasi-socialistic, 219
specialty-specific insurers, 226–227
supplemental extended reporting policy (SERP), 222
top five medical malpractice payments, 226t
Captive insurance agents, 216
Carnegie Foundation for Advancement of Teaching, 178
Cash value, universal life insurance, 13
Center for Peer Review Justice, 128–129
Centers for Medicare and Medicaid Services (CMS), 103–104
Certificates of Medical Necessity (CMNs), 125–126
rules for proper use of, 96–97
Certified Employee Benefits Specialist (CEBS), 310
Certified Financial Planner (CFP), 310
needs analysis, 58
Certified Insurance Counselor (CIC), 310
Certified Investment Management Counselor (CIMC), 310
Certified Medical Planner (CMP), 310
Certified Mutual Fund Consultant (CMFC), 310
CFOI (Bureau of Labor Statistics Census of Fatal Occupational Injuries), 151
Challenge for cause, 238–239
Charted Financial Consultant (CFC), 310
Charted Life Underwriter (CLU), 310
Child-care tax credit, 270–271
Children with special needs and medical error, 186–187
Child's investment income, tax considerations, 271
Child Support Enforcement Amendments (1984), 262
Child tax credit, 270
Civil asset forfeiture risks, 113
Civil Rights Act (1964), 102
Clinical Laboratory Improvement Amendments (CLIA), 91, 103–104
Clinton, Bill, 141
CME (Council on Medical Education), 178
COB (Coordination of benefit) information, 99
COBRA, 103
Codes
CPT and diagnosis codes, proper use and billing of, 92–93
E/M codes, 131
HCPCS codes, 99
standardized transaction and code set rule, 99–100
Collateral consequences, risk management, 126

Commissions, insurance agents, 307–308
Community property, 262, 286
Comparison of policies, 32–33
Compliance risk management
  introduction, 89–90
  process of compliance
    1. know which rules you have to follow, 90–91
    2. outline the rules in written policies and procedures, 91
    3. assess the organization's current compliance, 91
    4. training, communication, and enforcement, 91
    5. maintenance of the program, 91–92
Compliments, and sexual harassment, 140
Consumer Federation of America, malpractice premiums as percent of national health-care costs, 181
Continuous group insurance, 69
Contracts
  appropriate contracts, 131–132
  clauses, 31–32
  conditions, 31
  contract law, 29–30
  obligations, 31
  rights, 31
  signing in name of the corporation, 132
Controller, responsibilities, 167
Conversion feature, term policy, 7
Cooper, Cary, 158
Coordination of benefit (COB) information, 99
Co-pays, waiver of, 96
Copic Cos, 199
Corporations, 281
  and risk transfer, 5
Council on Ethical and Judicial Affairs, on restrictive agreements, 77
Council on Medical Education (CME), 178
Counsel. *See* Attorney
Covenants
  agreements restricting the practice of medicine, 77–78
  cy pres clause, 76
  as part of a medical employment contract, 75
  "reasonable" covenant terms, 75–76
  remedies for covenant breach
    award of actual damages proven after the fact, 76–77
    injunction, 77
    liquidated damages, 77, 78
  restrictive, defined, 73–74
  for the sale of a medical practice, 74–75
CPT codes, 92–93, 99
Crisis response procedures, 164

Cross-examination, 242
Cross purchase buy-sell agreement, 63
Custody of children
  joint legal custody, 260
  joint physical and legal custody, 260
  sole custody, 260
  split custody, 260
Cy pres clause, 76

D

Damages proven after the fact, 76–77
Dana Mediation Institute, cost of conflict to an organization, 169–171
Dandemis, 204
DAPTs (Domestic asset protection trusts), 295–297
DEA (Drug Enforcement Agency), 116–117
Death benefit settlement options, 18
Deductibles, waiver of, 96
Defendant, 232
Defensive medicine, 107
Demands or threats, sexual harassment, 144
Department of Health and Human Services, waiver of co-pays and deductibles, 96
Depositions, 236
Deselection risks, 126
"Dignity and respect" audit, 162–163
Directed verdict, 241
Direct examination, 242
Direct insurance agents, 216
Disability income insurance
  asset protection and, 280
  coordination of benefits, 24–25
  disability defined, 23–24
  elimination period, 24
  hazard category of the occupation, 25
  inflation protection, 25
  monthly benefit amount, 25
  partial disability, 24
  renewability, 25–26
  summary
    risk of disability among groups of people, 27
    statistics, 26
  taxation of benefits, 26
Discipline procedures, and dignity and respect for the employee, 163
Discovery process, 235
Disposable Worker, The: Living in a Job-Loss Economy, 163
Dividends, whole-life insurance, 12
Divorce
  asset protection trusts and, 299
  choosing a divorce attorney
    clues to look for, 258
    sources for, 257

tips
    attorney's philosophy, 257
    fees, 257
    handling your case, 258
    point of view, 257
    qualifications, 257
    referrals to others, 258
    work style, 257–258
domestic and spousal issues
    decline in standard of living, 252
    effects on children, 251–252
    financial issues of women in divorce, 252
do's and don'ts and pitfalls, 258–259
emotional upheaval of divorce, 255
factors leading to divorce, 254
mediation, benefits of, 255–256
older divorcing medical professionals, 272–274
other tax considerations
    child-care tax credit, 270–271
    child's investment income, 271
    child tax credit, 270
    earned income credit (EIC), 271
    education credits, 271
    exemptions for dependents, 269–270
    filing status, 268–269
    Jobs and Growth Tax Relief Reconciliation
        Act (2003), 271–272
overview of family and divorce law, 259–268
    child support and other financial issues,
        261–262
    community property states, 262
    custody options
        joint legal custody, 260
        joint physical and legal custody, 260
        sole custody, 260
        split custody, 260
    distribution of marital assets and liabilities,
        262–264
    equitable-distribution laws, 262–264
    marital assets
        business and professional practices, 264
        401(k) plans, other qualified plans, and
            individual retirement accounts (IRAs),
            265, 284–285
        pension plans (defined benefit plans),
            264
        real estate or marital residence, 265
    parenting time issues, 260–261
    spousal support or alimony and related tax
    issues
        alimony defined, 266
        alimony substitution trust, 267
        criteria for an award of alimony, 267–268
        "rehabilitative alimony," 268
        "reimbursement alimony," 268

    requirements for alimony, 266–267
prenuptial agreements (PNAs)
    described, 253
    premarital assets, 254
    Uniform Premarital Agreement Act (UPAA),
        253–254
    validity of, 254
    research on stable marriages, 255
Divorce Culture, The, 252
Divorce Revolution, The, 252
Doctor-employer liability, sexual harassment, 146
Documentation. *See* Medical Records
Documentation Guidelines for Evaluation and
    Management Services, 84, 111
Domestic asset protection trusts (DAPTs),
    295–297
Drug abuse, by physicians, 188
Drug Enforcement Agency (DEA) risks, 116–117
Dukes v. U.S. Healthcare, Inc., 121
Durable medical equipment (DME), authorization
    of, 96

E

Earned income credit (EIC), 271
"Economic credentialing," 82
Economic Growth and Tax Relief Reconciliation
    Act, 2001, 269, 270
Economic Recovery Tax Act (ERTA), 15–16
Edelen v. Osterman, 121
Education credit exemption, 271
Education debt load risks, 129–130
Electronic Medical Record (EMR), 83
    information about, 312–313
Electronic protected health information (EPHI),
    101
E/M codes, 131
Emergencies, establish emergency protocol with
    police, 164
Employee Assistance Program
    promotion of, 165
    utilization data, 162
Employee Retirement Income Security Act
    (ERISA), 102–103, 119, 121, 284–285
Enron, 282–283, 290
Entity purchase buy-sell agreement, 63
Environment, workplace violence and, 158
EOBs (Explanation of benefits) forms, 99
EPHI (Electronic protected health), 101
Equitable-distribution laws, 262–264
"Errors and omissions" insurance, 69
ERTA (Economic Recovery Tax Act), 15–16
Evaluating insurance companies and policies
    bankruptcy, 51–52
    financial ratings, 50–51, 51t
    lawsuits, 52

Excluded providers or entities, rules of compliance, 97
Executive bonus plan (162 plan), 64
Exhibits, trial, 242–243
Experience accuracy, 2
Expert witness, 128, 232–233
   disciplinary programs, 185
   risks, 128
Explanation of benefits forms (EOBs), 99

F

False Claims Act, 83, 85–86, 112
   for Medicare, 85
   qui tam action, 86
   "upcoding," 86
   U.S. v. Greenberg, 86
   U.S. v. Krizek, 85
   U.S. v. Lorenzo, 86
   "whistle-blower" provisions, 86
Family limited partnerships (FLPs), 292–294
Family Medical Leave Act, 103
Faragher v. City of Boca Raton, 159
Federal Retirement Equity Act (1984), 264
Federal Rules of Civil Procedure, 235
Fee-for-service models, 218–219
   hybrid capitation/reduced fee-for-service model, 224–225
   reduced fee-for-service model, 224
Fee only insurance consultant, 43
Final instructions to the jury, 244–245
Financial and economic costs, sexual harassment, 148–149
Financial ratings, insurance companies, 302–303, 302t
First Professional Insurance Company (Florida), 189
5-100 rule, 18
Fixed deferred annuity, 34
Flexner, Abraham, 178
Flexner report, 178
FLPs (Family limited partnerships), 292–294
Foreign asset protection trusts, 297–298
Fraudulent conveyances, avoiding, 289–290
Free look period, 30
Frequency distribution, 2
"Frivolous lawsuits," 183–184, 199
Full-time equivalent (FTE) staff members, 100
Fundamentals of Family Mediation, The, 256

G

Gatekeeper concept, 223
Gender-based harassment/animosity, 138, 144–145
General Accounting Office (GAO), on the practice of defensive medicine, 181

"General Duty Clause," (OSHA), 98
General liability insurance, 280
General Services Administration (GSA), 97
Geographic power, antitrust considerations, 118
Getting Divorced Without Ruining Your Life, 256
Gifting
   and asset protection, 287–288
   gift taxation, violating the 2 out of 3 rule, 21
Global Positioning System for security, 164
Gollier, Christian, 1
Goodman, Ernie, 239
Gottman, John M., 255
Griffith, Alan J., 168
Group life insurance, 17
GSA (General Services Administration), 97
"Guarantee fund," 52

H

Harvard University, 178
Hashem, Ahmad, 312–313
Haynes, John, 256
HCPCS codes, 99
Health and Human Services (Office of Civil Rights) risks, 117
Health Care Financing Agency (HCFA), statistical analysis, Medicare services, 130–131
Health Education Assistance Loan (HEAL), student numbers and default totals, 129–130
Health Forum-Statistics and Data, 312
Health Insurance Portability and Accountability Act (HIPAA)
   "federal health care offenses," 98
   health-care fraud, 111–112
   information about, 312–313
   limited English proficiency (LEP) compliance, 102
   Privacy Rule, 100–101, 117
   rules of compliance, 90, 98–99
   Security Rule, 101–102
   taxes on a viatical settlement, 56
   use of bounty hunters in pursuit of fraud, 112
   use of standardized forms, 99
Helppie, Richard D., 313
Herzlinger, Regina, 187
Hold Harmless Clause, 122
   avoiding risk and, 132
   contract capitulation dilemma, 124
   examples of, 122–124
   legal relationships, 221
Homeowners (and renters) insurance
   basic form, 44–45
   broad form, 45
   comprehensive form, 45
   inflation protection, 46
   liability protection, 44

modified coverage form, 45
other HO endorsements, 46
property and theft coverage, 44
replacement cost *vs.* actual cash value, 45–46
special form, 45
tenants form, 45
unit owners (condominium owners) form, 45
Homestead exemption, 291
Homicides in the workplace, 156–157
Hospitals, deaths and other medical errors
    occurring in, 187–188
Hospital Statistics, 312
Hostile work environment, sexual harassment, 138
Hung jury, 245
Hybrid capitation/reduced fee-for-service model,
    224–225

I

ICD-9 codes, 99
Illegal investment sales, insurance agents, 304–305
Immediate fixed annuity, 35–36
Immediate variable annuity, 36
"In camera," 239
"Incident to" rules, 94
Income-tax-free death benefit, 19
Independent insurance agents, 216
Independent physician's association (IPA),
    financial risk, 117
Individual Retirement Accounts (IRA), 36,
    284–285
    Roth IRA, 285
Information Technology (IT), 312–313
Injunction, 77
Injuries, in hospitals, 187
In limine motions, 236–237
In re: Stephan Jay Lawrence, 298
Institute of Medical Business Advisors, 314
Insurance agents
    hiring the right agent
        brokers *vs.* agents, 307
        commissions, 307–308
        education, 307
        experience, 307
        state corporation commission insurance
            department, 308–309
        titles, 306–307
    misdeeds by
        affinity fraud, 304
        illegal investment sales, 304–305
        promissory note scams, 304
    role of advisor/agent teamwork, 315–316
    titles and credentials, 306–307
        Certified Employee Benefits Specialist
            (CEBS), 310
        Certified Financial Planner (CFP), 307, 310

Certified Insurance Counselor (CIC), 310
Certified Investment Management Counselor
    (CIMC), 310
Certified Medical Planner (CMP), 307, 310
Certified Mutual Fund Consultant (CMFC),
    310
Charted Financial Consultant (ChFC), 307,
    310
Charted Life Underwriter (CLU), 307, 310
information about credentials, 311
life insurance agent, 309
Masters in Healthcare Administration
    (MHA), 311
Masters of Business Administration (MBA),
    311
Masters of Science in Financial Services
    (MSFS), 311
property and casualty agent, 309–310
types of, 216
why regulators target them
    agents have a built-in customer base, 305
    physicians and investors looking for yield and
        safety, 305
    what to do if approached about an
        investment, 306
Insurance company selection
    bankruptcy, 303
    companies monitoring insurance companies,
        301–302
    financial ratings, 302–303, 302t
    lawsuits, 304
Insurers, specialty-specific, 226–227
Interest rates, universal life, 13–14
Interest-sensitive whole life insurance, 17
Internal rate of return (IRR), 33
Internal Revenue Code Section 1035 exchange,
    54
Invitations, sexual harassment, 143–144
IPA (Independent physician's association),
    financial risk, 117
IRA. *See* Individual Retirement Accounts (IRA)
Irrevocable life insurance trusts (ILIT), 291–292
IRS Table PS 38 rates, 67

J

Job-loss procedures, and dignity and respect for
    the employee, 163
Jobs and Growth Tax Relief Reconciliation Act
    (JGTRRA) of 2003
    elimination of the marriage penalty, 271–272
    physician residents and young children, 272
    staying informed, 272
Johns Hopkins University, 178
Johnson, Dennis, 171
Joint first-to-die life insurance, 16–17

Joint tenancy with rights of survivorship
(JTWRO), 286
Jokes in the office, sexual harassment, 141–142
Joyce, Sherman, tort reform, 198
Judges, 233

K

Katt, Peter C., 69
Kenna, Frank, 159
Kennedy-Kassenbaum bill. *See* Health Insurance
Portability and Accountability Act (HIPAA)
Key person insurance, 61–62
Kongstvedt, Peter R., 313

L

Lao Kiun, 204
Last In First Out (LIFO) accounting rules
LIFO, 37
Law of Large Numbers, 1–2
Lawrence, Stephan Jay, 298
Lawrence v. Goldberg, 298
Lawsuits. *See also* Trial risks
against insurance companies, 52, 304
Layoff procedures, and dignity and respect for the
employee, 163
Lay witnesses, 232
Level term life insurance, 6–7
Liability coverage forms
claims-made, 222
occurrence, 222
Liability insurance
automobile insurance
bodily injury, 47
personal injury, 48
property damage, 48
homeowner's liability protection, 44
professional, 69
umbrella liability insurance, 49–50
Liability Risk Retention Act (LRRA), 219–220
Life cycle stages, 58–59
Life insurance. *See also* Business related insurance
agent, 309
asset protection and, 280
death benefit settlement options, 18
overview, 5
of common types, 10–11
permanent insurance
group, 17
interest-sensitive whole life, 17
joint first-to-die, 16–17
maturity dates, 8
premium-paying period, 8–9
the 5-100 rule, 18
single-premium, 17–18
survivorship life, 15–16

universal life, 12–14
variable, 14–15
whole-life (straight life or ordinary life),
9, 12
taxation and
gift taxation, violating the 2 out of 3 rule,
21
income-tax-free death benefit, 19
modified endowment contracts (MEC),
21–22
tax-deferred growth, 19–20
transfer-for-value problem, 19
withdrawals and loans, 20–21
term insurance
annual renewable (ART), 6
conversion feature, 7
decreasing, 7–8
defined, 6
level, 6–7
Regulation XXX (Triple X), 8, 16
summation, 8
Lifetime (viatical and senior) settlements, 55–58
guidelines, 56–57
overview, 55–56
regulating this industry, 57
LIFO (Last In First Out) accounting rules, 37
Limited English proficiency (LEP), rules and
regulations, 91, 102
Limited liability companies (LLCs), 281–283
Limited liability partnerships (LLPs), 281–283
Limited partnership (LP), 281
Liquidated damages, 77
Locum tenens physician, 92
Long-term care (LTC) insurance
activities of daily living (ADLs), 39–40
critical LTC policy features, 38–39
Medicare Home Health Services, 21–22
Medicare Skilled Nursing Care, 38
taxation, 40
Long-term care settings, workplace violence in,
155
Lustgarten, Gary, 185

M

Majewski, Elaine, 257, 258
Malpractice. *See* Medical malpractice
Managed care organizations (MCOs)
antitrust risks, 117
capitated fee-for-service model, 224–225
contractual risks, 119–120
liability factors, 225
"Mandated life insurance," 3
Marguelies, Sam, 256
Marital assets, divorce
business and professional practices, 264

401(K) plans, other qualified plans, and individual retirement accounts (IRAs), 265, 284–285
  pension plans (defined benefit plans), 264
  real estate or marital residence, 265
Market power, antitrust considerations, 118
Masters in Healthcare Administration (MHA), 311
Masters of Business Administration (MBA), 311
Masters of Science in Financial Services (MSFS), 311
McDondal, Homer, 251
MCOs. *See* Managed care organizations (MCOs)
Mediation Information and Resource, Center (MIRC), 256
Medical Association HCPCS codes, 99
Medical billing, legal statutes regarding, 85–86
Medical education and practice, history of, 178
Medical Group Management Association (MGMA), 180
Medical Information Bureau (MIB), 28–29
Medical Injury Compensation Reform Act (MICRA) caps, 189, 190t
Medical Liability Monitor Survey, malpractice premiums, 198
Medical malpractice. *See also* Self-regulation by physicians; Tort reform movement; Trial risks
  background
    "crisis states," 180
    "defensive medicine" practiced by physicians, 181–182
    earliest American malpractice case, 178
    increase in claims in the 1970s, 179
    physicians relocating to other states, 179–180, 216–217
    premiums
      cost of, as percentage of medical practice expenses, 180–181, 180t, 181t
      increases during 1970s, 179–180
      percent of national health-care costs, 181
  battery, defined, 280
  defined, 177, 178
  economic damages, 178
  as eighth leading cause of death, 186
  history of medical education and practice, 178
  insurance, 69, 177–178
  intentional tort, 280
  medical error
    defined, 178
    as leading cause of death, 186–187
    strategies for improving preventable errors, 186
  noneconomic damages, 178
  preventing and reducing incidents of malpractice
    honesty, 247

    medical records, 248
  punitive damages, 178
Medical necessity, 93, 95
  Certificates of Medical Necessity (CMNs), 96–97
Medical Records
  change in the function of, 82–83
  documentation guidelines, 84–85
  documentation rules, 92, 93t
  electronic medical record (EMR), 83, 312–313
  historic purpose of, 82
  preserving the patient's medical records, 230
  risks of inadequate documentation, 81–82, 248
  subjective reports *vs.* objective examination, 84
Medical risk management
  management degree programs, 314–315
  role of advisor/agent teamwork, 315–316
  societies and specialists
    American Board of Quality Assurance and Utilization Review Physicians (ABQAURP), 312
    American Society for Healthcare Risk Management (ASHRM), 312
    Application Service Providers (ASPs), 313
    Health Forum-Statistics and Data, 312
    HIPPA-compliant, Electronic Medical Record (EMR), Information Technology (IT), 312–313
    Hospital Statistics, 312
  textbook resources, 313–314
Medicare
  compliance, 81 (*See also* Rules of health care compliance)
  Medicare Home Health Services, 21–22
  Medicare Skilled Nursing Care, 38
  Part A, 4
  Part B, 4
  Safe Harbor regulations, 114–115, 116
  targeting audit candidates, 131
  5-year exclusion risks, 126
Medicare Anti-Fraud and Abuse Statute, 114
Memorandum of Understanding (MOU), 256
MGMA (Medical Group Management Association), 180
MIB (Medical Information Bureau), 28–29
MICRA (Medical Injury Compensation Reform Act) caps, 189, 190t
Mixed model or transitional system, reimbursement, 219
Modified Endowment Contract (MEC), 17, 21–22
Money laundering, 113
Monopolistic risks, 117
Moody's, 50–51, 51t, 301, 302t

N

Nader, Ralph, 201
National Association of Insurance Commissioners (NAIC), 8
National Board of Medical Examiners, 184
National Center for State Courts, tort filings, 179
National Conference of Insurance Guarantee Funds, 52, 303
National Council of Compensation Insurance, claims for workplace violence, 154
National Institute for Occupational Safety and Health (NIOSH), *Fact Sheet* on workplace violence, 155
National Organization of Life and Health Insurers Guaranty Associations (NOLHIGA), 51, 303
National Practitioner Databank (NPD), public access to, 201, 202
Natural disaster insurance, 280–281
Needs Analysis
  calculating needs, 58
  defined, 58
  stages of the life cycle, 58–59
  using a certified financial planner (CFP), 58
Negligence, 280
  defined, 49
  legal *vs.* commonly expressed, 232–233
Noncompete agreements. *See* Covenants
Nonexclusive provider panels, 118
Non obstante veredicto, 246
Nonphysician practitioners, rules of compliance, 93–94
Nonqualified salary continuation, 65
Nonworking spouses, Social Security benefits, 33
Normal retirement age (NRA), 3
North American Securities Administrators Association, 304
"No Weapons in the Workplace" policy, 161
Nurses
  level of education and death rates at hospitals, 187–188
  workplace violence and, 155

O

OASDI-HI. *See* Social Security (OASDI-HI)
Occupational Safety and Health Act (OSHA)
  and compliance, 90
  "General Duty Clause," 98
  specific standards for physicians, 116
  standards, 97–98
  violence in the workplace, 151, 153–154
  fines, 155
Offensive behavior, test for, 139
Offer of proof, 244
Office of the Inspector General (OIG)
  audits and evaluations, 2003, 111
  on certificates of medical necessity, 96–97
  excluded providers or entities, 97
  study of disciplinary actions, 185
Offshore trusts, 297–298
Omnibus Budget Reconciliation Act (1989), 115–116
Oncale v. Sundowner Offshore Services, Inc., 145
On-call risks, 129
Opening statements, 240–241
Optional purchase/wait and see/buy-sell agreement, 63
Order of evidence presentation, 241
Ordinary life insurance, 9, 12
OSHA. *See* Occupational Safety and Health Act (OSHA)
Outliers, statistical, 119

P

Parenting time issues, 260–261
Parrish, Gregg, 272
Partial disability benefits, 24
PATH (Physician at Teaching Hospital), documentation rules, 94–95
Patient's First Act (2003), 189
Patterson, Brian, 152
PCP medical groups
  liability factors, 225
  limits on referrals, 223–224
Pearson, Jessica, 255
Peer review risks, 128–129
Peremptory challenge, 239
"Perfect Storm, The," 204
Permanent life insurance
  the 5-100 rule, 18
  single-premium, 17–18
  survivorship life, 15–16
  universal life, 12–14
  variable, 14–15
  whole-life (straight life or ordinary life), 9, 12
Pharmaceutical doses, administered in error, 186
Physician at Teaching Hospital (PATH), documentation rules, 94–95
Physician networks, criteria, 118
Physician-owned medical malpractice mutual companies, 226–227
Physicians, relocating to other states because of high malpractice premiums, 179–180, 216–217
Plaintiffs, 232
PNAs. *See* Prenuptial agreements (PNAs)
Policy provisions
  the application, 27–28
  contract language
    clauses, 31–32
    conditions, 31

obligations, 31
rights, 31
contract law, 29–30
final underwriting decision, 29
free look period, 30
Medical Information Bureau (MIB), 28–29
policy comparisons, 32–33
the underwriting decision, 30
underwriting process, 28
Political Action Committee report (2002–2003),
malpractice insurance crisis, 226
Postoperative sepsis, 187
Practicing bare, avoiding medical or legal risks,
132–133
Preferential treatment, sexual harassment, 138
"Premium offset," 12
Premiums
medical malpractice, 189, 198, 201–202
cost of, as percentage of expenses, 180–181,
180t, 181t
increases during 1970s, 179–180
percent of national health-care costs, 181
premium-setting process, 217
whole-life insurance premiums, 12
Prenuptial agreements (PNAs)
described, 253
premarital assets, 254
Uniform Premarital Agreement Act (UPAA),
253–254
validity of, 254
Primum non nocere, 229
Prince Charming Isn't Coming, 252
Privacy Rule, 100–101
elements of privacy training, 101
Product power, antitrust considerations, 118
Professional courtesy and waiver of co-pays and
deductibles, 96
Promissory note scams, insurance agents, 304
Property and casualty agent, 309–310
Property & Casualty (P&C) insurance
automobile insurance
liability coverage
bodily injury, 47
personal injury, 48
property damage, 48
physical damage coverage
collision, 48
comprehensive, 48
repairs after the accidents, 49
umbrella liability insurance, 49–50
uninsured-underinsured motorists coverage,
49
boat insurance, 47
fee only insurance consultant, 43
homeowners (and renters) insurance

basic form, 44–45
broad form, 45
comprehensive form, 45
inflation protection, 46
liability protection, 44
modified coverage form, 45
other HO endorsements, 46
property and theft coverage, 44
replacement cost *vs.* actual cash value, 45–46
special form, 45
tenants form, 45
unit owners (condominium owners) form, 45
title insurance, 46
Protected health information (PHI), Privacy Rule,
100
Provider numbers, rules of compliance, 92
Provider (PCP) medical groups
liability factors, 225
limits on referrals, 223–224
Psychiatric settings, workplace violence in, 155
Public Citizen, 201
intradisciplinary protection, 185
Punitive damages, sexual harassment, 147–148

Q

"Qualified Domestic Relations Order (QDRO)",
264, 265
Quality of Health Care in America Committee of
the IOM
medical errors as leading cause of death,
186–187
strategies for improving preventable medical
errors, 186
Quasi-socialistic reimbursement model, 219
Quid pro quo harassment, 138
Qui tam action, 86

R

Rand Institute for Civil Justice, punitive damage
awards, 183
RBV (Resource based value) malpractice risk,
133–134
REB (Reportable economic benefit), 66–67
Rebuttal evidence, 241
Redirect examination, 242
Reduced fee-for-service model, 224
Reduction of risk, 5
Regulation XXX, 8, 16
Reimbursement
models
capitated, 219
fee-for-service, 218–219
mixed model or transitional system, 219
quasi-socialistic, 219
rules of compliance, 92

Relocating to other states
because of high malpractice premiums,
179–180, 216–217
those with debtor-friendly laws, 290–291
Replacement of policy
aspects to consider, 54–55
policy replacement: section 1035 exchanges, 54
process, 53
replacement defined, 53
replacement exception, 55
safeguards, 55
Reportable economic benefit (REB), 66–67
Reporting procedure, sexual harassment, 146
Required by law, 100, 105
Res Ipsa Loquitur, 233, 234
Resource based value (RBV), malpractice risk,
133–134
Retirement plans
401(K) plans, other qualified plans, and
individual retirement accounts (IRAs), 36, 265,
284–285
Social Security, 2–3
Risk management
avoiding medical or legal risks
appropriate contracts, 131–132
the bell-shaped normalization curve, 131
elimination of risky treatments, 133–134
practicing bare, 132–133
staff education and training, 133
statistical analysis and fraud investigations,
130–131
Balanced Budget Act (1997), 112
business practice litigation risks, 119
civil asset forfeiture risks, 113
collateral consequences, 126
contract capitulation dilemma, 124
deselection risks, 126
education debt load risks, 129–130
employee risks, 124–125
False Claims Act, 112
federal agency risks
antitrust rules, 117–118
Drug Enforcement Agency (DEA), 116–117
Environmental Protection Agency (EPA), 117
Occupational Safety and Health Agency
(OSHA), 116
Health and Human Services (Office of Civil
Rights), 117
health-care fraud risks
insurance fraud, 109
Medicare fraud, 109
misrepresentation, 109–110
Health Insurance Portability and Accountability
Act (HIPAA), 111–112
hearing before a hearing officer, 108–109

hearing before an administrative law judge, 109
malpractice risks, 110, 128
managed care contractual risks, 119–120
managed care lawsuits, historic bars to
ERISA, 121
implications for the physician, 122–124
lawyer options, 121–122
Medicare recoupment risks, 108–109
Medicare 5-year exclusion risks, 126
money laundering, 113
new practice risks
expert witness, 128
on-call, 129
peer review, 128–129
patterns of practice risk, 119
principles
risk assumption, 5
risk avoidance, 4–5
risk defined, 4
risk reduction, 5
risk transfer, 5
provider health-care fraud, 110–111
self-referral risks
Medicare Anti-Fraud and Abuse Statute, 114
Medicare Safe Harbor regulations, 114–115,
116
Stark Amendment to the Omnibus Budget
Reconciliation Act (1989), 115–116
state medical board actions, 127
vicarious risks
Certificates of Medical Necessity (CMNs),
125–126
employed physicians, 125
members of a group practice, 125
Risk retention groups (RRGs), 219–220, 226
Risky treatments, elimination of, 133–134
Rittle, Mary, 313
Roper Starch Worldwide Inc., 2
Rules of health care compliance
billing and reimbursement, 92
Clinical Laboratory Improvement Amendments
(CLIA), 103–104
documentation of medical records, 92, 93t
employment or services of excluded providers
or entities, 97
"incident to" rules, 94
limited English proficiency (LEP), 102
medical necessity and use of advance
beneficiary notices, 95
Occupational Safety and Health Act (OSHA),
97–98
personnel compliance and ERISA, 102–103
physicians at teaching hospitals, 94–95
privacy rule, 100–101

professional courtesy and waiver of co-pays and deductibles, 96
proper use and billing of CPT and diagnosis codes, 92–93
proper use of Certificates of Medical Necessity (CMNs), 96–97
provider numbers, 92
Security Rule, 101–102
standardized transaction and code set rule, 99–100
use of ancillary personnel "incident to" services, 93–94

S

Safe Harbor regulations, Medicare, 114–115, 116
Safety zones, financial risk, 117
Same-sex harassment, 145
Schwartz, Victor, 200
Second-to-die life policy, 67
Securities and Exchange Commission, 304
Security Prevention Through Environmental Design (SPTED), 163–164
Security Rule (HIPAA), 101–102
Security-sensitive areas, 163
Self-referral risks
    Medicare Anti-Fraud and Abuse Statute, 114
    Medicare Safe Harbor regulations, 114–115, 116
    Stark Amendment to the Omnibus Budget Reconciliation Act (1989), 115–116
Self-regulation by physicians
    is it always gross negligence, 186–188
        children with special needs and medical error, 186–187
        drug abuse and suicide of physicians, 188
        level of nurses' education and death rates at hospitals, 187–188
        limits on hours resident physicians can work, 188
        medical errors as leading cause of death, 186–187
        medical errors in hospitals, 187
        medical malpractice as eighth leading cause of death, 186
        pharmaceutical doses in error, 186
    questionable doctors: how does the public know, 185–186
    self-regulation, 185
    state licensing process, 184–185
    strategies for improving preventable medical errors, 186
Self-settled trusts, 288–289
Senior settlements, 55–58
SERP (Supplemental extended reporting) policy, 222

Sexist words, 140–141
Sexual harassment
    commonsense approach, 149
    defined, 137
    disciplinary actions, 147
    examples
        compliments, 140
        demands or threats, 144
        invitations, 143–144
        office jokes, 141–142
        sexist words, 140–141
        touching, 142–143
    financial and economic costs, 148–149
    gender-based animosity, 144–145
    hostile work environment, 138
    liability for supervisor's harassment, 146
    preferential treatment, 138
    punitive damages, 147–148
    reporting procedure, 146
    same-sex harassment, 145
    tangible employment action, 147
    test for offensive behavior, 139
    unreasonable interference with work performance, 139
"Short pay premium," 12
Sibik, Bob, 167
Single-premium life insurance, 17–18
Smith, Ken, 166–167
SOAP (subjective, objective, assessment, and plan), and documentation guidelines, 84
Social Security (OASDI-HI)
    black-out period, 3
    disability benefits, 3
    health insurance: Medicare, 4
    inflation adjustments, 4
    retirement benefits, 2–3
    Social Security rights of divorcing couples, 273
    survivor benefits, 3
Sole-proprietor buy-sell agreement, 63
Specialty-specific insurers, 226–227
Split-dollar plans
    concept of, 66
    employee-owned method, 67
    employer-owned method, 66–67
    summary, 67–68
SPTED (Security Prevention Through Environmental Design), 163–164
Staff education and training, risk management, 133
Standard of living, after divorce, 252
Standard & Poor's, 50–51, 51t, 301, 302t
Stanely, John, 199
Stanny, Barbara, 252
Stark Amendment to the Omnibus Budget Reconciliation Act (1989), 115–116
State medical board actions, 127

Statistical analysis and fraud investigations, risk management, 130–131

Straight life insurance, 9, 12

Stress management, and violence in the workplace, 158

Student loans, default on, 97

Subcontracting, and risk transfer, 5

Suicide, of physicians, 188

Supplemental extended reporting (SERP) policy, 222

Surgical tools left in patients, 226

Survivorship life insurance, 15–16

T

TAMRA 7-pay guideline, 22

Taxation
  of annuities
    nonqualified annuity, 37
    qualified annuity, 36–37
    wealth transfer issues, 37
  children and divorce considerations
    child-care tax credit, 270–271
    child's investment income, 271
    child tax credit, 270
    earned income credit (EIC), 271
    education credits, 271
    exemptions for dependents, 269–270
    filing status, 268–269
  of disability income benefits, 26
  of life insurance policies
    gift taxation, violating the 2 out of 3 rule, 21
    income-tax-free death benefit, 19
    modified endowment contracts (MEC), 21–22
    tax-deferred growth, 19–20
    transfer-for-value problem, 19
    withdrawals and loans, 20–21
  long-term care (LTC) insurance, 40
  taxes on a viatical settlement, 56

Tax-deferred growth, 19–20

Taxpayer Relief Act (1997), 265

"Tax Qualified Policies," 40

Tax Sheltered Annuities [403(b)], 36

Technology, changes in and the practice of medicine, 203–204

"Tenancy by the entirety," 285–286

Tenancy in common, advantages, 286–287

Termination procedures, and dignity and respect for the employee, 163

Term life insurance
  annual renewable (ART), 6
  conversion feature, 7
  decreasing, 7–8
  defined, 6
  level, 6–7

Regulation XXX (Triple X), 8, 16
  summation, 8

Texas, medical malpractice liability reform measures, 189, 196t

Textbook resources, medical risk management, 313–314

Thoennes, Nancy, 255

Title insurance, 46

To Err is Human: Building a Safer Health System, 186

Tort reform movement
  classification of damages
    compensatory, 182
    punitive, 182
  conclusion
    changes in technology and practice of medicine, 203–204
    summary, 202–203
    "The Perfect Storm," 204
  costs of U.S. tort system, 182, 183
  "frivolous lawsuits," 183–184, 199
    noneconomic damages as frivolous, 184
    punitive damage awards, 183
  intentional tort, 280
  medical malpractice liability reform measures, 189, 198–199
    countersuing for filing frivolous lawsuits, 199
    create compensation programs outside the courts, 199
    monetary caps, 189
      effect on premiums, 198
      on noneconomic damages, 189, 198
    other approaches to controlling premiums, 201–202
    patient legal protections, 199–201
      delayed timing issue, 201
      diminishing supply of malpractice insurers, 200
      disciplined physicians, patient access to data about, 201
      effects of underreserving and reliance on financial markets by insurers, 199–200
      practice of "venue shopping," 202
      statute of limitation on claims, 199
      traditional physician and insurance company-based arguments, 188
  medical malpractice liability reform measures by selected states, 190–197t
  "plaintiff-friendly statutes, 183
  suggested changes to existing laws, 183
  tort defined, 182
  tort lawsuits, 182–183
  tort liability and layering an organization, 284
  tort reform defined, 182

Touching, sexual harassment, 142–143

Transfer-for-value problem, tax considerations, 19
Transfer of property into spouse's name, 285
Transfer of risk, 5
Treatment, payment, or health-care operations (TPO), Privacy Rule, 100
Trial by jury, 234–235
Trial risks
  applicable standard of care, 234
  burden of proof, 233–234
  conclusion, 248–249
  depositions, 236
  discovery process, 235
  final instructions, 244–245
  hung jury, 245
  judgment *non obstante veredicto,* 246
  jury deliberations, 245
  jury selection
    alternate jurors, 237
    challenge for cause, 238–239
    examination of a juror "in camera," 239
    judge's queries, 237
    the jury pool, 237
    logistics, 239–240
    peremptory challenge, 239
    preliminary instructions to the jury, 240
    voir dire: questioning of jurors, 238
  motions *in limine,* 236–237
  opening statements, 240–241
  presentation of evidence
    cross-examination, 242
    directed verdict, 241
    direct examination, 242
    exhibits, 242–243
    objections, 243–244
    offer of proof, 244
    order of evidence presentation, 241
    rebuttal evidence, 241
    redirect examination, 242
    "sidebar," 243–244
    witnesses, 242
  preventing and reducing incidents of malpractice
    honesty, 247
    medical records, 248
  reasons for litigation, 229–230
  summation: closing arguments, 244
  the trial players
    counsel, 232
    defendant, 232
    doctrine of *Res Ipsa Loquitur,* 233, 234
    expert witnesses, 232–233
    judge and jury, 233
    lay witnesses, 232
    plaintiff, 232
  types of trials

  bench trial, 235
  trial by jury, 234–235
  the verdict, 246
  what to do if you are sued
    contact your malpractice insurance company, 230–231
    preserving the patient's medical records, 230
    secure personal counsel, 231–232
Triple X, 8, 16
Trusteed buy-sell agreement, 63–64
Trusts
  alimony substitution trust, 267
  asset protection trusts, 294–295
    and divorce, 299
    domestic asset protection trusts (DAPTs), 295–297
    foreign asset protection trusts, 297–298
  irrevocable life insurance trusts (ILIT), 291–292
  self-settled trusts, 288–289
Tying arrangements, 118

U

Ultimate Workplace Violence Prevention Policy, 160–161
Umbrella liability insurance
  examples of, 49–50
  negligence defined, 49
Underreserving by insurers, effects of, 199–200
Underwriting decisions, 29, 30
Uniform Premarital Agreement Act (UPAA), 253–254
Universal life insurance, 12–14
"Upcoding," 86
U.S. Agency for Healthcare Research, on hospital complications, 187
U.S. Centers for Disease Control and Prevention, on medical errors, 187
U.S. Health and Human Services (HHS), on rising malpractice premiums, 189
U.S. Supreme Court
  affirmative defense, sexual harassment, 146
  punitive damages for sexual harassment, 148
  same-sex harassment, 145
U.S. v. Greenberg, 86
U.S. v. Krizek, 85
U.S. v. Lorenzo, 86
Utilization review, 82

V

"Vanishing premium," 12, 13
Variable deferred annuity, 34–35
Variable life insurance, 14–15
VEBA (Voluntary Employee Benefit Association), 69

"Venue shopping," tort reform, 202
Viatical settlements, 55–58
Vicarious risks
  Certificates of Medical Necessity (CMNs), 125–126
  employed physicians, 125
  members of a group practice, 125
Violence in the workplace. *See also* Workplace Violence Prevention Committee
  analyzing the business aspect of an incident, 167–168
  assessing the risk
    homicide at work, 156–157
    nonfatal incidents, 157
  assessment, 173
  BMA survey on, 151–152
  case example: murder of doctor by medical center employee, 152–153
  contingency and crisis planning, 166–167
  contributing factors
    likelihood of a violent event, 157–158
    mental and emotional state of the individual, 158
    the setting or environment, 158
    stress, 158
  costs
    annual cost of workplace violence, 168–169, 169t
    hidden
      health costs, 171
      loss of skilled employees, 170
      lost work time, 171
      lowered job motivation, 171
      reduced decision-making quality, 170
      restructuring cost, 170
      sabotage, theft, and damage, 170–171
      wasted time, 170
    of implementing a prevention effort, 168–169, 169t
    of recovery after an incident, 171–173, 172t
  defined, 153–154
  financial risk management impact, 154–156
    historical data, 154–155
    prevention, 155–156
    risk mitigation plan, 156
    tracking the costs, 155
  further steps to take, 173–174
  perpetrators, 154
  prevention: the zero incident approach, 159, 160, 169t
Voir dire: questioning of jurors, 238
Voluntary Employee Benefit Association (VEBA), 69
Voluntary Profit Savings Plans [401(k)], 36, 265, 284

W

Walters, Tom, 167
Wealth transfer issues, annuities, 37
Weiss Ratings, 198, 199
Weitzman, Lenore, 252
Weston, Liz Pulliam, 304
"Whistle-blower" provisions for immunity, False Claims Act, 86
White, Bob, 189
Whitehead, Barbara Dafoe, 251
Whole-life insurance, 9, 12
"Who to call" list, workplace violence, 166
Wilson, Carol Ann, 259
Withdrawals and loans, tax considerations, 20–21
Wolfe, Sidney, 201
Workers' compensation, 68
Work performance, unreasonable interference with, 139
Workplace Violence Prevention Committee, 159–166
  cost of implementing a prevention effort, 168–169, 169t
  define nature of risk to the company, 161–162
  develop crisis response procedures, 164
  enhance hiring procedures, 164–165
  enhance physical security, 163–164
  establish emergency protocol with police, 164
  establish violence prevention policy, 160–161
  facility risk assessments, 162
  focus on eliminating at-risk behaviors, 160
  involve employees in the prevention effort, 165–166
  make an individual threat assessment, 163
  "No Weapons in the Workplace" policy, 161
  organizational violence assessments, 162–163
  participants, 159–160
  promote Employee Assistance Program, 165
  provide ongoing training, 165
  synchronize personnel, security, and safety policies, 164
  use of external resources, 166
  "who to call" list, 166
Workplace Violence Research Institute, annual cost of workplace violence, 154

Z

Zero incident approach, violence in the workplace, 159
  cost of implementing a policy, 169t
  establishing a policy, 160

Lightning Source UK Ltd.
Milton Keynes UK
UKOW051559251111

182708UK00008B/49/P